The Biml Book

Business Intelligence and Data
Warehouse Automation

Andy Leonard
Scott Currie
Jacob Alley
Martin Andersson
Peter Avenant
Bill Fellows

Simon Peck
Reeves Smith
Raymond Sondak
Benjamin Weissman
Cathrine Wilhelmsen

Apress®

The Biml Book

Andy Leonard
Farmville, Virginia, USA

Scott Currie
Greer, South Carolina, USA

Jacob Alley
Simpsonville, South Carolina, USA

Martin Andersson
Billeberga, Sweden

Peter Avenant
Erina, New South Wales,
Australia

Bill Fellows
Kansas City, Missouri, USA

Simon Peck
Christchurch, New Zealand

Reeves Smith
HIGHLANDS RANCH,
Colorado, USA

Raymond Sondak
Voorburg, The Netherlands

Benjamin Weissman
Nuernberg, Germany

Cathrine Wilhelmsen
Hagan, Norway

ISBN-13 (pbk): 978-1-4842-3134-0   ISBN-13 (electronic): 978-1-4842-3135-7
https://doi.org/10.1007/978-1-4842-3135-7

Library of Congress Control Number: 2017958634

Managing Director: Welmoed Spahr
Editorial Director: Todd Green
Acquisitions Editor: Jonathan Gennick
Development Editor: Laura Berendson
Coordinating Editor: Jill Balzano
Copy Editor: Mary Behr
Compositor: SPi Global
Indexer: SPi Global
Artist: SPi Global

Distributed to the book trade worldwide by Springer Science+Business Media New York, 233 Spring Street, 6th Floor, New York, NY 10013. Phone 1-800-SPRINGER, fax (201) 348-4505, e-mail orders-ny@springer-sbm.com, or visit www.springeronline.com. Apress Media, LLC is a California LLC and the sole member (owner) is Springer Science + Business Media Finance Inc (SSBM Finance Inc). SSBM Finance Inc is a **Delaware** corporation.

For information on translations, please e-mail rights@apress.com, or visit www.apress.com/rights-permissions.

Apress titles may be purchased in bulk for academic, corporate, or promotional use. eBook versions and licenses are also available for most titles. For more information, reference our Print and eBook Bulk Sales web page at www.apress.com/bulk-sales.

Any source code or other supplementary material referenced by the author in this book is available to readers on GitHub via the book's product page, located at www.apress.com/9781484231340. For more detailed information, please visit www.apress.com/source-code.

Printed on acid-free paper

For Christy.

—Andy Leonard

To those who possess "all the virtues of Man without his Vices"
and to one without equal who shared our journey for 16 years. Mac,
you will be missed.

—Scott Currie

Contents at a Glance

Contents

About the Authors

Andy Leonard is the founder and Chief Data Engineer at Enterprise Data & Analytics, an SSIS trainer, consultant, and developer; a Biml developer and BimlHero; SQL Server database and data warehouse developer, community mentor, engineer, and farmer. He is a co-author of *SQL Server Integration Services Design Patterns* and author of *Managing Geeks - A Journey of Leading by Doing*.

Scott Currie is the founder and CEO of Varigence, Inc. Scott has led the development at Varigence of Biml and the BimlStudio IDE. Before founding Varigence, Scott worked at Microsoft for seven years on the .NET Framework, Visual Studio, the C++ compiler, various customer connection initiatives, and internal BI/DW projects.

Jacob Alley is a software developer for Varigence, Inc., in Greenville, SC. He is a graduate of Florida State University and is currently enrolled in the Master's Computer Science program at Georgia Tech.

Martin Andersson lives in Landskrona, Sweden, and works as a consultant for SolidQ. He specializes in development and architecture design for the Microsoft SQL Server platform. As a former network technician, Martin took the leap over to databases in 2010 and continues to work with SQL Server to this day. Martin holds certifications for MSCE Business Intelligence and Data Vault Modeling. When he is not digging through ETL flows he can be found in front of a Kanban board planning his next project.

Peter Avenant is the Director of Technology and founder of Varigence Australia. He is a developer, trainer, and technical data architect with over 20 years' experience focusing on data warehousing. He was an early adopter of Biml and has given numerous community talks and training sessions on Biml worldwide. He is a certified data vault data modeler and creator of the data vault accelerator implemented within BimlFlex. He is the technical lead on the BimlFlex project, working closely with the BimlStudio development team to create a flexible, extensible, and completely customizable data warehouse framework.

Bill Fellows is the owner and principal architect at Sterling Data Consulting. He is a SQL Server MVP and has been a database developer for the past 16 years, with a focus on automation and ETL. He is the organizer of Kansas City's seven SQL Saturdays and maintains the SSIS tag on StackOverflow. Bill blogs at `ssis.science` and tweets under `@billinkc`.

Simon Peck is MCSE in SQL Server BI and has been working with SQL Server for 20 years. In March of 2016 he became the first person in the APAC region to become a Varigence-certified Biml expert (BimlHero). He has been fortunate enough to have worked for close to 50 organizations worldwide, including some of the leading Microsoft BI consultancies in Europe. He is also a co-leader of the Christchurch SQL User Group in New Zealand. In 2014, after nearly 20 years away, he returned home to New Zealand with his family and is keen to dust off his skis and motorbikes (and do some BI/DWH stuff).

Reeves Smith is an independent consultant and trainer with over 20 years of experience working with SQL Server on various development and data warehouse projects. He is a Microsoft Certified Master of SQL Server and SQL Server MVP. He holds a BS in Applied Mathematics from the University of Colorado and delivers technical presentations at international, regional, and local conferences and user groups. You can visit his blog at reevessmith.wordpress.com or follow him on Twitter at @SQLReeves.

Raymond Sondak is a technical architect, analytics consultant, and owner of Analyticsaholic. He is also the first BimlHero Certified Expert in the Netherlands. Raymond is an expert in agile end-to-end business intelligence and analytics implementation as well as automation focused on Microsoft technologies. His technical expertise extends from the Microsoft business intelligence and data platform to building cloud solutions with Microsoft Azure. He also delivers training and workshops on various subjects including Biml and is very passionate about sharing his knowledge. Raymond loves to enjoy life. When he is not behind his laptop you'll find him on adventure trips around the world with his wife; they're both foodies at heart.

Ben Weissman is the owner and founder of Solisyon, a consulting firm based in Germany and focused on business intelligence, business analytics, and data warehousing. He is the first German BimlHero and has been working with SQL Server since SQL Server 6.5. In his fight against stupid, repetitive tasks, he has developed numerous automation tools over the years to make his customers' lives easier. If he's not currently working with SQL Server, he is probably travelling to explore the world. Ben is also an MCSE, Charter Member of the Microsoft Professional Program for Big Data and Data Science, and a Certified Data Vault Data Modeler. You can find him online at http://biml-blog.de/ or @bweissman on Twitter.

Cathrine Wilhelmsen loves teaching and sharing knowledge. She works as a consultant, developer, and trainer, focusing on data warehouse and business intelligence projects. Her core skills are ETL, SSIS, Biml, and T-SQL development, but she enjoys everything from programming to data visualization. Outside of work, she's active in the SQL Server and PASS communities as a Microsoft Data Platform MVP, BimlHero Certified Expert, speaker, blogger, organizer, and chronic volunteer.

Acknowledgments

Andy Leonard: I thank God first for He leads me in right paths for his name's sake (Psalm 23:3). I thank Christy, my lovely bride, and our children, Stevie Ray, Emma, and Riley, for sacrificing some Dad time. Thanks to the awesome team at Enterprise Data & Analytics for their patience and hard work while I wrote: Bill Anton, Kent Bradshaw, Nick Harris, KeShawnda Lawrence, and Penny Trupe. We have an awesome team at Apress: Jill Balzano kept the wheels on the bus going 'round and 'round, and Jonathan Gennick is the best editor in the business. To my co-authors, Scott, Jacob, Martin, Peter, Bill, Simon, Reeves, Raymond, Ben, and Cathrine: thank you for putting up with me during the writing of this book. It has been an honor to write with you. Finally, I thank Scott for inventing Biml, allowing me the honor and privilege of being a BimlHero, patiently coaching on many topics (some technical), and being my friend.

Scott Currie: Thank you to everyone in the Biml community who has shared their insight and expertise with those who are new to data automation. Hopefully this book will ease your burden as Biml usage continues to grow. My eternal gratitude to my wife, Lydia, for her patience and grace this past year and my children, John, James, Sarah, Riley, and Helen, for granting their father the extra time at work to write this book. Dulcius ex asperis.

Jacob Alley: I would like to thank Amanda Tuttle for her unrelenting patience and love, and I would like to thank Scott Currie for affording me the opportunity to be a part of the Biml family.

Martin Andersson: For my best friend Tim, forever comrades in arms. For my father, for showing me that anything is possible. For Kristian, the struggle continues. Love and respect to Julia, Elisabeth, and Rosa for the support. Last but not least, thank you to Varigence for creating Biml.

Bill Fellows: I'd like to thank my co-authors for the opportunity to work on this project, Scott Currie for making development fun again with Biml, and Dr. James Bogan for igniting those sparks of fire so many years ago. Hilary, James, and Max: you are the reasons I get up in the morning and I love you all dearly.

Simon Peck: Marie, Oscar, Lenny, and Grace Peck for their support, love, and encouragement.

Reeves Smith: First and foremost, I would like to thank my wife, Amy, for supporting me through this effort. She took the kids on extra adventures alone to give me time to continue writing. She was selfless in all of this and I truly appreciate all the hard work it takes to raise three girls. Secondly, I want to thank my three girls, Marin, Gracynn, and Brynn, who missed out on the time with Dad. We will have to make it up. Finally, I want to thank Andy and the rest of the folks contributing to the book who gave additional help and motivation. (Yes, Ben, we are calling all of the additional communication "motivation.")

Raymond Sondak: I would like to thank my wife, Stacey, so I can do what I do, and my late sister, Sandra, with whom I share the credit on every goal I achieve. To Scott Currie, you're the man! For Andy's leadership and "The Biml Book" authors whose names are on the cover, you guys and girl rock!

Ben Weissman: Thank you to Scott for creating Biml. Thank you to Andy for including me on this project. Thank you to my awesome colleagues for delivering exceptional quality in our projects every day. And most importantly, thank you to Franzie and my family - for everything.

Cathrine Wilhelmsen: To my co-authors and fellow BimlHeroes, from the bottom of my heart, *thank you*. It has been an honor to write this book with you. Thank you for your hard work, the late nights writing and editing, and all the laughs we shared. A special thank you to Andy, Ben, and Martin; your support meant everything to me. (And to my dearest family, Cathe, Kjell, Jeanette, and Malin, I promise I won't be rambling about Biml during family dinners... for a while:) Glad i dere!)

Foreword

You have a long journey ahead of you to learn how to use Biml in your data integration projects. Before getting started, let's take a look at the upcoming chapters and what you will learn in each.

Who Is This Book For?

Anyone who is interested in Business Intelligence Markup Language (Biml), whether entirely new to the technology or a seasoned veteran, will likely find value and insight within these pages. There are, however, two audiences that will particularly benefit from this book.

First, those who are entirely new to Biml will learn everything from the very basics of writing Biml code to creating frameworks to more advanced Biml usage scenarios.

The second audience is those who have been coding with Biml for a while and are looking to take their skills to the next level through formal framework development, metadata development, or other more advanced topics. These readers might choose to skip or just skim some of the earlier chapters, but there is still much to learn from the later chapters, even for someone who has done a substantial amount of work with Biml already.

For both audiences, it is strongly recommended that you have a solid understanding of SQL Server and any SQL Server services, such as SSIS or SSAS, that you intend to use with Biml.

You should also be sure to install BIDS or SSDT for SQL Server 2005 or later.

How Is This Book Structured?

In the following sections, we will explore the chapter layout of this book. At a high level, there are four parts that guide you through the process of learning Biml, using Biml to build a framework, enhancing your Biml projects with a variety of additional capabilities, and providing a reference for additional topics of interest.

Part I: Learning Biml

In the first part of this book, we will focus on getting you up to speed on writing Biml solutions, assuming very little previous background with Biml or .NET coding. While these chapters are targeted primarily at those who are new to Biml, it is likely that even a seasoned Biml developer will pick up a few tips, tricks, and insights along the way. Note that we do not endeavor to create the most comprehensive primer for every aspect of Biml and BimlScript (which is the way to automate Biml). We will cover all of the basics, but if you feel that you need more details on XML syntax, C# syntax, VB syntax, or any other aspect of what we cover, there are excellent resources available online, both from the http://bimlscript.com community site, the http://varigence.com support and documentation site, and from third parties.

Chapter 1: Biml Tools

Before you can get started writing code, you must have your development environment set up with tools that enable you to author and build Biml code. There are a few great options–free and paid–to choose from. In this chapter, we'll give you a brief overview of each tool and provide some guidelines on how to choose among them.

Chapter 2: Introduction to the Biml Language

Once you have your tools set up, it's time to start writing some code. In the Introduction, you'll see some Biml code and we hope it gets you excited to get started writing your own code. To get you up to speed, here we're going to cover how all of the most critical language elements–the Biml language, BimlScript code nuggets, directives, and supplemental files–work together to build data solutions.

Chapter 3: Basic Staging Operations

Once you have a firm grasp on syntax, you're going to build your first Biml solution to stage data from a source system into a target system. This first real solution will take you step-by-step through the coding, building, and execution workflows. To ensure you focus on the mechanics of creating your first solution from scratch, it will not use any BimlScript code nuggets or .NET coding.

Chapter 4: Importing Metadata

Writing flat Biml by hand can get repetitive, so in this chapter you enhance your staging solution from Chapter 3 to use BimlScript code nuggets to automatically generate the staging targets and packages for all of the tables in your source system. As part of this process, we introduce some of the most important Biml utility methods for retrieving database schema metadata from relational databases.

Chapter 5: Reusing Code, Helper Classes, and Methods

At this point, you'll have written a decent amount of .NET code, and you're going to write even more in the next part of the book as you explore Biml frameworks. Consequently, in this chapter, you'll take a look at the various methods Biml offers to organize your code to enable easier authoring and maintenance.

Part II: Biml Frameworks

In the second part of this book, you will use everything you learned in the previous chapters to build a Biml framework. The idea behind a framework is to build a metadata store that holds all of your configuration information in addition to BimlScripts that will consume that metadata to create your solution. Once you have completed your framework, you will spend most of your data development time modeling, mapping, and writing business logic, because all of the plumbing that once consumed your workday is now handled automatically by the framework.

Chapter 6: A Custom Biml Framework

In this chapter, you will build a simple metadata database and custom BimlScripts to autogenerate a customizable data load solution. Once this sample is complete, you will be able to create entirely new data load solutions for arbitrarily large databases simply by modifying your metadata and rebuilding the framework code.

Chapter 7: Using Biml as an SSIS Design Patterns Engine

In the previous chapter, the custom Biml framework used a hardcoded data load pattern for the sake of simplicity. In this chapter, you will refactor the framework code to use an architecture where you can dynamically change the data load pattern on a table-by-table basis. This will enable you to develop a library of as many patterns as you need to support business requirements while preserving the maintainability of the code base.

Chapter 8: Integration with a Custom SSIS Execution Framework

Chapters 6 and 7 focused on the creation of build-time frameworks. These frameworks are responsible for building consistent data load packages. When you want to execute those packages, you also need an execution framework to manage the order in which packages execute and a variety of other runtime behaviors. In this chapter, we will present such an execution framework and show how to integrate it into the solution.

Chapter 9: Metadata Automation

So far, our approach for metadata management was to store it in database tables and retrieve it via direct SQL queries. This is a fine solution, but it experiences some management issues as the metadata store grows to include additional configuration. In this chapter, we will present a solution for modeling your metadata in a more reusable way, one that offers a variety of value-added services on top of your metadata store.

Chapter 10: Advanced Biml Frameworks and BimlFlex

Until now, in this part of the book, you built a functional Biml framework for your data solutions. Packaging that framework for deployment, providing extensibility points for third-party users, and protecting your code from unauthorized users still presents challenges. In this chapter, we show you how to solve these problems using the Biml bundles feature.

Additionally, we provide a brief overview of the BimlFlex bundle built by Varigence as a commercial product. This will give you a very clear picture of just how extensive your Biml framework capabilities can be with sufficient development investment. It will also give you a real-life example of how to build an out-of-the-box product using Biml.

Part III: Biml Topics

In the third part of the book, you explore a variety of Biml topics of general use to you throughout your Biml development activities, whether you are building a framework or developing an ad hoc solution.

Chapter 11: Biml and Analysis Services

Most of the code you've seen in this book and likely through other sources online focuses on using Biml to develop SQL scripts and SSIS packages. In this chapter, we show how to use Biml to automate SQL Server Analysis Services (SSAS) multidimensional cube and tabular model development. Additionally, we demonstrate how Biml can be used to reduce the overhead of SSAS multidimensional cube processing management by creating automated SSIS packages.

Chapter 12: Biml for T-SQL and Other Little Helpers

Many people assume Biml automation is only useful for building the core data transformation processes that you run on a recurring basis. While Biml can do this, it is also a great option for autogenerating single-use SQL scripts that would be tedious or difficult to code by hand. In this chapter, we show you various options for creating such scripts and demonstrate via several real-world examples.

Chapter 13: Documenting Your Biml Solution

An important, though often overlooked, part of any data solution is user-friendly documentation. In this chapter, we present several strategies to automatically generate high-quality documentation from your Biml code.

Chapter 14: Troubleshooting Metadata

Throughout the book, we have shown examples of using built-in Biml utility and library methods to solve a wide variety of common data automation tasks. In some cases, you will find that one of the provided utility methods does not quite meet your needs. The wonderful thing about Biml and BimlScript is that you have the option to return to first principles and build exactly what you need for the specific task at hand. In this chapter, we show an example of this principle in action. We directly read information schema tables in source databases to address project-specific needs around database schema discovery that are not supported by the built-in methods.

Chapter 15: Troubleshooting Biml

The samples shown in books are developed with the benefits of expert authors, plenty of time, and a technical review process to ensure the highest quality. When you first begin to write your own Biml code from scratch, you likely won't enjoy any of those benefits. When something goes wrong with your code, how should you go about finding and fixing the issue? In this chapter, we will show you several options for logging, diagnostics, and troubleshooting that should significantly improve your ability to hunt down and squash bugs in your code.

Part IV: Appendices

Even after reading this entire book, you're still just scratching the surface of what Biml can do to automate your data solutions and the flexibility Biml provides to author new approaches to common data integration problems. In the following appendices, we examine a few topics that expand on some ideas we developed earlier in the book. Our goal is to kickstart the next phase of your journey to mastering Biml.

Appendix A: Source Control

When using a human readable and writable coding language such as Biml, source control becomes a powerful tool for managing your project across multiple release cycles. In this chapter, you learn about some of the benefits of using source control and how to configure source control for BimlStudio.

Appendix B: Parallel Load Patterns in Biml

In Chapter 7, you learned how to create a modular system for choosing design patterns on a table-by-table basis. Since our focus was primarily on the modular pattern architecture, we only implemented two data load patterns. In this appendix, we give you samples of additional patterns to parallelize data flow and leverage the Change Data Capture (CDC) feature in SQL Server and SSIS.

Appendix C: Metadata Persistence

In Chapter 9, you learned how to build a Biml metadata model for your framework and how to interact with that metadata model. In this appendix, we expand that solution to include a completely generic mechanism for storing and retrieving any Biml metadata model to and from a database. This is a solution that will be useful for those who extensively use metadata models or develop multiple complementary Biml frameworks.

Conclusion

As you can see, you have a long journey filled with learning and new insights ahead of you. Let's get started!

Introduction

You will be more productive by using Biml for stupid data transfers... and more. This book will give you an idea of what Biml can do and how it is structured. Don't worry if some of the code samples look confusing or you don't understand it all at once. Instead of having you read multiple chapters just to get your first glimpse at Biml code, you will dive right in. But after that, you will take a step back and be guided through the process from the very basics to building the most advanced frameworks!

For those of you who continuously work with the SQL Server Integration Services (SSIS) to get data from A to B (no matter if it is to build a data warehouse or to achieve some other data integration goals), you will probably have figured that, despite the magic you do for your internal and external customers every day, a lot of what you do is just repeating yourself: create a staging table in your staging database based on the source table's structure and data types, and then build a simple package to load the data using SSIS. Many tables do not actually need your magic; they are simply data copy tasks. No more, no less.

Copying a table to staging is easy. The actual setup probably only takes 5 minutes, but doing so doesn't scale very well (from a human interaction point of view). To get the job done for two tables takes twice as long. For three tables, it takes three times as long, and so on.

Moreover, if the source schema changes or someone decides to convert the whole source database from non-Unicode to Unicode (and if that hasn't happened to you yet, it probably will at some point), you start touching and modifying all those single tasks one by one. It might only take 5 minutes per table to update your packages for these minor changes, but again, it does not scale. Even more important, it's tedious, boring, and the result is the same as before. Who wants to spend all that time on something that no one will care about (as long as it works)?

Having experienced that lack of appreciation and boredom, I was looking for a way to complete these repetitive and non-challenging tasks more quickly and easily, without cloning myself.

Let's take a minute to think about SSIS packages. In the end, they are eXtensible Markup Language (XML) files, which might contain a lot of XML as the packages become bigger and bigger. A .dtsx file that simply truncates a target table and then performs a dataflow task ends up around 400 lines of XML. Writing my own XML was no option; that became clear to me relatively quick. So effectively, I was looking for a tool that would write those .dtsx files for me.

Biml offered the answer to that question. In the end, Biml is also an XML format, so to avoid writing .dtsx (SSIS package files) XML, we are just writing a different dialect of XML. This doesn't seem to make too much sense at first sight, but if you look under the covers, it does! Why? Because Biml code is much easier to maintain due to almost no overhead. Biml is a markup language, designed by Varigence with the intention to automate development of Microsoft business intelligence (BI) objects like SSIS packages. Always keep that in mind: it is not an out-of-the box solution but rather a highly flexible language to automate. If you don't know how to solve a problem manually, Biml will not help you. But if you have a design pattern that you need to build multiple times, Biml will do just that!

Biml metadata for SSIS follows pretty much exactly the same patterns you already know from manual SSIS packages. A simple illustration of the types of database and SSIS assets you can create with Biml is shown in Figure F-1.

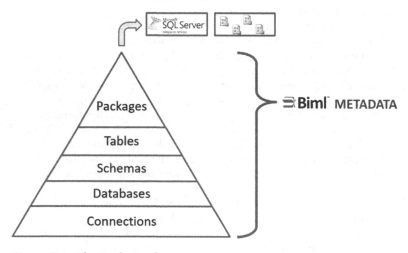

Figure F-1. *The Biml metadata structure*

A Biml file to generate that 400-line .dtsx file has less than 30 lines of code. It is easily readable on the screen, and it is easily manageable with your favorite text editor. So even basic functions like copying and pasting the code for those many dataflow tasks can result in saving a notable amount of time. However, that is just a small fraction of what you can achieve using Biml.

As coders, we want to avoid repeating ourselves, so we can make use of scripts (*code nuggets* containing variables, parameters, and loops) instead of having to copy and paste code repeatedly. This obviously also allows us to maintain one central codebase for annotations, transformations, etc.

In addition, one especially annoying, as in non-value adding, step is to actually create and maintain your destination tables based on the *metadata* in the underlying sources. Biml will take care of that for you, too!

Technically speaking, that means you build your Biml code, run it through the Biml compiler, and receive regular Microsoft BI objects or files, as shown in Figure F-2.

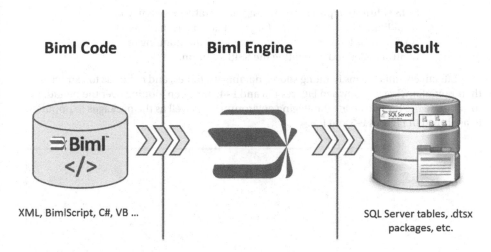

Biml Code   **Biml Engine**   **Result**

XML, BimlScript, C#, VB ...   SQL Server tables, .dtsx packages, etc.

Figure F-2. *The Biml compiler process*

Given the huge amount of resources available, including the community of very active Biml users as well as *BimlHero certified experts*[1] (many of whom were involved in this book), Biml is very easy to adopt, assuming you already consider yourself a good Microsoft BI and solid .NET developer.

So what's the catch? Well, there really is none besides the fact that, as always, there are multiple ways of achieving the same thing. You will have to figure out which patterns, practices, and approaches are right for solving your data development problems. Other than that, you will probably figure that some very complex, unique, or business-logic-heavy patterns are not actually a time saver in Biml, because Biml's strength is really the automation of repeatable tasks. It simply scales very well and therefore obviously adds most value in scenarios that require such scaling, compared to one-time tasks.

Getting back to the staging database scenario, let's identify, automate, and manage a handful of components:

> **One or more source databases:** This is probably out of your control so let's will treat it as a fixed variable.

> **Staging database:** You want Biml to manage and create the tables in your staging target automatically.

> **Metadata layer:** Depending on personal taste, this can be as simple as extended properties in your source database, an Excel file, a master data services solution (talking about oversizing things) or depending on the complexity, it might even be integrated in BimlStudio making use of Biml's metadata features. See more on this in Chapter 9.

---

[1]Become a Biml Hero Certified Expert!, https://varigence.com/Blog/Post/65

> **SSIS solution to populate the staging database:** Again, you want Biml to take care of that for you. The goal is that there is no human interaction required, except for maintaining the control tables and generating the SSIS solution.

Effectively, this means iterating source databases, tables, and columns to extract their metadata first, as shown in Figures F-3 and F-4, and then looping over the metadata to generate the Biml to create the staging environment as well as the packages to populate it, as shown in Figures F-5 and F-6.

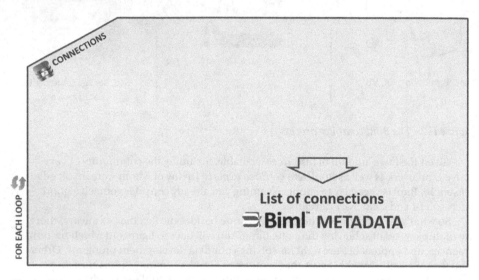

Figure F-3. *Step 1: Build your connections into Biml*

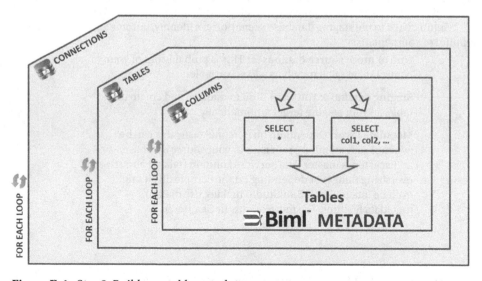

Figure F-4. *Step 2: Build your table metadata*

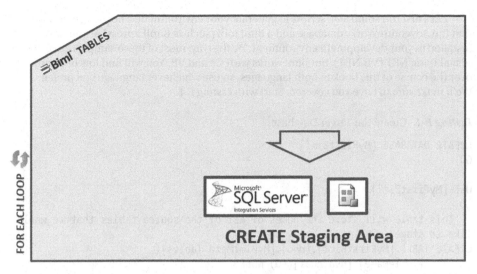

Figure F-5. *Step 3: Generate a package to generate your staging area*

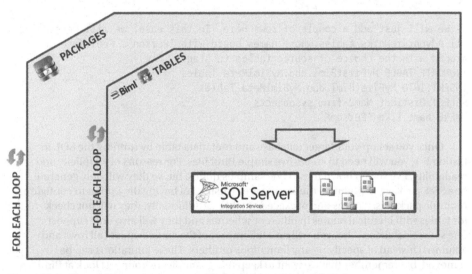

Figure F-6. *Step 4: Generate one or multiple packages to populate it*

Now, let's put that into code. Some of what you see may seem strange or simply unknown. Don't worry. This is just the beginning, and you'll build a greater understanding of how all this works over the course of the book.

Your main source database is going to be AdventureWorks[2] and for simplicity, you will maintain your metadata in dedicated tables residing in the SQL database to be used as your staging environment.

---

[2]CodePlex, SQL Server Database Product Samples, https://msftdbprodsamples.codeplex.com/

Let's first run some SQL scripts to generate your environment. The expectation is that the AdventureWorks database and a Biml tool (such as BimlExpress) are already installed in your development environment. By the way, most of these samples are using Visual Basic.NET (VB.NET), but Biml works with C# and VB. You will find lots of examples over the course of this book in both languages, so use whichever language you prefer. We'll make sure to have you covered. Start with Listing F-1.

Listing F-1. Create the Target Database

```
CREATE DATABASE [MyFirstBiml]
GO

USE [MyFirstBiml]
GO
-- This table will store the names of all of the source tables that we would
like to stage.
CREATE TABLE [MyFirstBiml].[dbo].[MyBimlMeta_Tables](
        [TableName] [nvarchar](50) NULL
) ON [PRIMARY]
GO

-- We will just add a couple of rows here. In this case, we will be staging
all AdventureWorks tables whose names begin with 'Person'. Feel free to play
around with the choice of source tables to stage!
TRUNCATE TABLE MyFirstBiml.dbo.MyBimlMeta_Tables
INSERT INTO MyFirstBiml.dbo.MyBimlMeta_Tables
SELECT Distinct Name from sysobjects
WHERE name like 'Person%'
```

Once you set up your target database and metadata table by running the SQL in Listing F-1, you will need to create five simple Biml files. For reasons of simplicity and readability, I've scaled down these code samples quite a bit, so they will only generate one SSIS package to populate the staging area (instead of having the option to configure multiple packages, such as one package per table). Additionally, they will not check for tables with identical names in different schemas and they will also only support one source database. Also, you will do a full import of the source tables (all rows and columns) instead of specifying any limitations or filters. These limitations can be removed, but remember that we want to keep things simple for your first look at Biml code. All the fun details will follow in the upcoming chapters.

01_Environment.biml

This Biml file will hold your database connection strings. In this very simple first example, they will just be static values. In a real-world scenario, you would want to retrieve your connection strings from control tables as well. See Listing F-2.

Listing F-2. 01_Environment.biml

```
<Biml xmlns="http://schemas.varigence.com/biml.xsd">
  <Connections>
    <OleDbConnection Name="Target"
 ConnectionString="Provider=SQLNCLI11;Server=(local);Initial
Catalog=MyFirstBiml;Integrated Security=SSPI;" />
    <OleDbConnection Name="AdventureWorks2014" ConnectionString="Provide
r=SQLNCLI11;Server=(local);Initial Catalog=AdventureWorks2014;Integrated
Security=SSPI;"/>
  </Connections>
  <Databases>
    <Database Name="MyFirstBiml" ConnectionName="Target" />
  </Databases>
  <Schemas>
    <Schema Name="dbo" DatabaseName="MyFirstBiml" />
  </Schemas>
</Biml>
```

02_BuildMeta.biml

This BimlScript file will retrieve the schema metadata from your source system, but only for those tables that were specified in your control table. These Biml table definitions will later be used by the Biml compiler to create the data definition language (DDL) to set up the staging tables as well as the data flow tasks to load them. Note how you're making use of additional .NET functions, using the System.Data namespace.

Also, you're orchestrating the way the Biml compiler will interpret your code by using the tier attribute in the first line. This is especially helpful when building a complex Biml solution where some files require the existence of other objects that are defined in other files. See Listing F-3.

Listing F-3. 02_BuildMeta.biml

```
<#@ template language="VB" tier="2" #>
<#@ import namespace="System.Data" #>
<#
dim targetConnection as AstDbConnectionNode = RootNode.Connections("Target")
dim SrcConn as AstDbConnectionNode = RootNode.Connections("AdventureWor
ks2014")
Dim ImportTables As new List(of String)
 #>
<Biml xmlns="http://schemas.varigence.com/biml.xsd">
  <Tables>
<# Dim DT as DataTable = ExternalDataAccess.GetDataTable(targetConnection.
ConnectionString, "SELECT [TableName]  FROM [MyBimlMeta_Tables]")
```

```
for each dr as datarow In dt.rows
  ImportTables.add(dr.item(0).ToString())
Next

dim ImportResult as ImportResults = srcconn.GetDatabaseSchema(nothing,Import
Tables,ImportOptions.ExcludeIdentity or ImportOptions.ExcludeForeignKey)

    for each table as AstTableNode in ImportResult.TableNodes #>
    <Table
Name="<#= srcconn.name #>_<#=table.Schema.Name#>_<#=table.Name#>"
SchemaName="MyFirstBiml.dbo">
      <Columns>
        <# for each column as AstTableColumnBaseNode in table.Columns    #>
        <#=column.GetBiml()#>
        <# next #>
      </Columns>
      <Annotations>
        <Annotation AnnotationType="Tag" Tag="SourceSchemaQualifiedName">
          <#=table.SchemaQualifiedName#>
        </Annotation>
      </Annotations>
    </Table>
    <# next #>
  </Tables>
</Biml>
```

03_Create_Staging.biml

This BimlScript file will generate your first SSIS package, which will simply drop and create all tables that you defined in the previous steps in your staging environment. While drop/create is not the pattern you will want to use for many scenarios, it is appropriate for most temporary staging targets. Furthermore, we'll cover incremental deployment strategies and other more complex loading patterns over the course of this book. See Listing F-4.

Listing F-4. 03_Create_Staging.biml (VB)

```
<#@ template tier="3" language="VB" #>
<Biml xmlns="http://schemas.varigence.com/biml.xsd">
  <Packages>
    <Package Name="01_CreateStaging">
      <Tasks>
        <# for each table as AstTableNode in RootNode.Tables #>
        <ExecuteSQL Name="CRE <#=table.Name#>" ConnectionName="Target">
          <DirectInput>
```

```
            <#=table.GetDropAndCreateDdl()#>
         </DirectInput>
       </ExecuteSQL>
       <# next #>
     </Tasks>
   </Package>
 </Packages>
</Biml>
```

By the way, as pointed out before, it is your choice whether you use VB or C# as your scripting language. You can even mix them within a solution (just not within a file) so Listing F-5 shows how this code file would look in C#.

Listing F-5. 03_Create_Staging.biml (C#)

```
<#@ template tier="3" #>
<Biml xmlns="http://schemas.varigence.com/biml.xsd">
  <Packages>
    <Package Name="01_CreateStaging">
      <Tasks>
        <# foreach (var table in RootNode.Tables) {  #>
        <ExecuteSQL Name="CRE <#=table.Name#>" ConnectionName="Target">
          <DirectInput>
            <#=table.GetDropAndCreateDdl()#>
          </DirectInput>
        </ExecuteSQL>
        <# } #>
      </Tasks>
    </Package>
  </Packages>
</Biml>
```

As you can see, they look very similar, so the choice comes down to personal likings and preferences.

04_Populate_Staging.biml

This BimlScript file (again in conjunction with the environment, control tables, and schema metadata) will generate your .dtsx files, named 02_Populate Tables.dtsx. This .dtsx will truncate and load the tables in your staging area. Note that it calls the code in the next BimlScript file listing. See Listing F-6.

■ **Note** For the Biml compiler to be able to build this package, the target tables have to exist! You must execute the package 01_CreateStaging.dtsx before you can compile the code.

Listing F-6. 04_Populate_Staging.biml

```
<#@ template tier="4" language="VB" #>
<Biml xmlns="http://schemas.varigence.com/biml.xsd">
  <Packages>
    <Package Name="02_Populate Tables">
      <Tasks>
        <# for each table as AstTableNode in RootNode.Tables #>
        <#=CallBimlScript("05_Populate_Table.biml", table) #>
        <# next #>
      </Tasks>
    </Package>
  </Packages>
</Biml>
```

05_Populate_Table.biml

Biml also has its own features for the templating and reuse of your Biml code. While
not strictly necessary, you can improve the readability of your code by separating
the per-table SSIS logic into its own Biml file. Then you can just call this file from the
04_Populate_Staging.biml script that you prepared earlier. It is not necessary in this
specific case, as you're not referencing this file multiple times from various locations in
your solution, but it does demonstrate your first reusable code pattern in your Biml. You
will learn more about this in Chapter 5. See Listing F-7.

Listing F-7. 05_Populate_Table.biml

```
<#@ template language="VB" #>
<#@ property name="table" type="AstTableNode" #>
<Container Name="Copy DataPatterns_<#=table.Schema.Name#>_<#=table.Name#>"
ConstraintMode="Linear">
  <Tasks>
    <ExecuteSQL Name="Truncate" ConnectionName="Target">
      <DirectInput>TRUNCATE TABLE <#=table.ScopedName#></DirectInput>
    </ExecuteSQL>
    <Dataflow Name="Copy <#=table.Schema.Name#>_<#=table.Name#>">
      <Transformations>
        <OleDbSource Name="Load" ConnectionName="AdventureWorks2014">
          <DirectInput>SELECT <#=table.GetColumnList()#> FROM
<#=table.GetTag("SourceSchemaQualifiedName")#>
          </DirectInput>
        </OleDbSource>
        <OleDbDestination Name="Set" ConnectionName="Target">
          <TableOutput TableName="<#=table.ScopedName#>" />
        </OleDbDestination>
      </Transformations>
    </Dataflow>
  </Tasks>
</Container>
```

So is this all you can do with Biml? NO!

So is Biml just for SSIS? NO!

Over the course of this book, you will become acquainted with the endless possibilities of Biml from complex SSIS scenarios, working with non-SQL server data, SQL Server Analysis Services (SSAS), data vault, the cloud, and even use cases for which you may have never–EVER–thought of Biml as a possibility.

Whether you're a Biml novice or just want to improve your skills, there are great things to learn in store for you!

Whatever it is you are doing, have fun Biml'ing!

—Ben Weissman

PART I

■ ■ ■

Learning Biml

CHAPTER 1

■ ■ ■

Biml Tools

Biml provides new and exciting perspectives on the world of business intelligence. As you further develop understanding of the concepts throughout this book, you'll need to choose from among the currently available tools to actually write and build your Biml code.

The purpose of this chapter is to introduce these tools and provide an overview of the main features of each tool along with the primary differentiators among them. From there, we will discuss a few key decision points and considerations in choosing the best tool for your next Biml project.

BimlExpress

BimlExpress is a free Visual Studio (also called VS, SSDT, and BIDS) extension built by Varigence specifically for Biml code development. BimlExpress extends the functionality of Visual Studio SSIS projects to author and build Biml code with a fully featured code editor, including syntax highlighting and IntelliSense, all from within the Visual Studio interface that you already use for your SSIS projects.

BimlExpress Installation

To get started using BimlExpress, first download it from the Varigence website at www.varigence.com/BimlExpress, as shown in Figure 1-1.

A. Leonard et al., *The Biml Book*, https://doi.org/10.1007/978-1-4842-3135-7_1

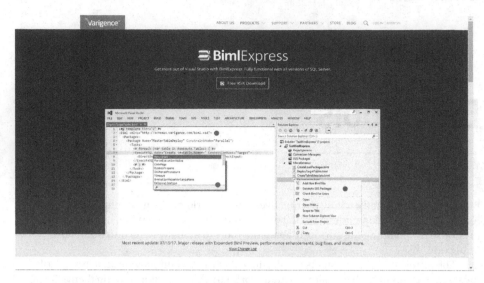

Figure 1-1. *The Varigence BimlExpress website*

Start the installation by executing the downloaded VSIX file. When the installation begins, the VSIX Installer window displays, as shown in Figure 1-2. You can choose which versions of Visual Studio will include the BimlExpress extension. Since Microsoft will sometimes label your data development installation of Visual Studio with the BIDS or SSDT brand, you might be unsure of which versions to select. You can find the Visual Studio version information for your SSDT or BIDS environment by clicking "About" in the SSDT/BIDS Help menu.

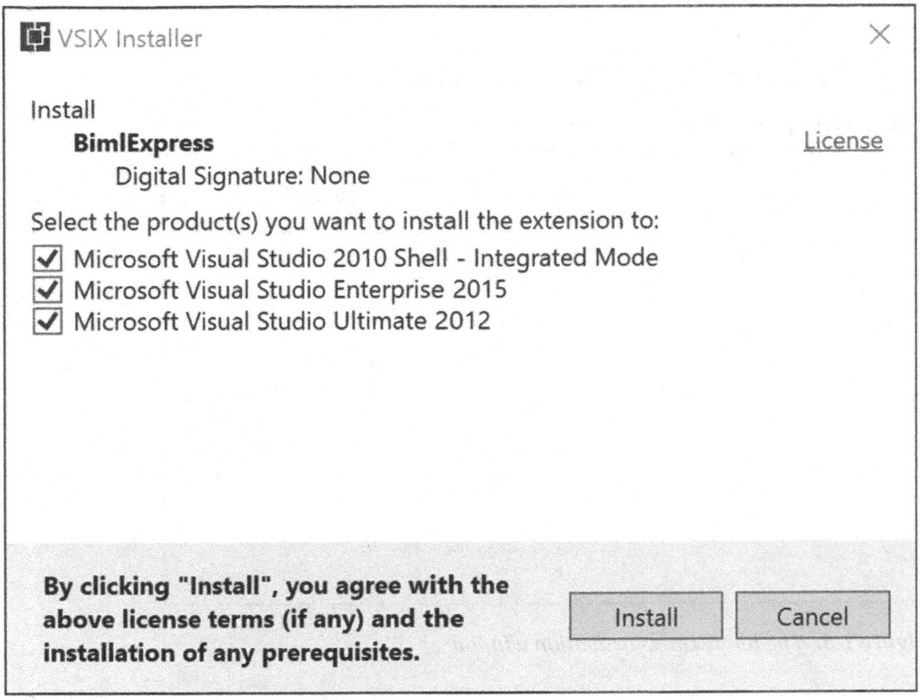

Figure 1-2. BimlExpress installation window

■ **Tip** If you would like to install the BimlExpress extension for all users, automate the installation in your IT processes, or take advantage of any of the other features available in Microsoft's VSIX installer workflow, you can instead use the command line VSIX installer that is shipped with Visual Studio. Check out Microsoft's documentation for VSIXInstaller.exe for more information.

After installing, but before you can use BimlExpress on your system, you need to request a software activation key by registering your name and e-mail address, as shown in Figure 1-3. Once BimlExpress is activated, you will be emailed a perpetual license by Varigence that allows you to use the software indefinitely. Registering and activating the product enables Varigence to track user counts of BimlExpress, prevent piracy of the Biml engine, and consequently provide better support for all users. If you are in an offline environment, you may need to visit Varigence.com to obtain a key directly. Additionally, Varigence.com provides options to generate a self-activating key that will work without any connection to the Internet.

Free BimlExpress Activation

×

Please enter your information to obtain a product key.
Varigence may contact you, but we will never sell your information to anyone.

* **First Name**	
* **Last Name**	
* **Email**	*The product key will be mailed to this address*
Phone	
PROMO	

I already have a product key
Copy machine code
Why do I have to provide this information?

Get Trial Key

Figure 1-3. The BimlExpress activation window

Once you have installed and activated BimlExpress, you will see a new BimlExpress toolbar available in Visual Studio, shown in Figure 1-4.

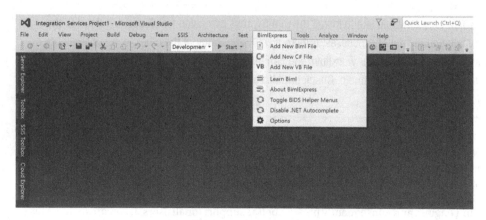

Figure 1-4. The BimlExpress toolbar

You can start your Biml code development by first creating a new SSIS project in Visual Studio. To add a new Biml file, you can right-click the project root node and select "Add New Biml File" from the context menu, or add a new Biml file using the BimlExpress menu. A new Biml file will be added to the `Miscellaneous` folder, as shown in Figure 1-5.

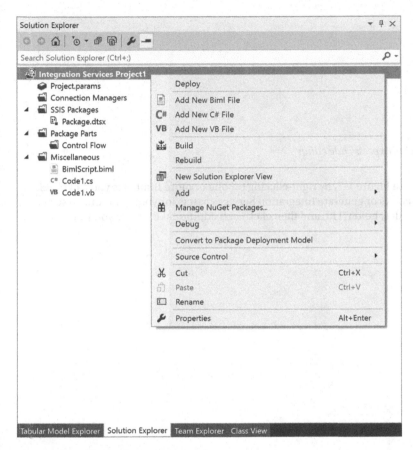

Figure 1-5. *The BimlExpress context menu*

Opening the Biml file will launch the Biml code editor, which includes syntax highlighting, code autocompletion, and quick info features for the Biml language. As shown in Figure 1-6, the Biml code editor is split into two panes: the top pane, which is the editor for your code, and the collapsible bottom pane, which is a preview of your expanded Biml code.

Figure 1-6. *BimlExpress code editor*

As shown in Figure 1-7, by right-clicking on one or more Biml files you can check Biml files for errors or generate Integration Services assets for your solution. To select multiple Biml files, hold CTRL and then click each additional Biml file you want to select.

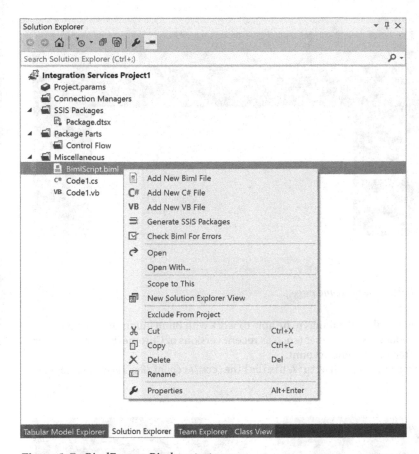

Figure 1-7. BimlExpress Biml context menu

BimlOnline

BimlOnline, shown in Figure 1-8, is another tool from Varigence for Biml code development. It is a web-based IDE to create and manage Biml projects online in your browser. With BimlOnline you can create and manage Biml projects with a full-featured code editor, a documentation generator, and an SSIS package importer, entirely from within your favorite modern web browser.

Figure 1-8. *BimlOnline welcome page*

You will need only three things to be able to work with BimlOnline: an Internet connection, a modern web browser (such as recent versions of Chrome, Firefox, Edge, or Opera), and a free BimlOnline account.

To create an account, visit `http://bimlonline.com/Account/Register`, as shown in Figure 1-9.

Figure 1-9. *BimlOnline registration page*

After registering, be sure to log in and optionally select "Remember Me" to avoid the need to log in from the same browser in the future, as shown in Figure 1-10.

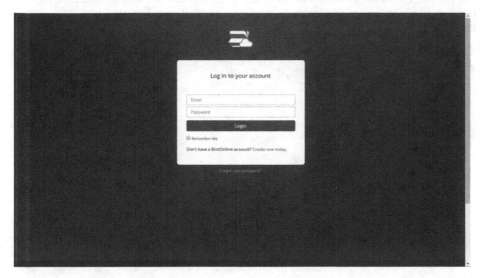

Figure 1-10. *The BimlOnline login page*

After you log into BimlOnline you can start your Biml code development by either creating a new Biml project, opening previous Biml project, or importing SSIS packages, as shown in Figure 1-11.

Figure 1-11. *The BimlOnline dashboard*

Once you have opened a project, you will notice three ribbon tabs at the top of the BimlOnline user interface: Add, Import, Build & Deploy. From the Add ribbon tab you can add empty Biml files or add files that have been filled out with sample code for relational, integration services, analysis services, and Biml metadata objects, as shown in Figure 1-12.

Figure 1-12. *The BimlOnline Add ribbon*

From the Import ribbon tab, you can import Integration Services assets like packages (.dtsx), project connection managers (.conmgr), project parameters (.params), and/or project deployment file (.ispac) to BimlOnline. All uploaded files will be automatically converted to Biml and you can either add the imported Biml to the current BimlOnline project or to a new project, as shown in Figure 1-13.

Figure 1-13. *The BimlOnline Import ribbon*

BimlOnline also allows you to publish your Biml project to a Visual Studio SSDT project via the Build & Deploy toolbar. To be able to do this you will need to use Google Chrome and install the Google Chrome extension called BimlChromeBuildAssistant that will allow you to build your SSIS project to your local machine, as shown in Figure 1-14.

Figure 1-14. *BimlOnline Build & Deploy ribbon*

To build your BimlOnline project, you need to do two things: prepare your environment and start the build process. To prepare your environment, you need to create an empty SSIS project on your local machine and add the full path of the `.dtproj` file to the Build Path in BimlStudio. After the preparation step, you can start the build process by first selecting the target build version and then clicking the Build button, as shown in Figure 1-15. Once the BimlOnline build is finished, new assets will be added to your local Visual Studio SSDT project.

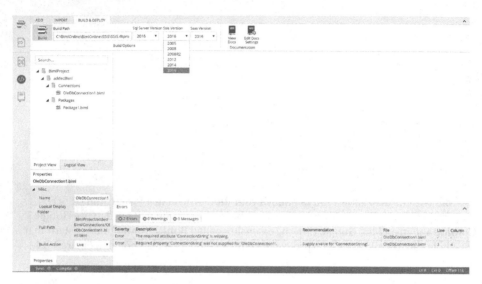

Figure 1-15. *BimlOnline Build & Deploy ribbon imported assets*

BimlStudio

The premier tool for designing and executing Biml and BimlScript is BimlStudio. It is an integrated development environment (IDE), much like Visual Studio/SQL Server Data Tools (SSDT)/Business Intelligence Designer Studio (BIDS), but it is specifically designed for development with Biml. BimlStudio, previously known as Mist, is a paid tool offered by Varigence. BimlStudio provides advanced code editing features, the ability to reverse engineer existing SSIS objects like packages and projects to Biml, visual designers for all Biml code, and a host of other features, which we summarize at the end of this chapter.

BimlStudio has a multiple document interface with a variety of tool windows. Like Visual Studio, each window is dockable, can be detached to different monitors, and supports independent zoom levels (use the slider in the status bar or CTRL + mousewheel to change the zoom level). In Figure 1-16, the top window is zoomed at 100% but the Biml code in the middle is zoomed at 150%, as displayed in the status bar in the bottom-right. Unlike BimlExpress, you don't have to build your code in order to see the output. As with other modern IDEs, BimlStudio will evaluate your code in the background and report back any errors, warnings, or information messages, and provide a live preview of objects that will be created when you invoke a build. Unlike Visual Studio, Biml Studio provides recommendations on how to resolve the four errors in the current project, as shown in Figure 1-16.

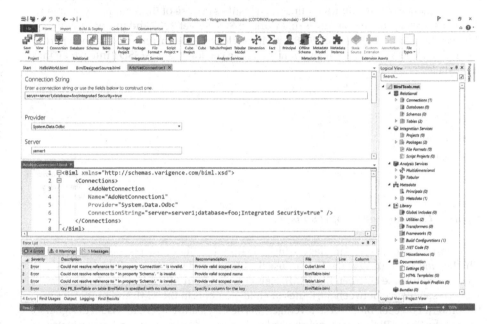

Figure 1-16. *The BimlStudio integrated development environment*

You can also see the rich ribbon structure at the top of BimlStudio. This is very similar to the Microsoft Office ribbon, which features contextual ribbons that appear when you perform specific tasks. For instance, when editing an SSIS Package, a Package Tools contextual ribbon group appears after Documentation. Edit an SSAS multidimensional cube, and that ribbon group is replaced with Cube Tools.

BimlStudio supports a project structure much like what you have used in BIDS and SSDT, all of which is saved under the project root node (`BimlTools.mst` in Figure 1-16). Double-clicking the project root node, or right-clicking and selecting Properties, will launch the project settings editor.

The most commonly modified project settings include Target Version selection and whether the SSIS packages should be built using the Project Deployment model (SSIS 2012 and above). If you work in a mixed version shop or provide consulting services, the convenience of this multi-targeting often justifies the use of BimlStudio. By changing the selector, you can emit packages that work on SQL Server 2005 and the exact same Biml can then target SQL Server 2016, all without leaving the current tool, as shown in Figure 1-17. The free Biml tools can only target the version of BIDS/SSDT into which they are installed.

Versions

SQL Server	SQL Server 2012 ▼	
SSAS Multidimensional	SSAS 2012 ▼	
SSAS Tabular	SSAS Tabular 2016 ▼	
SSIS	SSIS 2012 ▼	☐ Use Project Deployment *Disables Single Package* *Build & Run*

Figure 1-17. *BimlStudio project properties*

Biml is a homoiconic language, which means it has the same representation whether you are looking at the XML or use the object model. In other words, there is a 1:1 correspondence between Biml XML elements and Biml API objects, and a further 1:1 correspondence between attributes or child elements in the XML and properties in the Biml API objects. BimlStudio leverages this design feature to create visual designers against the Biml API that are synchronized with your code files. You can choose to use visual designers, code editors, or a combination of both, depending on what is most convenient for the task at hand. For example, we would much rather use the Connection String builder in BimlStudio than try to remember the correct syntax for an OLE DB connection. However, our preference is to write package-level code using the Biml Editor or Biml Designer. For instance, in Figure 1-16, if we made a change to the text, it would be reflected in the topmost editor and vice versa since they are different representations of the same underlying code. That is so cool!

BimlStudio has three different modes for working with code: Visual Designer, Biml Editor, and Biml Designer. The Visual Designer is analogous to the SSIS designer in SSDT. The Biml Editor is a fully featured Biml code editor. The Biml Designer is just like the Biml Editor but also includes a preview pane and a summary of errors/warnings for the file. In your project property settings, you can specify the "Default Action When Opening Item" from the Logical View tool window that shows all of the root objects in your solution. As shown in Figure 1-18, you have a variety of options to best suit your personal preferences.

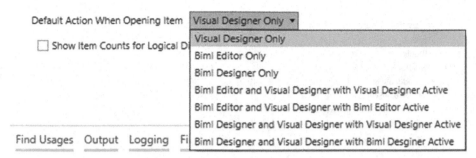

Figure 1-18. *BimlStudio default actions*

If you would prefer to make a different choice for any given open, simply right-click it to bring up a context menu that then allows you override the default editor experience, as shown in Figure 1-19.

View Designer

View Biml

View in BimlScript Designer

Figure 1-19. *BimlStudio Artifact context menu*

Logical vs. Project View

A BimlStudio project can be navigated using two different tool windows: the Logical View and the Project View. The Project View is straightforward; much like the Visual Studio Solution Explorer, it displays the files that comprise the project, as shown in Figure 1-20.

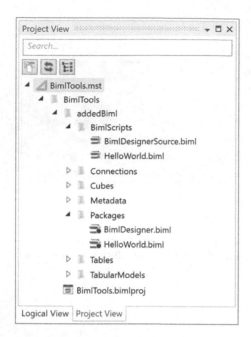

Figure 1-20. *Project View in BimlStudio*

In the above project, there are two files in the `BimlScripts` folder. Each of them when expanded will generate a Biml file that belongs to the Packages collection. The naming between a source Biml and the target does not have to be consistent. For example, expanding `HelloWorld.biml` results in a Biml file that defines an SSIS package also called HelloWorld. However, `BimlDesignerSource.biml` declares a package named BimlDesigner. The circle adornment indicates a script is live versus a reference file.

The concept of a Biml file being live or reference only has context within BimlStudio. In short, a live file is always compiled during the build process whereas a reference is only compiled on demand. That demand can be a direct request via Execute BimlScript or command line compilation, but it can also be an indirect call through another file's include statement or CallBimlScript. We will cover this in more depth in Chapter 5. BimlExpress only supports reference files as you must explicitly identify, via select/multi-select, the files to compile. If you find yourself stuck trying to debug a BimlScript with errors, changing it to a reference file allows you to "unbreak" the rest of the project while you sort out the issues.

The Logical View is for some a friendlier logical abstraction to the Biml projects. For example, in a complicated data warehouse solution, you might want to separate your staging packages from dimensional processing packages. That is easily accomplished in Logical View (and by specifying the `LogicalDisplayFolder` in your Biml). Think of it as a preview of which objects (tables, packages, projects) your Biml solution will create when you click the Build button, as shown in Figure 1-21. Also note that it is possible for a single Biml or BimlScript file to create a huge number of tables, packages, or other objects. The Project View will show the one Biml file. The Logical View will show the potentially numerous objects generated by that file.

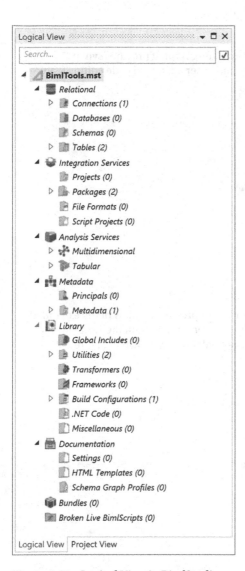

Figure 1-21. *Logical View in BimlStudio*

Biml Editor

The Biml Editor is the basic text editor for manipulating Biml. It provides syntax highlighting, quick info, code autocompletion, and other advanced code editing features. A sample is shown in Figure 1-22.

```
1  <Biml xmlns="http://schemas.varigence.com/biml.xsd">
2      <Packages>
3          <#
4              string packageName = "HelloWorld";
5          #>
6          <Package Name="<#= packageName #>" ProtectionLevel="DontSaveSensitive" />
7      </Packages>
8  </Biml>
9
```

Figure 1-22. *The Biml Editor*

Biml Designer

The Biml Designer provides a BimlScript editor with a preview window of the expanded contents. You can see that the expanded BimlScript does not contain the variable packageName because it has been replaced in the final Biml, as shown in Figure 1-23.

BimlScript Input Editor

```
1  <Biml xmlns="http://schemas.varigence.com/biml.xsd">
2      <Packages>
3          <#
4              string packageName = "HelloWorld";
5          #>
6          <Package Name="<#= packageName #>" ProtectionLevel="DontSaveSensitive" />
7      </Packages>
8  </Biml>
9
```

Preview Expanded BimlScript

```
1  <Biml xmlns="http://schemas.varigence.com/biml.xsd">
2      <Packages>
3          <Package Name="HelloWorld" ProtectionLevel="DontSaveSensitive" />
4      </Packages>
5  </Biml>
6
```

Figure 1-23. *Editing and previewing BimlScript*

Visual Designers

The Visual Designers provide a drag-and-drop experience for crafting your Biml objects. If you are new to Biml or not able to figure out what a property might be called, open up the Visual Designer and let the UI guide you. If you are stuck trying to figure out how to Biml something, you can also use the Import Tables or Import Packages facilities to render the working Biml for a given table or package that you have already created.

The designers are specific to the artifact they are modifying. As examples, there is a Package Designer that can help you to visualize the design of an SSIS package without coding in Biml, as shown in Figure 1-24.

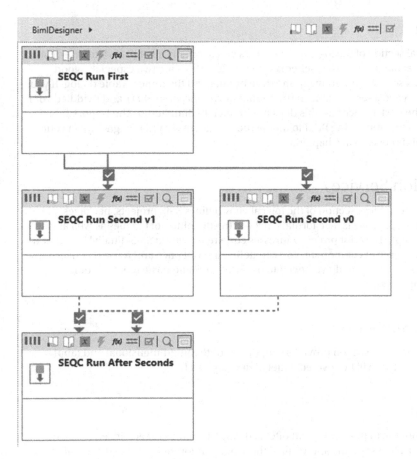

Figure 1-24. *The BimlStudio Visual Designer*

The table designer is shown in Figure 1-25.

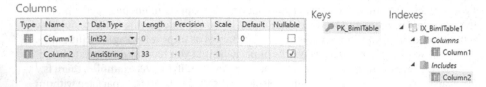

Figure 1-25. *BimlStudio Table Designer*

Relational

The Relational section of the logical view allows you to specify all of your database-related objects: connections, databases, schemas, and tables. There are two especially good features in this section: the Connection String builder and the Import Table dialog. If you have ever mistyped a server name in the connection manager in SSDT and twiddled your thumbs for the next 30 seconds, this does not happen in BimlStudio. The Import Table wizard creates the underlying Biml to model the tables, views, and foreign keys in your database. This is covered in Chapter 3.

Integration Services

The Integration Services section of the logical view defines SSIS projects, packages, file formats, and script projects. File formats include the definition of flat files as well as raw files. The concept of a script project addresses code reuse within SSIS–finally! Whether it is a script task or script component, you can define a script once and reuse it consistently across packages. No longer do you need to perform copy and paste reuse of your common script tasks.

Analysis Services

The Analysis Services section provides support for both multidimensional and tabular model projects. This will be covered in detail in Chapter 11.

Metadata

Metadata is unique to BimlStudio but offers advanced features for advanced users. An offline schema allows you to capture all of the schema information related to database tables, views, or query result sets. This can be invaluable for those providing consulting services; you can prepare an offline schema from the client's user context for systems that you cannot yet access. From here you can continue your work independent from client's system until your access request is granted or you are ready to provide working SSIS packages and SQL scripts that fit the client needs. The other types of Biml metadata are metadata models and the related metadata instances. These are formal abstractions for modelling the metadata that will drive your BimlScripts. For instance, instead of using a relational table in the foreword to store the list of tables we wanted to stage, we could have used a metadata model instead. We will cover the features and benefits in more detail for general metadata in Chapter 4 and the BimlStudio-specific metadata features in Chapter 9.

Library

The Library section contains everything that does not fit into the above categories. That is not to imply it is the "junk drawer." In fact, this is where your most powerful tools will be located. Your utilities will contain your powerful, reusable scripts. You might have scripts that codify your dimensional processing: Type 0, Type 1, Type 2, Type 6, or event handling or even audio files that you'd like to play while your project builds (as a fun diversion–not for any practical purpose). Anything that you can code can go in the utilities.

Transformers are also stored in the library. They allow you to modify the rendered Biml without having to change the original. For example, say the corporate standard is to name your data flow as "DFT Source Destination" and the developers delivered "Data Flow Task." Instead of manually renaming those tasks, changing their code, or rejecting it, you can apply a transformer after the fact to rename it all. A more realistic example of a transformer is a Kimball-style fact table load. If you designed a lookup pattern that assumed the reference dimension was populated prior to the fact table load, but later discovered this should actually be a late arriving dimension (or early arriving fact), you are potentially stuck with a bunch of work. Instead of recoding one or more entire data flows, you could instead apply a transformer to fix the issue across all of your packages that used that logic.

If you do not want to build your own patterns, frameworks are licensed bundles that provide turnkey solutions and are discussed in detail in Chapter 10.

If you have pure .NET code, VB, or C#, you can also add those files in and reference them as need be.

Documentation

Documentation is always the last item delivered in a project and so too in this chapter. BimlStudio already knows about the tables, packages, and cubes that you are delivering, so why not let it build the documentation? BimlStudio automatically creates a rich documentation UI for your project that displays the Logical View assets in a tree view with the ability to open each item for a rich display in the document area. As with all things Biml, it's fully customizable. Develop a template or stylesheet that reflects your corporate branding and you'll have a polished, interactive document to deliver at the end of your project. Chapter 13 will go into detail on the documentation capabilities.

Feature Comparison

Table 1-1 offers a summary of high-level features along with the Biml tools that support them. Depending on what you need to do, there should be a Biml tooling option to meet your needs.

Table 1-1. *BimlExpress, BimlOnline, and BimlStudio Feature Comparison*

Relational Databases	BimlExpress	BimlOnline	BimlStudio
Model relational database objects	X	X	X
Produce DDL for any ANSI SQL-compliant RDBMS	X	X	X
Import relational database objects from BimlScript code	X	X	X
Import relational database objects using visual UI	-	-	X
Integration Services (SSIS)			
Model SSIS packages	X	X	X
Generate SSIS packages (DTSX files)	X	X	X
Generate SSIS projects (DTProj, Params, ISPAC files)	-	-	X
Import SSIS packages and projects	-	X	X
Easier use of feature packs and third-party tasks/ components	-	-	X
Analysis Services (SSAS)			
Model SSAS cubes	-	-	X
Model SSAS tabular and PowerPivot	-	-	X
Generate SSAS cubes, tabular models, and PowerPivot	-	-	X
Import cubes, tabular models, and PowerPivot	-	-	X
Scripting			
Automate Biml with BimlScript code nuggets	X	X	X
Customize validation with your own errors and warnings	X	X	X
Use transformers to modify objects and inject patterns	-	-	X

(continued)

Table 1-1. (*continued*)

Relational Databases	BimlExpress	BimlOnline	BimlStudio
Organize transformers and BimlScripts into reusable frameworks	-	-	X
User Interface			
BimlScript code editor with advanced Intelliprompt	X	X	X
Visual Designers for all Biml objects	-	-	X
Live view of objects as you code	-	-	X
Automation			
Command line compiler	-	-	X
MSBuild support	-	-	X
API access from external applications	-	-	X
Extensibility			
Biml Bundle support for packaging and IP protection	-	-	X
Extend the Biml language	-	-	X
Extend BimlStudio UI	-	-	X
Redistribute BimlEngine binaries (OEM)	-	-	X
Host BimlEngine binaries in a value-added service (SaaS)	-	-	X
Metadata Management			
Create reusable models for metadata storage	-	-	X
Autogeneration of metadata entry UI based on metadata objects	-	-	X
Consistent and friendly API for accessing stored metadata	-	-	X
Plugin model allows storage of metadata anywhere	-	-	X

Summary

In this chapter, you were introduced to the different tools that you can use to start with your Biml development. Throughout the chapter, you looked at each tool and learned the features of the tool and how to use it.

In the next chapter, we will acquaint you with the basic elements and structure of the Biml language before we hop on to more advanced endeavours!

CHAPTER 2

■ ■ ■

Introduction to the Biml Language

Biml is an XML-based language that allows for faster development by creating more consistent and reliable code. Business Intelligence Markup Language (abbreviated as uppercase B, lowercase i, lowercase m, and lowercase l) uses XML along with code nuggets written in C# or Visual Basic to automate SQL Server Integration Services, Analysis Services, and Relational Database Objects.

Biml works in the design-time development environment, if you have any Biml tool like BimlExpress or BimlStudio installed (see Chapter 1), you won't need any additional software installed within your enterprise infrastructure. It is a design-time experience and outputs SQL scripts, Integration Services files, Analysis Services files (Multidimensional and Tabular), and other assets exactly as if they were created by hand. These projects/ scripts are then able to follow the standard operations workflow within your enterprise without any remaining dependency on Biml or BimlScript.

Figure 2-1 illustrates the Biml workflow starting with a tool that can work with Biml like BimlStudio, BimlExpress, or BimlOnline.

© Andy Leonard et al. 2017
A. Leonard et al., *The Biml Book*, https://doi.org/10.1007/978-1-4842-3135-7_2

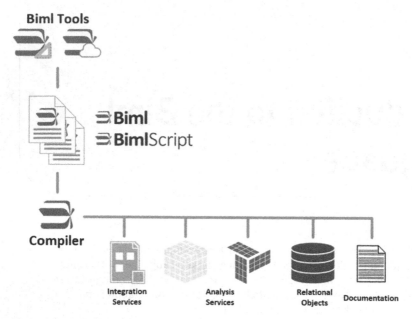

Figure 2-1. Biml workflow

Motivation

If you have worked with Microsoft business intelligence projects, you might be familiar with the fact that most of the files that are created within the development environment are stored in an XML format. What then would be the motivation to create an additional XML file to generate the above assets? There are two main reasons. First, the Microsoft file formats are designed to be read and written by graphical design tools. As a result, they tend to be very difficult to author and maintain by hand. Biml is designed to be human readable and writable, and that makes a huge difference. The second reason is automation. By creating a template/pattern in Biml, you are able to reuse that pattern over and over again to create new assets. This enables more consistent code with a focus on the pattern and not the reputation of creating multiple packages with a similar pattern.

There are projects that are very well suited for the use of Biml and those projects consist of patterns and repetition. This type of reusable pattern is often found within ETL (extract, transform, and load) projects. The staging pattern is often the exact same pattern applied to a different table, as seen in Figure 2-2.

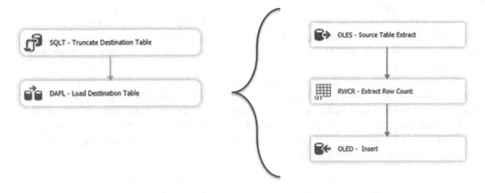

Figure 2-2. *Example of an integration services repeatable pattern for control flow and data flow*

We can also find repeating patterns and good use cases within Analysis Services, which will be discussed in Chapter 11.

Biml Language Structure

The Biml language can be broken down into two main components: Biml and BimlScript. Figure 2-3 illustrates the relationship between the Biml and BimlScript subsets of the language and provides a high-level overview of the syntax involved in using each aspect osf the language.

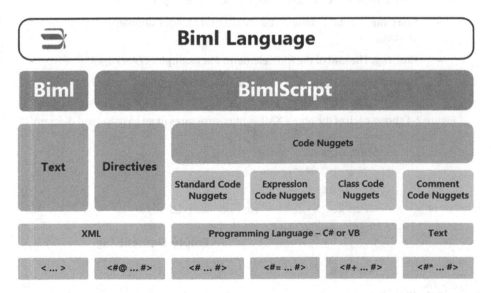

Figure 2-3. *Biml language diagram*

Biml refers to the XML sections within the code that define the elements that will be compiled into outputs for the Microsoft Business Intelligence stack. As a comparison to another technology, you can think of Biml as you would HyperText Markup Language (HTML). Creating static HTML pages is the same as creating a file that only contains Biml and not BimlScript.

BimlScript can be compared to Active Server Pages .NET (ASP.NET) or Hypertext Preprocessor (PHP). Like ASP.NET and PHP, which used server-side scripting to generate content prior to sending it to the client's web browser, BimlScript generates content in the design environment prior to rendering it as the final object you will use in your data solution.

Before moving on, we should have a quick review of XML syntax and usage because it is critical to writing Biml correctly.

■ **Note**   Biml is a T4-like language (T4 is Text Template Transformation Toolkit) which is based on a template text generation framework.

XML Introduction

Biml is an XML-based markup language, but before we discuss the Biml language elements, let's review some of the basic concepts and syntax of XML.

- **XML Element**: The item within a start or end tag. For example: `<Package>`

- **XML Attribute**: A name/value pair that exists within a start-tag or empty-element tag. Attributes are used to define more details of the element. For example: `<Package Name="Example" />`

- **Start Tag**: The beginning of the XML element. For example: `<Packages>`

- **End Tag**: The end of the XML element. For example: `</Packages>`

- **Empty-Element Tag**: An XML element with no content. For example: `<Package />`

Figure 2-4 shows each of the above XML syntax structures in an easy-to-read diagram.

Figure 2-4. *XML diagram*

If you want to learn more about XML than just these basics, check out the stairway to XML, which can be found at www.sqlservercentral.com/articles/Stairway+Series/ Introduction+to+XML/92780/ or www.bimlscript.com/walkthrough/Details/3109.

Biml

The Biml language is a dialect of XML, and the permitted elements, attributes, and structure of that dialect are defined in an XML schema. The Biml XML schema can be found at www.bimlscript.com/Content/Docs/biml.xsd.

All Biml files must start with the opening <Biml xmlns="http://schemas. varigence.com/biml.xsd"> element and end with the </Biml> element. Note that it is possible to create reusable Biml code fragments that do not have to begin with a Biml element, but those fragments must be included in a file, that itself contains a Biml root element, using an include declaration, CallBimlScript, etc. You will learn more about these methods in Chapter 5.

■ **Tip**   Just because the namespace is a URL, this does not mean that you need to be connected to the Internet for Biml to work!

Root Elements

The root elements are the building blocks for the any project. Anything that can be defined in a Biml project must start from a member of the root elements. Listing 2-1 shows the Packages root element. Others are shown in Figure 2-5.

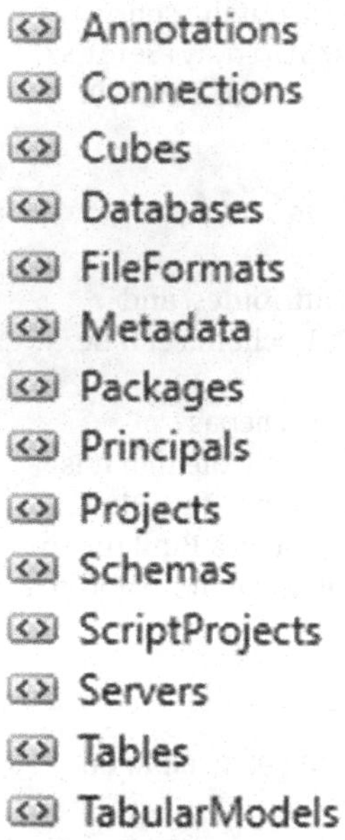

◁▷ Annotations

◁▷ Connections

◁▷ Cubes

◁▷ Databases

◁▷ FileFormats

◁▷ Metadata

◁▷ Packages

◁▷ Principals

◁▷ Projects

◁▷ Schemas

◁▷ ScriptProjects

◁▷ Servers

◁▷ Tables

◁▷ TabularModels

Figure 2-5. *Root elements*

Only some root elements will be covered in this chapter; if you need follow-up information, take a look at the Varigence online documentation for a complete list of objects within the root elements (`www.varigence.com/Documentation/Language/Index`). The most commonly used root elements are `Connections`, `FileFormats`, `Packages`, `Tables`, and `Schemas`.

Text Blocks

Text blocks are the sections of code that are copied "as-is" to the Biml compiler. These sections will not have any preprocessing applied prior to being sent to the Biml compiler.

Listing 2-1 is a Biml text block (the entire script) that gets copied directly to the Biml compiler and produces an Integration Services package named `Hello World.dtsx`.

Listing 2-1. A Simple Biml File with Only Text Blocks

```
<Biml xmlns="http://schemas.varigence.com/biml.xsd">
  <Packages>
    <Package Name="Hello World" />
  </Packages>
</Biml>
```

Listing 2-1 could be considered a Biml-only file and does not include any BimlScript language features.

Comments

Biml XML comments use the same syntax as regular XML comments. Like XML comments they are permitted to span more than one line. Comments cannot be placed inside another comment.

Listing 2-2 is a Biml XML comment that is used to document the code as well as comment out the creation of the Hello World package.

Listing 2-2. Biml XML Comments

```
<Biml xmlns="http://schemas.varigence.com/biml.xsd">
  <Packages>
    <!-- This is an XML Comment -->
    <!--
    <Package Name="Hello World" />
    -->
  </Packages>
</Biml>
```

■ **Note**   Biml XML comments do not stop BimlScript from the preprocessing phase. If a BimlScript needs to be commented out so that .NET code nuggets are not evaluated, use a Comment Control Block as described below.

Biml XML Comments were used extensively with the previously supported BIDSHelper add-in because of the highlighting issues associated with Biml code nuggets in the default BIDSHelper code editor for Biml and XML.

A First Package

If you compile the code in Listing 2-3, an empty package called MyFirstBimlPackage.dtsx is generated.

Listing 2-3. Biml Code for First Empty Package

```
<Biml xmlns="http://schemas.varigence.com/biml.xsd">
  <Packages>
    <Package Name="MyFirstBimlPackage"></Package>
  </Packages>
</Biml>
```

Not super exciting, so let's fill it with a little more content by adding a data flow and a container; see Listing 2-4.

Listing 2-4. Biml Code for a Package with a Container and a Data Flow

```
<Biml xmlns="http://schemas.varigence.com/biml.xsd">
  <Packages>
    <Package Name="MyFirstBimlPackage">
      <Tasks>
        <Dataflow Name="Dataflow1" />
        <Container Name="Container1" />
      </Tasks>
    </Package>
  </Packages>
</Biml>
```

You end up with the same package but it's not empty anymore. Instead, it now has a container and a dataflow (granted, both tasks are still empty); see Figure 2-6.

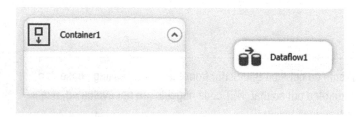

Figure 2-6. *Empty container and data flow created by Biml*

The important part here is that whenever you want Biml to actually create something inside your package, you wrap those tasks in the <Tasks> collection element. The same is true within a container, so if you want the dataflow to actually sit within our container, you would use the code shown in Listing 2-5.

Listing 2-5. Biml Code for a Package with a Dataflow within a Container

```
<Biml xmlns="http://schemas.varigence.com/biml.xsd">
  <Packages>
    <Package Name="MyFirstBimlPackage">
      <Tasks>
        <Container Name="Container1">
          <Tasks>
            <Dataflow Name="Dataflow1" />
          </Tasks>
        </Container>
      </Tasks>
    </Package>
  </Packages>
</Biml>
```

The logic within a data flow is similar: all the actual components will be authored into the <Transformations> collection element, as shown in Listing 2-6.

Listing 2-6. Biml Code for a Package Including an OLEDB Source and Destination

```
<Biml xmlns="http://schemas.varigence.com/biml.xsd">
  <Packages>
    <Package Name="MyFirstBimlPackage">
      <Tasks>
        <Container Name="Container1">
          <Tasks>
            <Dataflow Name="Dataflow1">
              <Transformations>
                <OleDbSource Name="Source"/>
                <OleDbDestination Name="Destination"/>
              </Transformations>
            </Dataflow>
          </Tasks>
        </Container>
      </Tasks>
    </Package>
  </Packages>
</Biml>
```

Referencing Objects by Name

Suppose you'd like to enhance your first version of the package by changing the simple sequence container to a ForEachFromVariable looping container. Consequently, you need to add both the container and a variable for that container to iterate over.

Before you change the container type, let's start by adding the variable, which works just as you would expect, as shown in Listing 2-7.

Listing 2-7. Biml Code for a Package Including a Variable

```
<Biml xmlns="http://schemas.varigence.com/biml.xsd">
  <Packages>
    <Package Name="MyFirstBimlPackage">
      <Tasks>
        <Dataflow Name="Dataflow1" />
        <Container Name="Container1">
          <Variables>
            <Variable Name="LoopVariable" DataType="String">abc</Variable>
          </Variables>
        </Container>
      </Tasks>
    </Package>
  </Packages>
</Biml>
```

35

Now you can change the Container to a ForEachFromVariableLoop element. As Biml allows us to reference an object by its name, you can simply set the variable to iterate over in your loop, as shown in Listing 2-8.

Listing 2-8. Biml Code for a Package Including a For Each Loop

```
<Biml xmlns="http://schemas.varigence.com/biml.xsd">
  <Packages>
    <Package Name="MyFirstBimlPackage">
      <Tasks>
        <Dataflow Name="Dataflow1" />
        <ForEachFromVariableLoop Name="Container1"
         VariableName="User.LoopVariable">
          <Variables>
            <Variable Name="LoopVariable" DataType="String">abc</Variable>
          </Variables>
        </ForEachFromVariableLoop>
      </Tasks>
    </Package>
  </Packages>
</Biml>
```

Building the above code will result in the package shown in Figure 2-7.

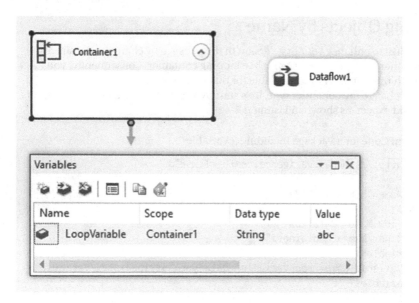

Figure 2-7. *Variable created by Biml*

You might have noticed that the variable was referenced as User.LoopVariable. As with Microsoft Business Intelligence Development Studio (BIDS) and SQL Server Data Tools (SSDT), SQL Server Integration Services (SSIS) variables are referenced using their namespace and their name; their default namespace is User, which you could override by using the Namespace attribute on the variable definition.

■ **Note**   As a general convention, any Biml attribute that references another object by name will have an attribute name that ends with "Name," such as VariableName in Listing 2-8.

References with Scoped Name

It is possible to have multiple variables with the same name, provided they are defined in different tasks, as shown in Listing 2-9.

Listing 2-9. Biml Code for a Package with Multiple Variables in Different Scopes

```
<Biml xmlns="http://schemas.varigence.com/biml.xsd">
  <Packages>
    <Package Name="MyFirstBimlPackage">
      <Variables>
        <Variable Name="LoopVariable" DataType="String">abc</Variable>
      </Variables>
      <Tasks>
        <Dataflow Name="Container1" />
        <ForEachFromVariableLoop Name="Boo" VariableName="User.LoopVariable">
          <Variables>
            <Variable Name="LoopVariable" DataType="String">abc</Variable>
          </Variables>
        </ForEachFromVariableLoop>
      </Tasks>
    </Package>
  </Packages>
</Biml>
```

This means that you have two instances of LoopVariable, so you potentially have to tell the Biml compiler which one you actually want to reference. This brings us to the notion of *scope* and *scoped names*. When you refer to an object by name, the Biml engine will automatically find the object with a matching name that is closest to the reference. In this case, since the instance of LoopVariable in Container1 is within the same object as the reference, while MyFirstBimlPackage's instance is on the parent object, the Biml compiler will use the Container1 instance. It's closer. And in many cases, this will be what you're looking for.

You can still use the variable defined in MyFirstBimlPackage though! To do so, you remove the ambiguity by using the scoped name of the target variable. This is just like in SQL where you can provide more context by writing SELECT * FROM adventureworks2014.Person.Person instead of just SELECT * FROM Person.Person. Just provide the additional context when needed, as shown in Listing 2-10.

Listing 2-10. Biml Code for a Package with a Scoped Reference to a Variable

```
<Biml xmlns="http://schemas.varigence.com/biml.xsd">
  <Packages>
    <Package Name="MyFirstBimlPackage">
      <Variables>
        <Variable Name="LoopVariable" DataType="String">abc</Variable>
      </Variables>
      <Tasks>
        <Dataflow Name="Dataflow1" />
        <ForEachFromVariableLoop Name="Container1" VariableName="MyFirstBiml
         Package.User.LoopVariable">
          <Variables>
            <Variable Name="LoopVariable" DataType="String">abc</Variable>
          </Variables>
        </ForEachFromVariableLoop>
      </Tasks>
    </Package>
  </Packages>
</Biml>
```

■ **Note**   Objects of the same type can never have the same scoped name. All references in Biml are restricted by the type of object you are referencing. For example, VariableName must reference a variable. Consequently, there aren't any cases where having objects of differing type with the same scoped name can actually cause conflicts.

More on the Biml Language

We will cover many more elements of Biml in this book, but we won't include the equivalent of reference documentation for Biml. If that's what you're looking for, Biml is fully documented on the varigence.com website at https://varigence.com/Documentation. Starting with the root node, the Biml documentation describes every language element, including its purpose, its attributes, child elements, required vs. optional configuration, and much more. The bimlscript.com site also has a guided walkthrough of all key Biml language elements for relational, SSIS, and SSIS targets, if you would prefer to see the language elements used in context of code samples.

Biml Script

BimlScript includes the programming language elements within a Biml script/file, which are generally referred to as *code nuggets* and *directives*. See Figure 2-3 for a diagram of how these language features interact with the rest of Biml. The code nuggets can be programmed using C# or Visual Basic. This means that BimlScript will automate major parts of your Biml code, so it will kind of automate your automation☺.

Of course, now that we're discussing the programmability aspects of the language, we need a Hello World example! Let's start with the earlier simple example of creating an empty package and add some code nuggets to create three Hello World packages.

Notice in Listing 2-11 there are two different types of code nuggets, the *control nugget* (`<# ... #>`) and the *text nugget* (`<#= ... #>`). Control nuggets allow you to place arbitrary C# or VB code that commonly define variables, loops, and conditional statements. Text nuggets contain an expression that will be evaluated as a string in the output Biml code.

Listing 2-11. Basic BimlScript File

```
<Biml xmlns="http://schemas.varigence.com/biml.xsd">
  <Packages>
    <# for (int i=1; i<=3; i++) { #>
    <Package Name="Hello World <#= i #>" />
    <# } #>
  </Packages>
</Biml>
```

To achieve the same result using Visual Basic, you need to declare the language first to the Biml Compiler (see *template directive*); see Listing 2-12.

Listing 2-12. Basic BimlScript File in Visual Basic

```
<#@ Template Language="VB" #>
<Biml xmlns="http://schemas.varigence.com/biml.xsd">
  <Packages>
    <# for i as integer = 1 to 3 #>
    <Package Name="Hello World <#= i #>" />
    <# next #>
  </Packages>
</Biml>
```

In each case, a for loop is created to iterate the variable i from 1 to 3. On each iteration, a package named Hello World.dtsx followed by the string value of i is created.

Code Nuggets

Code nuggets are the sections of code that contain C# or Visual Basic. Code nuggets can use any available .NET API and can reference objects in other Biml files through the RootNode object.

There are four types of code nuggets that will be discussed below: control code nuggets, text code nuggets, class code nuggets, and comment code nuggets.

Control Code Nuggets

Control code nuggets are sections of code that help in the generation of text for the Biml compiler. This capability enables you to use code nuggets to programmatically create Biml objects.

Control code nuggets have the following syntax: an opening <# followed by C# or VB code and ending with a closing #>, like so:

```
<# [C# or Visual Basic Code] #>
```

■ **Tip** There are multiple ways to use control code nuggets as well as two main stylistic coding methods: single line code termination, where each line of .NET code is placed in its own code nugget, and multiple line code termination, where a single code nugget may contain many lines of code. Both methods produce the same output, as shown in the two equivalent samples below, and represent only a coding preference selected by the developer.

```
<# var sqlString = "var sqlString = @"SELECT Something FROM dbo.Table"; #>

<# var conn = RootNode.OleDbConnections["Source"]; #>

<# var tables = ExternalDataAccess.GetDataTable(conn.ConnectionString,
sqlString); #>

<# var sqlString = "var sqlString = @"SELECT Something FROM dbo.Table";

    var conn = RootNode.OleDbConnections["Source"];

    var tables = ExternalDataAccess.GetDataTable(conn.ConnectionString,
    sqlString); #>
```

Text Code Nuggets

Text code nuggets are sections of code that evaluate an expression and then convert it to a string. This string is then inserted into the Biml output. The expression is evaluated first and then converted to a string. Unlike a standard control code nugget, text code nuggets can and must contain programming fragments that can be evaluated to a single string.

Text code nuggets have the following syntax: an opening <#= followed by C# or VB code and ending with a closing #>#>, as follows:

```
<#= [C# or Visual Basic Code] #>
```

■ **Note** Text code nuggets should not include the line terminators (e.g. a semicolon in C#) that are required with control code nuggets at the end of each line.

An example of a text code nugget that specifies the name of a package to use, Source, along with the current table name is shown in Listing 2-13.

Listing 2-13. Expression Control Block Example

```
<Package Name="Source <#=table.Name#>">
```

Class Code Nuggets

Class code nuggets allow .NET methods, properties, and other features to be added to the class that is autogenerated to process the BimlScript file. The code in class code nuggets is most commonly used to implement utility methods or helper classes that are consumed from within your other code nuggets. Generally, as you find your code being repeated across multiple code nuggets, it makes sense to refactor your code to move the common code into class code nuggets.

Class code nuggets have the following syntax: an opening <#+ followed by C# or VB code and ending with a closing #>, like so:

```
<#+ [C# or Visual Basic Code] #>
```

An example of a class code nugget that exposes the user-defined AllLower methods is shown in Listing 2-14.

Listing 2-14. Single File Class Feature Control Block Example

```
<Biml xmlns="http://schemas.varigence.com/biml.xsd">
  <Packages>
    <Package Name="<#= AllLower("CFCBExample") #>" >
  </Packages>
</Biml>

<#+
  private string AllLower(string Value)
  {
    return Value.ToLower();
  }
#>
```

A convenient option to keep your BimlScript files maintainable is to put your class code nuggets in a separate file that is pulled into your BimlScript file using an include directive. This is demonstrated in Listing 2-15 and Listing 2-16.

Listing 2-15. Class Feature Control Block Only File Example

```
<#+
  private string AllLower(string Value)
  {
    return Value.ToLower();
  }
#>
```

41

Listing 2-16. Class Feature Control Block with Include File Example

```
<#@ include file="ClassFeature.biml" #>

<Biml xmlns="http://schemas.varigence.com/biml.xsd">
  <Packages>
    <Package Name="<#= AllLower("CFCBExample") #>" >
  </Packages>
</Biml>
```

Comment Code Nuggets

Comment code nuggets allow comments within a BimlScript just like an XML comments but with the added benefit that comment code nuggets prevent contained BimlScript code nuggets from running. XML comments (`<!-- Comment -->`) will not stop a contained BimlScript from running.

Comment code nuggets have the following syntax: an opening `<#*` followed by any content or code and ending with a closing `*#>`, as shown in Listing 2-17.

Listing 2-17. Comment Code Nuggets

```
<#* [Text or C# or Visual Basic Code] *#>
```

A comment code nugget can be used anywhere and is a good way to comment out BimlScript code during testing. Comments in XML required additional comment syntax within the C# or Visual Basic code to prevent the code from running. See Listings 2-18 and 2-19.

Listing 2-18. C# Comment

```
<# //var importResult = conn.ImportDB("", "", ImportOptions.None); #>
```

Listing 2-19. Comment Control Block

```
<#* var importResult = conn.ImportDB("", "", ImportOptions.None); *#>
```

Both Listing 2-18 and Listing 2-19 achieve the same result, but Listing 2-20 does not stop the ImportDB method from executing.

Listing 2-20. XML Comment

```
<!--
<# var importResult = conn.ImportDB("", "", ImportOptions.
ExcludeForeignKey); #>
-- >
```

RootNode

RootNode is an application programming interface (API) to an in-memory representation of the objects within a Biml project. The RootNode works differently between BimlExpress and BimlStudio.

In BimlExpress, the RootNode API is only able to access objects within the selected files and after the Generate SSIS Packages menu option is selected.

BimlStudio can access all of the objects within the files (both live and reference) in a BimlStudio project.

■ **Note**   When using BimlExpress with Visual Studio the RootNode does not include all of the files in the project but only the files selected and then used in conjunction with the Generate SSIS Packages menu option.

Tiers

Tiers define which objects are available to the subsequent tiers during compilation. As noted in the section about the tier attribute of the template directive, tiers can be any numerical value, including negative numbers.

Any Biml file that contains no code nuggets and no directives defaults to tier 0. Any Biml file with code nuggets or directives defaults to tier 1.

Biml objects that are accessed through RootNode are not able to access other objects from the same or any higher tier. Listing 2-21 shows a basic use of tiers to access the connection objects from a separate Biml file.

Listing 2-21. Tier 0 File

```
<#@ template tier="0" #>

<Biml xmlns="http://schemas.varigence.com/biml.xsd">
  <Connections>
    <OleDbConnection Name="Source" ConnectionString="Provider=SQLOLEDB.1;
    Data Source=.;Initial Catalog=AdventureWorks;Integrated Security=SSPI;" />
    <OleDbConnection Name="Stage" ConnectionString="Provider=SQLOLEDB.1;
    Data Source=.;Initial Catalog=Stage; Integrated Security=SSPI;" />
  </Connections>
</Biml>
```

Listing 2-21 has two `OleDbConnection` objects that can be exposed to your BimlScript in later tiers. In Listing 2-22 (and Listing 2-23 for VB), you use the connection objects for your BimlScript to get all of the tables within the AdventureWorks database.

Listing 2-22. Tier 1 file That Accesses Biml Objects from Tier 0 and Creates Multiple Packages

```
<#@ template tier="1" #>

<#@ import namespace="Varigence.Biml.CoreLowerer.SchemaManagement" #>

<# var conn=RootNode.OleDbConnections["Source"]; #>
<# var tables=conn.GenerateTableNodes(); #>

<Biml xmlns="http://schemas.varigence.com/biml.xsd">
  <Packages>
    <# foreach (var table in tables) { #>
    <Package Name="Source <#= table.Name #>" >
      <Tasks>
        <Dataflow Name="Stage <#= table.Name #>" >
          <Transformations>
            <OleDbSource Name="Source <#= table.Name #>" ConnectionName="Source">
              <ExternalTableInput Table="[<#= table.Schema.Name #>].[<#=
              table.Name #>]" />
            </OleDbSource>
            <OleDbDestination Name="Destination" ConnectionName="Stage">
              <InputPath OutputPathName="Source <#= table.Name #>.Output" />
              <ExternalTableOutput Table="[<#= table.Schema.Name #>].[<#=
              table.Name #>]" />
            </OleDbDestination>
          </Transformations>
        </Dataflow>
      </Tasks>
    </Package>
    <# } #>
  </Packages>
</Biml>
```

Listing 2-23. Tier 1 File That Accesses Biml Objects from Tier 0 and Creates Multiple Packages in Visual Basic

```
<#@ template tier="1" language="VB" optionexplicit="false" #>

<#@ import namespace="Varigence.Biml.CoreLowerer.SchemaManagement" #>

<# Dim conn=RootNode.OleDbConnections("Source") #>
<# Dim tables=conn.GenerateTableNodes() #>
```

```
<Biml xmlns="http://schemas.varigence.com/biml.xsd">
  <Packages>
    <# for each tbl in tables #>
    <Package Name="Source <#= tbl.Name #>" >
      <Tasks>
        <Dataflow Name="Stage <#= tbl.Name #>" >
          <Transformations>
            <OleDbSource Name="Source <#= tbl.Name #>" ConnectionName="Source">
              <ExternalTableInput Table="[<#= tbl.Schema.Name #>].[<#= tbl.
              Name #>]" />
            </OleDbSource>
            <OleDbDestination Name="Destination" ConnectionName="Stage">
              <InputPath OutputPathName="Source <#= tbl.Name #>.Output" />
              <ExternalTableOutput Table="[<#= tbl.Schema.Name #>].[<#= tbl.
              Name #>]" />
            </OleDbDestination>
          </Transformations>
        </Dataflow>
      </Tasks>
    </Package>
    <# next #>
  </Packages>
</Biml>
```

There are a lot of different ways to work with Biml and the above example creates a separate package for each table. To create a single package with multiple dataflow would require a small change. Notice that the <# foreach (var table in tables) { #> line was moved three lines down to iterative over the Dataflow object and not the Package object; see Listings 2-24 and 2-25.

Listing 2-24. Tier 1 File That Accesses Biml Objects from Tier 0 and Creates One Package

```
<#@ template tier="1" #>

<#@ import namespace="Varigence.Biml.CoreLowerer.SchemaManagement" #>

<# var conn=RootNode.OleDbConnections["Source"]; #>
<# var tables=conn.GenerateTableNodes(); #>

<Biml xmlns="http://schemas.varigence.com/biml.xsd">
  <Packages>
    <#* Moved foreach From Here *#>
    <Package Name="Source All">
      <Tasks>
        <# foreach (var table in tables) { #>
        <Dataflow Name="Stage <#= table.Name #>" >
          <Transformations>
            <OleDbSource Name="Source <#= table.Name #>" ConnectionName="Source">
```

```
            <ExternalTableInput Table="[<#= table.Schema.Name #>].[<#=
              table.Name #>]" />
          </OleDbSource>
          <OleDbDestination Name="Destination" ConnectionName="Stage">
            <InputPath OutputPathName="Source <#= table.Name #>.Output" />
            <ExternalTableOutput Table="[<#= table.Schema.Name #>].[<#=
              table.Name #>]" />
          </OleDbDestination>
        </Transformations>
      </Dataflow>
      <# } #>
    </Tasks>
  </Package>
  </Packages>
</Biml>
```

Listing 2-25. *Tier 1 File That Accesses Biml Objects from Tier 0 and Creates One Package* *in Visual Basic*

```
<#@ template tier="1" language="VB" optionexplicit="false" #>

<#@ import namespace="Varigence.Biml.CoreLowerer.SchemaManagement" #>

<# Dim conn=RootNode.OleDbConnections("Source") #>
<# Dim tables=conn.GenerateTableNodes() #>

<Biml xmlns="http://schemas.varigence.com/biml.xsd">
  <Packages>
    <#* Moved foreach From Here *#>
    <Package Name="Source All" >
      <Tasks>
        <# for each tbl in tables #>
        <Dataflow Name="Stage <#= tbl.Name #>" >
          <Transformations>
            <OleDbSource Name="Source <#= tbl.Name #>" ConnectionName="Source">
              <ExternalTableInput Table="[<#= tbl.Schema.Name #>].[<#= tbl.
                Name #>]" />
            </OleDbSource>
            <OleDbDestination Name="Destination" ConnectionName="Stage">
              <InputPath OutputPathName="Source <#= tbl.Name #>.Output" />
              <ExternalTableOutput Table="[<#= tbl.Schema.Name #>].[<#= tbl.
                Name #>]" />
            </OleDbDestination>
          </Transformations>
        </Dataflow>
        <# next #>
      </Tasks>
    </Package>
  </Packages>
</Biml>
```

■ **Note**   Technically, we would not have needed the tier declaration for these samples. Any file that does not use BimlScript will automatically be in tier 0 by default whereas all files with BimlScript default to tier 1. Especially in the beginning, it helps to still explicitly declare them to make it more obvious in which order the Biml compiler will process the files.

What if you wanted to restrict the tables used to create packages? This is where a basic understanding of Language-Integrated Query (LINQ) can become very helpful.

If you want to learn more about LINQ, you should check out https://docs. microsoft.com/en-us/dotnet/csharp/programming-guide/concepts/linq/ introduction-to-linq for C# or https://docs.microsoft.com/en-us/dotnet/visual-basic/programming-guide/language-features/linq/introduction-to-linq for VB. You will also learn more about the functions used in this sample in Chapter 4.

Directives

Directives provide instructions to the Biml Engine on how to prepare the Biml file and generate outputs. Directives are typically the first code blocks or code nuggets in a Biml file, but most of them can appear wherever you prefer within the file. Multiple directives can be specified on a single Biml file.

The complete list of the names of the supported directives are shown in Figure 2-8.

- annotation
- assembly
- code
- dependency
- extension
- global
- import
- include
- output
- property
- target
- template

Figure 2-8. Directives list

We will discuss all of them in the sections that follow.

Directives have the following syntax: an opening < followed by the pound sign (#) and the @ with XML elements and attributes ending with a pound sign (#) followed by a closing >.

```
<#@ DirectiveName [AttributeName="AttributeValue"] ... #>
```

Annotation Directives

The annotation directive allows the placement of annotation information on an entire Biml file. This is primarily used for developer documentation purposes.

Annotation directives have the following syntax:

```
<#@ annotation annotationtype="CodeComment|Description|Documentation|Tag"
tag="Tag Name" text="Annotation Text" #>
```

The parameters for the annotation directive are

- AnnotationType: The type of annotation such as documentation or tag.

- Tag: If the annotation type is a tag, this specifies the value of that tag.

- Test: The string value that should be stored within the Biml file annotation.

Assembly Directives

The assembly directive allows the use of an external .NET assembly's code within your BimlScript. Think of an assembly as a container that adds additional types or code to the project. Referencing an assembly via a directive is equivalent to adding an assembly reference in a Visual Studio project. This enables the use of objects and methods in other .NET assemblies or custom-built assemblies. Common reasons to reference an assembly from your BimlScript include when you have some code you have already written that you would like to reuse or when you would like to use a software development kit (SDK) to retrieve metadata or other information from an existing source system. For instance, if you want to retrieve metadata from Microsoft Dynamics CRM or Salesforce to drive your BimlScript templates, you could use an assembly directive to reference their SDK assemblies.

Assembly directives have the following syntax:

```
<#@ assembly name="assembly strong name|assembly file name" #>
```

The following is an example of an assembly directive that adds the Event Log Messages assembly to the Biml file:

```
<#@ assembly name="C:\Program Files (x86)\Reference Assemblies\Microsoft\
Framework\.NETFramework\v4.0\EventLogMessages.dll " #>
```

The parameter for the assembly directive is

name: This is the location or the name of the assembly.

Considerations include

- The path to the assembly can be an absolute path, a path relative to the current file, a path relative to the Biml engine installation directory, or a fully qualified name of an assembly stored in the Windows Global Assembly Cache (GAC). It can also include environment variable references using the %EnvironmentVariableName% syntax.

- By default, the following assemblies are automatically referenced within any Biml project in Visual Studio, in addition to all of the Biml-specific assemblies required to write your code:

  - System.dll

  - System.Core.dll

  - System.Data.dll

  - System.Xml.dll

  - System.Xml.Linq.dll

  - WindowsBase.dll

■ **Note**   The System.IO namespace that is used for file interaction is located within the WindowsBase.dll and is not needed in an assembly directive because of the assemblies that are referenced by default in a Biml project. Using this namespace with the import directive is all that is needed to bring the System.IO namespace into scope. See the "Import Directive" section below for more details.

Code Directives

The code directive allows the use .NET code files to be used within your Biml projects. Code directives have the following syntax:

```
<#@ code file="CodeFile.cs" #>
```

The parameter for the code directive is

- File: The path to the .NET code file, which can be an absolute path, a path relative to the current file, or a path relative to the Biml engine installation directory. It can also include environment variable references using the %EnvironmentVariableName% syntax.

Considerations include

- A code file alternatively could be complied into a .NET DLL and then referenced with the assembly directive, but for most cases, that is a lot of unnecessary work. The code directive allows us to simply reference a code file without getting any other build processes involved.

Dependency Directives (BimlStudio Only)

The dependency directive is used with the feature that is only supported in BimlStudio called Live BimlScript. This directive allows BimlStudio to track dependencies among files so that a modification to one file only requires dependent files to be recompiled. BimlStudio will normally track dependencies automatically by examining `include` directives, tiers, and other information. Occasionally, a dynamic approach will be used (such as computing the filename that you use with `CallBimlScript`), which then requires you to explicitly declare the dependency to ensure correct Live previews.

Dependency directives have the following syntax:

```
<#@ dependency file="file name" #>
```

The parameter for the dependency directive is

- `File`: The path to the file on which the Biml file depends, which can be an absolute path, a path relative to the current file, or a path relative to the Biml engine installation directory. It can also include environment variable references using the `%EnvironmentVariableName%` syntax.

Considerations include

- You generally do not need to use this except within BimlStudio and when you are using an usual coding pattern that prevents BimlStudio from automatically detecting your dependencies. Even then, the dependency will not affect build output. It will only affect updates to the Live preview of objects in the BimlStudio Logical View, which can drift out-of-date if untracked dependencies are changed.

Extension Directives (BimlStudio Only)

The extension directive is used with a feature called Biml bundles that is only supported in BimlStudio.

A Biml bundle allows developers to combine a large amount of Biml code, usually as part of a framework, into an easily reusable file. A feature of a Biml bundle is to provide an extensibility mechanism for reusable frameworks so that they can be customized with new data adapters, proprietary business logic, and organization-specific or industry-specific patterns.

The extension directive enables the user to declare that the containing Biml file is intended to be used as one of these Biml bundle extensions. You will learn more about Biml bundles and extensions in Chapter 10.

Extension directives have the following syntax:

```
<#@ extension bundle="Bundle.bimlb" extensionpoint="ExtensionPointName" #>
```

The parameters for the extension directive are

- Bundle: The name of the Biml bundle being extended.

- ExtensionPoint: The name of the specific extension point within the Biml bundle that this file will satisfy

Global Directives

In some cases, you may want to use a certain piece of code or definition in every single file in your solution or in each directory. This is where the global directive comes into play.

Global directives have the following syntax:

```
<#@ global [active="True|False"] [location="top|bottom"]
[order="OrderNumber"] [scope="Global|Folder|FolderRecursive| LogicalDispl
ayFolder|LogicalDisplayFolderRecursive|Bundle|BundleExtension|NonBundle"] #>
```

The following is an example that will make VB your default language across the entire solution:

```
<#@ global #>
<#@ template language="VB" #>
```

The following example will simply add a comment on top of every Biml file:

```
<#@ global #>
<!-- Global Header -->
```

The global directive accepts up to four parameters, which are all optional, as they all have a default. The previous two examples omitted parameters and minimized the amount of code in the global file. Instead, you could combine both examples and manually specified all of the global directive parameters, as follows:

```
<#@ global active="True" location="top" order="0" scope="Global" #>
<#@ template language="VB" #>
<!-- Global Header -->
```

As the combined file shows, there is no restriction on how much code you can put into a global file. You can use it to declare variables, add namespaces, import global includes or code files, and much more. You are also permitted to have as many global files as you like, if you prefer to break them up.

The parameters for the global directive are

- `Active`: This is a simple *Boolean*, allowing you to enable or disable a certain global file.

- `Location`: This one accepts either "top" or "bottom" and defines if the content of that file is added at the beginning or the end of each file.

- `Order`: As you can add multiple files using the global directive, this property actually allows you to bring them in order.

- `applytocallbimlscript`: Another Boolean, controlling whether the global file should also affect files being called using `CallBimlScript`. The default value is True.

- `Scope`: Scope is probably confusing for those working with BimlExpress rather than BimlStudio. BimlStudio easily allows you to work with directories, etc. so this is where scope comes into play.

Options are

- `Global`: Will be applied to all files.

- `Folder/FolderRecursive`: Will only apply to all files within this folder or this folder including its subdirectories.

- `LogicalDisplayFolder/LogicalDisplayFolderRecursive`: Like `Folder`, except that it works for logical rather than physical folders in BimlStudio.

- `Bundle/BundleExtension/NonBundle`: This only comes into play when you're actually working with bundles. Again, you'll learn more about Biml bundles in Chapter 10.

Import Directives

The import directive brings a namespace into the scope of your code nuggets and provides access to the types in that namespace without providing a fully-qualified name. You can only import namespaces from assemblies that are currently referenced within the project. The import directive is the equivalent of adding the C# keyword `using` or the Visual Basic keyword `imports` in a .NET code file.

Import directives have the following syntax:

```
<#@ import namespace="namespace" #>
```

An example of the import directive that includes the Varigence.Biml.CoreLowerer. SchemaManagement namespace is as follows:

```
<#@ import namespace="Varigence.Biml.CoreLowerer.SchemaManagement" #>
```

This enables the Biml script to call the `SchemaManager.CreateConnectionNode()` function without using the fully qualified name.

```
<# var conn = SchemaManager.CreateConnectionNode( "SchemaProvider",
"Data Source=.....
```

Without the import directive, the same call would require the fully qualified name to create a reference to the `Varigence.Biml.CoreLowerer.SchemaManagement.SchemaManager.CreateConnectionNode()` function, as follows:

```
<# var conn = Varigence.Biml.CoreLowerer.SchemaManagement.SchemaManager.
CreateConnectionNode( "SchemaProvider", "Data Source=.....
```

The parameter for the import directive is

> `Namespace`: The namespace to be imported.

Include Directives

The include directive allows the insertion of text/code from another Biml file into the current file. The included files may also contain other include directives.

Include directives have the following syntax:

```
<#@ include file="filepath" #>
```

The parameter for the include directive is

> `File`: The path to the Biml fragment file to include, which can be an absolute path, a path relative to the current file, or a path relative to the Biml engine installation directory. It can also include environment variable references using the `%EnvironmentVariableName%` syntax.

Considerations include

- The Biml Compiler will replace the include directive with the full contents for the referenced file, exactly as if it was an automated copy/paste operation.

- This directive will need to be placed where the contents of the file will need to be replaced.

Property Directives

The property directive allows the use of `CallBimlScript`, which is like using a stored procedure within a Biml file. This will be discussed in more detail in Chapter 5.

Property directives have the following syntax:

```
<#@ property name="filepath" type=".NET type" required="True|False" #>
```

An example of a property directive that allows the passing a schema and table name from the calling Biml file to the called Biml file is

```
<#@ property name="SchemaName" type="String" #>
<#@ property name="TableName" type="String" #>
```

The parameters for the property directive are

- Name: The name of the property. A variable accessible to the code nuggets in the Biml file and containing the value passed in by the calling Biml file will be automatically created.

- Type: The full name of the .NET type, including namespace, if the namespace has not already been imported.

- Required: Specifies if this argument is required or optional. Optional arguments must be at the end of the arguments list.

Target Directives (BimlStudio Only)

The target directive is used with a feature called transformers that is only supported in BimlStudio. This directive allows BimlStudio to modify existing Biml objects. The target directive specifies that the containing Biml file is a transformer and allows you to configure options for what kinds of Biml objects the transformer should modify and what types of modifications should be made. This is a fairly advanced BimlStudio feature that you can learn more about online but will not be discussed further in this book.

Target directives have the following syntax:

```
<#@ target type="Biml object Name" mergemode="LocalMerge|LocalReplace|Local
MergeAndTypeReplace|RootAdd|RootMerge " exactmatch="True|False" #>
```

The parameters for the target directive are

- Type: The Biml object type that this transformer should attempt to modify.

- MergeMode: The type of transformation that can take place.

- ExactMatch: The type option should be an exact match or if subtypes of that type can also be transformed.

Template Directives

The template directive specifies how the Biml file will be processed. This directive has several attributes that allow configuration of the various aspects of the processing. The attributes that we will cover in this section are the tier, language, and designerbimlpath attributes.

The tier attribute specifies the explicit order in which Biml files are compiled, which is useful for multiple file builds. This is required when a Biml file needs to access objects defined in an earlier Biml file. Tiers can be any numerical value, including negative numbers.

There are two default tiers. Any Biml file that contains no code nuggets and no directives (also referred to as a "flat" Biml file) is in tier 0. Any Biml file with code nuggets or directives but without a specified tier will default to tier 1.

Tier 0 has one very special feature. For all other tiers, your Biml code can only reference objects that are defined in earlier tiers. Biml files in tier 0, however, can reference objects defined in any tier, including later tiers.

■ **Note**   Using Biml Live files in BimlStudio usually requires the use of the template directive or all of the live files be processed in the same tier.

Template directives have the following syntax:

```
<#@ template language="language" tier="tierNumber" designerbimlpath="" #>
```

The following example sets the Biml Script language to Visual Basic and places the Biml file in the first tier in the compilation order:

```
<#@ template language="VB" tier="0" #>
```

DesignerBimlPath is used for scenarios where you are defining a Biml fragment that you intend to use with either an include directive or CallBimlScript. BimlStudio and BimlExpress provide quick info, autocomplete, and a variety of other Biml editor features that depend on the code file being properly structured. But if you are working on a file that contains a Biml fragment for use with an include directive or CallBimlScript, the Biml editor will lack the proper context without the DesignerBimlPath and therefore won't be able to provide correct information. The DesignerBimlPath attribute can specify the XML path in which the fragment is expected to be included. For instance, if your fragment starts with an SSIS task, you could set a DesignerBimlPath of Biml/Packages/Package/Tasks.

The parameters for the template directive are

- Language: The .NET language that is being used in your BimlScript code nuggets. The default is set to C# and this option can be omitted if you are coding in C#. It is required for Visual Basic.

- Tier: The tier in which the Biml file should be compiled.

- DesignerBimlPath: This option allows you to specify the XML path from which the fragment in the current file will be used in order to enable advanced code editing features for the fragment.

- OptionExplicit: Only relevant if you chose VB as your language. This will set the "Option Explicit" compiler switch, as shown in the following example.

■ **Tip** If you chose Visual Basic as your programming language, make use of the addition parameter `optionexplicit` and set it to `False`. This means that you will no longer have to declare the type of every object and variable. An example of this is shown in Listing 2-26.

Listing 2-26. Basic BimlScript File in Visual Basic with Option Explicit

```
<#@ Template Language="VB" optionexplicit="False" #>
<Biml xmlns="http://schemas.varigence.com/biml.xsd">
  <Packages>
    <# for i = 1 to 3 #>
    <Package Name="Hello World <#= i #>" />
    <# next #>
  </Packages>
</Biml>
```

Summary

This chapter gave you an extended overview of Biml and its language elements. This forms the foundation for all upcoming chapters in which you will start building more complex data solutions using Biml. We will use these basics, enhance them with helper methods and metadata, and guide you through how to build better BI solutions faster with Biml. But enough theory; let's move on to how you can use Biml for basic staging operations!

CHAPTER 3

■ ■ ■

Basic Staging Operations

A staging area is commonly used as part of the standard data warehouse architecture. This "landing zone" (staging database) is the first entry point for the data coming to your data warehouse environment.

In this chapter you will use Biml, BimlScript, and Biml extension methods to generate SSIS packages that will

- Create DDL statements that create target tables in a staging database.

- Load data from a source database (AdventureWorks2014) to a staging database (Staging).

- Execute all stage load SSIS packages in parallel.

Basic Staging Load Pattern

There are many options for staging data. For simplicity in this chapter, we will use the following design rules:

- Temporary storage

- Volatile (not persisted)

- No transformations

- No aggregations

- Attributes will have the same name and data type as the source.

- One staging table per source table

- Additional attributes are allowed and include

  - Load date for data integration instrumentation

  - Hash key calculation for change detection

The staging database is a volatile data store that is not persisted. Data in the staging database will be erased before running a subsequent execution of the extract, transform, and load (ETL) process.

© Andy Leonard et al. 2017
A. Leonard et al., *The Biml Book*, https://doi.org/10.1007/978-1-4842-3135-7_3

A block diagram of the staging process is shown in Figure 3-1.

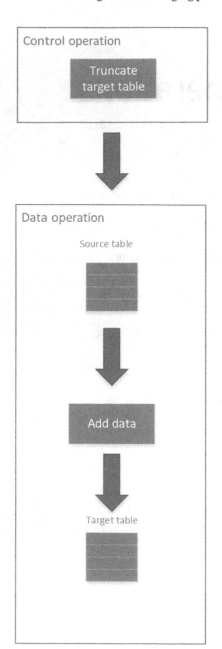

Figure 3-1. Staging process block diagram

You'll use the AdventureWorks2014 database as your source system, and then use Biml to extract object definitions from the source system. Your workflow proceeds to generate two types of SSIS packages based on the definitions. The first SSIS package creates the target objects. The second SSIS package loads data from the AdventureWorks2014 database to your staging database, as shown in Figure 3-2.

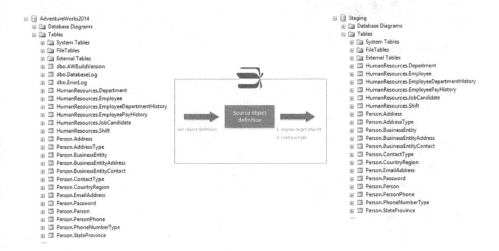

Figure 3-2. *Workflow overview*

Your two-step operation thus creates and then populates staging database objects.

Creating Basic Staging Operations Using BimlStudio

In staging, you land source data, unchanged, into a workspace that you fully control. You then modify the data as needed for use in your warehouse. It *would* be more efficient to transfer the data directly into the warehouse, modifying it in flight. However, one difference between theoretical and real world ETL is that data is dirty. Source data is flawed in ways you will not discover during development and that will break your data load. Staging provides a great inspection point for you to seek the answer to the question, "Is the issue bad source data, bad transformation logic, or something else?"

Creating Relational Hierarchy Artifacts

BimlStudio presents Biml developers with a lot of options. In this section, we show you how to model your relational artifacts (tables and views) in BimlStudio. To begin, you define your database connection and the target database.

Connections

In the Logical View, right-click Connections and hover over Add Connection to see a wealth of connection types that Biml supports out of the box, as shown in Figure 3-3.

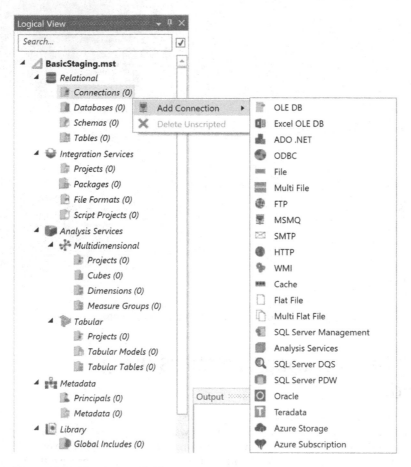

Figure 3-3. *Viewing available connection types*

Select OLE DB to open the OLE DB Connection Editor. In the Provider dropdown, select SQL Server Native Client 11.0 (or the SQL Server provider installed on your machine). Note that once you select this provider, the lower portion of the menu displays additional fields with which you may complete your connection string configuration. Our database is on a named instance of DEV2016 but your server name will vary. Specify your authentication method and click the Update link to the right of the Database dropdown. Clicking the Update link populates the dropdown with the names of discovered databases. Choose AdventureWorks2014, as shown in Figure 3-4.

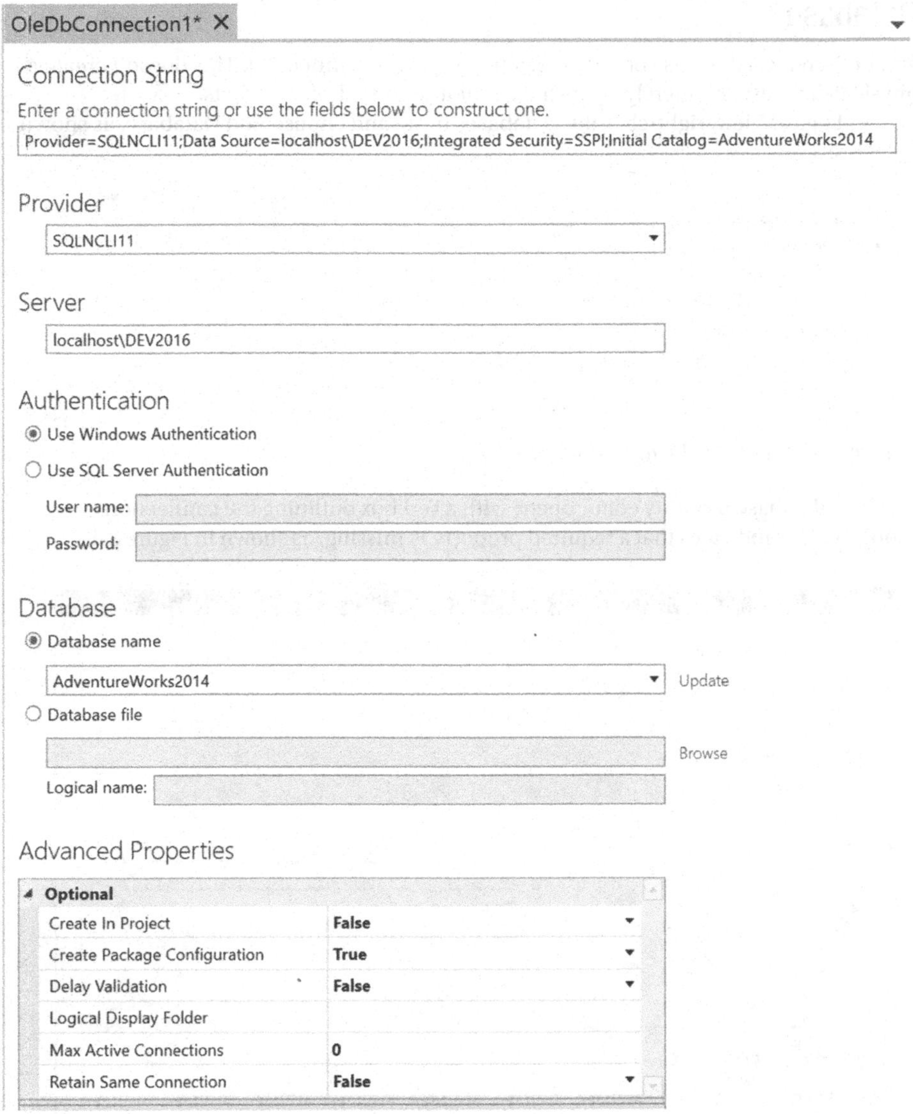

OleDbConnection1* ✕

Connection String

Enter a connection string or use the fields below to construct one.

Provider=SQLNCLI11;Data Source=localhost\DEV2016;Integrated Security=SSPI;Initial Catalog=AdventureWorks2014

Provider

SQLNCLI11 ▼

Server

localhost\DEV2016

Authentication

◉ Use Windows Authentication

○ Use SQL Server Authentication

User name:

Password:

Database

◉ Database name

AdventureWorks2014 ▼   Update

○ Database file

Browse

Logical name:

Advanced Properties

◢ Optional		
Create In Project	**False**	▼
Create Package Configuration	**True**	▼
Delay Validation	**False**	▼
Logical Display Folder		
Max Active Connections	0	
Retain Same Connection	**False**	▼

Figure 3-4. *Configuring the Biml OLE DB connection*

Ultimately, you are building a connection string. The choices you make in this editor are reflected in the topmost textbox. You may specify advanced properties or use different providers. The length and complexity of the connection string will reflect your changes. The OLE DB Connection String Editor is faster and easier than spending time combing through Books Online or www.connectionstrings.com.

Save and close the OLE DB Connection Editor. Rename the connection as AdventureWorks2014.

Databases

You next create a database object associated with your connection. This doesn't create a physical database; it's merely an abstract container for tabular artifacts.

In Logical View, right-click the Databases node and choose Add Database, as shown in Figure 3-5.

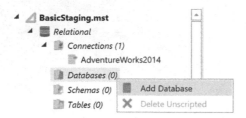

Figure 3-5. *Preparing to add a database*

The database property editor opens with a red box outlining the connection property. This indicates that a required property is missing, as shown in Figure 3-6.

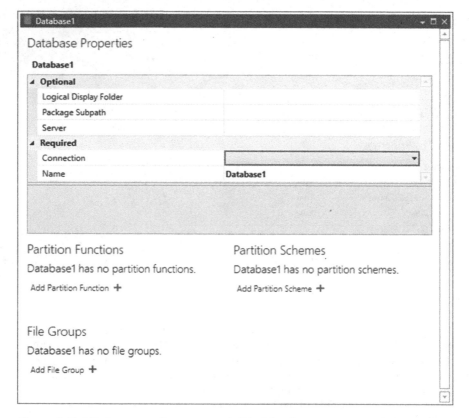

Figure 3-6. *Missing connection property in Biml database*

Associate the database to your connection by clicking the dropdown and selecting the AdventureWorks2014 connection you just configured. Set the Name property to AdventureWorks2014. When the database editor loses focus you may be prompted to rename the asset's Biml file; choose Yes. When complete, your database configuration should appear similar to that shown in Figure 3-7.

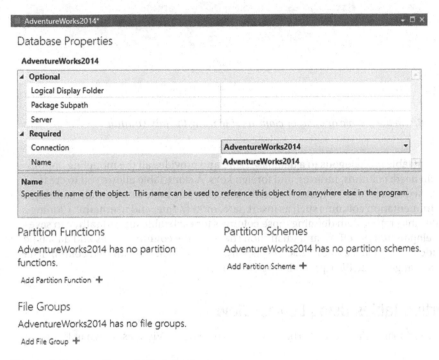

Figure 3-7. *A configured Biml database*

Importing Tables Using the Ribbon

The Home ribbon has a Relational section. Click the Table button to create tables or views, or to clone tables, as shown in Figure 3-8.

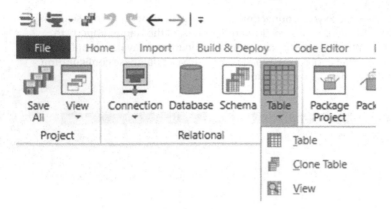

Figure 3-8. *Create a table or view, or clone a table using the table button*

A Biml table is analogous to a database table and provides all the modeling options you might need: columns, indexes, and foreign keys. A clone table allows you to create a table based on a prototype table. For example, a template table may contain auditing and instrumentation columns such as insert date, modify date, and username. Cloning a template table, rather than defining those columns for each table individually, can save you development time, effort, and frustration (because the column names and data types will be identical in each clone). This is especially helpful when the required column list is in flux; a change in one file ripples through to the rest.

Importing Tables Using Logical View

Tabular relational artifacts can also be added from the Logical View, as shown in Figure 3-9.

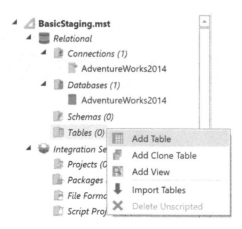

Figure 3-9. *Adding a table to the Biml relational hierarchy*

As stated earlier, BimlStudio presents Biml developers with many options. Some Biml developers prefer using the ribbon to create Biml relational hierarchy artifacts. Some Biml developers prefer using Logical View context menus. Other Biml developers prefer using IntelliSense-enabled BimlScript files.

Importing Tables Using the Import Ribbon

If you've already modeled your staging tables, you can import tables into Biml with a few mouse clicks. The BimlStudio ribbon's Import tab hosts an Import Tables button, as shown in Figure 3-10.

Figure 3-10. The BimlStudio Import ribbon

Logical View exposes Import Tables functionality in the same context menu you viewed earlier. As before, right-click Tables in the Relational header and select Import Tables, as shown in Figure 3-11.

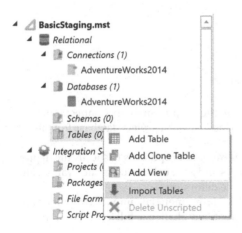

Figure 3-11. Importing tables from the Logical View

Summarizing Import Tables

Regardless of the method you choose, the Import Tables dialog displays as shown in Figure 3-12.

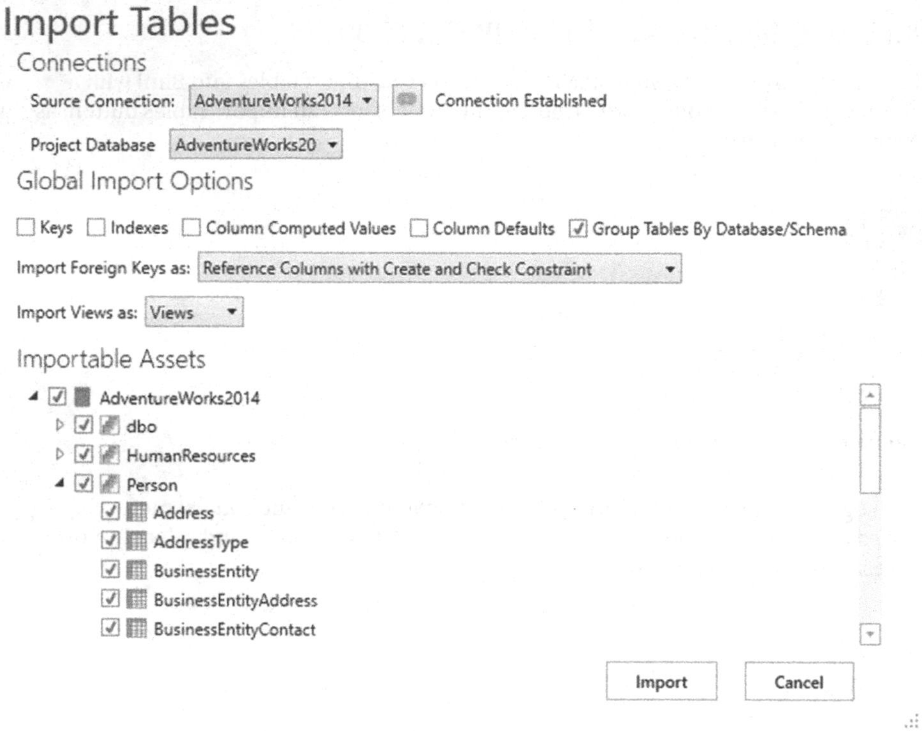

Import Tables

Connections

Source Connection: AdventureWorks2014 ▼   ⬤ Connection Established

Project Database AdventureWorks20 ▼

Global Import Options

☐ Keys ☐ Indexes ☐ Column Computed Values ☐ Column Defaults ☑ Group Tables By Database/Schema

Import Foreign Keys as: Reference Columns with Create and Check Constraint   ▼

Import Views as: Views ▼

Importable Assets

◢ ☑ ▦ AdventureWorks2014
　▷ ☑ ▨ dbo
　▷ ☑ ▨ HumanResources
　◢ ☑ ▨ Person
　　☑ ▦ Address
　　☑ ▦ AddressType
　　☑ ▦ BusinessEntity
　　☑ ▦ BusinessEntityAddress
　　☑ ▦ BusinessEntityContact

[Import]   [Cancel]

Figure 3-12. *The BimlStudio Import Tables dialog*

Begin by selecting a source connection from the dropdown. If the Connection Established indicator turns green, you may proceed. Select a project database from its dropdown.

The global import options provide checkboxes and dropdowns to specify the depth of table metadata imported. Checkboxes for keys, indexes, column computed values, and column defaults determine the detail of the table definition.

The obvious benefit of eliminating detail is a faster metadata import. Dropping and creating tables in a continuous build environment may challenge full fidelity with the source unless all the options are selected.

Checking "Group Tables By Database/Schema" results in the population of the Logical Display Name Biml attribute as tables are imported. Tables are sorted by table name and then schema name. When importing larger, multi-schema databases, the impact can be significant. Figure 3-13 compares import results not grouped, and then grouped in logical display folders.

Figure 3-13. *Imported tables, not grouped and grouped*

Creating SSIS Packages

One purpose of Biml is to develop SSIS packages. Package creation functionality shares many similarities with table creation. In this section, you'll create an SSIS package that truncates and reloads a staging table.

Creating Packages Using the Ribbon

The ribbon on the Home tab allows you to create an SSIS project, package, or package part (SQL Server 2016 and above). The Home ribbon also allows you to define file formats and script projects. A file format is used with Flat File SSIS connection managers. The file format describes the design and layout of a file, such as

- Comma-separated values (CSV) with ten columns
- Fixed-width text file without headers 200 bytes wide

A script project defines the Visual Studio Tools for Applications (VSTA) code used in a script task (control flow task) or script component (data flow component). Once defined, a script project may be consumed by any SSIS package referencing the script project by name.

The Package Project, Package, Package Part, File Format, and Script Project buttons reside in the Integration Services section of the Home tab ribbon, as shown in Figure 3-14.

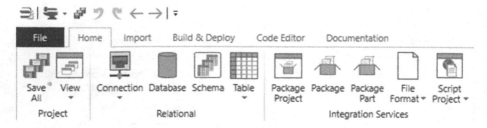

Figure 3-14. *The Integration Services section of the Home tab ribbon*

Creating Packages Using Logical View

Right-click any collection found in the Integration Services node of the Logical View to display a context menu that will allow you to add a new entity. Figure 3-15 shows the right-clicking of the Packages node to display Add Package or Import Packages on the context menu.

Figure 3-15. *The Logical View Integration Services Packages context menu*

Configuring SSIS Package Tasks and Components

A new SSIS package, when first opened in the Biml designer, will appear similar to that shown in Figure 3-16.

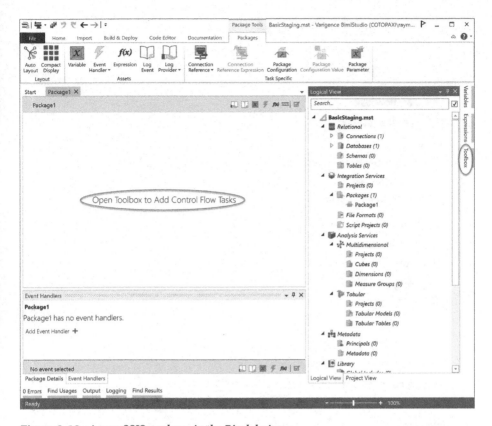

Figure 3-16. *A new SSIS package in the Biml designer*

You may click the "Open Toolbox to Add Control Flow Tasks" link or the Toolbox tab (circled in Figure 3-16) to open the Toolbox tab. Click a control flow element to display available tasks, as shown in Figure 3-17.

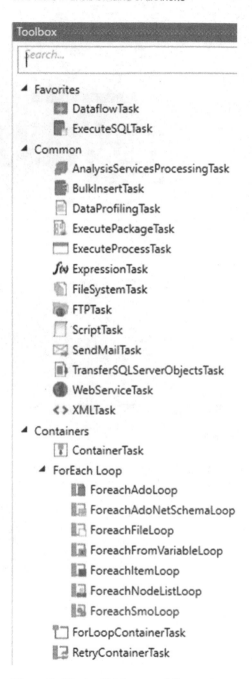

Figure 3-17. *Available control flow tasks*

Click inside a data flow element to display available data flow components, as shown in Figure 3-18.

Figure 3-18. *Available data flow components*

Drag a data flow task onto the package surface. Click inside the data flow task to display available data flow components. Drag or double-click an OLEDBSource from Favorites, and then drag or double-click a RowCount from Common. Drag the connector line from OLEDBSource1 to RowCount2, as shown in Figure 3-19.

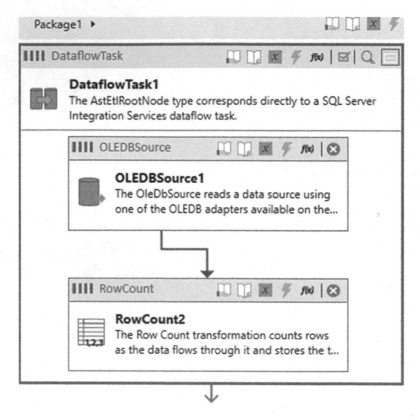

Figure 3-19. *Adding a data flow task and two components*

Using the Biml designer is similar to creating an SSIS package using SQL Server Data Tools (SSDT). SSDT displays red circles containing white X's on your OLE DB Source and Row Count components because they are missing required elements; see Figure 3-20.

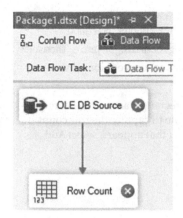

Figure 3-20. *Viewing the design in SSDT*

Let's return to BimlStudio and fix those errors. Double-click OLEDBSource1 to open the Package Details section. Select AdventureWorks2014 from the Connection dropdown. The Method dropdown contains five values that reflect four values available in the SSIS OLE DB Source adapter Data Access Mode property:

1. Direct, "SQL command" in SSIS

2. Variable , "SQL command from variable" in SSIS

3. Table, the Biml Tables collection in the Biml Relational Hierarchy (see Logical View)

4. TableFromVariable, "Table name or view name variable" in SSIS

5. External, "Table or view" in SSIS

Select Table from the Method dropdown to populate the Table dropdown with a list of tables in the AdventureWorks2014 database. Select [AdventureWorks2014].[Sales]. [Currency]. It is a Biml and SSIS best practice to give your tasks and components useful names; in this case, it's OLESRC Sales_Currency, as shown in Figure 3-21.

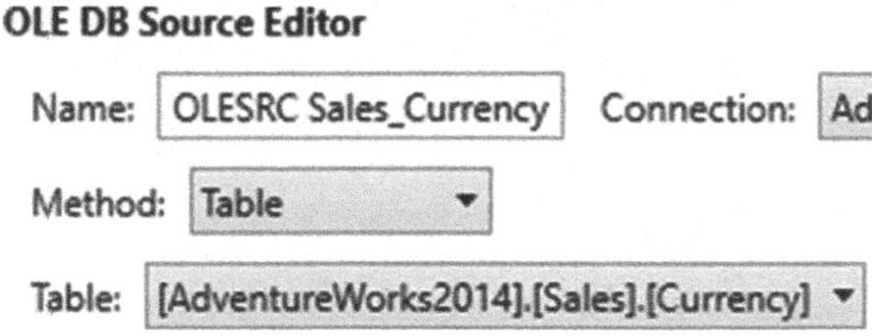

OLE DB Source Editor

Name: | OLESRC Sales_Currency | Connection: | AdventureWorks2014 ▼ |

Method: | Table ▼ |

Table: | [AdventureWorks2014].[Sales].[Currency] ▼ |

Figure 3-21. *The OLE DB source editor*

■ **Tip**   Jamie Thomson's "SSIS Best Practises and Naming Conventions" is a good reference for SSIS naming conventions; go to `http://sqlblog.com/blogs/jamie_thomson/archive/2012/01/29/suggested-best-practises-and-naming-conventions.aspx`.

Double-click the RowCount to view properties. A red rectangle around the `Variable` property indicates this property is required. Create a variable to capture the row count value. Right-click the data flow task and in the context menu that appears, select Add Variable, as shown in Figure 3-22.

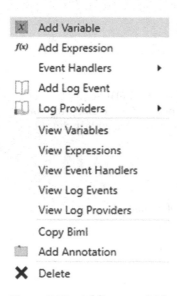

Figure 3-22. Adding a variable

When the Variables window displays, specify RowCountSource as the name, Int32 as the type, and 0 as the value, as shown in Figure 3-23.

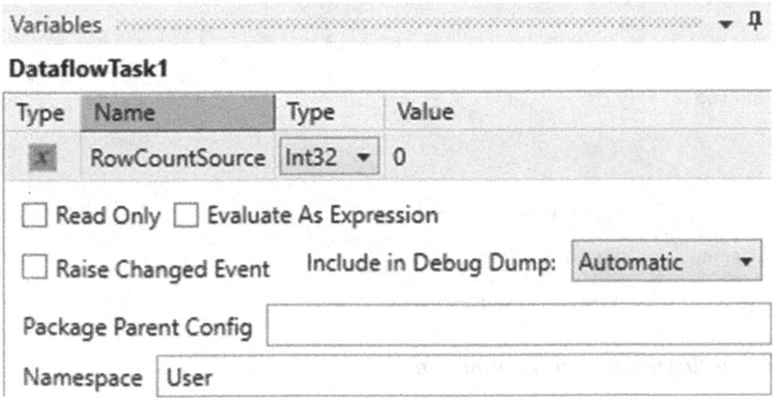

Variables ·· ▼ ႕

DataflowTask1

Type	Name	Type	Value
✕	RowCountSource	Int32 ▼	0

☐ Read Only ☐ Evaluate As Expression

☐ Raise Changed Event   Include in Debug Dump: | Automatic ▼ |

Package Parent Config [   ]

Namespace [User   ]

Figure 3-23. Configuring the RowCountSource variable

Biml surfaces SSIS properties that are buried within Visual Studio, and namespace is one of those properties. Instead of organizing variables in the default User namespace, you may categorize them with a more meaningful namespace.

Consider ETL instrumentation captured during an ETL execution. Metrics may include

- Source row count

- Inserted row count

- Updated row count

- Unchanged row count

- Error row count

- Load date

- Process name

Isolating instrumentation metrics and execution variables into an Audit or Technical namespace is a good–if not best–practice.

Returning to the demo, add an Audit transformation after the RowCount to capture the package name and the execution start time. Double-click the Audit transformation to open the Audit editor. Right-click Type and choose Add Audit twice. Specify ProcessName as the name and select Package Name from the Audit Type dropdown. Repeat for LoadDate (name) and Execution Start Time (audit type), as show in Figure 3-24.

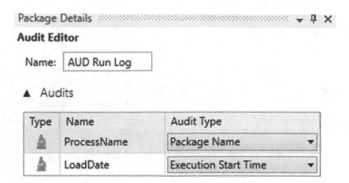

Figure 3-24. Configuring the audit transformation

When staging data it is helpful if the target table's structure matches the structure of the source table to minimize data type conversion and truncations errors. Biml's clone table functionality duplicates the structure of a source table. In your Logical View Relational section, right-click the Tables node and choose Add Clone Table. In the property editor, specify the name, schema, and table in the Required section. Name your table StageSalesCurrency, select AdventureWorks2014.dbo from the Schema dropdown, and select AdventureWorks2014.Sales.Currency from the Table dropdown, as shown in Figure 3-25.

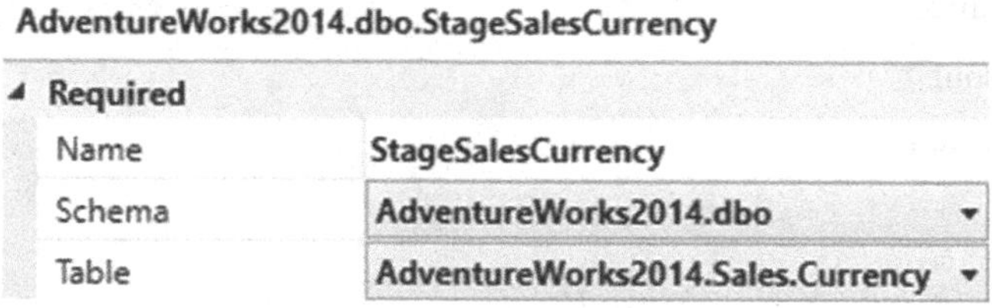

AdventureWorks2014.dbo.StageSalesCurrency

⊿ Required	
Name	**StageSalesCurrency**
Schema	**AdventureWorks2014.dbo** ▾
Table	**AdventureWorks2014.Sales.Currency** ▾

Figure 3-25. Configuring a Biml clone table

Biml clone table functionality makes it easy to capture audit data in your staging data. In the body of the clone table, click the Add Table Column option, as shown in Figure 3-26.

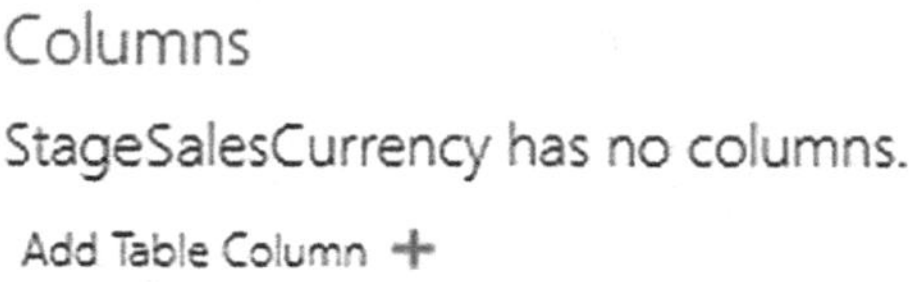

Columns

StageSalesCurrency has no columns.

Add Table Column ✚

Figure 3-26. Preparing to add a column

Add a column named ProcessName of string data type with a length of 128. Right-click Type and click Add Table Column to add another column named LoadDate of DateTime data type, as shown in Figure 3-27.

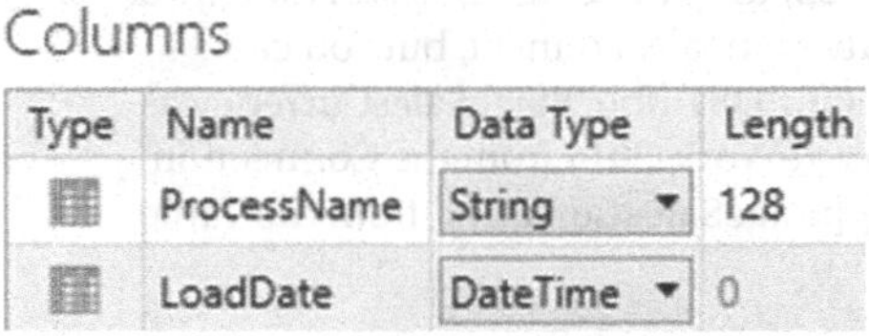

Columns

Type	Name	Data Type	Length
▦	ProcessName	String ▾	128
▦	LoadDate	DateTime ▾	0

Figure 3-27. *Adding ETL instrumentation metrics columns*

Your table is in-memory. Right-click the clone table, select Copy SQL Script, and click the first option: Drop and Create DDL to generate Transact-SQL for a physical table. Your clipboard now contains the script shown in Listing 3-1.

Listing 3-1. Generate Drop and Create DLL for Physical Table

```
SET ANSI_NULLS ON
SET QUOTED_IDENTIFIER ON
GO


-------------------------------------------------------------------
IF EXISTS (SELECT * from sys.objects WHERE object_id = OBJECT_ID(N'[dbo].
[StageSalesCurrency]') AND type IN (N'U'))
DROP TABLE [dbo].[StageSalesCurrency]
GO

CREATE TABLE [dbo].[StageSalesCurrency]
(
-- Columns Definition
        [CurrencyCode] nchar(3) NOT NULL
,       [Name] nvarchar(50) NOT NULL
,       [ModifiedDate] datetime NOT NULL
,       [ProcessName] nvarchar(128) NOT NULL
,       [LoadDate] datetime NOT NULL

-- Constraints

)
ON "default"
WITH (DATA_COMPRESSION = NONE)
GO
-------------------------------------------------------------------
```

Open SQL Server Management Studio (SSMS), connect to your staging database, paste the Transact-SQL into a new query window, and run that script to create the staging table.

The last step in your data flow task is to add an OLE DB destination. Within the data flow task, select AUD Run Log. In the Toolbox, drag the OLEDBDestination into the data flow. Data flow components should automatically connect, but you can always manually connect components. Specify OLEDST dbo_StageSalesCurrency as the OLEDBDestination name and select AdventureWorks2014 from the Connection dropdown. Select [AdventureWorks2014].[dbo].[StageSalesCurrency] from the Table dropdown, as shown in Figure 3-28.

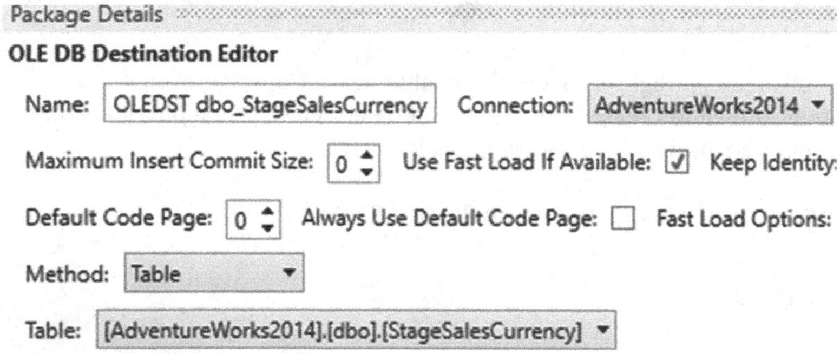

Figure 3-28. *Configuring an OLE DB destination*

Your data flow now reads data from your source table, counts the number of rows read, enriches the data flow with audit data, and then stores source data plus audit instrumentation to a new table. The final step is to ensure your target table is empty before the data begins loading.

Click the background of the control flow anywhere outside of your data flow task to select the control flow. Drag an Execute SQL task from the Toolbox and connect the green arrow (an on-success precedence constraint) from the Execute SQL task to your data flow task. Double-click the Execute SQL task to open the editor. Set the Name property to "SQL Truncate Target" and select AdventureWorks2014 from the Connection dropdown. Add the following Transact-SQL in the Query textbox:

```
TRUNCATE TABLE dbo.StageSalesCurrency;
```

Your Execute SQL Editor should now appear as shown in Figure 3-29.

Execute Sql Editor

Name: | SQL Truncate Target | Connection: | AdventureWorks2014 ▾ |

Result Set: | None ▾ | Code Page: | 1252 ⬍ | Bypass Prepare: ☑

Method: | Direct ▾ |

T-SQL Editor

  Connection: AdventureWorks2014   ⬤   Connection Established

Query

```
1   TRUNCATE TABLE dbo.StageSalesCurrency;
```

Figure 3-29. *Configuring the SQL Truncate Target Execute SQL task*

Your SSIS package should now appear as shown in Figure 3-30.

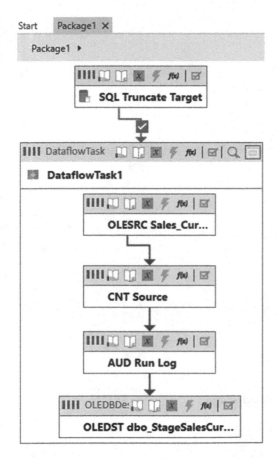

Figure 3-30. *An SSIS package in the Biml designer*

Building an SSIS Package

To build an SSIS package, right-click Package1 in Logical View and select Build & Open in BIDS. The end result should be the Biml presentation of the SSIS package in Visual Studio, as shown in Figure 3-31.

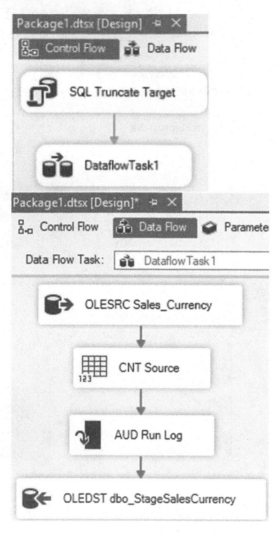

Figure 3-31. *Your SSIS package open in Visual Studio*

In BimlStudio, right-click Package1 and select View Biml. In less than 40 lines of Biml, you've described that same SSIS Package as shown in Listing 3-2.

Listing 3-2. Generated Biml Code from Biml Designer

```
<Biml xmlns="http://schemas.varigence.com/biml.xsd">
  <Packages>
    <Package Name="Package1">
      <Tasks>
        <Dataflow Name="DataflowTask1">
          <Transformations>
            <OleDbSource Name="OLESRC Sales_Currency" ConnectionName=
              "AdventureWorks2014" ValidateExternalMetadata="true">
              <TableInput TableName="AdventureWorks2014.Sales.Currency" />
            </OleDbSource>
            <RowCount Name="CNT Source" VariableName="User.RowCountSource" />
            <OleDbDestination Name="OLEDST dbo_StageSalesCurrency"
              ConnectionName="AdventureWorks2014">
              <TableOutput TableName="AdventureWorks2014.dbo.
                StageSalesCurrency" />
              <InputPath OutputPathName="AUD Run Log.Output" />
            </OleDbDestination>
            <Audit Name="AUD Run Log">
              <InputPath OutputPathName="CNT Source.Output" />
              <Audits>
                <Audit Name="ProcessName" AuditType="PackageName" />
                <Audit Name="LoadDate" AuditType="ExecutionStartTime" />
              </Audits>
            </Audit>
          </Transformations>
          <Variables>
            <Variable Name="RowCountSource" DataType="Int32">0</Variable>
          </Variables>
          <PrecedenceConstraints>
            <Inputs>
              <Input OutputPathName="SQL Truncate Target.Output" />
            </Inputs>
          </PrecedenceConstraints>
        </Dataflow>
        <ExecuteSQL Name="SQL Truncate Target" ConnectionName="AdventureWorks2014">
          <DirectInput>TRUNCATE TABLE dbo.StageSalesCurrency;</DirectInput>
        </ExecuteSQL>
      </Tasks>
    </Package>
  </Packages>
</Biml>
```

BimlStudio provides a graphical design experience for building Biml without having to learn additional languages to solve the business problem. Instead, development focuses on the familiar interface while the designer transcribes the Biml. In the next section, you'll learn how to build similar packages using the free BimlExpress tool, which does not include a graphical designer.

Creating Basic Staging Operations Using BimlExpress

In this section, we demonstrate how to create basic staging operations using BimlExpress, a free Visual Studio extension for SSDT, which is available for download from `https://varigence.com/bimlexpress`.

As with BimlStudio, you may also create a staging database and SSIS packages with BimlExpress. You first create a new database named Staging and use the `GetDatabaseSchema` extension method to import an in-memory representation of AdventureWorks tables. You generate two types of SSIS packages:

- An SSIS package to create tables

- An SSIS package to load AdventureWorks2014 source data to your Staging database

A block diagram of the workflow is shown in Figure 3-32.

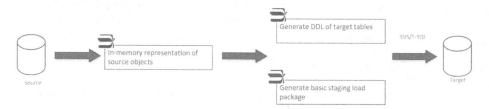

Figure 3-32. *Staging workflow block diagram*

Creating Relational Hierarchy Artifacts

In this section, you create a new database and an in-memory representation of the tables. You next generate SSIS packages with a DROP and CREATE TABLE script.

Creating the Database Using Transact-SQL

You create a database named Staging and the following five schemas: HumanResources, Person, Production, Purchasing, and Sales. Execute the following Transact-SQL script using the code in Listing 3-3 in SSMS to create the initial environment.

Listing 3-3. Transact-SQL Script to Create Database and Schema

```
CREATE DATABASE Staging
GO
USE Staging
GO
CREATE SCHEMA HumanResources
GO
CREATE SCHEMA Person
GO
CREATE SCHEMA Production
GO
CREATE SCHEMA Purchasing
GO
CREATE SCHEMA Sales
GO
```

Configuring the BimlExpress Database and Schemas

To prepare your staging environment with Biml, you first define in-memory Biml objects that will represent the Staging database. In Solution Explorer, right-click the project name and click Add New Biml File. Rename the new Biml file as 1-2-CreateEnvironment.biml and add the Biml shown in Listing 3-4.

Listing 3-4. Create In-Memory Biml Objects

```
<#@ template tier="10" #>
<Biml xmlns="http://schemas.varigence.com/biml.xsd">
  <Connections>
    <OleDbConnection Name="Source" ConnectionString="Provider=SQLNCLI11;
      Server=localhost\DEV2016;Initial Catalog=AdventureWorks2014;Integrated
      Security=SSPI;" CreateInProject="true" />
    <OleDbConnection Name="Target" ConnectionString="Provider=SQLNCLI11;
      Server=localhost\DEV2016;Initial Catalog=Staging;Integrated
      Security=SSPI;" CreateInProject="true" />
  </Connections>
  <Databases>
    <Database Name="Staging" ConnectionName="Target" />
  </Databases>
  <Schemas>
    <Schema Name="HumanResources" DatabaseName="Staging" />
    <Schema Name="Person" DatabaseName="Staging" />
    <Schema Name="Production" DatabaseName="Staging" />
    <Schema Name="Purchasing" DatabaseName="Staging" />
    <Schema Name="Sales" DatabaseName="Staging" />
  </Schemas>
</Biml>
```

In this Biml you define connection strings for the source and target database, the staging database, and the staging database schemas. These configurations will be used later in the process to create the physical tables using an SSIS package.

Connections are defined in the <Connections> tag. Within the <Connections> tag, you can define multiple connections. In this case you are defining two OLE DB connections with SQL Server Native Client 11.0 as the OLE DB provider: AdventureWorks2014 database as your source database and Staging database as your target staging environment.

To build your staging database objects based on the AdventureWorks database, you define database and schema objects in Biml (defined in <Database> and <Schema> tags) to contain table objects (defined in <Table> tags).

The tier attribute of template directive specifies the explicit order the Biml files are compiled.

Configuring the Target Tables

Add a new Biml file named 1-2-CreateBimlTableObject.biml to create an in-memory Biml representation of AdventureWorks tables objects based on the definitions extracted with GetDatabaseSchema extension method.

This Biml file contains two directives. The import directive brings object namespace into the scope of the project and the template directive with tier attributes specifies the explicit order in which Biml files are compiled. See Listings 3-5 and 3-6.

Listing 3-5. Create an In-Memory Biml Representation of AdventureWorks Tables (C#)

```
<#@ template tier="20" #>
<#@ import namespace="Varigence.Biml.CoreLowerer.SchemaManagement"  #>
<#
var sourceConnection = RootNode.OleDbConnections["Source"];
var includedSchemas = new List<string>{"HumanResources","Person","Production
","Purchasing","Sales"};
var importResult = sourceConnection.GetDatabaseSchema(includedSchemas, null,
ImportOptions.ExcludeForeignKey | ImportOptions.ExcludeColumnDefault |
ImportOptions.ExcludeViews);
#>
<Biml xmlns="http://schemas.varigence.com/biml.xsd">
  <Tables>
    <# foreach (var table in importResult.TableNodes) { #>
    <Table Name="<#=table.Name#>" SchemaName="Staging.<#=table.Schema#>">
      <Columns>
        <# foreach (var column in table.Columns) { #>
            <#=column.GetBiml()#>
        <# } #>
        <Column Name="LoadDateTime" DataType="DateTime2"/>
      </Columns>
    </Table>
    <# } #>
  </Tables>
</Biml>
```

Listing 3-6. Create an In-Memory Biml Representation of AdventureWorks Tables (VB)

```
<#@ template tier="20" language="VB" optionexplicit="False" #>
<#@ import namespace="Varigence.Biml.CoreLowerer.SchemaManagement"  #>
<#
Dim sourceConnection = RootNode.OleDbConnections("Source")
Dim includedSchemas as new List(of String) from {"HumanResources","Person","
Production","Purchasing","Sales"}
Dim importResult = sourceConnection.GetDatabaseSchema(includedSchemas,
nothing, ImportOptions.ExcludeForeignKey or ImportOptions.
ExcludeColumnDefault or ImportOptions.ExcludeViews)
#>
<Biml xmlns="http://schemas.varigence.com/biml.xsd">
  <Tables>
    <# for each tbl in importResult.TableNodes #>
    <Table Name="<#=tbl.Name#>" SchemaName="Staging.<#=tbl.Schema#>">
      <Columns>
        <# for each column in tbl.Columns #>
            <#=column.GetBiml()#>
        <# next #>
        <Column Name="LoadDateTime" DataType="DateTime2"/>
      </Columns>
    </Table>
    <# next #>
  </Tables>
</Biml>
```

You start by defining three variables:

- sourceConnection: Holds the connection to the source system.

- includedSchemas: Contains a list of schema names.

- importResult: Holds AdventureWorks2014 metadata.

GetDatabaseSchema is an extension method that imports metadata from a database schema. This method has optional parameters including IncludedSchemas, IncludedTables, and ImportOptions. For your staging load area, and to show how to make use of GetDatabaseSchema parameters, include all tables with schemas defined in the includedSchemas variable and exclude some properties of the tables as defined in the ImportOptions parameter.

Table are defined in a <Tables> tag based on the metadata you collect using GetDatabaseSchema. For each table in TableNodes collection you can now loop through all columns by calling GetBiml(), which converts column items into Biml.

Building the Table Deployment SSIS Package

Let's next add a Biml file named 1-x-DeployTableObject.biml to generate an SSIS package named DeployTable.dtsx. This SSIS package will execute drop and create table script for each table objects, as illustrated in Listings 3-7 and 3-8.

Listing 3-7. Create Table Deployment SSIS Package (C#)

```
<#@ template tier="30" #>
<Biml xmlns="http://schemas.varigence.com/biml.xsd">
  <Packages>
    <Package Name="DeployTable" ConstraintMode="Parallel">
      <Tasks>
        <# foreach (var table in RootNode.Tables) { #>
        <ExecuteSQL Name="Create <#=table.Name#>" ConnectionName="Target">
          <DirectInput><#=table.GetDropAndCreateDdl()#></DirectInput>
        </ExecuteSQL>
        <# } #>
      </Tasks>
    </Package>
  </Packages>
</Biml>
```

Listing 3-8. Create Table Deployment SSIS Package (VB)

```
<#@ template tier="30" language="VB" optionexplicit="False" #>
<Biml xmlns="http://schemas.varigence.com/biml.xsd">
  <Packages>
    <Package Name="DeployTable" ConstraintMode="Parallel">
      <Tasks>
        <# for each tbl in RootNode.Tables #>
        <ExecuteSQL Name="Create <#=tbl.Name#>" ConnectionName="Target">
          <DirectInput><#=tbl.GetDropAndCreateDdl()#></DirectInput>
        </ExecuteSQL>
        <# next #>
      </Tasks>
    </Package>
  </Packages>
</Biml>
```

For each in-memory Biml tables representation in RootNode, you call the GetDropAndCreateDdl() extension method that will generate Transact-SQL DDL to drop and create a table object. This generated drop and create Transact-SQL DDL will then be executed by Execute SQL Task control flow from the SSIS package DeployTable.dtsx.

Creating the Staging Load SSIS Package

In this section, you will use the database metadata collected from GetDatabaseSchema to build your load staging logic and mapping.

Add a new Biml script named x-2-CreateLoadPackage.biml, as shown in Listing 3-9 and 3-10, to create two types of packages: an SSIS package in your staging area that will read data from a single AdventureWorks table and load the data to a target table, and an SSIS workflow that will execute all staging load packages in parallel.

Listing 3-9. Create SSIS Staging Packages and Workflow Package (C#)

```
<#@ template tier="40" #>
<Biml xmlns="http://schemas.varigence.com/biml.xsd">
  <Packages>
    <# foreach (var table in RootNode.Tables) { #>
    <Package Name="Load_Staging_<#=table.Schema#>_<#=table.Name#>"
     ConstraintMode="Linear">
      <Tasks>
        <ExecuteSQL Name="Truncate_<#=table.Schema#>_<#=table.Name#>"
         ConnectionName="Target">
            <DirectInput>TRUNCATE TABLE [<#=table.Schema#>].[<#=table.
            Name#>]</DirectInput>
        </ExecuteSQL>
        <Dataflow Name="DFT_Load_<#=table.Schema#>_<#=table.Name#>">
          <Transformations>
            <OleDbSource Name="DBS_<#=table.Schema#>_<#=table.Name#>"
             ConnectionName="Source">
              <DirectInput>SELECT <#=table.GetColumnList(c => c.Name
              != "LoadDateTime")#> FROM [<#=table.Schema#>].[<#=table.
              Name#>]</DirectInput>
            </OleDbSource>
            <!-- Derived Columns Standard Values -->
              <DerivedColumns Name="DCT_StandardValues">
                    <Columns>
                            <Column Name="LoadDateTime"
                            DataType="DateTime2" Scale="7">
                            (DT_DBTIMESTAMP2,7)GETDATE()</Column>
                    </Columns>
              </DerivedColumns>
            <OleDbDestination Name="DBD_<#=table.Schema#>_<#=table.Name#>"
             ConnectionName="Target">
                <ExternalTableOutput Table="[<#=table.Schema#>].[<#=table.
                Name#>]"></ExternalTableOutput>
            </OleDbDestination>
          </Transformations>
        </Dataflow>
      </Tasks>
    </Package>
```

```
    <# } #>
    <Package Name="Workflow_Load_Staging" ConstraintMode="Parallel">
        <Tasks>
            <# foreach (var table in RootNode.Tables) { #>
            <ExecutePackage Name="EPT Load_Staging_<#=table.
            Schema#>_<#=table.Name#>">
                <ExternalProjectPackage Package="Load_Staging_<#=table.
                    Schema#>_<#=table.Name#>.dtsx"/>
            </ExecutePackage>
            <# } #>
        </Tasks>
    </Package>
  </Packages>
</Biml>
```

Listing 3-10. Create SSIS Staging Packages and Workflow Package (VB)

```
<#@ template tier="40" language="VB" optionexplicit="False" #>
<Biml xmlns="http://schemas.varigence.com/biml.xsd">
  <Packages>
    <# for each tbl in RootNode.Tables #>
    <Package Name="Load_Staging_<#=tbl.Schema#>_<#=tbl.Name#>"
     ConstraintMode="Linear">
      <Tasks>
        <ExecuteSQL Name="Truncate_<#=tbl.Schema#>_<#=tbl.Name#>"
         ConnectionName="Target">
            <DirectInput>TRUNCATE TABLE [<#=tbl.Schema#>].[<#=tbl.Name#>]
            </DirectInput>
        </ExecuteSQL>
        <Dataflow Name="DFT_Load_<#=tbl.Schema#>_<#=tbl.Name#>">
          <Transformations>
            <OleDbSource Name="DBS_<#=tbl.Schema#>_<#=tbl.Name#>"
             ConnectionName="Source">
              <DirectInput>SELECT <#=tbl.GetColumnList(function(c) c.Name <>
              "LoadDateTime")#> FROM [<#=tbl.Schema#>].[<#=tbl.Name#>]
              </DirectInput>
            </OleDbSource>
            <!-- Derived Columns Standard Values -->
              <DerivedColumns Name="DCT_StandardValues">
                  <Columns>
                          <Column Name="LoadDateTime"
                          DataType="DateTime2" Scale="7">
                          (DT_DBTIMESTAMP2,7)GETDATE()</Column>
                  </Columns>
              </DerivedColumns>
            <OleDbDestination Name="DBD_<#=tbl.Schema#>_<#=tbl.Name#>"
             ConnectionName="Target">
```

```
                <ExternalTableOutput Table="[<#=tbl.Schema#>].[<#=tbl.
                    Name#>]"></ExternalTableOutput>
                </OleDbDestination>
              </Transformations>
            </Dataflow>
          </Tasks>
        </Package>
        <# next #>
        <Package Name="Workflow_Load_Staging" ConstraintMode="Parallel">
            <Tasks>
                <# for each tbl in RootNode.Tables #>
                <ExecutePackage Name="EPT Load_Staging_<#=tbl.Schema#>_<#=tbl.
                  Name#>">
                    <ExternalProjectPackage Package="Load_Staging_<#=tbl.
                      Schema#>_<#=tbl.Name#>.dtsx"/>
                </ExecutePackage>
                <# next #>
            </Tasks>
        </Package>
      </Packages>
</Biml>
```

You generate the SSIS loading packages by looping through the RootNode.Tables object. You create an SSIS package for each Biml table in RootNode.Tables. Every package starts with a TRUNCATE TABLE statement defined in an <ExecuteSQL> task to ensure the target table does not contain data before you begin the load. You define a data flow task that contains an OLE DB source, a Derived Columns transformation, and an OLE DB destination. Biml *automatically maps* source columns to target columns if the columns have the same name. If the column names are different, you need to explicitly map source columns to target columns, which you can do in Biml by specifying <Columns> Biml.

Generating Staging Load and Workflow SSIS Packages

You are now ready to generate SSIS packages that load your basic staging environment. You create a Deploy SSIS package that contains Transact-SQL DDL scripts in SSIS Execute SQL tasks to create target staging tables. You also create Staging Load SSIS packages.

You are using the Biml file naming standard discussed in an earlier chapter because you need to build your Biml solution in multiple steps and numbering schemes help.

You first build the following files:

- 1-2-CreateEnvironment.biml

- 1-2-CreateBimlTableObject.biml

- 1-x-DeployTableObject.biml

To build, multi-select the files in Solution Explorer, right-click, and click Generate SSIS Packages.

After building the files, the DeployTable.dtsx SSIS package is created. DeployTable. dtsx contains an Execute SQL task with CREATE TABLE DDL per metadata definitions in script 1-2-CreateBimlTableObject.biml. Executing this package creates all target tables, as shown in Figure 3-33.

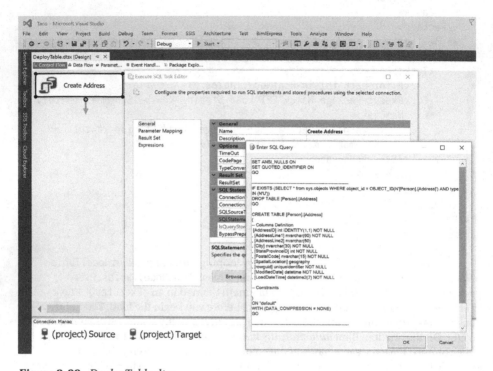

Figure 3-33. *DeployTable.dtsx*

You next build the following files:

- 1-2-CreateEnvironment.biml

- 1-2-CreateBimlTableObject.biml

- x-2-CreateLoadPackage.biml

A staging load SSIS package is created for each target table, as shown in Figure 3-34.

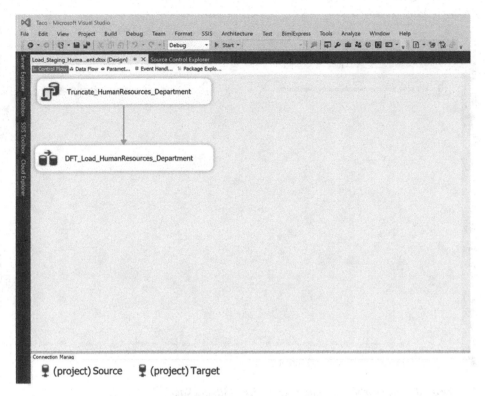

Figure 3-34. *A staging load SSIS package*

Each staging load SSIS package contains an Execute SQL task that truncates the staging table and a data flow task that loads data from an AdventureWorks table to your corresponding staging table.

The Workflow_Load_Staging.dtsx SSIS package contains Execute Package tasks that execute each staging load SSIS package in parallel, as shown in Figure 3-35.

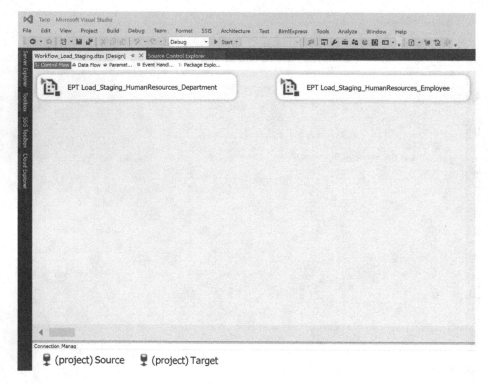

Figure 3-35. *The Workflow_Load_Staging.dtsx SSIS package*

Summary

In this chapter we demonstrated and discussed how to use Biml, BimlScript, and Biml extension methods to generate SSIS packages that

- Create DDL statements that create target tables in a staging database.

- Load data from a source database (AdventureWorks2014) to a staging database (Staging).

- Execute all stage load SSIS packages in parallel.

The next chapter will lead you to different ways of extracting metadata from source systems using BimlScript!

CHAPTER 4

■ ■ ■

Importing Metadata

Now that you have a good understanding of the Biml language and the various tools you can use to write and build Biml code, let us take a closer look at one of the most fundamental features of Biml: importing metadata from source systems and source files. This is a critically important task for most projects because it is used in autogeneration of staging and is usually also part of the metadata story for later phases of the data integration.

Figure 4-1 shows the available SSIS connection managers in SQL Server Data Tools (*left*) and Connections in BimlStudio (*right*). As you can see, both SSIS and Biml can work with a wide range of source systems and files. This chapter will focus on the most commonly used sources, and you will learn how to import metadata from SQL Server, Excel files, and flat files.

© Andy Leonard et al. 2017
A. Leonard et al., *The Biml Book*, https://doi.org/10.1007/978-1-4842-3135-7_4

Type	Description
ADO	Connection manager for ADO connections
ADO.NET	Connection manager for ADO.NET connections
CACHE	Connection manager for cache
DQS	Connection manager for DQS server
EXCEL	Connection manager for Excel files
FILE	Connection manager for files
FLATFILE	Connection manager for flat files
FTP	Connection manager for FTP connections
Hadoop	Connection manager for Hadoop
HTTP	Connection manager for HTTP connections
MSMQ	Connection manager for the Message Queue task
MSOLAP100	Connection manager for Analysis Services connections
MULTIFILE	Connection manager for multiple files
MULTIFLATFILE	Connection manager for multiple flat files
ODATA	Connection Manager for OData services
ODBC	Connection manager for ODBC connections
OLEDB	Connection manager for OLE DB connections
SMOServer	Connection manager for SQL Server transfer tasks
SMTP	Connection manager for the Send Mail task
SQLMOBILE	Connection manager for SQL Server Compact connections
WMI	Connection manager for the WMI tasks

Figure 4-1. SSIS and Biml connection managers

SQL Server

There are three core Biml methods for importing metadata from SQL Server: ImportTableNodes, ImportDB, and GetDatabaseSchema.

They all return an ImportResults object that contains schema, table, and view metadata, including columns, indexes, keys, constraints, and defaults. Certain objects can be excluded by passing an ImportOptions parameter. The main differences among these three methods are the kind of parameters they accept, how these parameters can be used to filter what source metadata is returned, and the methods used to retrieve the metadata from the database.

ImportTableNodes and ImportDB

ImportTableNodes is restricted to importing a single schema and the tables/views belonging to that schema. ImportDB can import all schemas, tables, and views, or a subset of these. You choose which objects to import by passing parameters to the methods.

The parameters work as filters to get one or more objects. In both cases, the metadata is retrieved by performing a *SchemaOnly* execution of a SELECT * FROM Table query on each of the imported tables. This will generally produce metadata with data type mappings that exactly match the behavior of SSIS data flow source components. Note that this might not match the data types that would be used in relational modeling contexts. For that case, GetDatabaseSchema, which you will learn more about below, may be the better option.

ImportTableNodes

ImportTableNodes requires two string parameters, Schema and TableFilter, and has an optional parameter named ImportOptions that can be used to exclude specific objects. See Table 4-1.

Table 4-1. ImportTableNodes Parameters

Parameter	Description	Examples
Schema	String that must be the name of a specific schema; it can't be an empty string, and it can't use wildcards.	"Sales"
TableFilter	String that can be empty or null to import all tables/views in the schema; it can be the name of a specific table/view in the schema, and it can use wildcards to import a set of tables/views in the schema.	" " "SalesOrderDetail" "SalesOrderHeader" "%Order%"
ImportOptions	A special parameter that can be used to exclude specific objects.	None ExcludeCheckConstraint ExcludeColumnDefault ExcludeForeignKey ExcludeIdentity ExcludeIndex ExcludePrimaryKey ExcludeUniqueKey ExcludeViews

To import the schema and tables/views filtered by both Schema and TableFilter:

```
ImportTableNodes(Schema, TableFilter)
```

To import the schema, and tables/views filtered by both Schema and TableFilter; also to exclude objects specified in ImportOptions:

```
ImportTableNodes(Schema, TableFilter, ImportOptions)
```

ImportDB

ImportDB does not require any parameters, but it can take two optional string parameters named SchemaFilter and TableFilter, and has an additional optional parameter named ImportOptions that can be used to exclude specific objects.

To import all schemas, tables, and views:

```
ImportDB()
```

To import schemas filtered by SchemaFilter, and tables/views filtered by both SchemaFilter and TableFilter:

```
ImportDB(SchemaFilter, TableFilter)
```

To import schemas filtered by SchemaFilter, and tables/views filtered by both SchemaFilter and TableFilter; also to exclude objects specified in ImportOptions:

```
ImportDB (SchemaFilter, TableFilter, ImportOptions)
```

See Table 4-2.

Table 4-2. *ImportDB Parameters*

Parameter	Description	Examples
SchemaFilter	String parameter that can be empty or null to import all schemas, it can be the name of a specific schema, and it can use wildcards to import a set of schemas.	" " "Production" "P%"
TableFilter	String parameter that can be empty or null to import all tables/views, it can be the name of a specific table/view, and it can use wildcards to import a set of tables/views. If the SchemaFilter parameter is not empty, the tables/views are restricted to those schemas.	" " "Product" "ProductCategory" "ProductSubcategory" "Product%"
ImportOptions	A special parameter that can be used to exclude specific objects.	None ExcludeCheckConstraint ExcludeColumnDefault ExcludeForeignKey ExcludeIdentity ExcludeIndex ExcludePrimaryKey ExcludeUniqueKey ExcludeViews

A Note on Wildcards in Parameters

The SchemaFilter and TableFilter parameters can use wildcards. The wildcard characters allowed are the same as the ones used in the T-SQL *LIKE* statement:

- The percent sign (%) for zero or more characters

- Underscore (_) for a single character

- Brackets ([ ]) for a single character in a range or set

- Brackets ([^]) for a single character not in a range or set

If object names contain characters that are used as wildcards, such as underscores in table names, you can treat wildcards as literals by enclosing them in brackets. If you have two tables, Product_Category and ProductXCategory, and you pass the TableFilter parameter "Product_Category", both tables will be returned because the underscore is treated as a wildcard. You must pass the parameter "Product[_]Category" to treat the underscore as a literal to only return the first table.

Using ImportDB

Listing 4-1 shows how to use ImportDB to import *all* metadata from the AdventureWorks2014 database. It creates a package that drops and creates all the imported tables in a Staging database.

First, you create a connection to your source database by calling SchemaManager. CreateConnectionNode() and passing the connection name and connection string as parameters. You save this connection in a variable called sourceConnection.

Then you import the metadata by calling sourceConnection.ImportDB(), and save the imported results in a variable called sourceMetadata.

Finally, you create your SSIS package and loop over all the tables in your metadata. For each table in your metadata, you create an Execute SQL task to drop and create that table in your Staging database. The GetDropAndCreateDdl() method creates the SQL statement for you.

Listing 4-1. ImportDB

```
<# var sourceConnection = SchemaManager.CreateConnectionNode("AW2014", "Data
Source=.;Initial Catalog=AdventureWorks2014;Provider=SQLNCLI11;Integrated
Security=SSPI;"); #>

<# var sourceMetadata = sourceConnection.ImportDB(); #>

<Biml xmlns="http://schemas.varigence.com/biml.xsd">
  <Connections>
    <OleDbConnection Name="Staging" ConnectionString="Data Source=.;Initial
      Catalog=Staging;Provider=SQLNCLI11;Integrated Security=SSPI;" />
  </Connections>
```

```
<Packages>
  <Package Name="DropAndCreateStagingTables">
    <Tasks>
      <# foreach (var table in sourceMetadata.TableNodes) { #>
      <ExecuteSQL Name="Drop and Create <#=table.Schema#> <#=table.Name#>"
       ConnectionName="Staging">
        <DirectInput><#=table.GetDropAndCreateDdl()#></DirectInput>
      </ExecuteSQL>
      <# } #>
    </Tasks>
  </Package>
</Packages>
</Biml>
```

Using ImportDB without any parameters imports *all* metadata from the source database, including identity columns, constraints, indexes, and keys. The resulting Biml code from `<#=table.GetDropAndCreateDdl()#>` for the Product table is shown in Listing 4-2.

Listing 4-2. Result of ImportDB

```
<ExecuteSQL Name="Drop and Create Production Product"
ConnectionName="Staging">
  <DirectInput>
    SET ANSI_NULLS ON
    SET QUOTED_IDENTIFIER ON
    GO


    -------------------------------------------------------------------
    IF EXISTS (SELECT * from sys.objects WHERE object_id = OBJECT_
    ID(N'[Production].[Product]') AND type IN (N'U'))
    DROP TABLE [Production].[Product]
    GO

    CREATE TABLE [Production].[Product]
    (
    -- Columns Definition
    [ProductID] int IDENTITY(1,1) NOT NULL
    ,[Name] nvarchar(50) NOT NULL
    ,[ProductNumber] nvarchar(25) NOT NULL
    ,[MakeFlag] bit NOT NULL
    ,[FinishedGoodsFlag] bit NOT NULL
    ,[Color] nvarchar(15)
    ,[SafetyStockLevel] smallint NOT NULL
    ,[ReorderPoint] smallint NOT NULL
    ,[StandardCost] money NOT NULL
    ,[ListPrice] money NOT NULL
    ,[Size] nvarchar(5)
```

```
,[Weight] decimal(8,2)
,[DaysToManufacture] int NOT NULL
,[ProductLine] nchar(2)
,[Class] nchar(2)
,[Style] nchar(2)
,[SellStartDate] datetime NOT NULL
,[SellEndDate] datetime
,[DiscontinuedDate] datetime
,[rowguid] uniqueidentifier NOT NULL
,[ModifiedDate] datetime NOT NULL

-- Constraints
,CONSTRAINT [PK_Product_ProductID] PRIMARY KEY CLUSTERED
(
[ProductID] Asc) WITH(PAD_INDEX = OFF,IGNORE_DUP_KEY = OFF) ON "default"

)
ON "default"
WITH (DATA_COMPRESSION = NONE)
GO

---------------------------------------------------------------------

ALTER TABLE [Production].[Product] ADD CONSTRAINT [DF_Product_MakeFlag]
DEFAULT (((1))) FOR [MakeFlag]
GO
ALTER TABLE [Production].[Product] ADD CONSTRAINT [DF_Product_
FinishedGoodsFlag] DEFAULT (((1))) FOR [FinishedGoodsFlag]
GO
ALTER TABLE [Production].[Product] ADD CONSTRAINT [DF_Product_rowguid]
DEFAULT ((newid())) FOR [rowguid]
GO
ALTER TABLE [Production].[Product] ADD CONSTRAINT [DF_Product_
ModifiedDate] DEFAULT ((getdate())) FOR [ModifiedDate]
GO

CREATE UNIQUE CLUSTERED INDEX [PK_Product_ProductID] ON [Production].
[Product]
(
[ProductID] Asc
)

WITH
(
PAD_INDEX = OFF,
SORT_IN_TEMPDB = OFF,
DROP_EXISTING = OFF,
IGNORE_DUP_KEY = OFF,
```

```
ONLINE = OFF
)
ON "default"
GO
CREATE UNIQUE NONCLUSTERED INDEX [AK_Product_ProductNumber] ON
[Production].[Product]
(
[ProductNumber] Asc
)

WITH
(
PAD_INDEX = OFF,
SORT_IN_TEMPDB = OFF,
DROP_EXISTING = OFF,
IGNORE_DUP_KEY = OFF,
ONLINE = OFF
)
ON "default"
GO
CREATE UNIQUE NONCLUSTERED INDEX [AK_Product_Name] ON [Production].
[Product]
(
[Name] Asc
)

WITH
(
PAD_INDEX = OFF,
SORT_IN_TEMPDB = OFF,
DROP_EXISTING = OFF,
IGNORE_DUP_KEY = OFF,
ONLINE = OFF
)
ON "default"
GO
CREATE UNIQUE NONCLUSTERED INDEX [AK_Product_rowguid] ON [Production].
[Product]
(
[rowguid] Asc
)

WITH
(
PAD_INDEX = OFF,
SORT_IN_TEMPDB = OFF,
DROP_EXISTING = OFF,
IGNORE_DUP_KEY = OFF,
```

```
   ONLINE = OFF
   )
   ON "default"
   GO

</DirectInput>
</ExecuteSQL>
```

Using ImportDB with ImportOptions

In a typical staging environment, you don't want to keep identity columns, constraints, indexes, and keys, and you don't want to create any tables based on source views. To exclude all of these objects from your imported metadata, you can pass the ImportOptions parameter after passing the Schema and TableFilter parameters. In Listing 4-3, you leave the Schema and TableFilter parameters blank to import all objects. Each ImportOption is separated by the pipe (|) character.

Listing 4-3. ImportDB with ImportOptions

```
<# var sourceConnection = SchemaManager.CreateConnectionNode("AW2014", "Data
Source=.;Initial Catalog=AdventureWorks2014;Provider=SQLNCLI11;Integrated
Security=SSPI;"); #>

<# var sourceMetadata = sourceConnection.ImportDB("", "", ImportOptions.
ExcludeCheckConstraint | ImportOptions.ExcludeColumnDefault | ImportOptions.
ExcludeForeignKey | ImportOptions.ExcludeIdentity | ImportOptions.
ExcludeIndex | ImportOptions.ExcludePrimaryKey | ImportOptions.
ExcludeUniqueKey | ImportOptions.ExcludeViews); #>

<Biml xmlns="http://schemas.varigence.com/biml.xsd">
  <Connections>
    <OleDbConnection Name="Staging" ConnectionString="Data Source=.;Initial
    Catalog=Staging;Provider=SQLNCLI11;Integrated Security=SSPI;" />
  </Connections>
  <Packages>
    <Package Name="DropAndCreateStagingTables">
      <Tasks>
        <# foreach (var table in sourceMetadata.TableNodes) { #>
          <ExecuteSQL Name="Drop and Create <#=table.Schema#> <#=table.
          Name#>" ConnectionName="Staging">
            <DirectInput><#=table.GetDropAndCreateDdl()#></DirectInput>
          </ExecuteSQL>
        <# } #>
      </Tasks>
    </Package>
  </Packages>
</Biml>
```

The resulting code from <#=table.GetDropAndCreateDdl()#> for the Product table is shown in Listing 4-4.

Listing 4-4. Result of ImportDB with ImportOptions

```
<ExecuteSQL Name="Drop and Create Production Product"
ConnectionName="Staging">
  <DirectInput>
    SET ANSI_NULLS ON
    SET QUOTED_IDENTIFIER ON
    GO


    -------------------------------------------------------------------

    IF EXISTS (SELECT * from sys.objects WHERE object_id = OBJECT_ID
    (N'[Production].[Product]') AND type IN (N'U'))
    DROP TABLE [Production].[Product]
    GO

    CREATE TABLE [Production].[Product]
    (
    -- Columns Definition
    [ProductID] int NOT NULL
    ,[Name] nvarchar(50) NOT NULL
    ,[ProductNumber] nvarchar(25) NOT NULL
    ,[MakeFlag] bit NOT NULL
    ,[FinishedGoodsFlag] bit NOT NULL
    ,[Color] nvarchar(15)
    ,[SafetyStockLevel] smallint NOT NULL
    ,[ReorderPoint] smallint NOT NULL
    ,[StandardCost] money NOT NULL
    ,[ListPrice] money NOT NULL
    ,[Size] nvarchar(5)
    ,[SizeUnitMeasureCode] nchar(3)
    ,[WeightUnitMeasureCode] nchar(3)
    ,[Weight] decimal(8,2)
    ,[DaysToManufacture] int NOT NULL
    ,[ProductLine] nchar(2)
    ,[Class] nchar(2)
    ,[Style] nchar(2)
    ,[ProductSubcategoryID] int
    ,[ProductModelID] int
    ,[SellStartDate] datetime NOT NULL
    ,[SellEndDate] datetime
    ,[DiscontinuedDate] datetime
    ,[rowguid] uniqueidentifier NOT NULL
    ,[ModifiedDate] datetime NOT NULL
```

```
-- Constraints

)
ON "default"
WITH (DATA_COMPRESSION = NONE)
GO


-----------------------------------------------------------------------

</DirectInput>
</ExecuteSQL>
```

ImportTableNodes and ImportDB work well for certain use cases. But what if you want to exclude one specific schema, such as dbo? What if you only want to import a few tables in different schemas, such as the Product tables and the SalesOrder tables?

Limitations of ImportTableNodes and ImportDB

The main limitation of ImportTableNodes and ImportDB is that you can't specify a collection of schemas, tables, or views to import. You can only specify patterns by using wildcards. For example, you can import all tables that begin with a *P* by using a wildcard, but you can't choose to import just the three tables Customer, Employee, and Person. Additionally, since these methods perform the equivalent of a SELECT * in *SchemaOnly* mode, they can be quite slow when importing a large number of tables, especially against underpowered servers.

The solution to both of these limitations is to instead use the GetDatabaseSchema method.

GetDatabaseSchema

GetDatabaseSchema can import all schema information or just the schema information for specific collections of schemas, tables, and views. In addition to importing metadata, it is also possible to specify options to control the Biml generated from the imported schemas, tables, and views. Additionally, GetDatabaseSchema will use the information schema tables (or equivalent features) for the source provider type to capture the schema information and perform type mappings. Note that this approach, while faster and more flexible, may produce results that are different from the ImportDB and ImportTableNodes methods and may also differ from the type mappings applied by SSIS dataflow source components.

GetDatabaseSchema has several overloaded methods that can take one or more parameters. The three most important parameters are IncludedSchemas, IncludedTables, and ImportOptions; they define which objects to include and exclude from the imported results. There is also an optional TimeOut parameter that is offered for each combination of overloaded parameters. See Table 4-3.

Table 4-3. *GetDatabaseSchema Parameters*

Parameter	Description	Examples

IncludedSchemas	Collection of strings that specifies the schemas to import. It can be null and it can be an empty collection. In this chapter, we will use List<string>.	null
		new List<string>()
		new List<string>{
		"Production"
		}

IncludedTables	Collection of strings that specifies tables/views to import. It can be null and it can be an empty collection. In this chapter, we will use List<string>.	null
		new List<string>()
		new List<string>{
		"Product",
		"ProductCategory",
		"ProductSubcategory"
		}

ImportOptions	A special parameter that can be used to exclude specific objects.	None ExcludeCheckConstraint ExcludeColumnDefault ExcludeForeignKey ExcludeIdentity ExcludeIndex ExcludePrimaryKey ExcludeUniqueKey ExcludeViews
TimeOut	Integer that specifies the connection timeout in seconds. It can be null to use the default timeout of 30 second. It can be 0 to run with no timeout.	null 0 1000
AddColumnAnnotations	Boolean that specifies whether or not to include source column metadata in Biml annotations.	True False
DatabaseNode	AstDatabaseNode that specifies the destination database in Biml.	RootNode. Databases["Staging"]

To import all metadata:

```
GetDatabaseSchema()
```

To import all metadata and set a timeout for the queries run during import:

```
GetDatabaseSchema(TimeOut)
```

To import all metadata and exclude objects specified in ImportOptions:

```
GetDatabaseSchema(ImportOptions)
```

To import all metadata, exclude objects specified in ImportOptions, and set a timeout for the queries run during import:

```
GetDatabaseSchema(ImportOptions, TimeOut)
```

To import specified schemas, tables, and/or views; also, exclude objects specified in ImportOptions:

```
GetDatabaseSchema(IncludedSchemas, IncludedTables, ImportOptions)
```

To import specified schemas, tables, and/or views; exclude objects specified in ImportOptions; and set a timeout for the queries run during import:

```
GetDatabaseSchema(IncludedSchemas, IncludedTables, ImportOptions, TimeOit)
```

To import specified schemas, tables, and/or views; exclude objects specified in ImportOptions; choose whether or not to include source column metadata as Biml annotations; and set a timeout for the queries run during import:

```
GetDatabaseSchema(IncludedSchemas, IncludedTables, ImportOptions,
AddColumnAnnotations, TimeOut)
```

To define the destination database; import specified schemas, tables, and/or views; exclude objects specified in ImportOptions; choose whether or not to include source column metadata as Biml annotations; and set a timeout for the queries run during import:

```
GetDatabaseSchema(DatabaseNode, IncludedSchemas, IncludedTables,
ImportOptions, AddColumnAnnotations, TimeOut)
```

Using GetDatabaseSchema to Import Specified Schemas and Tables

If you want to import just a few tables, you can use GetDatabaseSchema.

First, you create two lists containing string values only, named includedSchemas and includedTables. You choose to create these objects first and then pass them as parameters to make the example more readable, but it is also possible to create these lists inside the GetDatabaseSchema() method, as shown in the comments in Listing 4-5.

Then you create the connection to your source database and import the metadata by calling sourceConnection.GetDatabaseSchema() and passing in your included schemas, included tables, and ImportOptions.

Listing 4-5. GetDatabaseSchema (C#)

```
<#
  var includedSchemas = new List<string>{"Production", "Sales"};
  var includedTables = new List<string>{"Product", "ProductCategory",
  "ProductSubcategory", "SalesOrderDetail", "SalesOrderHeader"};

  var sourceConnection = SchemaManager.CreateConnectionNode("AW2014", "Data
Source=.;Initial Catalog=AdventureWorks2014;Provider=SQLNCLI11;Integrated
Security=SSPI;");

  var sourceMetadata = sourceConnection.GetDatabaseSchema(includedSchemas,
  includedTables, ImportOptions.ExcludeCheckConstraint | ImportOptions.
  ExcludeColumnDefault | ImportOptions.ExcludeForeignKey | ImportOptions.
  ExcludeIdentity | ImportOptions.ExcludeIndex | ImportOptions.
  ExcludePrimaryKey | ImportOptions.ExcludeUniqueKey | ImportOptions.
  ExcludeViews);
#>
<#*

  /* If you prefer to create the lists inline, you can use the following
     code instead: */

  var sourceMetadata = sourceConnection.GetDatabaseSchema(new List<string>
  {"Production", "Sales"}, new List<string>{"Product", "ProductCategory",
  "ProductSubcategory", "SalesOrderDetail", "SalesOrderHeader"}, ImportOptions.
  ExcludeCheckConstraint | ImportOptions.ExcludeColumnDefault | ImportOptions.
  ExcludeForeignKey | ImportOptions.ExcludeIdentity | ImportOptions.
  ExcludeIndex | ImportOptions.ExcludePrimaryKey | ImportOptions.
  ExcludeUniqueKey | ImportOptions.ExcludeViews);
*#>

<Biml xmlns="http://schemas.varigence.com/biml.xsd">
  <Connections>
    <OleDbConnection Name="Staging" ConnectionString="Data Source=.;Initial
    Catalog=Staging;Provider=SQLNCLI11;Integrated Security=SSPI;" />
  </Connections>
  <Packages>
    <Package Name="DropAndCreateStagingTables">
      <Tasks>
        <# foreach (var tbl in sourceMetadata.TableNodes) { #>
        <ExecuteSQL Name="Drop and Create <#=tbl.Schema#> <#= tbl.Name#>"
         ConnectionName="Staging">
          <DirectInput><#= tbl.GetDropAndCreateDdl()#></DirectInput>
        </ExecuteSQL>
        <# } #>
```

```
        </Tasks>
      </Package>
    </Packages>
  </Biml>
```

If you want to use VB as your programming language, the code will look like Listing 4-6.

Listing 4-6. GetDatabaseSchema (VB)

```
<#@ template language="VB" optionexplicit="False" #>
<#
  Dim includedSchemas as new List(of String) from { "Production", "Sales" }
  Dim includedTables as new List(of String) from {"Product",
  "ProductCategory", "ProductSubcategory", "SalesOrderDetail",
  "SalesOrderHeader"}

  Dim sourceConnection = SchemaManager.CreateConnectionNode("AW2014", "Data
  Source=.;Initial Catalog=AdventureWorks2014;Provider=SQLNCLI11;Integrated
  Security=SSPI;")

  Dim sourceMetadata = sourceConnection.GetDatabaseSchema(includedSchemas,
  includedTables, ImportOptions.ExcludeCheckConstraint or ImportOptions.
  ExcludeColumnDefault or ImportOptions.ExcludeForeignKey or ImportOptions.
  ExcludeIdentity or ImportOptions.ExcludeIndex or ImportOptions.
  ExcludePrimaryKey or ImportOptions.ExcludeUniqueKey or ImportOptions.
  ExcludeViews)
#>

<Biml xmlns="http://schemas.varigence.com/biml.xsd">
  <Connections>
    <OleDbConnection Name="Staging" ConnectionString="Data Source=.;Initial
    Catalog=Staging;Provider=SQLNCLI11;Integrated Security=SSPI;" />
  </Connections>
  <Packages>
    <Package Name="DropAndCreateStagingTables">
      <Tasks>
        <# for each tbl in sourceMetadata.TableNodes #>
        <ExecuteSQL Name="Drop and Create <#=tbl.Schema#> <#= tbl.Name#>"
         ConnectionName="Staging">
          <DirectInput><#= tbl.GetDropAndCreateDdl()#></DirectInput>
        </ExecuteSQL>
        <# next #>
      </Tasks>
    </Package>
  </Packages>
</Biml>
```

If you compare the two code samples, you will see some differences:

1. You need to declare the VB language explicitly in a template directive, and we recommend setting the VB specific attribute optionexplicit to False. Setting this attribute to false means that the Visual Basic compiler will no longer require you to declare every object or variable's type explicitly.

   With optionexplicit="False", instead of

   ```
   <# for each tbl as AstTableNode in sourceMetadata.TableNodes #>
   ```

   you can just write

   ```
   <# for each tbl in sourceMetadata.TableNodes #>
   ```

   This makes your code easier to read, but it also means that you don't need to remember every single object type, which is quite handy especially if you're just getting used to the Biml language and its elements.

   More about option explicit at https://docs.microsoft.com/en-us/dotnet/visual-basic/language-reference/statements/option-explicit-statement.

2. The syntax to define the lists and the for each loop is different.

3. To pass multiple ImportOptions, you use or instead of pipes (|).

4. You don't need to use semicolons at the end of each line.

By keeping these simple rules in mind, you can easily translate most C# code to VB code or vice versa.

The resulting output, regardless of coding language, looks like Listing 4-7. Only the first *Drop and Create* statement is shown in full.

Listing 4-7. Result of GetDatabaseSchema

```
<Biml xmlns="http://schemas.varigence.com/biml.xsd">
 <Connections>
  <OleDbConnection Name="Staging" ConnectionString="Data Source=.;Initial
   Catalog=Staging;Provider=SQLNCLI11;Integrated Security=SSPI;" />
 </Connections>
 <Packages>
  <Package Name="DropAndCreateStagingTables">
   <Tasks>
    <ExecuteSQL Name="Drop and Create Production Product"
     ConnectionName="Staging">
     <DirectInput>
      SET ANSI_NULLS ON
      SET QUOTED_IDENTIFIER ON
      GO
```

```
-----------------------------------------------------------------------
IF EXISTS (SELECT * from sys.objects WHERE object_id =
OBJECT_ID(N'[Production].[Product]') AND type IN (N'U'))
DROP TABLE [Production].[Product]
GO

CREATE TABLE [Production].[Product]
(
-- Columns Definition
[ProductID] int NOT NULL
, [Name] nvarchar(50) NOT NULL
, [ProductNumber] nvarchar(25) NOT NULL
, [MakeFlag] bit NOT NULL
, [FinishedGoodsFlag] bit NOT NULL
, [Color] nvarchar(15)
, [SafetyStockLevel] smallint NOT NULL
, [ReorderPoint] smallint NOT NULL
, [StandardCost] money NOT NULL
, [ListPrice] money NOT NULL
, [Size] nvarchar(5)
, [SizeUnitMeasureCode] nchar(3)
, [WeightUnitMeasureCode] nchar(3)
, [Weight] decimal(8,2)
, [DaysToManufacture] int NOT NULL
, [ProductLine] nchar(2)
, [Class] nchar(2)
, [Style] nchar(2)
, [ProductSubcategoryID] int
, [ProductModelID] int
, [SellStartDate] datetime NOT NULL
, [SellEndDate] datetime
, [DiscontinuedDate] datetime
, [rowguid] uniqueidentifier NOT NULL
, [ModifiedDate] datetime NOT NULL

-- Constraints

)
ON "default"
WITH (DATA_COMPRESSION = NONE)
GO

-----------------------------------------------------------------------

</DirectInput>
</ExecuteSQL>
<ExecuteSQL Name="Drop and Create Production ProductCategory"
ConnectionName="Staging">
```

```
      <DirectInput>...</DirectInput>
      </ExecuteSQL>
      <ExecuteSQL Name="Drop and Create Production ProductSubcategory"
      ConnectionName="Staging">
      <DirectInput>...</DirectInput>
      </ExecuteSQL>
      <ExecuteSQL Name="Drop and Create Sales SalesOrderDetail"
      ConnectionName="Staging">
      <DirectInput>...</DirectInput>
      </ExecuteSQL>
      <ExecuteSQL Name="Drop and Create Sales SalesOrderHeader"
      ConnectionName="Staging">
        <DirectInput>...</DirectInput>
      </ExecuteSQL>
    </Tasks>
  </Package>
 </Packages>
</Biml>
```

Using GetDatabaseSchema with Column Annotations

As your Biml solution grows, you may want to store source metadata information for later use. For example, you may want to create facts and dimensions with different data types than your source system, and then handle conversions in the fact and dimension loading packages. To do this, you can store source metadata in Biml annotations.

Biml annotations are not the same as SSIS annotations. While SSIS annotations are used to create comments inside your packages, Biml annotations are used to store and pass code between Biml files. The following is an example of a Biml annotation named SourceDatabase, where you store the value "AdventureWorks2014":

```
<Annotations>
  <Annotation Tag="SourceDatabase">AdventureWorks2014</Annotation>
</Annotations
```

GetDatabaseSchema has an AddColumnAnnotations parameter that will add source datatype metadata to your Biml code so that you can override the datatype mappings based on raw source system information in the rare cases where you need to implement custom datatype mapping logic.

Listing 4-8 shows how to use two tiered Biml files to import metadata from the AdventureWorks2014 database. The first file defines the connections and databases. The second file imports metadata including column annotations.

Environment.biml: In this file, you specify your connections and database.

Listing 4-8. Environment File

```
<#@ template tier="0" #>
<Biml xmlns="http://schemas.varigence.com/biml.xsd">
  <Connections>
    <OleDbConnection Name="AW2014" ConnectionString="Data Source=.;Initial
      Catalog=AdventureWorks2014;Provider=SQLNCLI11.1;Integrated
      Security=SSPI;" />
    <OleDbConnection Name="Staging" ConnectionString="Data Source=.;Initial
      Catalog=Staging;Provider=SQLNCLI11.1;Integrated Security=SSPI;" />
  </Connections>
  <Databases>
    <Database Name="Staging" ConnectionName="Staging" />
  </Databases>
</Biml>
```

TableMetadata.biml: In this file, you use RootNode.OleDbConnections["AW2014"] to get the connection named AW2014 from your environment file.

You then use the following version of GetDatabaseSchema:

```
GetDatabaseSchema(DatabaseNode, IncludedSchemas, IncludedTables,
ImportOptions, AddColumnAnnotations, TimeOut)
```

You pass RootNode.Databases["Staging"] as your destination database, then your included schemas, included tables and ImportOptions, and finally you say that you want to add the column annotations (true) and that you don't want to specify a timeout (null).

Finally, you use schema.GetBiml() and table.GetBiml() to view the schema and table metadata, as shown in Listing 4-9.

Listing 4-9. Build Metadata (C#)

```
<#@ template tier="1" #>
<#
  var includedSchemas = new List<string>{"Production"};
  var includedTables = new List<string>{"Product", "ProductCategory",
  "ProductSubcategory"};

  var sourceConnection = RootNode.OleDbConnections["AW2014"];

  var sourceMetadata = sourceConnection.GetDatabaseSchema(RootNode.
  Databases["Staging"], includedSchemas, includedTables, ImportOptions.
  ExcludeCheckConstraint | ImportOptions.ExcludeColumnDefault |
  ImportOptions.ExcludeForeignKey | ImportOptions.ExcludeIdentity |
  ImportOptions.ExcludeIndex | ImportOptions.ExcludePrimaryKey |
  ImportOptions.ExcludeUniqueKey | ImportOptions.ExcludeViews, true, null);
#>
```

```
<Biml xmlns="http://schemas.varigence.com/biml.xsd">
  <Schemas>
    <# foreach (var schema in sourceMetadata.SchemaNodes) { #>
<#= schema.GetBiml()#>
    <# } #>
  </Schemas>
  <Tables>
    <# foreach (var tbl in sourceMetadata.TableNodes) { #>
<#= tbl.GetBiml()#>
    <# } #>
  </Tables>
</Biml>
```

If you want to use VB as your programming language, the code will look like Listing 4-10.

Listing 4-10. Build Metadata (VB)

```
<#@ template language="VB" optionexplicit="False" #>
<#
  Dim includedSchemas as new List(of String) from { "Production" }
  Dim includedTables as new List(of String) from {"Product",
  "ProductCategory", "ProductSubcategory"}

  Dim sourceConnection = RootNode.OleDbConnections("AW2014")

  Dim sourceMetadata = sourceConnection.GetDatabaseSchema(RootNode.
  Databases("Staging"), includedSchemas, includedTables, ImportOptions.
  ExcludeCheckConstraint or ImportOptions.ExcludeColumnDefault or
  ImportOptions.ExcludeForeignKey or ImportOptions.ExcludeIdentity
  or ImportOptions.ExcludeIndex or ImportOptions.ExcludePrimaryKey or
  ImportOptions.ExcludeUniqueKey or ImportOptions.ExcludeViews, true, nothing)
#>

<Biml xmlns="http://schemas.varigence.com/biml.xsd">
  <Schemas>
    <# for each schema in sourceMetadata.SchemaNodes #>
      <#=schema.GetBiml()#>
    <# next #>
  </Schemas>
  <Tables>
    <# for each tbl in sourceMetadata.TableNodes #>
      <#= tbl.GetBiml()#>
    <# next #>
  </Tables>
</Biml>
```

If you compare the two code samples again, you will see some additional differences between C# and VB.

1. Instead of null, you use nothing.

2. Instead of [ ], you use ( ).

The resulting output, again regardless of code language, looks like Listing 4-11. Only the first column is shown with the additional annotations from the AddColumnAnnotations option.

Listing 4-11. Result of Your Metadata Collection

```
<Biml xmlns="http://schemas.varigence.com/biml.xsd">
 <Schemas>
  <Schema Name="Production" DatabaseName="Staging" />
  <Schema Name="Sales" DatabaseName="Staging" />
 </Schemas>
 <Tables>
  <Table Name="Product" SchemaName="Staging.Production">
   <Columns>
    <Column Name="ProductID">
     <Annotations>
      <Annotation Tag="GetDatabaseSchema.RawProviderType">56</Annotation>
      <Annotation Tag="GetDatabaseSchema.RawDataTypeId">56</Annotation>
      <Annotation Tag="GetDatabaseSchema.RawDataType">int</Annotation>
      <Annotation Tag="GetDatabaseSchema.RawLength">4</Annotation>
      <Annotation Tag="GetDatabaseSchema.RawPrecision">10</Annotation>
      <Annotation Tag="GetDatabaseSchema.RawScale">0</Annotation>
      <Annotation Tag="GetDatabaseSchema.SizeInBytes">4</Annotation>
     </Annotations>
    </Column>
    <Column Name="Name" DataType="String" Length="50" />
    <Column Name="ProductNumber" DataType="String" Length="25" />
    <Column Name="MakeFlag" DataType="Boolean" />
    <Column Name="FinishedGoodsFlag" DataType="Boolean" />
    <Column Name="Color" DataType="String" Length="15" IsNullable="true" />
    <Column Name="SafetyStockLevel" DataType="Int16" />
    <Column Name="ReorderPoint" DataType="Int16" />
    <Column Name="StandardCost" DataType="Currency" />
    <Column Name="ListPrice" DataType="Currency" />
    <Column Name="Size" DataType="String" Length="5" IsNullable="true" />
    <Column Name="SizeUnitMeasureCode" DataType="StringFixedLength"
     Length="3" IsNullable="true" />
    <Column Name="WeightUnitMeasureCode" DataType="StringFixedLength"
     Length="3" IsNullable="true" />
    <Column Name="Weight" DataType="Decimal" Precision="8" Scale="2"
     IsNullable="true" />
    <Column Name="DaysToManufacture" />
    <Column Name="ProductLine" DataType="StringFixedLength" Length="2"
     IsNullable="true" />
```

```
    <Column Name="Class" DataType="StringFixedLength" Length="2"
     IsNullable="true" />
    <Column Name="Style" DataType="StringFixedLength" Length="2"
     IsNullable="true" />
    <Column Name="ProductSubcategoryID" IsNullable="true" />
    <Column Name="ProductModelID" IsNullable="true" />
    <Column Name="SellStartDate" DataType="DateTime" />
    <Column Name="SellEndDate" DataType="DateTime" IsNullable="true" />
    <Column Name="DiscontinuedDate" DataType="DateTime" IsNullable="true" />
    <Column Name="rowguid" DataType="Guid" />
    <Column Name="ModifiedDate" DataType="DateTime" />
   </Columns>
  </Table>
  <Table Name="ProductCategory" SchemaName="Staging.Production">
   <Columns>
    ...
   </Columns>
  </Table>
  <Table Name="ProductSubcategory" SchemaName="Staging.Production">
   <Columns>
    ...
   </Columns>
  </Table>
  <Table Name="SalesOrderDetail" SchemaName="Staging.Sales">
   <Columns>
    ...
   </Columns>
  </Table>
  <Table Name="SalesOrderHeader" SchemaName="Staging.Sales">
   <Columns>
    ...
   </Columns>
  </Table>
 </Tables>
</Biml>
```

Which Method Should I Use?

The main limitation of ImportTableNodes and ImportDB is that you can't specify a collection of schemas, tables, or views to import. You can only specify patterns by using wildcards. For example, you can import all tables that begin with a *P* by using a wildcard, but you can't choose to import just the three tables Customer, Employee, and Person. GetDatabaseSchema allows you to specify collections of schemas, tables, and views to import and it has some additional options to get source metadata.

Additionally, you can use GetDatabaseSchema if you need faster performance, the alternative datatype mappings from the information schema method it uses to retrieve metadata, or require the raw datatype metadata for custom type mapping logic.

Excel

When it comes to working with Excel as a data source, you can make use of the GetDatabaseSchema method that you have already learned about. First, start by declaring a source connection as well as a target database and schema to load the data to.

Your Excel connection will need a driver, some extra properties as well as the filename, as shown in Listing 4-12.

Listing 4-12. Environment Definition for an Excel Source

```
Biml xmlns="http://schemas.varigence.com/biml.xsd">
  <Connections>
    <ExcelConnection Name="MyExcel" ConnectionString="Provider=Microsoft.
    ACE.OLEDB.12.0;Data Source=C:\Flatfiles\XLS\MyExcel.xlsx;Extended
    Properties=&quot;Excel 12.0 XML;HDR=YES&quot;;" />
    <OleDbConnection Name="Target" ConnectionString="Data
    Source=localhost;initial catalog=MySimpleBiml_Destination;provider=SQLN
    CLI11;integrated security=SSPI"/>
  </Connections>
  <Databases>
    <Database Name="MySimpleBiml_Destination" ConnectionName="Target"/>
  </Databases>
  <Schemas>
    <Schema Name="dbo" DatabaseName="MySimpleBiml_Destination"/>
  </Schemas>
</Biml>
```

Because Excel does not really have a database schema for its tables, you will need to assign one manually. Otherwise, you can use the methods and functionality that you have seen previously. This example just assigns the first schema within *RootNode* to all tables coming from Excel; obviously, this is something that you may want to modify to fit your exact needs. See Listing 4-13.

Listing 4-13. GetDatabaseSchema on Excel (C#)

```
<Biml xmlns="http://schemas.varigence.com/biml.xsd">
  <Tables>
    <#
    var xls = RootNode.Connections["MyExcel"];
    var ImportResult = xls.GetDatabaseSchema();
    foreach (var tbl in ImportResult.TableNodes) {
      tbl.Schema = RootNode.Schemas[0];#>
      <#= tbl.GetBiml() #>
    <# } #>
  </Tables>
</Biml>
```

Or, in Visual Basic, use the code in Listing 4-14.

Listing 4-14. GetDatabaseSchema on Excel (VB)

```
<#@ template language="VB" optionexplicit="False"#>
<Biml xmlns="http://schemas.varigence.com/biml.xsd">
  <Tables>
    <#
    Dim XLS = RootNode.Connections("MyExcel")
    Dim ImportResult = XLS.GetDatabaseSchema()
    for each tbl in ImportResult.TableNodes
      tbl.Schema = RootNode.Schemas(0)#>
      <#= tbl.GetBiml() #>
    <# next #>
  </Tables>
</Biml>
```

The other potential issue that may result from reading the metadata from Excel is that Excel has, by default, no way of actually making sure that data types are being adhered to, so you may run into conversion issues when eventually loading the data. In this case, we recommend enriching the metadata based on an extended metadata model to modify the detected data types as needed. You can learn more about this in Chapter 14.

Flat Files

Biml can also be used to create packages that load data from flat files. Let us look at the basics first.

Basic Biml Elements for Flat Files

When working with flat files, you will need at least one flat file connection as well as a flat file format. The flat file format will define top-level attributes of the file structure. The major attributes are

- Name
- Codepage
- Unicode
- ColumnNamesInFirstDataRow

If you have imported flat files using SSIS before, this should align with what you have seen there. In addition to these main attributes, each file format will specify one or more columns which will be defined by attributes such as

- Name
- DataType

- Length

- Delimiter

The flat file connection, on the other hand, is simply a link between a file (physical path on disk) and the file format to be applied when working with that file. A full flat file environment could look like Listing 4-15.

Listing 4-15. Environment File for Flat Files

```
<Biml xmlns="http://schemas.varigence.com/biml.xsd">
  <FileFormats>
    <FlatFileFormat Name="MyFlatFile" CodePage="1252" ColumnNamesInFirstData
    Row="true" IsUnicode="false">
      <Columns>
        <Column Name="Warehouse" DataType="String" Length="50"
         Delimiter="Semicolon" />
        <Column Name="Item" DataType="String" Length="50"
         Delimiter="Semicolon" />
        <Column Name="Inventory" DataType="Int64" Delimiter="CRLF" />
      </Columns>
    </FlatFileFormat>
  </FileFormats>
  <Connections>
    <FlatFileConnection Name="MyFlatFile" FilePath="C:\myFlatfile.csv"
    FileFormat="MyFlatFile" />
  </Connections>
</Biml>
```

Listing 4-15 would be enough metadata to actually read from or write to a flat file with three columns (Warehouse, Item, and Inventory).

To actually perform the read/write, you will need to define a connection, a target relational <Table>, and a package to perform the copy. In Listing 4-16, you define the relational connection and target table.

Listing 4-16. Environment File for Flat Files Including a Dummy Table

```
<Biml xmlns="http://schemas.varigence.com/biml.xsd">
  <Connections>
    <OleDbConnection Name="Target" ConnectionString="Data Source=localhost;
     initial catalog=MyBiml_Flatfiles;provider=SQLNCLI11;
     integrated security=SSPI"></OleDbConnection>
  </Connections>
  <Databases>
    <Database Name="MyBiml_Flatfiles" ConnectionName="Target"></Database>
  </Databases>
  <Schemas>
    <Schema Name="dbo" DatabaseName="MyBiml_Flatfiles"></Schema>
  </Schemas>
```

117

```
  <Tables>
    <Table Name="TBL_MyFlatFile" SchemaName="MyBiml_Flatfiles.dbo">
      <Columns>
        <Column Name="Warehouse" DataType="String" Length="50" />
        <Column Name="Item" DataType="String" Length="50" />
        <Column Name="Inventory" DataType="Int64" />
      </Columns>
    </Table>
  </Tables>
</Biml>
```

In Listing 4-17, you create a package that loads the flat file into the target table you created earlier.

Listing 4-17. Data Flow Using a Flat File Source

```
<Biml xmlns="http://schemas.varigence.com/biml.xsd">
  <Packages>
    <Package Name="Load FF">
      <Tasks>
        <Dataflow Name="Load My Flatfile">
          <Transformations>
            <FlatFileSource ConnectionName="MyFlatFile" Name="MyFlatFile"/>
            <OleDbDestination Name="Dest" ConnectionName="Target">
              <TableOutput TableName="MyBiml_Flatfiles.dbo.TBL_MyFlatFile" />
            </OleDbDestination>
          </Transformations>
        </Dataflow>
      </Tasks>
    </Package>
  </Packages>
</Biml>
```

You can learn more advanced techniques for handling metadata with flat files in Chapter 14.

Summary

In this chapter, you learned about one of the most fundamental features of Biml: importing metadata from source systems and source files. Besides the Biml language itself, this might be the most important feature to master. By using methods like GetDatabaseSchema(), GetBiml(), and DropAndCreateDdl(), you can let Biml do the hard work of mapping columns and data types, and even create T-SQL scripts for you. This allows you to write short and simple code to automate database creation and package generation. Because you let Biml do the hard work, it will also handle any source metadata additions or changes for you, so all you have to do is regenerate and rerun your scripts and packages. There is no need for you to manually maintain a data dictionary for this anymore.

In the next chapter, you will learn how to organize your Biml code and make it reusable.

CHAPTER 5

■ ■ ■

Reusing Code, Helper Classes, and Methods

In Chapter 3, you learned how to use tiered Biml files to create a basic staging environment. For a single project, this might be all you need. However, once your solution grows and you need to use Biml for more complex scenarios, you may start to see some of your code repeated in multiple files.

One of the reasons for using Biml is to avoid doing the same manual tasks over and over again. Similarly, you don't want to repeat the same Biml code over and over again either. A rule of thumb is that if we have to copy and paste our Biml code more than two times, we should think about a way to refactor our code and optimize it for reuse instead.

By following the Don't Repeat Yourself (DRY) software engineering principle and creating code that is centralized and reusable, we can update code once and quickly apply the changes in many projects across multiple solutions.

You have already learned how to use tiered Biml files to separate code into multiple files that can be reused in multi-step processes. In this chapter, we will go through how to use include files and the `CallBimlScript` methods, how to create your own helper classes and methods, and finally how to use C# and VB code files to turn your helper methods into extension methods that can help simplify your Biml code.

Include Files

You can think of include files as an automated copy and paste. The include directive specifies which file to include. When your Biml code compiles, all code from the included file is copied and replaces the include directive. It is important that the included file only contains code that can replace the include directive without causing syntax errors. In Listing 5-1, the include directive is used inside `<Variables></Variables>`, so the included file must only contain `<Variable>` elements.

© Andy Leonard et al. 2017
A. Leonard et al., *The Biml Book*, https://doi.org/10.1007/978-1-4842-3135-7_5

Package.biml: You specify the include directive with the file path to the Variables.biml file. See Listing 5-1.

Listing 5-1. Package with Include Directive

```
<Biml xmlns="http://schemas.varigence.com/biml.xsd">
  <Packages>
    <Package Name="Package">
      <Variables>
        <#@ include file="Variables.biml" #>
      </Variables>
      <Tasks>
        ...
      </Tasks>
    </Package>
  </Packages>
</Biml>
```

Variables.biml: Since this is a code fragment, you only specify the variables you want to include. See Listing 5-2.

Listing 5-2. Included File

```
<Variable Name="NewRows" DataType="Int32">0</Variable>
<Variable Name="ChangedRows" DataType="Int32">0</Variable>
<Variable Name="UnchangedRows" DataType="Int32">0</Variable>
```

When you compile the Biml, the end result looks like Listing 5-3.

Listing 5-3. Result After Processing Through the Biml Compiler

```
Biml xmlns="http://schemas.varigence.com/biml.xsd">
  <Packages>
    <Package Name="Package">
      <Variables>
        <Variable Name="NewRows" DataType="Int32">0</Variable>
        <Variable Name="ChangedRows" DataType="Int32">0</Variable>
        <Variable Name="UnchangedRows" DataType="Int32">0</Variable>
      </Variables>
      <Tasks>
        ...
      </Tasks>
    </Package>
  </Packages>
</Biml>
```

Include files are not limited to .biml files. It is also possible to include .txt files, .sql files, .cs files, .vb files, and so on. This gives you the flexibility of working with the included files in the code editor of your choice, for example using SQL Server Management Studio (SSMS) with its IntelliSense when working on .sql files.

By using include files, you can manage code fragments in separate files and include them where needed. When you need to make changes, you update just the one code fragment instead of having to update multiple files. This reduces the risk of manual errors and makes your code easier to maintain.

Using Include Files to Control Logging

In Listing 5-4, you create a simple *Truncate/Load* package for your staging tables.

The TruncateLoadPackages.biml file has an include directive referencing LogRows.biml just after the data flow task, which creates an Execute SQL task.

Listing 5-4. Practical Example Making Use of the Include Directive

```
<#
  var destinationSchema = "AW2014";
  var sourceConnection = SchemaManager.CreateConnectionNode("Source",
  @"Data Source=.;Initial Catalog=AdventureWorks2014;Provider=SQLNCLI11;
  Integrated Security=SSPI;");
  var sourceMetadata = sourceConnection.GetDatabaseSchema
  (ImportOptions.ExcludeViews);
#>
<Biml xmlns="http://schemas.varigence.com/biml.xsd">
  <Connections>
    <OleDbConnection Name="Admin" ConnectionString="Data Source=.;
    Initial Catalog=Admin;Provider=SQLNCLI11;Integrated Security=SSPI;" />
    <OleDbConnection Name="AW2014" ConnectionString="Data Source=.;
    Initial Catalog=AdventureWorks2014;Provider=SQLNCLI11.1;Integrated
    Security=SSPI;" />
    <OleDbConnection Name="Staging" ConnectionString="Data Source=.;
    Initial Catalog=Staging;Provider=SQLNCLI11.1;Integrated Security=SSPI;" />
  </Connections>
  <Packages>
    <# foreach (var table in sourceMetadata.TableNodes) { #>
    <Package Name="Load_<#=destinationSchema#>_<#=table.Schema#>_
    <#=table.Name#>" ConstraintMode="Linear">
      <Variables>
        <Variable Name="NewRows" DataType="Int32">0</Variable>
      </Variables>
      <Tasks>
        <ExecuteSQL Name="Truncate <#=table.Schema#> <#=table.Name#>"
        ConnectionName="Staging">
          <DirectInput>TRUNCATE TABLE <#=destinationSchema#>.
          <#=table.Schema#>_<#=table.Name#>
```

```
        </DirectInput>
      </ExecuteSQL>
      <Dataflow Name="Load <#=table.Schema#> <#=table.Name#>">
        <Transformations>
          <OleDbSource Name="Source <#=table.Schema#> <#=table.Name#>"
          ConnectionName="WWI">
            <ExternalTableInput Table="<#=table.SchemaQualifiedName#>" />
          </OleDbSource>
          <DerivedColumns Name="Add LoadDate">
            <Columns>
              <Column Name="LoadDate" DataType="DateTime">@
              [System::StartTime]</Column>
            </Columns>
          </DerivedColumns>
          <RowCount Name="Count NewRows" VariableName="User.NewRows" />
          <OleDbDestination Name="Destination <#=table.Schema#>
          <#=table.Name#>" ConnectionName="Staging">
            <ExternalTableOutput Table="<#=destinationSchema#>.<#=table.
            Schema#>_<#=table.Name#>" />
          </OleDbDestination>
        </Transformations>
      </Dataflow>
      <#@ include file="LogRows.biml" #>
    </Tasks>
  </Package>
  <# } #>
  </Packages>
</Biml>
```

See Listing 5-5 for the LogRows.biml file.

Listing 5-5. File to Be Included

```
ExecuteSQL Name="Log Rows" ConnectionName="Admin">
  <DirectInput>INSERT INTO dbo.SSISLog (StartTime, PackageName, NewRows)
  VALUES (?, ?, ?)</DirectInput>
  <Parameters>
    <Parameter Name="0" VariableName="System.StartTime" DataType="DateTime2"
    Length="-1" />
    <Parameter Name="1" VariableName="System.PackageName"
    DataType="AnsiString" Length="-1" />
    <Parameter Name="2" VariableName="User.NewRows" DataType="AnsiString"
    Length="-1" />
  </Parameters>
</ExecuteSQL>
```

Now imagine that you also had `IncrementalLoadPackages.biml`, referencing the same `LogRows.biml` file. If you needed to change your logging pattern to include a new parameter, you would only need to update `LogRows.biml` once, and be confident that your logging pattern would be consistent across your different packages.

CallBimlScript

`CallBimlScript` is a more advanced method that allows you to pass parameters from a *caller* file to a *callee* file, similar to a stored procedure in SQL. Inside the callee file, you can use the parameters as regular variables and to control logic, returning different code fragments based on the input parameters.

You can use `CallBimlScript` with any Biml file without defining or passing any parameters. This is similar to using an include directive. To create a callable Biml file that accepts parameters, you have to add *property directives* to the file. The order you specify the properties (parameters) is the order you need to pass them when you call the file.

`CallBimlScript` is used within a text code nugget (that starts with the equal sign `<#= ... #>`). Text code nuggets first parse the content inside the block as a string, and then the text code nugget is replaced by that string. It is important that the callee only contains code that can replace the text code nugget without causing syntax errors. In Listing 5-6, `CallBimlScript` is used inside `<Variables></Variables>`, so the included file must only contain `<Variable>` elements.

`Callee.biml`: You specify two properties (parameters). The first is a required Boolean that specifies if you want to use prefixes or not in your variable names, and the second is an optional String that defines the prefix you want to use. You then use the shorthand code for an if/else statement (`UsePrefix ? Prefix : null`) in your variable names: if `UsePrefix` is `True`, insert the `Prefix` string, else insert *null* (nothing).

Listing 5-6. Callee

```
<#@ property name="UsePrefix" type="Boolean" required="True" #>
<#@ property name="Prefix" type="String" #>
<Variable Name="<#=UsePrefix ? Prefix : null#>NewRows"
DataType="Int32">0</Variable>
<Variable Name="<#=UsePrefix ? Prefix : null#>ChangedRows"
DataType="Int32">0</Variable>
<Variable Name="<#=UsePrefix ? Prefix : null#>UnchangedRows"
DataType="Int32">0</Variable>
```

Caller.biml: You use CallBimlScript twice. In the first package, you want to use a *Var_* prefix in your variable names. In the second package, you don't want to use any prefixes in your variable names. See Listing 5-7.

Listing 5-7. Caller

```
<Biml xmlns="http://schemas.varigence.com/biml.xsd">
  <Packages>
    <Package Name="UsePrefixes">
      <Variables>
        <#=CallBimlScript("Callee.biml", true, "Var_")#>
      </Variables>
    </Package>
    <Package Name="DontUsePrefixes">
      <Variables>
        <#=CallBimlScript("Callee.biml", false)#>
      </Variables>
    </Package>
  </Packages>
</Biml>
```

The resulting expanded Biml looks like Listing 5-8.

Listing 5-8. Result of CallBimlScript

```
<Biml xmlns="http://schemas.varigence.com/biml.xsd">
  <Packages>
    <Package Name="UsePrefixes">
      <Variables>
        <Variable Name="Var_NewRows" DataType="Int32">0</Variable>
        <Variable Name="Var_ChangedRows" DataType="Int32">0</Variable>
        <Variable Name="Var_UnchangedRows" DataType="Int32">0</Variable>
      </Variables>
    </Package>
    <Package Name="DontUsePrefixes">
      <Variables>
        <Variable Name="NewRows" DataType="Int32">0</Variable>
        <Variable Name="ChangedRows" DataType="Int32">0</Variable>
        <Variable Name="UnchangedRows" DataType="Int32">0</Variable>
      </Variables>
    </Package>
  </Packages>
</Biml>
```

You are not limited to passing simple data types like *Int32*s, *Strings*, or *Booleans*. You can pass any kind of object, like a List<string> or even Biml API objects, for example for a table (AstTableNode).

Using CallBimlScript to Control Logging

In a previous example, you saw how to use include files to control logging in a package. You pulled the code for the Execute SQL file into your main file by using an include directive. By using `CallBimlScript`, you can turn this logic around and pass a parameter that specifies whether or not you want to include the Execute SQL task.

`Callee.biml:` The *callee* file creates a *Truncate/Load* package for your staging tables. It accepts six parameters: the table metadata (`AstTableNode`) that you want to use to generate the package, the admin connection, source connection and destination connection, the destination schema, and whether or not to include the logging task or not. You can reuse this callee file in all your projects with a Truncate/Load pattern simply by passing in different parameters. If you want to change the pattern, for example if you want to add a second derived column, you will only have to change it in this one callee Biml file. See Listing 5-9.

Listing 5-9. Practical Example of a Callee

```
<#@ property name="table" type="AstTableNode" #>
<#@ property name="adminConnection" type="String" #>
<#@ property name="sourceConnection" type="String" #>
<#@ property name="destinationConnection" type="String" #>
<#@ property name="destinationSchema" type="String" #>
<#@ property name="includeLogRows" type="Boolean" #>

<Package Name="Load_<#=destinationSchema#>_<#=table.Schema#>_<#=table.
Name#>" ConstraintMode="Linear">
  <Variables>
    <Variable Name="NewRows" DataType="Int32">0</Variable>
  </Variables>
  <Tasks>
    <ExecuteSQL Name="SQL Truncate <#=table.Schema#> <#=table.Name#>" Connec
    tionName="<#=destinationConnection#>">
                        <DirectInput>TRUNCATE TABLE
                        <#=destinationSchema#>.<#=table.Schema#>_<#=table.Name#>
                        </DirectInput>
    </ExecuteSQL>
    <Dataflow Name="Load <#=table.Schema#> <#=table.Name#>">
      <Transformations>
        <OleDbSource Name="Source <#=table.Schema#> <#=table.Name#>"
        ConnectionName="<#=sourceConnection#>">
          <ExternaltableInput table="<#=table.SchemaQualifiedName#>" />
        </OleDbSource>
        <DerivedColumns Name="Add LoadDate">
          <Columns>
            <Column Name="LoadDate" DataType="DateTime">@
            [System::StartTime]</Column>
          </Columns>
        </DerivedColumns>
```

```
        <RowCount Name="Count NewRows" VariableName="User.NewRows" />
        <OleDbDestination Name="Destination <#=table.Schema#>
        <#=table.Name#>" ConnectionName="<#=destinationConnection#>">
          <ExternaltableOutput table="<#=destinationSchema#>.
          <#=table.Schema#>_<#=table.Name#>" />
        </OleDbDestination>
      </Transformations>
    </Dataflow>
    <# if (includeLogRows) { #>
      <ExecuteSQL Name="Log Rows" ConnectionName="<#=adminConnection#>">
          <DirectInput>INSERT INTO dbo.SSISLog (StartTime, PackageName,
          NewRows) VALUES (?, ?, ?)</DirectInput>
        <Parameters>
          <Parameter Name="0" VariableName="System.StartTime"
          DataType="DateTime2" Length="-1" />
          <Parameter Name="1" VariableName="System.PackageName"
          DataType="AnsiString" Length="-1" />
          <Parameter Name="2" VariableName="User.NewRows" DataType="Int32"
          Length="-1" />
        </Parameters>
      </ExecuteSQL>
    <# } #>
  </Tasks>
</Package>
```

Caller.biml: The caller file now only contains the specific connection information and the CallBimlScript code. Compare the parameters passed with the properties defined in the Callee.biml file. See Listing 5-10.

Listing 5-10. Caller

```
<#
  var destinationSchema = "AW2014";
  var sourceConnection = SchemaManager.CreateConnectionNode("Source", @"Data
  Source=.;Initial Catalog=AdventureWorks2014;Provider=SQLNCLI11;Integrated
  Security=SSPI;");
  var sourceMetadata = sourceConnection.GetDatabaseSchema
  (ImportOptions.ExcludeViews);
#>
<Biml xmlns="http://schemas.varigence.com/biml.xsd">
  <Connections>
    <OleDbConnection Name="Admin" ConnectionString="Data Source=.;
    Initial Catalog=Admin;Provider=SQLNCLI11;Integrated Security=SSPI;" />
    <OleDbConnection Name="AW2014" ConnectionString="Data Source=.;Initial Ca
    talog=AdventureWorks2014;Provider=SQLNCLI11;Integrated Security=SSPI;" />
    <OleDbConnection Name="Staging" ConnectionString="Data Source=.;Initial
    Catalog=Staging;Provider=SQLNCLI11;Integrated Security=SSPI;" />
  </Connections>
```

```
<Packages>
    <# foreach (var table in sourceMetadata.TableNodes) { #>
      <#=CallBimlScript(
          "Callee.biml",
          table,      /* Table */
          "Admin",    /* AdminConnection */
          "AW2014",   /* SourceConnection */
          "Staging",  /* DestinationConnection */
          "AW2014",   /* DestinationSchema */
          true        /* IncludeLogRows */
      )#>
    <# } #>
  </Packages>
</Biml>
```

CallBimlScript: is a great helper method for reusing and organizing your code, but it mainly works in one direction. The caller can pass parameters to the callee, and the callee returns Biml code. There is no simple way for the callee to communicate with the caller, except for the returned Biml code.

CallBimlScriptWithOutput

Just like with CallBimlScript, you can use CallBimlScriptWithOutput to pass parameters from the caller to the callee and get Biml code in return. In addition, CallBimlScriptWithOutput can return a dynamic object from the callee to the caller. This object can contain anything you want, from simple strings to Biml API objects.

There are countless scenarios where this comes in handy. For example, you can have CallBimlScriptWithOutput return Biml code for a control flow task, and then have the callee return a dynamic object that determines the output path to be used in a later step.

Using CallBimlScriptWithOutput

The simplified example in Listing 5-11 shows how to use CallBimlScriptWithOutput to create and use a dynamic object.

StaticTable.biml: You first define a static table that you want to pass from the caller to the callee. If you are trying this in an existing Biml environment, you can use any of your previously created tables instead.

Listing 5-11. Static Biml File to Prepare a Lab Environment for This Example

```
<Biml xmlns="http://schemas.varigence.com/biml.xsd">
  <Connections>
    <OleDbConnection Name="Local" ConnectionString="Data Source=.;Initial Ca
    talog=LocalDB;Provider=SQLNCLI11;Integrated Security=SSPI;" />
  </Connections>
  <Databases>
```

```
    <Database Name="LocalDB" ConnectionName="Local" />
  </Databases>
  <Schemas>
    <Schema Name="dbo" DatabaseName="LocalDB" />
  </Schemas>
  <Tables>
    <Table Name="StaticTable" SchemaName="LocalDB.dbo">
      <Columns>
        <Column Name="StringColumn" DataType="String" />
        <Column Name="IntColumn" DataType="Int32" />
        <Column Name="IntColumn" DataType="Int32" />
        <Column Name="DateColumn" DataType="Date" />
      </Columns>
    </Table>
  </Tables>
</Biml>
```

Callee.biml: In the callee, you specify your parameters and your Biml code. (In this simplified example, you only return one comment line.) In addition, you specify your dynamic CustomOutput object and add your custom properties. You can't rename CustomOutput, but you can name the custom properties anything you want and assign any kind of object to them.

In Listings 5-12 (C#) and 5-13 (VB), you create the property ColumnCount with the number of columns in the table, and the property TableDescription, which creates a custom description for the table.

Listing 5-12. Callee with Output (C#)

```
<#@ property name="table" type="AstTableNode" #>

<!-- Biml Code -->

<#
  CustomOutput.ColumnCount = table.Columns.Count;
  CustomOutput.TableDescription = table.Name + " has " + table.Columns.Count
+ " columns.";
#>
```

Listing 5-13. Callee with Output (VB)

```
<#@ template language="VB" optionexplicit="False" #>
<#@ property name="table" type="AstTableNode" #>

<!-- Biml Code -->
```

```
<#
  CustomOutput.ColumnCount = table.Columns.Count
  CustomOutput.TableDescription = table.Name & " has " & table.Columns.Count
& " columns"
#>
```

Caller.biml: In the caller, you create a dynamic object that will contain the CustomOutput from the callee. You can name this object anything you like in the caller file; in this example you name it outputObject.

Then you use CallBimlScriptWithOutput, pass in the dynamic object, and then pass in the rest of the parameters, as shown in Listings 5-14 (C#) and 5-15 (VB).

Listing 5-14. Caller with Output (C#)

```
<Biml xmlns="http://schemas.varigence.com/biml.xsd">

  <# dynamic outputObject; #>
  <#=CallBimlScriptWithOutput("Callee.biml", out outputObject,
  RootNode.Tables["StaticTable"]) #>

    <!-- <#=outputObject.ColumnCount#> -->
    <!-- <#=outputObject.TableDescription#> -->

</Biml>
```

Listing 5-15. Caller with Output (VB)

```
<#@ template language="VB" optionexplicit="False" #>
<Biml xmlns="http://schemas.varigence.com/biml.xsd">

    <# Dim outputObject #>
    <#=CallBimlScriptWithOutput("Callee.biml", outputObject,
    RootNode.Tables("StaticTable")) #>

    <!-- <#=outputObject.ColumnCount#> -->
    <!-- <#=outputObject.TableDescription#> -->

</Biml>
```

The resulting code looks like Listing 5-16.

Listing 5-16. Result of CallBimlScriptWithOutput

```
Biml xmlns="http://schemas.varigence.com/biml.xsd">
        <!-- Biml Code -->
        <!-- 4 -->
        <!-- StaticTable has 4 columns -->
</Biml>
```

Helper Classes and Methods

In this section, we will explain how to create helper classes and methods in C# and VB. For those who are new to programming, we recommend first reading the C# Primer chapter on BimlScript.com at http://bimlscript.com/walkthrough/Details/3117.

There are three ways to create classes and methods in Biml. You can use inline class code nuggets, included files with class code nuggets, or code files.

Helper Method: Check If Annotation Exists

Biml *annotations* and *ObjectTags* are key/value pairs that can be used to store and pass code between Biml files. Annotations can only contain String values, while ObjectTags can contain objects. Listing 5-17 shows how to create and retrieve both annotations and ObjectTags.

Listing 5-17. Annotations in Biml

```
<OleDbConnection Name="AdventureWorks2014" ConnectionString="...">
  <Annotations>
    <Annotation Tag="StagingSchema">AW2014</Annotation>
  </Annotations>
</OleDbConnection>

//Getting Annotations:
RootNode.OleDbConnections["AdventureWorks2014"].GetTag("StagingSchema");

//Creating ObjectTags:
RootNode.OleDbConnections["AdventureWorks2014"].ObjectTag["SchemaFilter"] =
new List<string>{"Production","Sales"};

//Getting ObjectTags:
    RootNode.OleDbConnections["Destination"].ObjectTag["Filter"];
```

You can use annotations or ObjectTags to store metadata to be used later in your solution. To make your solution robust, you should check that the annotation or ObjectTag exists before trying to execute code. Instead of writing this check many times, you can create a helper class and helper method to simplify your code.

Creating the Helper Class and Method

For the first version, create a class named HelperClass. It has a method named TagExists that accepts two parameters and returns a bool. The first parameter is of type AstNode (the base type for all Biml API objects); this is the element you want to check. The second parameter is of type string; this is the name of the tag whose existence you are checking.

If the element has either an annotation with the name specified that is not an empty string, or an ObjectTag that contains the key with the name specified, the method returns true; the tag exists. Otherwise, it returns false; the tag does not exist. See Listing 5-18.

Listing 5-18. First Version of the Helper Class

```
public static class HelperClass {
  public static bool TagExists(AstNode node, string tag) {
    if (node.GetTag(tag) != "" || node.ObjectTag.ContainsKey(tag)) {
      return true;
    }
    return false;
  }
}
```

The first version of your code is quite verbose for a simple *if/else* statement. Let's simplify it, step by step.

In the second version of your code, you change the full *if* statement to the shorthand conditional operator: condition ? first_expression : second_expression;. You evaluate the condition (does the node contain either an annotation or an ObjectTag?), and return either true or false. See Listing 5-19.

Listing 5-19. Second Version of the Helper Class

```
public static class HelperClass {
  public static bool TagExists(AstNode node, string tag) {
    return (node.GetTag(tag) != "" || node.ObjectTag.ContainsKey(tag)) ?
    true : false;
  }
}
```

Finally, since you know that the result of your condition (does the node contain either an annotation or an ObjectTag?) is always true or false, you can remove the conditional operator completely. See Listing 5-20.

Listing 5-20. Third Version of the Helper Class

```
public static class HelperClass {
  public static bool TagExists(AstNode node, string tag) {
    return node.GetTag(tag) != "" || node.ObjectTag.ContainsKey(tag);
  }
}
```

This third version of the code works for methods that return a bool. If you need to return a different kind of object, you may have to use a more verbose syntax like the previous examples.

Now that you have created your helper class and helper method, how do you use it?

Inline Class Code Nuggets

The first way you can use your helper class and method is to create an inline class feature control block. You can then call HelperClass.TagExists() in your BimlScript, as shown in Listing 5-21.

Listing 5-21. Helper as Inline Class

```
<Biml xmlns="http://schemas.varigence.com/biml.xsd">
  <# foreach (var table in RootNode.Tables) { #>
    <# if (HelperClass.TagExists(table, "StagingSchema")) { #>
      ...
    <# } #>
  <# } #>
</Biml>

<#+
public static class HelperClass {
  public static bool TagExists(AstNode node, string tag) {
    return (node.GetTag(tag) != "" || node.ObjectTag.ContainsKey(tag));
  }
}
#>
```

When you use an inline class code nugget, you can only use the code in that one Biml file.

Included Files with Class Code Nuggets

The second way you can use your helper class and method is to move the class code nugget to a separate file and include it where needed, as shown in Listings 5-22 and 5-23.

Listing 5-22. MainFile.biml

```
<#@ include file="HelperClass.biml" #>

<Biml xmlns="http://schemas.varigence.com/biml.xsd">
  <# foreach (var table in RootNode.Tables) { #>
    <# if (HelperClass.TagExists(table, "StagingSchema")) { #>
      ...
    <# } #>
  <# } #>
</Biml>
```

Listing 5-23. HelperClass.biml

```
<#+
public static class HelperClass {
  public static bool TagExists(AstNode node, string tag) {
    return (node.GetTag(tag) != "" || node.ObjectTag.ContainsKey(tag));
  }
}
#>
```

Code Files

The third way you can use your helper class and method is to move your code to a separate *code file*. Notice that you now use the code directive instead of the include directive, and that you no longer need to use the class code nuggets <#+   #> in the code file. See Listings 5-24 and 5-25.

Listing 5-24. MainFile.biml

```
<#@ code file="HelperClass.cs" #>

<Biml xmlns="http://schemas.varigence.com/biml.xsd">
  <# foreach (var table in RootNode.Tables) { #>
    <# if (HelperClass.TagExists(table, "StagingSchema")) { #>
      ...
    <# } #>
  <# } #>
</Biml>
```

Listing 5-25. HelperClass.cs

```
public static class HelperClass {
  public static bool TagExists(AstNode node, string tag) {
    return (node.GetTag(tag) != "" || node.ObjectTag.ContainsKey(tag));
  }
}
```

Using code files is the most sophisticated and reusable way of creating helper classes and methods in Biml. But in all the examples so far, you need to know the name of the helper class, and use it to call your helper method: HelperClass.TagExists(table, "StagingSchema"). By converting your helper method to an *extension method*, you can simplify your code even further.

Extension Methods

By creating an extension method, you can make it look like the method you have defined belongs to an already defined object instead of a helper class. You have already used several extension methods, probably without realizing that they were in fact extension methods.

The best known extension method might be GetBiml(). You can use this extension method on any element of type AstNode, for example RootNode.GetBiml() to get the Biml for your entire project, RootNode.Tables["Table"].GetBiml() to get the Biml for a table, RootNode.Tables["Table"].Columns["Column"].GetBiml() to get the Biml for a column, and so on.

Another extension method is GetDatabaseSchema(), which allows you to import metadata from any connection of type AstConnectionBaseNode, such as an OLE DB connection.

Even GetDropAndCreateDdl() is an extension method. You can't really tell that these methods are extension methods, and not "real" methods that belong to the objects you're working with.

To turn your helper method into an extension method, all you need to do is to add the keyword *this* in front of the first parameter. This parameter type specifies what kind of object you want to make it look like the method belongs to; see Listing 5-26.

Listing 5-26. HelperClass.cs

```
public static class HelperClass {
  public static bool TagExists(this AstNode node, string tag) {
    return (node.GetTag(tag) != "" || node.ObjectTag.ContainsKey(tag));
  }
}
```

Now that you have turned your helper method into an extension method, you can simplify your Biml code as well. You no longer need to specify the name of the helper class, and instead of passing in the object as a parameter, you call the method on the object, as shown in Listing 5-27.

Listing 5-27. MainFile.biml

```
<#@ code file="HelperClass.cs" #>

<Biml xmlns="http://schemas.varigence.com/biml.xsd">
  <# foreach (var table in RootNode.Tables) { #>
    <# if (table.TagExists("StagingSchema")) { #>
    ...
    <# } #>
  <# } #>
</Biml>
```

Using the VB Extension Method

As you can see, Biml comes with countless functions and methods out of the box. But sometimes there is just this one additional method that would come in handy.

For instance, say you have a couple of flat file formats defined in your Biml solution and now want to use Biml again to create the target tables in your SQL database. That means you need to convert an AstFlatFileFormatNode into an AstTableNode. Unfortunately, you can't just call a method like ToAstTableNode on an AstFlatFileFormatNode—or can you?

The little piece of Biml in Listing 5-28 will generate the tables within your RootNode.

Listing 5-28. Biml File Using an Extension Method to Get an AstTableNode from a Flat File Format

```
<#@ template language="VB" optionexplicit="true" #>
<#@ code file="FlatFileExtensions.vb" #>
<# Dim UseSchema = rootnode.schemas(0) #>
<Biml xmlns="http://schemas.varigence.com/biml.xsd">
    <Tables>
    <# for each tbl in rootnode.flatfileformats #>
        <#= tbl.ToAstTableNode(UseSchema).GetBiml #>
    <# next #>
    </Tables>
</Biml>
```

An AstTableNode requires a schema to be valid, which is the only information that you can't get from the AstFlatFileFormatNode so you define a variable called UseSchema and pass it to your ToAstTableNode extension method.

But... how does that extension method work?

Let's take a look at the code file in Listing 5-29.

Listing 5-29. Code File with the Flat File Extension Methods

```
Imports Varigence.Languages.Biml
Imports Varigence.Languages.Biml.FileFormat
Imports Varigence.Languages.Biml.Table
Imports System.Runtime.CompilerServices

Module FlatFileExtension
    <Extension()>
    Public Function ToAstTableNode(FlatFile As AstFlatFileFormatNode,
    Schema As AstSchemaNode) As AstTableNode
        Dim BimlTable As New AstTableNode(Nothing)
        BimlTable.Name = "FF_" + FlatFile.name
        BimlTable.Schema = schema
        For Each flatFileColumn As astflatfilecolumnnode In FlatFile.Columns
            Dim tableColumn As New AstTableColumnNode(Nothing)
            tableColumn.Name = flatFileColumn.Name
            tableColumn.DataType = flatFileColumn.DataType
            tableColumn.Length = flatFileColumn.Length
            tableColumn.Precision = flatFileColumn.Precision
            tableColumn.Scale = flatFileColumn.Scale
            tableColumn.CodePage = flatFileColumn.CodePage
            BimlTable.Columns.Add(tableColumn)
        Next
        Return BimlTable
    End Function
End Module
```

There are only a few minor things to take care of:

1. `Imports System.Runtime.CompilerServices` : This is required by VB for an extension method to actually work.

2. Rather than specifying a class, you're using a module.

3. Immediately before your extension method, you flag it using `<Extension()>`.

4. By default, an extension method will take the object that it's called from as its first parameter so you're defining two input parameters but you're only passing the schema as parameter when you call the extension method.

Once that is understood, the method itself is pretty straight forward:

- Create a new `AstTableNode`.

- Assign a name and a schema to it.

- For each column in the flat file format, add a column to the `AstTableNode` and assign the format's properties to it.

- Return the table.

That's it. You can now call the `ToAstTableNode` on your `AstFlatFileFormatNode`!

Summary

This chapter was all about making your code smarter and better organized. Instead of reinventing the wheel over and over again, copying and pasting the same code multiple times, and producing many different versions of similar code, you have isolated your functions and ended up with reusable code that is much easier to manage and read.

Now that you have the right tools, metadata, and code helpers in place, let us take a look at how you can build a custom Biml framework.

PART II

Biml Frameworks

CHAPTER 6

■■■

A Custom Biml Framework

In this chapter you are going to build a moderately complex solution: a custom Biml metadata-driven framework. We write *moderately* because everyone brings their own experience and comfort level with them to any project. Some will enjoy working with metadata; others will type a lot. Although the code you will build in the demonstrations qualifies as "moderately complex," the solution itself is a relatively simple example of a Biml framework.

This solution consists of a database that contains metadata, which you will build, and a couple Biml files that read and respond to that metadata. As with all solutions, ours is not the only way to build anything. We're positive there are other ways to provide the same functionality, and we're pretty sure some of those ways are better.

The purpose of this chapter is to discuss and demonstrate one way to build a custom Biml framework. Note that while you are directly using database tables to store your metadata, Biml provides an abstraction for metadata called Biml metadata models. To avoid introducing too much at once, we won't use them here, but you can learn about Biml metadata models and how to use them for automation in Chapter 9.

For the demonstration purposes we are using Visual Studio 2015 and BimlExpress Build 5.0.61815.0. If you are using different versions of either Visual Studio (SQL Server Data Tools) or BimlExpress, your user experience may differ.

What Is a Framework?

According to the dictionary integrated into Microsoft® Word a framework /'frām,wərk/ is "a basic conceptional structure (as of ideas)" or "a skeletal, openwork, or structural frame." A Biml framework is a structure that contains the building blocks of an application, in this case, a data integration application that uses SSIS.

How does it work? Biml files contain BimlScript that connects to metadata stored in a database and use that metadata to construct Biml artifacts such as databases, schemas, tables, SSIS packages, and T-SQL scripts.

© Andy Leonard et al. 2017

A. Leonard et al., *The Biml Book*, https://doi.org/10.1007/978-1-4842-3135-7_6

Why Use Metadata?

Biml often uses metadata as the source for data-related objects. Although metadata collection is beyond the scope of this chapter, there are several methods we can use to extract relational metadata from a database and some methods are covered in detail in Chapter 4. We cover Biml metadata in Chapter 9.

■ **Andy Note**   I will share, however, that I use a rather clunky SSIS package similar to the package I describe in a blog post found at http://andyleonard.blog/2008/08/28/ssis-design-pattern-collect-enterprise-sql-server-database-metadata-with-ssis/. The post is titled "SSIS Design Pattern - Collect Enterprise SQL Server Database Metadata with SSIS." In fact, I used this very package as a starting point for my Biml Metadata Loader SSIS package. My Biml Metadata Loader SSIS package only works with SQL Server but can be easily modified to work with other database engines.

Regardless of which method you choose for storing metadata, you will need to persist it. Precisely which metadata will you need to store? It depends, which is the standard answer to any data-related question, equivalent to the answer "42" in *The Hitchhiker's Guide to the Galaxy* (Adams, 1979).

We humbly submit you begin by storing metadata related to the *Biml relational hierarchy* because Biml relational hierarchy metadata is used by Biml to generate much of its output.

The Biml Relational Hierarchy

In this section we discuss and demonstrate the *Biml relational hierarchy*. The Biml relational hierarchy is at the heart of much of the automation we accomplish using Biml. It is a "Biml-izied" version of relational database objects:

- Connections
- Databases
- Schemas
- Tables
- Columns (included in the Table Biml)

These database objects appear in the BimlStudio Logical View, as shown in Figure 6-1.

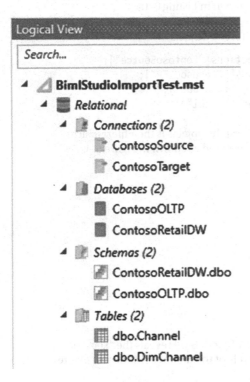

Figure 6-1. *Viewing the Biml relational hierarchy in Logical View*

Although the objects are related in a hierarchy, they appear "flat" similar to the bulleted listing above. The flat representation is intentional and reveals one aspect of the relationship between the relational database objects, shown in Figure 6-2.

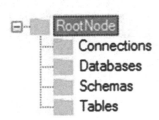

Figure 6-2. *Viewing the "flat" aspect of Biml relational hierarchy objects*

143

We can address the Biml relational database objects programmatically by addressing them directly from the RootNode object, as shown in Listing 6-1.

Listing 6-1. Addressing Biml Relational Hierarchy Objects

```
var sourceConnection = RootNode.Connections["ContosoSource"];
var sourceDatabase = RootNode.Databases["ContosoOLTP"];
var sourceSchema = RootNode.Schemas["Contoso.dbo"];
var sourceTable = RootNode.Tables["dbo.Channel"];
```

Another aspect of the Biml relational hierarchy objects is their hierarchical relationship to each other, which can be represented as shown in Figure 6-3.

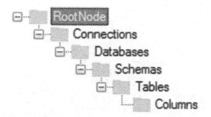

Figure 6-3. *The Biml relational hierarchy*

Examining the Biml relational hierarchy object's Biml reveals the "keys" of the hierarchical relationship, shared between levels of the hierarchy, shown in Figure 6-4.

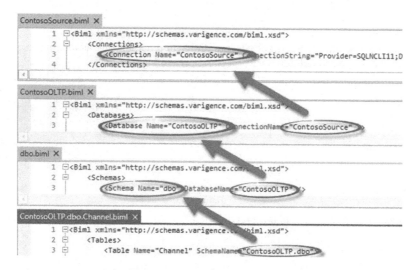

Figure 6-4. *Viewing the relational database hierarchy in Biml*

Figure 6-4 shows a connection named ContosoSource that contains a database named ContosoOLTP. The dbo Schema resides in the ContosoOLTP database, and a table named Channel is found in the dbo (named ContosoOLTP.dbo) schema.

Examining the Channel table's Biml further, you see the columns metadata, shown in Figure 6-5.

```
ContosoOLTP.dbo.Channel.biml ×
1   <Biml xmlns="http://schemas.varigence.com/biml.xsd">
2     <Tables>
3       <Table Name="Channel" SchemaName="ContosoOLTP.dbo">
4         <Columns>
5           <Column Name="ID" IdentityIncrement="1" />
6           <Column Name="Label" DataType="String" Length="100" />
7           <Column Name="Name" DataType="String" Length="20" IsNullable="true" />
8           <Column Name="Description" DataType="String" Length="50" IsNullable="true" />
9           <Column Name="LastUpdatedDate" DataType="Date" IsNullable="true" />
10        </Columns>
11      </Table>
12    </Tables>
13  </Biml>
```

Figure 6-5. *Viewing the Channel table's Biml*

Figures 6-4 and 6-5 provide different, but equally valid, views of a populated Biml Relational Hierarchy.

In this section we discussed and demonstrated the Biml relational hierarchy. In the next section, let's examine how you might persist the Biml relational hierarchy in a database.

Storing the Relational Biml Hierarchy Metadata in a Database

In Chapter 4, you examined some of the many ways to import Biml relational hierarchy metadata using methods exposed by the Varigence.Biml.CoreLowerer. SchemaManagement namespace. In this section you'll examine one example of how you might store Biml relational hierarchy metadata in a custom database for use within Biml projects. One reason you may want to store Biml relational hierarchy metadata is to dynamically map source columns to destination columns when the columns have different names and data types. Some things you gain by describing the whole schema and mappings in a database rather than just doing it all with source schema discovery and cobbling together the mappings are the following:

- The database is more reliable.

- You can do change detection if your sources or targets have their schemas modified.

- You can store additional metadata like Slowly Changing Dimension type and late/early arrivals easily.

145

- You can specify mappings and have the database enforce integrity (so you avoid bogus mappings to missing columns).

- You can add business logic to those mappings because you have a place to put it.

Creating a Database and Schema for Custom Biml Relational Hierarchy Metadata

To demonstrate, let's create a database named BRMetadata to host your metadata using the following Transact-SQL statement:

```
Create Database BRMetadata
```

Let's next create a schema named di (for data integration) in the BRMetadata database using the following Transact-SQL statements:

```
Use BRMetadata
go

Create Schema di
```

Creating a Table for Custom Biml Relational Hierarchy Connections Metadata

Let's now build custom tables to contain your Biml relational hierarchy metadata. You begin by creating a table to hold connections, constructed using the Transact-SQL statement in Listing 6-2.

Listing 6-2. Creating the Di.Connections Table

```
Create Table [di].[Connections]
  (
        ConnectionID int identity(1,1) Not NULL
        Constraint PK_Connections Primary Key
      , ConnectionName varchar(255) Not NULL
      , ConnectionString varchar(255) Not NULL
  )
```

You have a table to store connections. It still has that new table smell. Awesome. Let's add some metadata using the following Transact-SQL statement (note that your connection string values will *not* match mine); see Listing 6-3.

Listing 6-3. Populating the Di.Connections Table

```
Insert Into [di].[Connections]
(ConnectionName
,ConnectionString)
Values
 ('ContosoSource'
 ,'Provider=SQLNCLI11;Data Source=vmDemo\MBF;Integrated
Security=SSPI;Initial Catalog=ContosoOLTP;')
,('ContosoTarget'
 ,'Provider=SQLNCLI11;Data Source=vmDemo\MBF;Integrated
Security=SSPI;Initial Catalog=ContosoRetailDW;')
```

This Transact-SQL inserts metadata for two connections into your BRMetadata. di.Connections table. The connections are named ContosoSource and ContosoTarget and they are aimed at the ContosoOLTP and ContosoRetailDW databases, respectively.

Creating a Table for Custom Biml Relational Hierarchy Database Metadata

Let's continue by creating and populating a table to hold metadata for the next level in the Biml relational hierarchy, databases. The Transact-SQL statements in Listing 6-4 build and insert records into the [di].[Databases] table.

Listing 6-4. Creating and Populating the Di.Databases Table

```
Create Table [di].[Databases]
   (
          DatabaseID int identity(1,1) Not NULL
          Constraint PK_Databases Primary Key
        , ConnectionID int Not Null
          Constraint FK_Databases_Connections Foreign Key
            References [di].[Connections](ConnectionID)
        , DatabaseName varchar(255) Not NULL
   )
   go
```

```
Insert Into [di].[Databases]
(ConnectionID
,DatabaseName)
Values
 ((Select ConnectionID From [di].[Connections] Where ConnectionName =
'ContosoSource')
 ,'ContosoOLTP')
,((Select ConnectionID From [di].[Connections] Where ConnectionName =
'ContosoTarget')
 ,'ContosoRetailDW')
```

This Transact-SQL inserts metadata for two databases into your BRMetadata.
di.Databases table. The databases are named ContosoOLTP, which is related to the
ContosoSource connection, and ContosoRetailDW, which is related to the ContosoTarget
connection.

Creating a Table for Custom Biml Relational Hierarchy Schema Metadata

Let's continue by creating and populating a table to hold metadata for the next level in the
Biml relational hierarchy: schemas. The Transact-SQL statements in Listing 6-5 build and
insert records into the [di].[Schemas] table.

Listing 6-5. Creating and Populating the Di.Schemas Table

```
Create Table [di].[Schemas]
  (
           SchemaID int identity(1,1) Not NULL
           Constraint PK_Schemas Primary Key
         , DatabaseID int Not Null
           Constraint FK_Schemas_Databases Foreign Key
           References [di].[Databases](DatabaseID)
         , SchemaName varchar(255) Not NULL
  )
 go

Insert Into [di].[Schemas]
(DatabaseID
,SchemaName)
Values
 ((Select DatabaseID From [di].[Databases] Where DatabaseName =
 'ContosoOLTP')
 ,'dbo')
,((Select DatabaseID From [di].[Databases] Where DatabaseName =
'ContosoRetailDW')
 ,'dbo')
```

This Transact-SQL inserts metadata for two schemas into your BRMetadata.di.Schemas table. The schemas are both named dbo. One is related to the ContosoOLTP database, the other to the ContosoRetailDW database.

Creating a Table for Custom Biml Relational Hierarchy Tables Metadata

Let's next create and populate a table to hold metadata for the level beneath schemas in the Biml relational hierarchy: tables. The Transact-SQL statements in Listing 6-6 build and insert records into the [di].[Tables] table.

Listing 6-6. Creating and Populating the Di.Tables Table

```
Create Table [di].[Tables]
  (
          TableID int identity(1,1) Not NULL
          Constraint PK_Tables Primary Key
        , SchemaID int Not Null
          Constraint FK_Tables_Schemas Foreign Key
            References [di].[Schemas](SchemaID)
        , TableName varchar(255) Not NULL
  )
  go

Insert Into [di].[Tables]
(SchemaID
,TableName)
Values
 ((Select SchemaID From [di].[Schemas] Where DatabaseID = (Select DatabaseID
 From [di].[Databases] Where DatabaseName = 'ContosoOLTP'))
 ,'Channel')
,((Select SchemaID From [di].[Schemas] Where DatabaseID = (Select DatabaseID
 From [di].[Databases] Where DatabaseName = 'ContosoRetailDW'))
 ,'DimChannel')
```

This Transact-SQL inserts metadata for two tables, ContosoOLTP.dbo.Channel and ContosoRetailDW.dbo.DimChannel, into your BRMetadata.di.Tables table.

Creating a Table for Custom Biml Relational Hierarchy Columns Metadata

Let's next create and populate a table to hold metadata for the lowest level of the Biml relational hierarchy: columns. The Transact-SQL statements in Listing 6-7 build and insert records into the [di].[Columns] table.

Listing 6-7. Creating and Populating the Di.Columns Table

```
Create Table [di].[Columns]
  (
          ColumnID int identity(1,1) Not NULL
          Constraint PK_Columns Primary Key
        , TableID int Not Null
          Constraint FK_Columns_Tables Foreign Key
          References [di].[Tables](TableID)
        , ColumnName varchar(255) Not NULL
        , DataType  varchar(255) Not NULL
        , [Length] int Not NULL
        , IsNullable bit Not NULL
        , IsIdentity bit Not NULL
  )
 go

Insert Into [di].[Columns]
(TableID
,ColumnName
,DataType
,[Length]
,IsNullable
,IsIdentity
)
Values
 ((Select TableID From [di].[Tables] Where TableName = 'Channel')
 ,'Label', 'String', 100, 0, 0)
,((Select TableID From [di].[Tables] Where TableName = 'Channel')
 ,'Name', 'String', 20, 1, 0)
,((Select TableID From [di].[Tables] Where TableName = 'Channel')
 ,'Description', 'String', 50, 1, 0)
,((Select TableID From [di].[Tables] Where TableName = 'Channel')
 ,'LastUpdatedDate', 'Date', 0, 1, 0)
,((Select TableID From [di].[Tables] Where TableName = 'DimChannel')
 ,'ChannelLabel', 'String', 100, 0, 0)
,((Select TableID From [di].[Tables] Where TableName = 'DimChannel')
 ,'ChannelName', 'String', 20, 1, 0)
,((Select TableID From [di].[Tables] Where TableName = 'DimChannel')
 ,'ChannelDescription', 'String', 50, 1, 0)
,((Select TableID From [di].[Tables] Where TableName = 'DimChannel')
 ,'UpdateDate', 'DateTime', 0, 1, 0)
```

This Transact-SQL inserts metadata for columns in two tables, – ContosoOLTP.dbo. Channel and ContosoRetailDW.dbo.DimChannel, into your BRMetadata.di.Columns table. Note that the data types you store are *not* SQL Server data types; they are Biml data types.

For more information about translating SQL Server and Biml data types, please see Cathrine Wilhelmsen's *excellent* blog post titled "SQL Server, SSIS, and Biml Data Types" at www. cathrinewilhelmsen.net/2014/05/27/sql-server-ssis-and-biml-data-types/.

Creating a Table for Mappings Metadata

If you've done traditional ETL (extract, transform, and load) work, you may be familiar with a mapping document. Many enterprises use Excel to create ETL mapping documentation and it often looks similar to that shown in Figure 6-6.

| Source | | | | | Target | | | | |
Instance	Database	Schema	Table	Column	Instance	Database	Schema	Table	Column
				Label					ChannelLabel
vmDemo\MBF	ContosoOLTP	dbo	Channel	Name	vmDemo\MBF	ContosoRetailDW	dbo	DimChannel	ChannelName
				Description					ChannelDescription
				LastUpdatedDate					UpdateDate

Figure 6-6. An ETL mapping document in Excel

The goal of the Mappings table is to "map" the columns from the source to the target. The BRMetadata.di.Mappings table pulls the Biml relational hierarchy metadata together to create the data equivalent of a mapping document. The Mappings table contains an identity column (MappingsID), and columns to hold the source and target ColumnID values. The ColumnID values will suffice because they reference their respective tables, which reference their respective schemas, which reference their respective databases, which reference their respective connections.

The Transact-SQL statements in Listing 6-8 build and insert records into the [di].[Mappings] table.

Listing 6-8. Creating and Populating the Di.Mappings Table

```
Create Table [di].[Mappings]
    (
            MappingID int identity(1,1) Not NULL
            Constraint PK_Mappings Primary Key
        , SourceColumnID int Not Null
            Constraint FK_Mappings_SourceColumns Foreign Key
            References [di].[Columns](ColumnID)
        , TargetColumnID int Not Null
            Constraint FK_Mappings_TargetColumns Foreign Key
            References [di].[Columns](ColumnID)
```

```
         , IsBusinessKey bit Not Null
           Constraint DF_Mappings_IsBusinessKey
              Default(0)
   )

Insert Into [di].[Mappings]
(SourceColumnID
,TargetColumnID
,IsBusinessKey)
Values
  (1, 5, 1)
 ,(2, 6, 0)
 ,(3, 7, 0)
 ,(4, 8, 0)
```

With the Mappings metadata loaded, it's possible to write a query that returns a dataset that appears remarkably similar to that found in the mapping document shown in Figure 6-5. In fact, let's store this query in a view by executing the Transact-SQL statement in Listing 6-9.

Listing 6-9. Creating the Di.MetadataMappings View

```
Create View [di].[metadataMappings]
As

Select scn.ConnectionName As SourceConnectionName
, sd.DatabaseName As SourceDatabaseName
, ss.SchemaName As SourceSchemaName
, st.TableName As SourceTableName
, st.TableID As SourceTableID
, sc.ColumnName As SourceColumnName
, sc.ColumnID As SourceColumnID
, tcn.ConnectionName As TargetConnectionName
, td.DatabaseName As TargetDatabaseName
, ts.SchemaName As TargetSchemaName
, tt.TableName As TargetTableName
, tt.TableID As TargetTableID
, tc.ColumnName As TargetColumnName
, tc.ColumnID As TargetColumnID
, m.IsBusinessKey
From [di].[Mappings] As m
Join [di].Columns sc
  On sc.ColumnID = m.SourceColumnID
Join [di].[Tables] As st
  On st.TableID = sc.TableID
Join [di].[Schemas] As ss
  On ss.SchemaID = st.SchemaID
Join [di].[Databases] As sd
```

```
  On sd.DatabaseID = ss.DatabaseID
Join [di].[Connections] As scn
  On scn.ConnectionID = sd.ConnectionID
Join [di].Columns As tc
  On tc.ColumnID = m.TargetColumnID
Join [di].Tables As tt
  On tt.TableID = tc.TableID
Join [di].[Schemas] As ts
  On ts.SchemaID = tt.SchemaID
Join [di].[Databases] As td
  On td.DatabaseID = ts.DatabaseID
Join [di].[Connections] As tcn
  On tcn.ConnectionID = td.ConnectionID
```

Executing the Transact-SQL query `Select * From [di].[metadataMappings]` should return results similar to those shown in Figure 6-7.

SourceConnectionName	SourceDatabaseName	SourceSchemaName	SourceTableName	SourceColumnName	TargetConnectionName	TargetDatabaseName	TargetSchemaName	TargetTableName	TargetColumnName	IsBusinessKey
ContosoSource	ContosoOLTP	dbo	Channel	Label	ContosoTarget	ContosoRetailDW	dbo	DimChannel	ChannelLabel	1
ContosoSource	ContosoOLTP	dbo	Channel	Name	ContosoTarget	ContosoRetailDW	dbo	DimChannel	ChannelName	0
ContosoSource	ContosoOLTP	dbo	Channel	Description	ContosoTarget	ContosoRetailDW	dbo	DimChannel	ChannelDescription	0
ContosoSource	ContosoOLTP	dbo	Channel	LastUpdatedDate	ContosoTarget	ContosoRetailDW	dbo	DimChannel	UpdateDate	0

Figure 6-7. *Viewing results of the mapping query*

You now have enough Biml relational hierarchy metadata stored in your database to use in a Biml project.

In this section, you examined one example of how you might store Biml relational hierarchy metadata in a custom database for use within Biml projects. In the next section, you'll see how you might use the metadata stored in your custom Biml relational hierarchy database to build Biml relational hierarchy objects in Biml.

Using the Relational Database Metadata to Build the Biml Relational Hierarchy

In this previous section, you examined one example of storing Biml relational hierarchy metadata in a custom database. In this section, you put your stored metadata to use! Open SQL Server Data Tools (SSDT) and create a new Integration Services project. You can name your SSIS project whatever you like; we named ours Chapter7.

As previously stated, we are using Visual Studio 2015 and BimlExpress Build 5.0.61815.0. If you are using different versions of either Visual Studio (SQL Server Data Tools) or BimlExpress, your user experience may differ.

Add a new Biml file and rename it to LoadBimlRelationalHierarchy.biml, as shown in Figure 6-8.

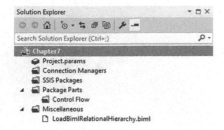

Figure 6-8. *Viewing the Chapter7 project and LoadBimlRelationalHierarchy.biml file*

The LoadBimlRelationalHierarchy.biml file opens with default open and close Biml tags, as shown in Figure 6-9.

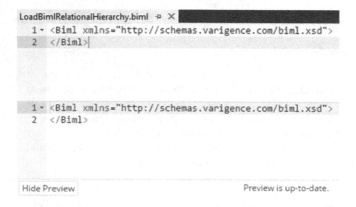

Figure 6-9. *Creating a new Biml file*

You are going to need to access the BRMetadata database you designed and populated earlier, so let's add import directives to use the .Net Framework's System.Data namespace. When added, your code should appear as shown in Listing 6-10 (with the newly-added code highlighted).

Listing 6-10. Starting the LoadBimlRelationalHierarchy.biml File

```
<#@ import namespace="System.Data" #>
<# string connectionString = @"Provider=SQLNCLI11;Data Source=vmDemo\
MBF;Integrated Security=SSPI;Initial Catalog=BRMetadata;"; #>
<Biml xmlns="http://schemas.varigence.com/biml.xsd">
</Biml>
```

In addition to the directives, you declare and initialize a variable named connectionString that contains a connection string to your BRMetadata database. Please note that your connection string will almost certainly differ.

Building Biml Connection Tags from Metadata

Let's add more BimlScript to read your connections metadata and use it to build Biml connections. Add a BimlScript code block after the opening Biml tag that contains the (highlighted) BimlScript shown in Listing 6-11.

Listing 6-11. Building Biml Connection Tags from Metadata

```
<#@ import namespace="System.Data" #>
<# string connectionString = @"Provider=SQLNCLI11;Data Source=vmDemo\
MBF;Integrated Security=SSPI;Initial Catalog=BRMetadata;"; #>
<Biml xmlns="http://schemas.varigence.com/biml.xsd">
  <!-- Connections -->
  <# var dataTable = ExternalDataAccess.GetDataTable(connectionString,
  "Select ConnectionName, ConnectionString From [di].[Connections]"); #>
  <Connections>
    <# foreach (DataRow row in dataTable.Rows) { #>
    <Connection Name="<#=row["ConnectionName"]#>" ConnectionString="<#=row
    ["ConnectionString"]#>" />
    <# } #>
  </Connections>
</Biml>
```

When added, your Biml file should appear similar to that shown in Figure 6-10.

```
1   <#@ import namespace="System.Data" #>
2   <# string connectionString = @"Provider=SQLNCLI11;Data Source=vmDemo\MBF;Integrated Security=SSPI;Initial Catalog=BRMetadata"; #>
3 ▾ <Biml xmlns="http://schemas.varigence.com/biml.xsd">
4     <!-- Connections -->
5     <# var dataTable = ExternalDataAccess.GetDataTable(connectionString, "Select ConnectionName, ConnectionString From [di].[Connections]"); #>
6 ▾   <Connections>
7       <# foreach (DataRow row in dataTable.Rows) { #>
8       <Connection Name="<#=row["ConnectionName"]#>" ConnectionString="<#=row["ConnectionString"]#>" />
9       <# } #>
10    </Connections>
11  </Biml>
```

Figure 6-10. *Connections BimlScript added*

At Line 5 you use a built-in BimlScript utility method called ExternalDataAccess. GetDataTable, which handles all of the database access drudgery for you. You simply supply your connection string and your query and get back a dataTable with the query execution results. On line 6 you pop out of BimlScript and write a Connections opening tag. On lines 7-9 you iterate over the rows in your dataTable and create a Biml connection for each, using the ConnectionName and ConnectionString columns to populate the Biml connection objects.

After saving the LoadBimlRelationalHierarchy.biml file, the Preview pane displays the Biml connections, as shown in Figure 6-11.

```
<Biml xmlns="http://schemas.varigence.com/biml.xsd">
  <Connections>
    <Connection Name="ContosoSource" ConnectionString="Provider=SQLNCLI11;Data Source=vmDemo\MBF;Integrated Security=SSPI;Initial Catalog=ContosoOLTP;" />
    <Connection Name="ContosoTarget" ConnectionString="Provider=SQLNCLI11;Data Source=vmDemo\MBF;Integrated Security=SSPI;Initial Catalog=ContosoRetailDW;" />
  </Connections>
</Biml>
```

***Figure 6-11.** Viewing the preview with Biml connection tags*

At this point in the demonstration, the LoadBimlRelationalHierarchy.biml file is generating valid Biml from metadata. How cool!

Building Biml Database Tags from Metadata

You can leverage the BimlScript code pattern you built for retrieving Biml connection metadata from the BRMetadata database to retrieve Biml database metadata. Add the highlighted portions shown in Listing 6-12 to retrieve Biml Database metadata.

***Listing 6-12.** Building Biml Database Tags from Metadata*

```
<#@ import namespace="System.Data" #>
<# string connectionString = @"Provider=SQLNCLI11;Data Source=vmDemo\
MBF;Integrated Security=SSPI;Initial Catalog=BRMetadata;"; #>
<Biml xmlns="http://schemas.varigence.com/biml.xsd">
  <!-- Connections -->
  <# var dataTable = ExternalDataAccess.GetDataTable(connectionString,
  "Select ConnectionName, ConnectionString From [di].[Connections]"); #>
  <Connections>
    <# foreach (DataRow row in dataTable.Rows) { #>
    <Connection Name="<#=row["ConnectionName"]#>" ConnectionString="<#=row["
    ConnectionString"]#>" />
    <# } #>
  </Connections>

  <!-- Databases -->
  <# dataTable = ExternalDataAccess.GetDataTable(connectionString, "Select
d.DatabaseName, c.ConnectionName From [di].[Databases] As d Join [di].
[Connections] As c On c.ConnectionID = d.ConnectionID"); #>
  <Databases>
    <# foreach (DataRow row in dataTable.Rows) { #>
      <Database Name="<#=row["DatabaseName"]#>" ConnectionName="<#=row
["ConnectionName"]#>" />
    <# } #>
  </Databases>
</Biml>
```

When added, your Biml file should appear similar to that shown in Figure 6-12.

```
1   <#@ import namespace="System.Data" #>
2   <# string connectionString = @"Provider=SQLNCLI11;Data Source=vmDemo\MBF;Integrated Security=SSPI;Initial Catalog=BRMetadata"; #>
3 ▾ <Biml xmlns="http://schemas.varigence.com/biml.xsd">
4     <!-- Connections -->
5     <# var dataTable = ExternalDataAccess.GetDataTable(connectionString, "Select ConnectionName, ConnectionString From [di].[Connections]"); #:
6 ▾  <Connections>
7       <# foreach (DataRow row in dataTable.Rows) { #>
8         <Connection Name="<#=row["ConnectionName"]#>" ConnectionString="<#=row["ConnectionString"]#>" />
9       <# } #>
10     </Connections>
11
12     <!-- Databases -->
13     <# dataTable = ExternalDataAccess.GetDataTable(connectionString, "Select d.DatabaseName, c.ConnectionName From [di].[Databases] As d Join |
14 ▾  <Databases>
15       <# foreach (DataRow row in dataTable.Rows) { #>
16         <Database Name="<#=row["DatabaseName"]#>" ConnectionName="<#=row ["ConnectionName"]#>" />
17       <# } #>
18     </Databases>
19   </Biml>
```

Figure 6-12. *Databases BimlScript added*

As with the Connections BimlScript, the Databases BimlScript calls the ExternalDataAccess.GetDataTable utility method at line 13 that queries the BRMetadata database and populates the dataTable variable with the results. On line 14 you jump out of BimlScript and write a Biml Databases opening tag. On Line 15 you start a foreach loop to iterate the rows returned to the dataTable variable. On line 16 you write the Biml for database artifacts.

After saving the LoadBimlRelationalHierarchy.biml file, the Preview pane displays the Biml databases, as shown in Figure 6-13.

```
<Biml xmlns="http://schemas.varigence.com/biml.xsd">
  <Connections>
    <Connection Name="ContosoSource" ConnectionString="Provider=SQLNCLI11;Data Source=vmDemo\MBF;
    <Connection Name="ContosoTarget" ConnectionString="Provider=SQLNCLI11;Data Source=vmDemo\MBF;
  </Connections>
  <Databases>
    <Database Name="ContosoOLTP" ConnectionName="ContosoSource" />
    <Database Name="ContosoRetailDW" ConnectionName="ContosoTarget" />
  </Databases>
</Biml>
```

Figure 6-13. *Viewing the preview with Biml Databases tags*

Building Biml Schema Tags from Metadata

You can leverage the BimlScript code pattern you built for retrieving Biml connection and database metadata from the BRMetadata database to retrieve Biml schema metadata. Add the highlighted portions shown in Listing 6-13 to retrieve Biml schema metadata.

Listing 6-13. Building Biml Schema Tags from Metadata

```
<#@ import namespace="System.Data" #>
<# string connectionString = @"Provider=SQLNCLI11;Data Source=vmDemo\
MBF;Integrated Security=SSPI;Initial Catalog=BRMetadata;"; #>
<Biml xmlns="http://schemas.varigence.com/biml.xsd">
  <!-- Connections -->
  <# var dataTable = ExternalDataAccess.GetDataTable(connectionString,
   "Select ConnectionName, ConnectionString From [di].[Connections]"); #>
  <Connections>
    <# foreach (DataRow row in dataTable.Rows) { #>
    <Connection Name="<#=row["ConnectionName"]#>" ConnectionString="
    <#=row["ConnectionString"]#>" />
    <# } #>
  </Connections>

  <!-- Databases -->
  <# dataTable = ExternalDataAccess.GetDataTable(connectionString, "Select
   d.DatabaseName, c.ConnectionName From [di].[Databases] As d Join [di].
   [Connections] As c On c.ConnectionID = d.ConnectionID"); #>
  <Databases>
    <# foreach (DataRow row in dataTable.Rows) { #>
      <Database Name="<#=row["DatabaseName"]#>" ConnectionName=
        "<#=row ["ConnectionName"]#>" />
    <# } #>
  </Databases>

  <!-- Schemas -->
  <# dataTable = ExternalDataAccess.GetDataTable(connectionString, "Select
   s.SchemaName, d.DatabaseName From [di].[Schemas] As s Join [di].
   [Databases] As d On d.DatabaseID = s.DatabaseID"); #>
  <Schemas>
    <# foreach (DataRow row in dataTable.Rows) { #>
      <Schema Name="<#=row["SchemaName"]#>" DatabaseName="<#=row
      ["DatabaseName"]#>" />
    <# } #>
  </Schemas>
</Biml>
```

When added, your Biml file should appear similar to that shown in Figure 6-14.

```
1  <#@ import namespace="System.Data" #>
2  <# string connectionString = @"Provider=SQLNCLI11;Data Source=vmDemo\MBF;Integrated Security=SSPI;Initial Catalog=BRMetadata"; #>
3  <Biml xmlns="http://schemas.varigence.com/biml.xsd">
4    <!-- Connections -->
5    <# var dataTable = ExternalDataAccess.GetDataTable(connectionString, "Select ConnectionName, ConnectionString From [di].[Connections]"); #
6    <Connections>
7      <# foreach (DataRow row in dataTable.Rows) { #>
8      <Connection Name="<#=row["ConnectionName"]#>" ConnectionString="<#=row["ConnectionString"]#>" />
9      <# } #>
10   </Connections>
11
12   <!-- Databases -->
13   <# dataTable = ExternalDataAccess.GetDataTable(connectionString, "Select d.DatabaseName, c.ConnectionName From [di].[Databases] As d Join |
14   <Databases>
15     <# foreach (DataRow row in dataTable.Rows) { #>
16     <Database Name="<#=row["DatabaseName"]#>" ConnectionName="<#=row ["ConnectionName"]#>" />
17     <# } #>
18   </Databases>
19
20   <!-- Schemas -->
21   <# dataTable = ExternalDataAccess.GetDataTable(connectionString, "Select s.SchemaName, d.DatabaseName From [di].[Schemas] As s Join [di].[C
22   <Schemas>
23     <# foreach (DataRow row in dataTable.Rows) { #>
24     <Schema Name="<#=row["SchemaName"]#>" DatabaseName="<#=row ["DatabaseName"]#>" />
25     <# } #>
26   </Schemas>
27 </Biml>
```

Figure 6-14. *Schemas BimlScript added*

As with the Connections and Databases BimlScript, the Schemas BimlScript starts with a `ExternalDataAccess.GetDataTable` call to retrieve schemas metadata from the BRMetadata database on line 21. On Line 22 you jump out of BimlScript and write a Schemas opening tag. On lines 23-25 you iterate the dataset in dataTable to write Biml Schema tags for each row returned by the query.

After saving the `LoadBimlRelationalHierarchy.biml` file, the Preview pane displays the Biml schemas, as shown in Figure 6-15.

```
<Biml xmlns="http://schemas.varigence.com/biml.xsd">
  <Connections>
    <Connection Name="ContosoSource" ConnectionString="Provider=SQLNCLI11;Data Source=vmDemo\MBF
    <Connection Name="ContosoTarget" ConnectionString="Provider=SQLNCLI11;Data Source=vmDemo\MBF
  </Connections>
  <Databases>
    <Database Name="ContosoOLTP" ConnectionName="ContosoSource" />
    <Database Name="ContosoRetailDW" ConnectionName="ContosoTarget" />
  </Databases>
  <Schemas>
    <Schema Name="dbo" DatabaseName="ContosoOLTP" />
    <Schema Name="dbo" DatabaseName="ContosoRetailDW" />
  </Schemas>
</Biml>
```

Figure 6-15. *Viewing the preview with Biml Schema tags*

Building Biml Table Tags from Metadata

With tables, you depart from the BimlScript code pattern you built for retrieving Biml connection, database, and schema metadata from the BRMetadata database to retrieve Biml table metadata as shown in the highlighted portions in Listing 6-14.

Listing 6-14. Building Biml Table Tags from Metadata

```
<#@ import namespace="System.Data" #>
<# string connectionString = @"Provider=SQLNCLI11;Data Source=vmDemo\
MBF;Integrated Security=SSPI;Initial Catalog=BRMetadata;"; #>
<Biml xmlns="http://schemas.varigence.com/biml.xsd">
  <!-- Connections -->
  <# var dataTable = ExternalDataAccess.GetDataTable(connectionString,
   "Select ConnectionName, ConnectionString From [di].[Connections]"); #>
  <Connections>
    <# foreach (DataRow row in dataTable.Rows) { #>
    <Connection Name="<#=row["ConnectionName"]#>"
     ConnectionString="<#=row["ConnectionString"]#>" />
    <# } #>
  </Connections>

  <!-- Databases -->
  <# dataTable = ExternalDataAccess.GetDataTable(connectionString, "Select
   d.DatabaseName, c.ConnectionName From [di].[Databases] As d Join [di].
   [Connections] As c On c.ConnectionID = d.ConnectionID"); #>
  <Databases>
    <# foreach (DataRow row in dataTable.Rows) { #>
      <Database Name="<#=row["DatabaseName"]#>" ConnectionName="
       <#=row ["ConnectionName"]#>" />
    <# } #>
  </Databases>

  <!-- Schemas -->
  <# dataTable = ExternalDataAccess.GetDataTable(connectionString, "Select
   s.SchemaName, d.DatabaseName From [di].[Schemas] As s Join [di].
   [Databases] As d On d.DatabaseID = s.DatabaseID"); #>
  <Schemas>
    <# foreach (DataRow row in dataTable.Rows) { #>
      <Schema Name="<#=row["SchemaName"]#>" DatabaseName="<#=row
      ["DatabaseName"]#>" />
    <# } #>
  </ Schemas >
```

```
  <!-- Tables -->
<# var tableQuery = @"
Select distinct mm.SourceDatabaseName + '.' + mm.SourceSchemaName As
SourceQualifiedSchemaName
  , mm.SourceSchemaName, mm.SourceTableName, mm.SourceTableID, mm.SourceTableName
  , mm.TargetDatabaseName + '.' + mm.TargetSchemaName As TargetQualifiedSchemaName
  , mm.TargetSchemaName, mm.TargetTableName, mm.TargetTableID
From [di].[metadataMappings] As mm;";
  dataTable = ExternalDataAccess.GetDataTable(connectionString, tableQuery); #>
      <Tables>
        <# foreach(DataRow row in dataTable.Rows) { #>
        <# var sourceTableId = row["SourceTableID"].ToString(); #>
        <# var targetTableId = row["TargetTableID"].ToString(); #>
        <Table Name="<#=row["SourceTableName"]#>" SchemaName="<#=row["Source
        QualifiedSchemaName"]#>">
          <Annotations>
            <Annotation Tag="MappedTableID"><#=targetTableId#></Annotation>
            <Annotation Tag="MappedTableName"><#=row["TargetTableName"]#>
            </Annotation>
          </Annotations>
        </Table>
        <Table Name="<#=row["TargetTableName"]#>" SchemaName="<#=row["Target
        QualifiedSchemaName"]#>">
          <Annotations>
            <Annotation Tag="MappedTableID"><#=sourceTableId#></Annotation>
            <Annotation Tag="MappedTableName"><#=row["SourceTableName"]#>
            </Annotation>
          </Annotations>
        </Table>
        <# } #>
    </Tables>
</Biml>
```

When added, your Biml file should appear similar to that shown in Figure 6-16.

```
1   <#@ import namespace="System.Data" #>
2   <# string connectionString = @"Provider=SQLNCLI11;Data Source=vmDemo\MDF;Integrated Security=SSPI;Initial Catalog=BRMetadata"; #>
3 ▾ <Biml xmlns="http://schemas.varigence.com/biml.xsd">
4       <!-- Connections -->
5       <# var dataTable = ExternalDataAccess.GetDataTable(connectionString, "Select ConnectionName, ConnectionString From [di].[Connections]");
6 ▾     <Connections>
7           <# foreach (DataRow row in dataTable.Rows) { #>
8           <Connection Name="<#=row["ConnectionName"]#>" ConnectionString="<#=row["ConnectionString"]#>" />
9           <# } #>
10      </Connections>
11
12      <!-- Databases -->
13      <# dataTable = ExternalDataAccess.GetDataTable(connectionString, "Select d.DatabaseName, c.ConnectionName From [di].[Databases] As d Jo:
14 ▾    <Databases>
15          <# foreach (DataRow row in dataTable.Rows) { #>
16          <Database Name="<#=row["DatabaseName"]#>" ConnectionName="<#=row ["ConnectionName"]#>" />
17          <# } #>
18      </Databases>
19
20      <!-- Schemas -->
21      <# dataTable = ExternalDataAccess.GetDataTable(connectionString, "Select s.SchemaName, d.DatabaseName From [di].[Schemas] As s Join [di]
22 ▾    <Schemas>
23          <# foreach (DataRow row in dataTable.Rows) { #>
24          <Schema Name="<#=row["SchemaName"]#>" DatabaseName="<#=row ["DatabaseName"]#>" />
25          <# } #>
26      </Schemas>
27
28      <!-- Tables -->
29      <# var tableQuery = @"
30  Select distinct mm.SourceDatabaseName + '.' + mm.SourceSchemaName As SourceQualifiedSchemaName
31      , mm.SourceSchemaName, mm.SourceTableName, mm.SourceTableID, mm.SourceTableName
32      , mm.TargetDatabaseName + '.' + mm.TargetSchemaName As TargetQualifiedSchemaName
33      , mm.TargetSchemaName, mm.TargetTableName, mm.TargetTableID
34  From [di].[metadataMappings] As mm;";
35      dataTable = ExternalDataAccess.GetDataTable(connectionString, tableQuery); #>
36 ▾        <Tables>
37              <# foreach(DataRow row in dataTable.Rows) { #>
38              <# var sourceTableId = row["SourceTableID"].ToString(); #>
39              <# var targetTableId = row["TargetTableID"].ToString(); #>
40 ▾            <Table Name="<#=row["SourceTableName"]#>" SchemaName="<#=row["SourceQualifiedSchemaName"]#>">
41 ▾                <Annotations>
42                      <Annotation Tag="MappedTableID"><#=targetTableId#></Annotation>
43                      <Annotation Tag="MappedTableName"><#=row["TargetTableName"]#></Annotation>
44                  </Annotations>
45              </Table>
46 ▾            <Table Name="<#=row["TargetTableName"]#>" SchemaName="<#=row["TargetQualifiedSchemaName"]#>">
47 ▾                <Annotations>
48                      <Annotation Tag="MappedTableID"><#=sourceTableId#></Annotation>
49                      <Annotation Tag="MappedTableName"><#=row["SourceTableName"]#></Annotation>
50                  </Annotations>
51              </Table>
52              <# } #>
53          </Tables>
54  </Biml>
```

Figure 6-16. *Tables BimlScript added*

On lines 29-34 you declare and initialize a variable (tableQuery) to contain your Transact-SQL query that retrieves table metadata from the BRMetadata database. On line 35 you call the utility method ExternalDataAccess.GetDataTable, passing it the connectionString and tableQuery variables. On line 37 you begin a foreach loop to iterate the resulting dataset. On lines 38-39 you declare and initialize two variables, sourceTableId and targetTableId. On lines 40-45 you build the source tables returned to the dataTable variable. On lines 46-51 you build the target tables returned to the dataTable variable. On lines 41-44 and 47-50 you add Biml annotations that contain two tags: MappedTableID and MappedTableName.

■ **Note** You can think of Biml annotations as being like extended properties or custom attributes you add to Biml artifacts. You use Biml annotations here to store mapping attributes for Biml tables. In the next subsection you will use Biml annotations to store mapping attributes for business keys, which are values that uniquely identify rows in both the source and target tables. If you plan to dive into Biml, do yourself a favor and get very comfortable using Biml annotations.

You will rely on these Biml annotations when you build SSIS packages in the next section.

After saving the `LoadBimlRelationalHierarchy.biml` file, the Preview pane displays the Biml tables, as shown in Figure 6-17.

```
<Biml xmlns="http://schemas.varigence.com/biml.xsd">
  <Connections>
    <Connection Name="ContosoSource" ConnectionString="Provider=SQLNCLI11;Data Source=vmDemo\MBF
    <Connection Name="ContosoTarget" ConnectionString="Provider=SQLNCLI11;Data Source=vmDemo\MBF
  </Connections>
  <Databases>
    <Database Name="ContosoOLTP" ConnectionName="ContosoSource" />
    <Database Name="ContosoRetailDW" ConnectionName="ContosoTarget" />
  </Databases>
  <Schemas>
    <Schema Name="dbo" DatabaseName="ContosoOLTP" />
    <Schema Name="dbo" DatabaseName="ContosoRetailDW" />
  </Schemas>
  <Tables>
    <Table Name="Channel" SchemaName="ContosoOLTP.dbo">
      <Annotations>
        <Annotation AnnotationType="Tag" Tag="MappedTableID">2</Annotation>
        <Annotation AnnotationType="Tag" Tag="MappedTableName">DimChannel</Annotation>
      </Annotations>
    </Table>
    <Table Name="DimChannel" SchemaName="ContosoRetailDW.dbo">
      <Annotations>
        <Annotation AnnotationType="Tag" Tag="MappedTableID">1</Annotation>
        <Annotation AnnotationType="Tag" Tag="MappedTableName">Channel</Annotation>
      </Annotations>
    </Table>
  </Tables>
</Biml>
```

Figure 6-17. *Viewing the preview with Biml Table tags*

Building Biml Column Tags from Metadata

You can leverage the BimlScript code pattern you built for retrieving Biml connection, database, schema, and table metadata from the BRMetadata database to retrieve Biml column metadata. There is a twist however: Biml column metadata is embedded within Biml tables. Add the highlighted portions shown in Listing 6-15 to retrieve Biml column metadata.

Listing 6-15. Building Biml Column Tags from Metadata

```
<#@ import namespace="System.Data" #>
<# string connectionString = @"Provider=SQLNCLI11;Data Source=vmDemo\
MBF;Integrated Security=SSPI;Initial Catalog=BRMetadata;"; #>
<Biml xmlns="http://schemas.varigence.com/biml.xsd">
<!-- Connections -->
  <# var dataTable = ExternalDataAccess.GetDataTable(connectionString,
   "Select ConnectionName, ConnectionString From [di].[Connections]"); #>
  <Connections>
    <# foreach (DataRow row in dataTable.Rows) { #>
    <Connection Name="<#=row["ConnectionName"]#>" ConnectionString="<#=row["
      ConnectionString"]#>" />
    <# } #>
  </Connections>

  <!-- Databases -->
  <# dataTable = ExternalDataAccess.GetDataTable(connectionString, "Select
   d.DatabaseName, c.ConnectionName From [di].[Databases] As d Join [di].
   [Connections] As c On c.ConnectionID = d.ConnectionID"); #>
  <Databases>
    <# foreach (DataRow row in dataTable.Rows) { #>
      <Database Name="<#=row["DatabaseName"]#>" ConnectionName="<#=row
      ["ConnectionName"]#>" />
    <# } #>
  </Databases>

  <!-- Schemas -->
  <# dataTable = ExternalDataAccess.GetDataTable(connectionString, "Select
   s.SchemaName, d.DatabaseName From [di].[Schemas] As s Join [di].
   [Databases] As d On d.DatabaseID = s.DatabaseID"); #>
  <Schemas>
    <# foreach (DataRow row in dataTable.Rows) { #>
      <Schema Name="<#=row["SchemaName"]#>" DatabaseName="<#=row ["DatabaseName"]#>" />
    <# } #>
  </Schemas>

  <!-- Tables -->
<# var tableQuery = @"
Select distinct mm.SourceDatabaseName + '.' + mm.SourceSchemaName As
SourceQualifiedSchemaName
  , mm.SourceSchemaName, mm.SourceTableName, mm.SourceTableID, mm.SourceTableName
  , mm.TargetDatabaseName + '.' + mm.TargetSchemaName As TargetQualifiedSchemaName
  , mm.TargetSchemaName, mm.TargetTableName, mm.TargetTableID
From [di].[metadataMappings] As mm;";
```

```
var columnsQuery = @"
Select mm.SourceTableID, mm.SourceColumnName
  , sc.DataType As SourceDataType, sc.[Length] As SourceLength
  , sc.IsNullable As SourceIsNullable, mm.TargetTableID, mm.TargetTableName
  , mm.TargetColumnName, tc.DataType As TargetDataType
  , tc.[Length] As TargetLength, tc.IsNullable As TargetIsNullable
  , mm.IsBusinessKey
From [di].[metadataMappings] As mm
Join [di].[Columns] sc
  On sc.ColumnID = mm.SourceColumnID
Join [di].[Columns] tc
  On tc.ColumnID = mm.TargetColumnID ";

  dataTable = ExternalDataAccess.GetDataTable(connectionString, tableQuery);
  var colTable = ExternalDataAccess.GetDataTable(connectionString,
  columnsQuery); #>
  <Tables>
    <# foreach(DataRow row in dataTable.Rows) { #>
    <# var sourceTableId = row["SourceTableID"].ToString(); #>
    <# var targetTableId = row["TargetTableID"].ToString(); #>
    <Table Name="<#=row["SourceTableName"]#>" SchemaName="<#=row["Source
    QualifiedSchemaName"]#>">
      <Columns>
        <# foreach(var scr in colTable.Rows.OfType<DataRow>().Where(r =>
        r["SourceTableID"].ToString()==sourceTableId)) { #>
        <Column Name="<#=scr["SourceColumnName"]#>"
                DataType="<#=scr["SourceDataType"]#>"
                Length="<#=scr["SourceLength"]#>"
                IsNullable="<#=scr["SourceIsNullable"]#>">
          <Annotations>
            <Annotation Tag="IsBusinessKey"><#=scr["IsBusinessKey"]#>
            </Annotation>
            <Annotation Tag="MappedColumnName"><#=scr["TargetColumnName"]#>
            </Annotation>
          </Annotations>
        </Column>
        <# } #>
      </Columns>
      <Annotations>
        <Annotation Tag="MappedTableID"><#=targetTableId#></Annotation>
        <Annotation Tag="MappedTableName"><#=row["TargetTableName"]#>
        </Annotation>
      </Annotations>
    </Table>
    <Table Name="<#=row["TargetTableName"]#>" SchemaName="<#=row["Target
    QualifiedSchemaName"]#>">
      <Columns>
```

```
<# foreach(var scr in colTable.Rows.OfType<DataRow>().Where(r => r
["TargetTableID"].ToString()==targetTableId)) { #>
<Column Name="<#=scr["TargetColumnName"]#>"
        DataType="<#=scr["TargetDataType"]#>"
        Length="<#=scr["TargetLength"]#>"
        IsNullable="<#=scr["TargetIsNullable"]#>">
  <Annotations>
    <Annotation Tag="IsBusinessKey"><#=scr["IsBusinessKey"]#>
    </Annotation>
    <Annotation Tag="MappedColumnName"><#=scr["SourceColumnName"]#>
    </Annotation>
  </Annotations>
</Column>
<# } #>
</Columns>
<Annotations>
  <Annotation Tag="MappedTableID"><#=sourceTableId#></Annotation>
  <Annotation Tag="MappedTableName"><#=row["SourceTableName"]#>
  </Annotation>
</Annotations>
</Table>
<# } #>
</Tables>
</Biml>
```

Please note that there are *four* locations where Biml and BimlScript are added.

When added, your Biml file should appear similar to that shown in Figures 6-18a and 6-18b (shown in two figures so the code is legible).

166

```
48
49    dataTable = ExternalDataAccess.GetDataTable(connectionString, tableQuery);
50    var colTable = ExternalDataAccess.GetDataTable(connectionString, columnsQuery);#>
51        <Tables>
52            <# foreach(DataRow row in dataTable.Rows) { #>
53            <# var sourceTableId = row["SourceTableID"].ToString(); #>
54            <# var targetTableId = row["TargetTableID"].ToString(); #>
55            <Table Name="<#=row["SourceTableName"]#>" SchemaName="<#=row["SourceQualifiedSchemaName"]#>">
56                <Columns>
57                    <# foreach(var scr in colTable.Rows.OfType<DataRow>().Where(r => r["SourceTableID"].ToString()==sourceTableId)) { #>
58                    <Column Name="<#=scr["SourceColumnName"]#>"
59                            DataType="<#=scr["SourceDataType"]#>"
60                            Length="<#=scr["SourceLength"]#>"
61                            IsNullable="<#=scr["SourceIsNullable"]#>">
62                        <Annotations>
63                          <Annotation Tag="IsBusinessKey"><#=scr["IsBusinessKey"]#></Annotation>
64                          <Annotation Tag="MappedColumnName"><#=scr["TargetColumnName"]#></Annotation>
65                        </Annotations>
66                    </Column>
67                    <# } #>
68                </Columns>
69                <Annotations>
70                  <Annotation Tag="MappedTableID"><#=targetTableId#></Annotation>
71                  <Annotation Tag="MappedTableName"><#=row["TargetTableName"]#></Annotation>
72                </Annotations>
73            </Table>
74            <Table Name="<#=row["TargetTableName"]#>" SchemaName="<#=row["TargetQualifiedSchemaName"]#>">
75                <Columns>
76                    <# foreach(var scr in colTable.Rows.OfType<DataRow>().Where(r => r["TargetTableID"].ToString()==targetTableId)) { #>
77                    <Column Name="<#=scr["TargetColumnName"]#>"
78                            DataType="<#=scr["TargetDataType"]#>"
79                            Length="<#=scr["TargetLength"]#>"
80                            IsNullable="<#=scr["TargetIsNullable"]#>">
81                        <Annotations>
82                          <Annotation Tag="IsBusinessKey"><#=scr["IsBusinessKey"]#></Annotation>
83                          <Annotation Tag="MappedColumnName"><#=scr["SourceColumnName"]#></Annotation>
84                        </Annotations>
85                    </Column>
86                    <# } #>
87                </Columns>
88                <Annotations>
89                  <Annotation Tag="MappedTableID"><#=sourceTableId#></Annotation>
90                  <Annotation Tag="MappedTableName"><#=row["SourceTableName"]#></Annotation>
91                </Annotations>
92            </Table>
93            <# } #>
94        </Tables>
95    </Biml>
```

Figure 6-18a. *Top half with Columns BimlScript added*

```
48
49    dataTable = ExternalDataAccess.GetDataTable(connectionString, tableQuery);
50    var colTable = ExternalDataAccess.GetDataTable(connectionString, columnsQuery);#>
51 ▾    <Tables>
52         <# foreach(DataRow row in dataTable.Rows) { #>
53         <# var sourceTableId = row["SourceTableID"].ToString(); #>
54         <# var targetTableId = row["TargetTableID"].ToString(); #>
55 ▾        <Table Name="<#=row["SourceTableName"]#>" SchemaName="<#=row["SourceQualifiedSchemaName"]#>">
56 ▾          <Columns>
57               <# foreach(var scr in colTable.Rows.OfType<DataRow>().Where(r => r["SourceTableID"].ToString()==sourceTableId)) { #>
58 ▾            <Column Name="<#=scr["SourceColumnName"]#>"
59                     DataType="<#=scr["SourceDataType"]#>"
60                     Length="<#=scr["SourceLength"]#>"
61                     IsNullable="<#=scr["SourceIsNullable"]#>">
62 ▾              <Annotations>
63                 <Annotation Tag="IsBusinessKey"><#=scr["IsBusinessKey"]#></Annotation>
64                 <Annotation Tag="MappedColumnName"><#=scr["TargetColumnName"]#></Annotation>
65                </Annotations>
66              </Column>
67              <# } #>
68            </Columns>
69 ▾          <Annotations>
70             <Annotation Tag="MappedTableID"><#=targetTableId#></Annotation>
71             <Annotation Tag="MappedTableName"><#=row["TargetTableName"]#></Annotation>
72            </Annotations>
73          </Table>
74 ▾        <Table Name="<#=row["TargetTableName"]#>" SchemaName="<#=row["TargetQualifiedSchemaName"]#>">
75 ▾          <Columns>
76               <# foreach(var scr in colTable.Rows.OfType<DataRow>().Where(r => r["TargetTableID"].ToString()==targetTableId)) { #>
77 ▾            <Column Name="<#=scr["TargetColumnName"]#>"
78                     DataType="<#=scr["TargetDataType"]#>"
79                     Length="<#=scr["TargetLength"]#>"
80                     IsNullable="<#=scr["TargetIsNullable"]#>">
81 ▾              <Annotations>
82                 <Annotation Tag="IsBusinessKey"><#=scr["IsBusinessKey"]#></Annotation>
83                 <Annotation Tag="MappedColumnName"><#=scr["SourceColumnName"]#></Annotation>
84                </Annotations>
85              </Column>
86              <# } #>
87            </Columns>
88 ▾          <Annotations>
89             <Annotation Tag="MappedTableID"><#=sourceTableId#></Annotation>
90             <Annotation Tag="MappedTableName"><#=row["SourceTableName"]#></Annotation>
91            </Annotations>
92          </Table>
93          <# } #>
94        </Tables>
95    </Biml>
```

Figure 6-18b. *Bottom half with Columns BimlScript added*

To build the columns metadata you insert four snippets of Biml and BimlScript. The first snippet declares and initializes a variable named columnsQuery on lines 36-47. The second snippet of BimlScript is the declaration and initialization of the colTable variable on line 50, which calls ExternalDataAccess.GetDataTable to populate the variable with columns metadata from the BRMetadata database. After declaring and initializing variables to contain sourceTableId and targetTableId on lines 53 and 54, you iterate the source table column in the third BimlScript snippet using a foreach loops and some Language Integrated Query (Linq) to first filter for source columns in lines 57-67. You use annotations to store column attributes for business keys and the mapped target column name on lines 63 and 64. You repeat the columns metadata iteration, with a Linq filter for target columns, in your fourth snippet of BimlScript on lines 76-86. You use annotations to store column attributes for business keys and the mapped source column name on lines 82 and 83. After the business key and mapped column name Biml annotations you close the Biml Column tags on lines 68 and 85, respectively.

After saving the LoadBimlRelationalHierarchy.biml file, the Preview pane displays the Biml columns, as shown in Figure 6-19.

```
 1 ▾  <Biml xmlns="http://schemas.varigence.com/biml.xsd">
 2 ▾    <Connections>
 3        <Connection Name="ContosoSource" ConnectionString="Provider=SQLNCLI11;Data Source=vmDemo\MBF;Int
 4        <Connection Name="ContosoTarget" ConnectionString="Provider=SQLNCLI11;Data Source=vmDemo\MBF;Int
 5      </Connections>
 6 ▾    <Databases>
 7        <Database Name="ContosoOLTP" ConnectionName="ContosoSource" />
 8        <Database Name="ContosoRetailDW" ConnectionName="ContosoTarget" />
 9      </Databases>
10 ▾    <Schemas>
11        <Schema Name="dbo" DatabaseName="ContosoOLTP" />
12        <Schema Name="dbo" DatabaseName="ContosoRetailDW" />
13      </Schemas>
14 ▾    <Tables>
15 ▾      <Table Name="Channel" SchemaName="ContosoOLTP.dbo">
16 ▾        <Columns>
17 ▾          · <Column Name="Label" DataType="String" Length="100" >
18 ▾            <Annotations>
19              <Annotation AnnotationType="Tag" Tag="IsBusinessKey">true</Annotation>
20              <Annotation AnnotationType="Tag" Tag="MappedColumnName">ChannelLabel</Annotation>
21            </Annotations>
22          </Column>
23 ▾          <Column Name="Name" DataType="String" Length="20" IsNullable="true" >
24 ▾            <Annotations>
25              <Annotation AnnotationType="Tag" Tag="MappedColumnName">ChannelName</Annotation>
26            </Annotations>
27          </Column>
28 ▾          <Column Name="Description" DataType="String" Length="50" IsNullable="true" >
29 ▾            <Annotations>
30              <Annotation AnnotationType="Tag" Tag="MappedColumnName">ChannelDescription</Annotation>
31            </Annotations>
32          </Column>
33 ▾          <Column Name="LastUpdatedDate" DataType="Date" IsNullable="true" >
34 ▾            <Annotations>
35              <Annotation AnnotationType="Tag" Tag="MappedColumnName">UpdateDate</Annotation>
36            </Annotations>
37          </Column>
38        </Columns>
39 ▾      <Annotations>
40          <Annotation AnnotationType="Tag" Tag="MappedTableID">2</Annotation>
41          <Annotation AnnotationType="Tag" Tag="MappedTableName">DimChannel</Annotation>
42        </Annotations>
43      </Table>
44 ▾    <Table Name="DimChannel" SchemaName="ContosoRetailDW.dbo">
45 ▾      <Columns>
46 ▾        <Column Name="ChannelLabel" DataType="String" Length="100" >
47 ▾          <Annotations>
48            <Annotation AnnotationType="Tag" Tag="IsBusinessKey">true</Annotation>
49            <Annotation AnnotationType="Tag" Tag="MappedColumnName">Label</Annotation>
50          </Annotations>
51        </Column>
52 ▾        <Column Name="ChannelName" DataType="String" Length="20" IsNullable="true" >
53 ▾          <Annotations>
54            <Annotation AnnotationType="Tag" Tag="MappedColumnName">Name</Annotation>
55          </Annotations>
56        </Column>
57 ▾        <Column Name="ChannelDescription" DataType="String" Length="50" IsNullable="true" >
58 ▾          <Annotations>
59            <Annotation AnnotationType="Tag" Tag="MappedColumnName">Description</Annotation>
60          </Annotations>
61        </Column>
62 ▾        <Column Name="UpdateDate" DataType="DateTime" IsNullable="true" >
63 ▾          <Annotations>
64            <Annotation AnnotationType="Tag" Tag="MappedColumnName">LastUpdatedDate</Annotation>
65          </Annotations>
66        </Column>
67      </Columns>
68 ▾    <Annotations>
69        <Annotation AnnotationType="Tag" Tag="MappedTableID">1</Annotation>
70        <Annotation AnnotationType="Tag" Tag="MappedTableName">Channel</Annotation>
71      </Annotations>
72      </Table>
73    </Tables>
74  </Biml>
```

Figure 6-19. *Viewing the preview with Biml Column tags*

A good way to test your Biml and BimlScript is to build or expand the Biml file.
In Solution Explorer, right-click the LoadBimlRelationalHierarchy.biml file and
click "Generate SSIS Packages." If your Biml or BimlScript contains an error, it may be
displayed in a dialog; the error will definitely be displayed in the Output window. If all
goes well, your SSDT Output window will display Biml compiler output indicating that
the Biml expansion completed, as shown in Figure 6-20.

Figure 6-20. *Viewing the Biml compiler output in the SSDT Output window*

In this section you used BimlScript to retrieve metadata from the BRMetadata
database to build and populate the Biml relational hierarchy. In the next section, you
leverage the Biml relational hierarchy and use the mappings metadata to build a simple
SSIS package.

Using the Relational Database Metadata to Build Packages

In the previous section, you built and populated the Biml relational hierarchy from
metadata stored in a database named BRMetadata. In this section, you will use the freshly-
populated Biml relational hierarchy, along with the mappings metadata, to build an SSIS
package that loads new rows into the ContosoRetailDW.dbo.DimChannel table.

As you worked your way through the last section, you may have been curious about
why we used Biml annotations to store attributes about Biml tables and some Biml
columns. We took this approach to eliminate the need for more trips to the BRMetadata
database as we build SSIS packages from the Biml relational hierarchy.

Building an SSIS Package

Let's build an SSIS Package to demonstrate! Begin by creating a new Biml file and rename
it CreatePackages.biml. On line 1, add a template directive to inform the Biml compiler
that this file is to be executed *after* LoadBimlRelationalHierarchy.biml, by adding the
highlighted directive shown in Listing 6-16.

Listing 6-16. Starting the CreatePackages.biml Biml File

```
<#@ template tier="20"#>
<Biml xmlns="http://schemas.varigence.com/biml.xsd">
</Biml>
```

Why tier 20? When building more complex solutions, it is best practice to number your Biml files by 10's to preserve the option of adding some other Biml file between two existing Biml files in execution order.

Let's next add Biml Packages open and close tags; see Listing 6-17.

Listing 6-17. Adding the Packages Biml Tags

```
<#@ template tier="20"#>
<Biml xmlns="http://schemas.varigence.com/biml.xsd">
    <Packages></Packages>
</Biml>
```

Adding the Biml Package Tag

Let's next add a BimlScript code block and Biml Package open and close tags, as shown highlighted in Listing 6-18.

Listing 6-18. Adding BimlScript to Read the Biml Relational Hierarchy and Build an SSIS Package

```
<#@ template tier="20"#>
<Biml xmlns="http://schemas.varigence.com/biml.xsd">
    <Packages>
    <#
    var sourceConnection = "ContosoSource";
    var targetConnection = "ContosoTarget";
    foreach(var tgtTable in RootNode.Tables.Where(t => t.Connection.Name ==
      targetConnection)) {
        var sourceTable = tgtTable.GetTag("MappedTableName");
        var srcTable = RootNode.Tables[sourceTable];
        #>
    <Package Name="Load <#=tgtTable.Name#>" ProtectionLevel="EncryptSensitive
     WithUserKey">
    </Package>
    <# } #>
    </Packages>
</Biml>
```

Your CreatePackages.biml file should appear as shown in Figure 6-21.

```
1   <#@ template tier="20"#>
2 ▾ <Biml xmlns="http://schemas.varigence.com/biml.xsd">
3 ▾     <Packages>
4           <#
5           var sourceConnection = "ContosoSource";
6           var targetConnection = "ContosoTarget";
7           foreach(var tgtTable in RootNode.Tables.Where(t => t. Connection.Name == targetConnection)) {
8               var sourceTable = tgtTable.GetTag("MappedTableName");
9               var srcTable = RootNode.Tables[sourceTable];
10              #>
11 ▾          <Package Name="Load <#=tgtTable.Name#>" ProtectionLevel="EncryptSensitiveWithUserKey">
12          </Package>
13          <# } #>
14      </Packages>
15  </Biml>
```

Figure 6-21. *Viewing CreatePackages.biml with target table BimlScript*

The BimlScript you added starts on line 4 with a code block start tag. On lines 5 and 6 you declare and initialize two variables, sourceConnection and targetConnection. You iterate RootNode.Tables starting on line 7, using Linq to filter for target tables. On lines 9 and 10, you declare and initialize the variables sourceTable and srcTable.

■ **Note** Want to learn more about LINQ? Microsoft has a series of articles at the Getting Started with LINQ in C# web page at https://docs.microsoft.com/en-us/dotnet/csharp/programming-guide/concepts/linq/getting-started-with-linq.

You use a Where query operator method (Microsoft's terminology, not ours) in concert with a *lambda expression* to filter the results returned to the tgtTable enumerator. In this case, the lambda expression t => t.Connection.Name == targetConnection can be read "t such that t's connection name matches the value of the targetConnection variable." The lambda expression configures the enumeration of the foreach loop to only return AstTableNodes where the connection name property of the Biml connection for the Biml database for the Biml schema for the Biml table matches the value of the targetConnection variable. To learn more about lambda expressions and query operator methods, read the articles on the Getting Started with LINQ in C# web page at https://docs.microsoft.com/en-us/dotnet/csharp/programming-guide/concepts/linq/getting-started-with-linq.

On line 9 you read the MappedTableName tag of the target table and store this value in the sourceTable variable. On line 11 you set the srcTable variable to the table in the RootNode.Tables collection with the same name stored in the sourceTable variable. We wrote about RootNode at the beginning of this chapter.

On lines 12-13 you build a Biml SSIS package. Please note two items:

1. You derive the name of the SSIS package from the name of the target table to be loaded, naming your SSIS package "Load *<target table name>*."

2. You set the package ProtectionLevel property to the default for SSDT SSIS packages, EncryptSensitiveWithUserKey. On line 16 you close the foreach loop.

What happens when you save, compile, and update the Biml file? If CreatePackages.biml is the only file open, the results appear as shown in Figure 6-22.

```
<Biml xmlns="http://schemas.varigence.com/biml.xsd">
  <Packages></Packages>
</Biml>
```

Figure 6-22. Viewing the results of CreatePackages.biml compile with Biml package

You may be looking at the Preview pane and wondering, "What gives? Where's my Biml SSIS package?" Fair questions.

To build your empty SSIS package, return to Solution Explorer. Multi-select LoadBimlRelationalHierarchy.biml and CreatePackages.biml. Right-click the selected files and click Generate SSIS Packages, as shown in Figure 6-23.

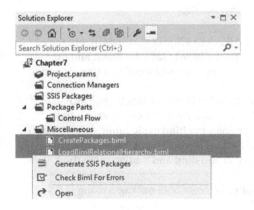

Figure 6-23. Generating an SSIS package

If all goes as planned, an SSIS package named Load DimChannel.dtsx will appear in Solution Explorer's SSIS Packages virtual folder. If you open Load DimChannel.dtsx and start the debugger (F5, or Debug ➤ Start Debugging) this package should execute and succeed as shown in Figure 6-24.

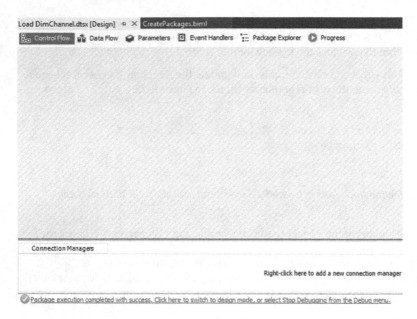

Figure 6-24. *Successful execution of an empty SSIS package*

Why do you need to multi-select both Biml files? LoadBimlRelationalHierarchy.biml populates the Biml relational hierarchy from the BRMetadata database, and then CreatePackages.biml enumerates the contents of the Biml relational hierarchy in order to build the SSIS package.

In BimlStudio, you can execute the LoadBimlRelationalHierarchy.biml to populate the Biml relational hierarchy *and then* preview the results of an expanded CreatePackages.biml file. Is there no way to preview the Biml using BimlExpress? Yes. If you open and update the preview for LoadBimlRelationalHierarchy.biml, the Preview pane in BimlExpress will show you updates as you add Biml and BimlScript to the CreatePackages.biml file.

The Biml and BimlScript you are developing to create SSIS packages using BimlExpress works the same in BimlStudio. There are differences between BimlStudio and BimlExpress, but those differences don't impact your project. Let's transfer your code to BimlStudio to prove it.

Moving the Project to BimlStudio

Open BimlStudio and create a new project named BimlBookBimlBookChapter7BimlStudio. Create a new utility named `LoadBimlRelationalHierarchy.biml`, copy your Biml and BimlScript code from the SSDT/BimlExpress project's `LoadBimlRelationalHierarchy.biml` file, and paste it into the BimlStudio version. Repeat this action for the `CreatePackages.biml` file.

When you initially preview the `CreatePackages.biml` file in BimlStudio, you see results similar to those you witnessed in BimlExpress (with LoadBimlRelationalHierarchy. biml open and updated), as shown in Figure 6-25.

```
1   <#@ template tier="20"#>
2   <Biml xmlns="http://schemas.varigence.com/biml.xsd">
3       <Packages>
4           <#
5           var sourceConnection = "ContosoSource";
6           var targetConnection = "ContosoTarget";
7           foreach(var tgtTable in RootNode.Tables.Where(t => t.Connection.Name == targetConnection)) {
8               var sourceTable = tgtTable.GetTag("MappedTableName");
9               var srcTable = RootNode.Tables[sourceTable];
10          #>
11          <Package Name="Load <#=tgtTable.Name#>" ProtectionLevel="EncryptSensitiveWithUserKey">
12          </Package>
13          <# } #>
14      </Packages>
15  </Biml>
```

Preview Expanded BimlScript

```
1   <Biml xmlns="http://schemas.varigence.com/biml.xsd">
2       <Packages>
3       </Packages>
4   </Biml>
```

***Figure 6-25.** Viewing the preview of CreatePackages.biml in BimlStudio*

Note that the Biml relational hierarchy, visualized in BimlStudio in Logical View, is not yet populated, as shown in Figure 6-26.

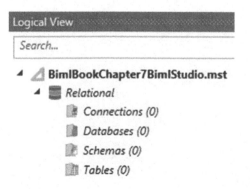

***Figure 6-26.** Viewing an empty Biml relational hierarchy in Logical View*

You can execute the `LoadBimlRelationalHierarchy.biml` file, as shown in Figure 6-27.

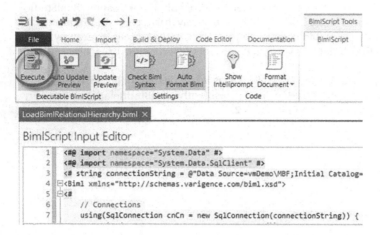

Figure 6-27. *Executing the LoadBimlRelationalHierarchy.biml file*

Executing `LoadBimlRelationalHierarchy.biml` populates the Biml relational hierarchy. You can see the results in Logical View, as shown in Figure 6-28.

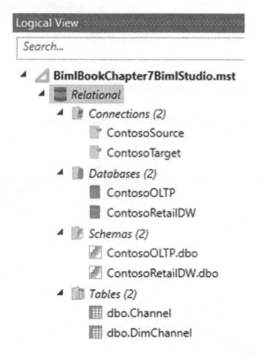

Figure 6-28. *A populated Biml relation hierarchy in Logical View*

If you convert the `LoadBimlRelationalHierarchy.biml` file to a Live Biml script, artifacts in the Biml relational hierarchy are generated automatically.

If you update the preview of `CreatePackages.biml`, you can now view the Biml SSIS package, as shown in Figure 6-29.

Preview Expanded BimlScript

```
1   <Biml xmlns="http://schemas.varigence.com/biml.xsd">
2       <Packages>
3           <Package Name="Load DimChannel" ProtectionLevel="EncryptSensitiveWithUserKey">
4           </Package>
5       </Packages>
6   </Biml>
```

Figure 6-29. *Previewing the Biml SSIS package*

You may continue this demonstration in either BimlExpress or BimlStudio. You will achieve the same results in the end (and we will prove it). Let's proceed for now in BimlStudio.

You must now consider the requirements of your load. There are many ways to build SSIS packages to load data. Some data is never updated, only new rows are added to the source that must be transmitted to the target. Some data includes new and updated rows at the source. The new rows must be added and the updated rows updated at the target. Some data may be deleted at the source and you may want to indicate that these rows have been deleted in the target. Your SSIS design pattern must match your load requirements.

■ **Note**   To learn more about SSIS design patterns, please read *SQL Server Integration Services Design Patterns* (`www.amazon.com/Server-Integration-Services-Design-Patterns/dp/1484200837`).

Based on certain requirements (in the author's mind and nowhere else...), let's' build an SSIS package that loads only new data, but also adds ETL (extract, transform, and load) instrumentation metadata to the load process.

Adding the Tasks and Dataflow Tags

To continue the demonstration, let's next add Biml Tasks opening and closing tags to the `CreatePackages.biml` file in BimlStudio. While we're at it, let's also add opening and closing tags for a Biml Dataflow. Your Biml and BimlScript should now appear as shown in Listing 6-19 (highlighted new syntax).

Listing 6-19. Adding the Tasks and Dataflow Tags

```
<#@ template tier="20"#>
<Biml xmlns="http://schemas.varigence.com/biml.xsd">
  <Packages>
  <#
    var sourceConnection = "ContosoSource";
    var targetConnection = "ContosoTarget";
    foreach(var tgtTable in RootNode.Tables.Where(t => t. Connection.Name ==
     targetConnection)) {
        var sourceTable = tgtTable.GetTag("MappedTableName");
        var srcTable = RootNode.Tables[sourceTable];
      #>
      <Package Name="Load <#=tgtTable.Name#>" ProtectionLevel="EncryptSensitive
      WithUserKey">
        <Tasks>
          <Dataflow Name="DFT Load <#=tgtTable.Name#>">
          </Dataflow>
        </Tasks>
      </Package>
      <# } #>
  </Packages>
</Biml>
```

In BimlStudio, your Biml and BimlScript now appear as shown in Figure 6-30.

```
 1   <#@ template tier="20"#>
 2  ⊟<Biml xmlns="http://schemas.varigence.com/biml.xsd">
 3  ⊟    <Packages>
 4  ⊟    <#
 5        var sourceConnection = "ContosoSource";
 6        var targetConnection = "ContosoTarget";
 7        foreach(var tgtTable in RootNode.Tables.Where(t => t.Connection.Name == targetConnection)) {
 8            var sourceTable = tgtTable.GetTag("MappedTableName");
 9            var srcTable = RootNode.Tables[sourceTable];
10            #>
11  ⊟    <Package Name="Load <#=tgtTable.Name#>" ProtectionLevel="EncryptSensitiveWithUserKey">
12  ⊟        <Tasks>
13                <Dataflow Name="DFT Load <#=tgtTable.Name#>">
14                </Dataflow>
15            </Tasks>
16        </Package>
17        <# } #>
18        </Packages>
19   </Biml>
```

Figure 6-30. *Viewing CreatePackages.biml with Dataflow*

Your newly-added Biml and BimlScript starts on line 12 with a Biml Tasks tag. On line 13 you add a Biml Dataflow tag and set the Name attribute to "DFT Load *<target table name>*." On lines 14 and 15 you close the Dataflow and Tasks tags, respectively.

The BimlScript Preview pane in BimlStudio now reflects your latest additions, as shown in Figure 6-31.

```
<Biml xmlns="http://schemas.varigence.com/biml.xsd">
    <Packages>
        <Package Name="Load DimChannel" ProtectionLevel="EncryptSensitiveWithUserKey">
            <Tasks>
                <Dataflow Name="DFT Load DimChannel">
                </Dataflow>
            </Tasks>
        </Package>
    </Packages>
</Biml>
```

Figure 6-31. *Previewing CreatePackages.biml Biml with Dataflow*

Adding the Transformations Tag and Your First Dataflow Component

Let's next add Biml Transformations opening and closing tags to the CreatePackages.biml file in BimlStudio, along with your first Dataflow component, an OLE DB Source adapter. Your Biml and BimlScript now appears as shown in Listing 6-20 (highlighted new syntax).

Listing 6-20. Adding the Transformations Tag and the First Dataflow Component

```
<#@ template tier="20"#>
<Biml xmlns="http://schemas.varigence.com/biml.xsd">
  <Packages>
  <#
    var sourceConnection = "ContosoSource";
    var targetConnection = "ContosoTarget";
    foreach(var tgtTable in RootNode.Tables.Where(t => t.Schema.Database.
    Connection.Name == targetConnection)) {
        var sourceTable = tgtTable.GetTag("MappedTableName");
        var srcTable = RootNode.Tables[sourceTable];
      #>
    <Package Name="Load <#=tgtTable.Name#>" ProtectionLevel="EncryptSensitive
    WithUserKey">
      <Tasks>
        <Dataflow Name="DFT Load <#=tgtTable.Name#>">
          <Transformations>
            <OleDbSource Name="OLEDBSrc <#=sourceTable#>" ConnectionName=
            "<#=sourceConnection#>">
              <DirectInput><#=srcTable.GetSelectSql()#></DirectInput>
            </OleDbSource>
          </Transformations>
        </Dataflow>
      </Tasks>
```

```
    </Package>
    <# } #>
  </Packages>
</Biml>
```

In BimlStudio, your Biml and BimlScript now appear as shown in Figure 6-32.

```
1   <#@ template tier="20"#>
2   <Biml xmlns="http://schemas.varigence.com/biml.xsd">
3       <Packages>
4           <#
5       var sourceConnection = "ContosoSource";
6       var targetConnection = "ContosoTarget";
7       foreach(var tgtTable in RootNode.Tables.Where(t => t.Connection.Name == targetConnection)) {
8           var sourceTable = tgtTable.GetTag("MappedTableName");
9           var srcTable = RootNode.Tables[sourceTable];
10          #>
11          <Package Name="Load <#=tgtTable.Name#>" ProtectionLevel="EncryptSensitiveWithUserKey">
12              <Tasks>
13                  <Dataflow Name="DFT Load <#=tgtTable.Name#>">
14                      <Transformations>
15                          <OleDbSource Name="OLEDBSrc <#=sourceTable#>" ConnectionName="<#=sourceConnection#>">
16                              <DirectInput><#=srcTable.GetSelectSql()#></DirectInput>
17                          </OleDbSource>
18                      </Transformations>
19                  </Dataflow>
20              </Tasks>
21          </Package>
22          <# } #>
23      </Packages>
24  </Biml>
```

Figure 6-32. *Viewing CreatePackages.biml with an OLE DB source adapter*

Your newly-added Biml and BimlScript starts on lines 14 and 18 with Biml Transformations open and close tags. On lines 15-17 you add a Biml OLE DB source and set the Name attribute to "OLEDBSrc *source table name*." Note that you set the value of the DirectInput tag for the OLE DB source adapter by calling the GetSelectSql() method of the srcTable variable. This is why you went to the trouble to set up the srcTable variable.

The BimlScript Preview pane in BimlStudio now reflects the latest additions, as shown in Figure 6-33.

```
<Biml xmlns="http://schemas.varigence.com/biml.xsd">
    <Packages>
        <Package Name="Load DimChannel" ProtectionLevel="EncryptSensitiveWithUserKey">
            <Tasks>
                <Dataflow Name="DFT Load DimChannel">
                    <Transformations>
                        <OleDbSource Name="OLEDBSrc Channel" ConnectionName="ContosoSource">
                            <DirectInput>SELECT [Label]
                            ,[Name]
                            ,[Description]
                            ,[LastUpdatedDate]
                            FROM [dbo].[Channel]
                            </DirectInput>
                        </OleDbSource>
                    </Transformations>
                </Dataflow>
            </Tasks>
        </Package>
    </Packages>
</Biml>
```

Figure 6-33. *Previewing CreatePackages.biml Biml with OLE DB Source adapter*

Adding a Lookup Transformation

Next, let's add a lookup transformation to the CreatePackages.biml file in BimlStudio. Your Biml and BimlScript now appear as shown in Listing 6-21 (highlighted new syntax).

Listing 6-21. Adding a Lookup Transformation

```
<#@ template tier="20"#>
<Biml xmlns="http://schemas.varigence.com/biml.xsd">
  <Packages>
    <#
    var sourceConnection = "ContosoSource";
    var targetConnection = "ContosoTarget";
    foreach(var tgtTable in RootNode.Tables.Where(t => t.Connection.Name ==
    targetConnection)) {
      var sourceTable = tgtTable.GetTag("MappedTableName");
      var srcTable = RootNode.Tables[sourceTable];
      var keyCols = srcTable.Columns.Where(c => c.GetTag("IsBusinessKey").
      ToLower() == "true");
      var mappedKeyColNames = keyCols.Select(c =>
      c.GetTag("MappedColumnName"));
```

181

```
      var lkupSelect = "Select [" + string.Join("],[", mappedKeyColNames) +
      "] From " + tgtTable.SchemaQualifiedName;
      var lkupWhere = string.Join("] = ?\nAnd [refTable].[",
      mappedKeyColNames);
        #>
   <Package Name="Load <#=tgtTable.Name#>" ProtectionLevel="EncryptSensitive
   WithUserKey">
     <Tasks>
       <Dataflow Name="DFT Load <#=tgtTable.Name#>">
         <Transformations>
           <OleDbSource Name="OLEDBSrc <#=sourceTable#>"
           ConnectionName="<#=sourceConnection#>">
             <DirectInput><#=srcTable.GetSelectSql()#></DirectInput>
           </OleDbSource>
           <Lookup Name="LkUp Correlate" OleDbConnectionName="<#=target
           Connection#>" NoMatchBehavior="RedirectRowsToNoMatchOutput">
             <Parameters>
               <# foreach(var keyCol in keyCols) { #>
                   <Parameter SourceColumn="<#=keyCol.Name#>" />
                   <# } #>
             </Parameters>
             <Inputs>
               <# foreach(var keyCol in keyCols) { #>
               <Column SourceColumn="<#=keyCol.Name#>"
               TargetColumn="<#=keyCol.GetTag("MappedColumnName")#>" />
               <# } #>
             </Inputs>
             <DirectInput><#=lkupSelect#></DirectInput>
             <ParameterizedQuery>select * from (<#=lkupSelect#>) [refTable]
             where [refTable].[<#=lkupWhere#> = ?</ParameterizedQuery>
           </Lookup>
         </Transformations>
       </Dataflow>
     </Tasks>
   </Package>
   <# } #>
 </Packages>
</Biml>
```

In BimlStudio, the Biml and BimlScript now appear as shown in Figure 6-34.

```
1    <#@ template tier="20"#>
2    <Biml xmlns="http://schemas.varigence.com/biml.xsd">
3      <Packages>
4        <#
5        var sourceConnection = "ContosoSource";
6        var targetConnection = "ContosoTarget";
7        foreach(var tgtTable in RootNode.Tables.Where(t => t.Connection.Name == targetConnection)) {
8          var sourceTable = tgtTable.GetTag("MappedTableName");
9          var srcTable = RootNode.Tables[sourceTable];
10         var keyCols = srcTable.Columns.Where(c => c.GetTag("IsBusinessKey").ToLower() == "true");
11         var mappedKeyColNames = keyCols.Select(c => c.GetTag("MappedColumnName"));
12         var lkupSelect = "Select [" + string.Join("],[", mappedKeyColNames) + "] From " + tgtTable.SchemaQualifiedName;
13         var lkupWhere = string.Join("] = ?\nAnd [refTable].[", mappedKeyColNames);
14         #>
15       <Package Name="Load <#=tgtTable.Name#>" ProtectionLevel="EncryptSensitiveWithUserKey">
16         <Tasks>
17           <Dataflow Name="DFT Load <#=tgtTable.Name#>">
18             <Transformations>
19               <OleDbSource Name="OLEDBSrc <#=sourceTable#>" ConnectionName="<#=sourceConnection#>">
20                 <DirectInput><#=srcTable.GetSelectSql()#></DirectInput>
21               </OleDbSource>
22               <Lookup Name="LkUp Correlate" OleDbConnectionName="<#=targetConnection#>" NoMatchBehavior="RedirectRowsToNoMatchOutput">
23                 <Parameters>
24                   <# foreach(var keyCol in keyCols) { #>
25                   <Parameter SourceColumn="<#=keyCol.Name#>" />
26                 <# } #>
27                 </Parameters>
28                 <Inputs>
29                   <# foreach(var keyCol in keyCols) { #>
30                   <Column SourceColumn="<#=keyCol.Name#>" TargetColumn="<#=keyCol.GetTag("MappedColumnName")#>" />
31                 <# } #>
32                 </Inputs>
33                 <DirectInput><#=lkupSelect#></DirectInput>
34                 <ParameterizedQuery>select * from (<#=lkupSelect#>) [refTable] where [refTable].[<#=lkupWhere#> = ?</ParameterizedQuery>
35               </Lookup>
36             </Transformations>
37           </Dataflow>
38         </Tasks>
39       </Package>
40       <# } #>
41     </Packages>
42   </Biml>
```

Figure 6-34. *Viewing CreatePackages.biml with a lookup transformation*

The newly-added Biml and BimlScript starts and ends on lines 22 and 35 with Biml Lookup open and close tags. You're using a static name for the lookup transformation, "LkUp Correlate," because the operation of correlation with the target is fairly generic. You use the value of the targetConnection variable in the OleDbConnectionName attribute of the Lookup tag, and you set the NoMatchBehavior to "RedirectRowsToNoMatchOutput."

In the next portion of the Biml lookup transformation configuration, parameters, you chose a string collection to represent related pairs of column names. The variable named keyCols is declared on line 10 to contain only columns that are configured (in Mappings metadata) as business key columns. A foreach loop begins on line 24, enumerating the keyCols collection. On line 25 you jump out of BimlScript to build the Biml Parameter tag, supplying the name of the source column, previously identified as a business key, to the SourceColumn attribute. You close the Parameter tag on line 27.

On line 28 you start the next portion of the Biml lookup transformation: inputs. You enumerate the keyCols collection and build a Biml Column tag for each, setting the SourceColumn attribute to the keyCols.Name value and the TargetColumn attribute to the value found in the Biml annotation MappedColumnName using keyCols. GetTag("MappedColumnName"). The Inputs tag is closed on line 32.

The next portion of the Biml lookup transformation is the DirectInput tag. You construct the DirectInput query in a variable named lkupSelect on line 12. The DirectInput open and close tags are on line 33 and you write the contents of the lkupSelect variable into the DirectInput tag on the same line.

The next portion of the Biml lookup transformation is the ParameterizedQuery. You construct the Where clause of the ParameterizedQuery in a variable named lkupWhere on line 13. The ParameterizedQuery open and close tags are on line 34 along with the ParameterizedQuery using the lkupSelect variable value to populate the refTable sub-select statement and the lkupWhere variable for the Where clause of the ParameterizedQuery.

The BimlScript Preview pane in BimlStudio now reflects the latest additions, as shown in Figure 6-35.

```
<Biml xmlns="http://schemas.varigence.com/biml.xsd">
    <Packages>
        <Package Name="Load DimChannel" ProtectionLevel="EncryptSensitiveWithUserKey">
            <Tasks>
                <Dataflow Name="DFT Load DimChannel">
                    <Transformations>
                        <OleDbSource Name="OLEDBSrc Channel" ConnectionName="ContosoSource">
                            <DirectInput>SELECT [Label]
                                ,[Name]
                                ,[Description]
                                ,[LastUpdatedDate]
                                FROM [dbo].[Channel]
                            </DirectInput>
                        </OleDbSource>
                        <Lookup Name="LkUp Correlate" OleDbConnectionName="ContosoTarget" NoMatchBehavior="RedirectRowsToNoMatchOutput">
                            <InputPath OutputPathName="OLEDBSrc Channel.Output" />
                            <Parameters>
                                <Parameter SourceColumn="Label" />
                            </Parameters>
                            <Inputs>
                                <Column SourceColumn="Label" TargetColumn="ChannelLabel" />
                            </Inputs>
                            <DirectInput>
                                Select [ChannelLabel] From [dbo].[DimChannel]
                            </DirectInput>
                            <ParameterizedQuery>select * from (Select [ChannelLabel] From [dbo].[DimChannel]) [refTable]
                                where [refTable].[ChannelLabel] = ?
                            </ParameterizedQuery>
                        </Lookup>
                    </Transformations>
                </Dataflow>
            </Tasks>
        </Package>
    </Packages>
</Biml>
```

Figure 6-35. *Previewing CreatePackages.biml Biml with a lookup transformation*

Adding a Derived Column Transformation

Let's next add a derived columns transformation to the CreatePackages.biml file in BimlStudio. Your Biml and BimlScript now appears as shown in Listing 6-22 (highlighted new syntax).

Listing 6-22. Adding a Derived Column Transformation

```
<#@ template tier="20"#>
<Biml xmlns="http://schemas.varigence.com/biml.xsd">
  <Packages>
    <#
    var sourceConnection = "ContosoSource";
    var targetConnection = "ContosoTarget";
    foreach(var tgtTable in RootNode.Tables.Where(t => t.Connection.Name ==
    targetConnection)) {
      var sourceTable = tgtTable.GetTag("MappedTableName");
      var srcTable = RootNode.Tables[sourceTable];
      var keyCols = srcTable.Columns.Where(c => c.GetTag("IsBusinessKey").
      ToLower() == "true");
      var mappedKeyColNames = keyCols.Select(c =>
      c.GetTag("MappedColumnName"));
      var lkupSelect = "Select [" + string.Join("],[", mappedKeyColNames) + "]
      From " + tgtTable.SchemaQualifiedName;
      var lkupWhere = string.Join("] = ?\nAnd [refTable].[", mappedKeyColNames);
        #>
    <Package Name="Load <#=tgtTable.Name#>" ProtectionLevel="EncryptSensitive
    WithUserKey">
      <Tasks>
        <Dataflow Name="DFT Load <#=tgtTable.Name#>">
          <Transformations>
            <OleDbSource Name="OLEDBSrc <#=sourceTable#>"
            ConnectionName="<#=sourceConnection#>">
              <DirectInput><#=srcTable.GetSelectSql()#></DirectInput>
            </OleDbSource>
            <Lookup Name="LkUp Correlate" OleDbConnectionName="<#=target
            Connection#>" NoMatchBehavior="RedirectRowsToNoMatchOutput">
              <Parameters>
                <# foreach(var keyCol in keyCols) { #>
                    <Parameter SourceColumn="<#=keyCol.Name#>" />
                <# } #>
              </Parameters>
              <Inputs>
                <# foreach(var keyCol in keyCols) { #>
                <Column SourceColumn="<#=keyCol.Name#>"
                TargetColumn="<#=keyCol.GetTag("MappedColumnName")#>" />
                <# } #>
              </Inputs>
              <DirectInput><#=lkupSelect#></DirectInput>
              <ParameterizedQuery>select * from (<#=lkupSelect#>) [refTable]
              where [refTable].[<#=lkupWhere#>] = ?</ParameterizedQuery>
            </Lookup>
            <DerivedColumns Name="DER ETL Instrumentation">
              <InputPath OutputPathName="LkUp Correlate.NoMatch" />
```

```xml
                <Columns>
                    <Column Name="ETLLoadID" DataType="Int32">(DT_I4)@
                    [System::ServerExecutionID]</Column>
                    <Column Name="LoadDate" DataType="Date">@[System::StartTime]
                      </Column>
                </Columns>
            </DerivedColumns>
          </Transformations>
        </Dataflow>
      </Tasks>
    </Package>
    <# } #>
  </Packages>
</Biml>
```

In BimlStudio, the Biml and BimlScript now appear as shown in Figure 6-36.

```
1    <#@ template tier="20"#>
2    <Biml xmlns="http://schemas.varigence.com/biml.xsd">
3      <Packages>
4        <#
5        var sourceConnection = "ContosoSource";
6        var targetConnection = "ContosoTarget";
7        foreach(var tgtTable in RootNode.Tables.Where(t => t.Connection.Name == targetConnection)) {
8            var sourceTable = tgtTable.GetTag("MappedTableName");
9            var srcTable = RootNode.Tables[sourceTable];
10           var keyCols = srcTable.Columns.Where(c => c.GetTag("IsBusinessKey").ToLower() == "true");
11           var mappedKeyColNames = keyCols.Select(c => c.GetTag("MappedColumnName"));
12           var lkupSelect = "Select [" + string.Join("],[", mappedKeyColNames) + "] From " + tgtTable.SchemaQualifiedName;
13           var lkupWhere = string.Join("] = ?\nAnd [refTable].[", mappedKeyColNames);
14           #>
15       <Package Name="Load <#=tgtTable.Name#>" ProtectionLevel="EncryptSensitiveWithUserKey">
16         <Tasks>
17           <Dataflow Name="DFT Load <#=tgtTable.Name#>">
18             <Transformations>
19               <OleDbSource Name="OLEDBSrc <#=sourceTable#>" ConnectionName="<#=sourceConnection#>">
20                 <DirectInput><#=srcTable.GetSelectSql()#></DirectInput>
21               </OleDbSource>
22               <Lookup Name="LkUp Correlate" OleDbConnectionName="<#=targetConnection#>" NoMatchBehavior="RedirectRowsToNoMatchOutput">
23                 <Parameters>
24                   <# foreach(var keyCol in keyCols) { #>
25                   <Parameter SourceColumn="<#=keyCol.Name#>" />
26                   <# } #>
27                 </Parameters>
28                 <Inputs>
29                   <# foreach(var keyCol in keyCols) { #>
30                   <Column SourceColumn="<#=keyCol.Name#>" TargetColumn="<#=keyCol.GetTag("MappedColumnName")#>" />
31                   <# } #>
32                 </Inputs>
33                 <DirectInput><#=lkupSelect#></DirectInput>
34                 <ParameterizedQuery>select * from (<#=lkupSelect#>) [refTable] where [refTable].[<#=lkupWhere#>] = ?</ParameterizedQuery>
35               </Lookup>
36               <DerivedColumns Name="DER ETL Instrumentation">
37                 <InputPath OutputPathName="LkUp Correlate.NoMatch" />
38                 <Columns>
39                   <Column Name="ETLLoadID" DataType="Int32">(DT_I4)@[System::ServerExecutionID]</Column>
40                   <Column Name="LoadDate" DataType="Date">@[System::StartTime]</Column>
41                 </Columns>
42               </DerivedColumns>
43             </Transformations>
44           </Dataflow>
45         </Tasks>
46       </Package>
47       <# } #>
48     </Packages>
49   </Biml>
```

Figure 6-36. *Viewing CreatePackages.biml with a derived columns transformation*

The newly-added Biml and BimlScript starts and ends on lines 36 and 42 with DerivedColumns open and close tags. As with the lookup transformation, you chose a static name for the derived columns transformation, "DER ETL Instrumentation." All Biml in the derived columns transformation is hard-coded in this example. Two columns are added to your data flow:

1. ETLLoadID: Derived from the value of the System::ServerExecutionID SSIS variable, converted from an eight-byte integer to a four-byte integer (short-sighted, we know; the better solution is to update the ETLLoadID column in the target table to bigint).

2. LoadDate: Derived from the System::StartTime SSIS variable.

The BimlScript Preview pane in BimlStudio now reflects the latest additions, as shown in Figure 6-37.

```
<Biml xmlns="http://schemas.varigence.com/biml.xsd">
    <Packages>
        <Package Name="Load DimChannel" ProtectionLevel="EncryptSensitiveWithUserKey">
            <Tasks>
                <Dataflow Name="DFT Load DimChannel">
                    <Transformations>
                        <OleDbSource Name="OLEDBSrc Channel" ConnectionName="ContosoSource">
                            <DirectInput>SELECT [Label]
                                ,[Name]
                                ,[Description]
                                ,[LastUpdatedDate]
                                FROM [dbo].[Channel]
                            </DirectInput>
                        </OleDbSource>
                        <Lookup Name="LkUp Correlate" OleDbConnectionName="ContosoTarget" NoMatchBehavior="RedirectRowsToNoMatchOutput">
                            <InputPath OutputPathName="OLEDBSrc Channel.Output" />
                            <Parameters>
                                <Parameter SourceColumn="Label" />
                            </Parameters>
                            <Inputs>
                                <Column SourceColumn="Label" TargetColumn="ChannelLabel" />
                            </Inputs>
                            <DirectInput>
                                Select [ChannelLabel] From [dbo].[DimChannel]
                            </DirectInput>
                            <ParameterizedQuery>select * from (Select [ChannelLabel] From [dbo].[DimChannel]) [refTable]
                                where [refTable].[ChannelLabel] = ?
                            </ParameterizedQuery>
                        </Lookup>
                        <DerivedColumns Name="DER ETL Instrumentation">
                            <InputPath OutputPathName="LkUp Correlate.NoMatch" />
                            <Columns>
                                <Column Name="ETLLoadID" DataType="Int32">(DT_I4)@[System::ServerExecutionID]</Column>
                                <Column Name="LoadDate" DataType="Date">@[System::StartTime]</Column>
                            </Columns>
                        </DerivedColumns>
                    </Transformations>
                </Dataflow>
            </Tasks>
        </Package>
    </Packages>
</Biml>
```

Figure 6-37. *Previewing CreatePackages.biml Biml with a derived columns transformation*

Adding an Ole DB Destination Adapter

Next, let's next add an OLE DB destination adapter to the CreatePackages.biml file in BimlStudio. Your Biml and BimlScript now appears as shown in Listing 6-23 (highlighted new syntax).

Listing 6-23. Adding an Ole DB Destination

```
<#@ template tier="20"#>
<Biml xmlns="http://schemas.varigence.com/biml.xsd">
  <Packages>
    <#
    var sourceConnection = "ContosoSource";
    var targetConnection = "ContosoTarget";
    foreach(var tgtTable in RootNode.Tables.Where(t => t.Connection.Name ==
    targetConnection)) {
      var sourceTable = tgtTable.GetTag("MappedTableName");
      var srcTable = RootNode.Tables[sourceTable];
      var keyCols = srcTable.Columns.Where(c => c.GetTag("IsBusinessKey").
      ToLower() == "true");
      var mappedKeyColNames = keyCols.Select(c =>
      c.GetTag("MappedColumnName"));
      var lkupSelect = "Select [" + string.Join("],[", mappedKeyColNames) +
      "] From " + tgtTable.SchemaQualifiedName;
      var lkupWhere = string.Join("] = ?\nAnd [refTable].[",
      mappedKeyColNames);
        #>
    <Package Name="Load <#=tgtTable.Name#>" ProtectionLevel="EncryptSensitive
    WithUserKey">
      <Tasks>
        <Dataflow Name="DFT Load <#=tgtTable.Name#>">
          <Transformations>
            <OleDbSource Name="OLEDBSrc <#=sourceTable#>"
            ConnectionName="<#=sourceConnection#>">
              <DirectInput><#=srcTable.GetSelectSql()#></DirectInput>
            </OleDbSource>
            <Lookup Name="LkUp Correlate" OleDbConnectionName="<#=target
            Connection#>" NoMatchBehavior="RedirectRowsToNoMatchOutput">
              <Parameters>
                <# foreach(var keyCol in keyCols) { #>
                  <Parameter SourceColumn="<#=keyCol.Name#>" />
                  <# } #>
              </Parameters>
              <Inputs>
```

```
          <# foreach(var keyCol in keyCols) { #>
          <Column SourceColumn="<#=keyCol.Name#>"
          TargetColumn="<#=keyCol.GetTag("MappedColumnName")#>" />
          <# } #>
        </Inputs>
        <DirectInput><#=lkupSelect#></DirectInput>
        <ParameterizedQuery>select * from (<#=lkupSelect#>) [refTable]
        where [refTable].[<#=lkupWhere#>] = ?</ParameterizedQuery>
      </Lookup>
      <DerivedColumns Name="DER ETL Instrumentation">
        <InputPath OutputPathName="LkUp Correlate.NoMatch" />
        <Columns>
          <Column Name="ETLLoadID" DataType="Int32">(DT_I4)@
          [System::ServerExecutionID]</Column>
          <Column Name="LoadDate" DataType="Date">@
          [System::StartTime]</Column>
        </Columns>
      </DerivedColumns>
      <OleDbDestination Name="OLEDBDest <#=tgtTable.Name#>"
      ConnectionName="<#=targetConnection#>">
        <Columns>
          <# foreach(var c in srcTable.Columns) { #>
          <Column SourceColumn="<#=c.Name#>" TargetColumn="<#=c.
          GetTag("MappedColumnName")#>" />
          <# } #>
        </Columns>
        <ExternalTableOutput Table="<#=tgtTable.SchemaQualifiedName#>" />
      </OleDbDestination>
      </Transformations>
    </Dataflow>
   </Tasks>
  </Package>
  <# } #>
 </Packages>
</Biml>
```

In BimlStudio, the Biml and BimlScript now appear as shown in Figure 6-38.

```
1   <#@ template tier="20"#>
2   <Biml xmlns="http://schemas.varigence.com/biml.xsd">
3     <Packages>
4       <#
5       var sourceConnection = "ContosoSource";
6       var targetConnection = "ContosoTarget";
7       foreach(var tgtTable in RootNode.Tables.Where(t => t.Connection.Name == targetConnection)) {
8         var sourceTable = tgtTable.GetTag("MappedTableName");
9         var srcTable = RootNode.Tables[sourceTable];
10        var keyCols = srcTable.Columns.Where(c => c.GetTag("IsBusinessKey").ToLower() == "true");
11        var mappedKeyColNames = keyCols.Select(c => c.GetTag("MappedColumnName"));
12        var lkupSelect = "Select [" + string.Join("],[", mappedKeyColNames) + "] From " + tgtTable.SchemaQualifiedName;
13        var lkupWhere = string.Join("] = ?\nAnd [refTable].[", mappedKeyColNames);
14        #>
15        <Package Name="Load <#=tgtTable.Name#>" ProtectionLevel="EncryptSensitiveWithUserKey">
16          <Tasks>
17            <Dataflow Name="DFT Load <#=tgtTable.Name#>">
18              <Transformations>
19                <OleDbSource Name="OLEDBSrc <#=sourceTable#>" ConnectionName="<#=sourceConnection#>">
20                  <DirectInput><#=srcTable.GetSelectSql()#></DirectInput>
21                </OleDbSource>
22                <Lookup Name="LkUp Correlate" OleDbConnectionName="<#=targetConnection#>" NoMatchBehavior="RedirectRowsToNoMatchOutput">
23                  <Parameters>
24                    <# foreach(var keyCol in keyCols) { #>
25                    <Parameter SourceColumn="<#=keyCol.Name#>" />
26                    <# } #>
27                  </Parameters>
28                  <Inputs>
29                    <# foreach(var keyCol in keyCols) { #>
30                    <Column SourceColumn="<#=keyCol.Name#>" TargetColumn="<#=keyCol.GetTag("MappedColumnName")#>" />
31                    <# } #>
32                  </Inputs>
33                  <DirectInput><#=lkupSelect#></DirectInput>
34                  <ParameterizedQuery>select * from (<#=lkupSelect#>) [refTable] where [refTable].[<#=lkupWhere#> = ?</ParameterizedQuery>
35                </Lookup>
36                <DerivedColumns Name="DER ETL Instrumentation">
37                  <InputPath OutputPathName="LkUp Correlate.NoMatch" />
38                  <Columns>
39                    <Column Name="ETLLoadID" DataType="Int32">(DT_I4)@[System::ServerExecutionID]</Column>
40                    <Column Name="LoadDate" DataType="Date">@[System::StartTime]</Column>
41                  </Columns>
42                </DerivedColumns>
43                <OleDbDestination Name="OLEDBDest <#=tgtTable.Name#>" ConnectionName="<#=targetConnection#>">
44                  <Columns>
45                    <# foreach(var c in srcTable.Columns) { #>
46                    <Column SourceColumn="<#=c.Name#>" TargetColumn="<#=c.GetTag("MappedColumnName")#>" />
47                    <# } #>
48                  </Columns>
49                  <ExternalTableOutput Table="<#=tgtTable.SchemaQualifiedName#>" />
50                </OleDbDestination>
51              </Transformations>
52            </Dataflow>
53          </Tasks>
54        </Package>
55        <# } #>
56      </Packages>
57   </Biml>
```

Figure 6-38. *Viewing CreatePackages.biml with an OLE DB Destination*

The newly-added Biml and BimlScript starts and ends on lines 43 and 50 with OleDbDestination open and close tags. On line 43 you define the Name attribute as "OLEDBDest *<target table name>*" and the ConnectionName attribute is set to targetConnection. The Biml Columns open and close tags are found on lines 44 and 48, respectively. On line 45, you start a foreach loop to enumerate the srcTable.Columns collection. On line 46, you use attributes of the srcTable.Columns collection and Biml annotations to build the individual Biml Column tags for the OLE DB destination adapter. On line 49 you configure the Biml ExternalTableOutput tag, aiming the OLE DB destination at the SchemaQualifiedName property of the target table.

The BimlScript Preview pane in BimlStudio now reflects the latest additions, as shown in Figure 6-39.

```
<Biml xmlns="http://schemas.varigence.com/biml.xsd">
    <Packages>
        <Package Name="Load DimChannel" ProtectionLevel="EncryptSensitiveWithUserKey">
            <Tasks>
                <Dataflow Name="DFT Load DimChannel">
                    <Transformations>
                        <OleDbSource Name="OLEDBSrc Channel" ConnectionName="ContosoSource">
                            <DirectInput>SELECT [Label]
                                ,[Name]
                                ,[Description]
                                ,[LastUpdatedDate]
                                FROM [dbo].[Channel]
                            </DirectInput>
                        </OleDbSource>
                        <Lookup Name="LkUp Correlate" OleDbConnectionName="ContosoTarget" NoMatchBehavior="RedirectRowsToNoMatchOutput">
                            <InputPath OutputPathName="OLEDBSrc Channel.Output" />
                            <Parameters>
                                <Parameter SourceColumn="Label" />
                            </Parameters>
                            <Inputs>
                                <Column SourceColumn="Label" TargetColumn="ChannelLabel" />
                            </Inputs>
                            <DirectInput>
                                Select [ChannelLabel] From [dbo].[DimChannel]
                            </DirectInput>
                            <ParameterizedQuery>select * from (Select [ChannelLabel] From [dbo].[DimChannel]) [refTable]
                                where [refTable].[ChannelLabel] = ?
                            </ParameterizedQuery>
                        </Lookup>
                        <DerivedColumns Name="DER ETL Instrumentation">
                            <InputPath OutputPathName="LkUp Correlate.NoMatch" />
                            <Columns>
                                <Column Name="ETLLoadID" DataType="Int32">(DT_I4)@[System::ServerExecutionID]</Column>
                                <Column Name="LoadDate" DataType="Date">@[System::StartTime]</Column>
                            </Columns>
                        </DerivedColumns>
                        <OleDbDestination Name="OLEDBDest DimChannel" ConnectionName="ContosoTarget">
                            <InputPath OutputPathName="DER ETL Instrumentation.Output" />
                            <Columns>
                                <Column SourceColumn="Label" TargetColumn="ChannelLabel" />
                                <Column SourceColumn="Name" TargetColumn="ChannelName" />
                                <Column SourceColumn="Description" TargetColumn="ChannelDescription" />
                                <Column SourceColumn="LastUpdatedDate" TargetColumn="UpdateDate" />
                            </Columns>
                            <ExternalTableOutput Table="[dbo].[DimChannel]" />
                        </OleDbDestination>
                    </Transformations>
                </Dataflow>
            </Tasks>
        </Package>
    </Packages>
</Biml>
```

Figure 6-39. *Previewing CreatePackages.biml Biml with an OLE DB destination*

Testing the CreatePackages.biml File

You moved to BimlStudio so you could preview the progress of your Biml as you built up the CreatePackages.biml file. Let's copy the contents of the CreatePackages.biml file from BimlStudio and paste them into your BimlExpress solution in SSDT.

Save the Chapter7 project and then multi-select the `CreatePackages.biml` and `LoadBimlRelationalHierarchy.biml` files in Solution Explorer. Right-click the selected files and click Generate SSIS Packages, as shown in Figure 6-40.

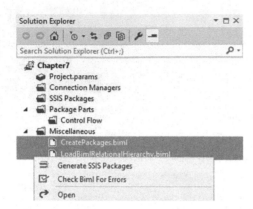

Figure 6-40. *Generating SSIS packages*

If all goes as planned, you should see an SSIS package named `Load DimChannel.dtsx`, as shown in Figure 6-41.

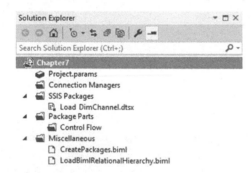

Figure 6-41. *The Load DimChannel.dtsx SSIS package*

If you open the Load DimChannel.dtsx SSIS package, view the data flow task, and execute the SSIS package in the debugger. The package should execute and succeed, as shown in Figure 6-42.

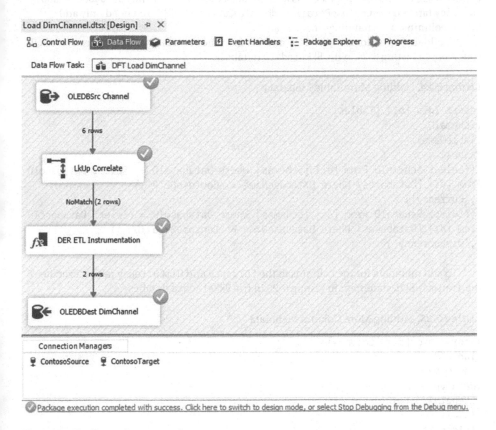

Figure 6-42. *Execution success!*

In this section, you read metadata from the Biml relational hierarchy to build an SSIS package that loads new rows into the ContosoRetailDW.dbo.DimChannel table. In the end, you built a single SSIS package. Only one.

In the next section, you'll see more value in your custom Biml framework solution by adding metadata for a second table.

Load Currency Metadata

In the last section you completed the Biml and BimlScript required to build a single SSIS package... or did you? Actually, you built a Biml framework that builds SSIS packages from any metadata you choose to load into the BRMetadata database. Let's test this assertion.

Just Add Metadata...

If you look at the metadata currently stored in the BRMetadata database, you see connections, databases, and schemas already present for loading the ContosoOLTP.dbo. Currency table to the ContosoRetailDW.dbo.DimCurrency table. You need only add tables, columns, and mappings metadata.

To add metadata for the Currency and DimCurrency tables, execute the Transact-SQL statement in Listing 6-24 in the BRMetadata database.

Listing 6-24. Adding More Table Metadata

```
Insert Into [di].[Tables]
(SchemaID
,TableName)
Values
 ((Select SchemaID From [di].[Schemas] Where DatabaseID = (Select DatabaseID
From [di].[Databases] Where DatabaseName = 'ContosoOLTP'))
 ,'Currency')
,((Select SchemaID From [di].[Schemas] Where DatabaseID = (Select DatabaseID
From [di].[Databases] Where DatabaseName = 'ContosoRetailDW'))
 ,'DimCurrency')
```

To add metadata for the columns in the Currency and DimCurrency tables, execute the Transact-SQL statement in Listing 6-25 in the BRMetadata database.

Listing 6-25. Adding More Column Metadata

```
Insert Into [di].[Columns]
(TableID
,ColumnName
,DataType
,[Length]
,IsNullable
,IsIdentity
)
Values
 ((Select TableID From [di].[Tables] Where TableName = 'Currency')
 ,'CurrencyLabel', 'String', 10, 0, 0)
,((Select TableID From [di].[Tables] Where TableName = 'Currency')
 ,'CurrencyName', 'String', 20, 0, 0)
,((Select TableID From [di].[Tables] Where TableName = 'Currency')
 ,'CurrencyDescription', 'String', 50, 0, 0)
,((Select TableID From [di].[Tables] Where TableName = 'Currency')
 ,'UpdateDate', 'DateTime', 0, 1, 0)
,((Select TableID From [di].[Tables] Where TableName = 'DimCurrency')
 ,'CurrencyLabel', 'String', 100, 0, 0)
,((Select TableID From [di].[Tables] Where TableName = 'DimCurrency')
 ,'CurrencyName', 'String', 20, 0, 0)
```

```
,((Select TableID From [di].[Tables] Where TableName = 'DimCurrency')
 ,'CurrencyDescription', 'String', 50, 0, 0)
,((Select TableID From [di].[Tables] Where TableName = 'DimCurrency')
 ,'UpdateDate', 'DateTime', 0, 1, 0)
```

To add metadata for the column mappings in the Currency and DimCurrency tables, execute the Transact-SQL statement in Listing 6-26 in the BRMetadata database.

Listing 6-26. Adding More Mapping Metadata

```
Insert Into [di].[Mappings]
(SourceColumnID
,TargetColumnID
,IsBusinessKey)
Values
 (9, 13, 1)
,(10, 14, 0)
,(11, 15, 0)
,(12, 16, 0)
```

Once this metadata has been loaded, return to the Chapter7 SSIS project in SSDT.

Regenerate the SSIS packages by multi-selecting the LoadBimlRelationalHierarchy.biml and CreatePackages.biml files, right-clicking the selection, and clicking Generate SSIS Packages.

If all goes as planned, you will see a dialog that warns you the code is attempting to overwrite the Load DimChannel.dtsx package, as shown in Figure 6-43.

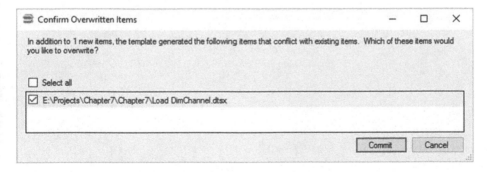

Figure 6-43. *Confirm load DimChannel.dtsx overwrite*

Click the Commit button to overwrite the Load DimChannel.dtsx SSIS package. A second or so later you should see the Load DimCurrency.dtsx SSIS package appear in Solution Explorer, as shown in Figure 6-44.

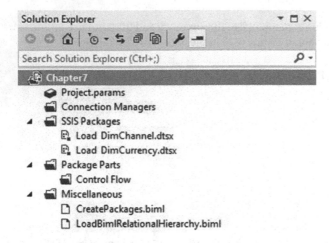

Figure 6-44. The Load DimCurrency.dtsx SSIS package

As before, let's open the Load DimCurrency.dtsx SSIS package and execute it in the SSDT debugger. It should succeed, as shown in Figure 6-45.

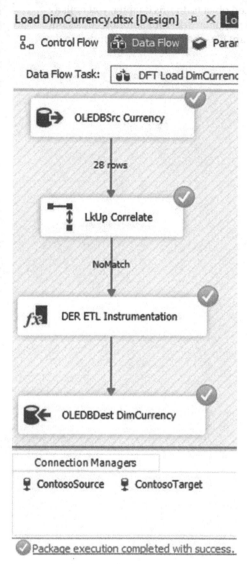

Figure 6-45. Success!

What does this test tell you? You can build SSIS packages using this new-rows-only design pattern by simply supplying connections, databases, schemas, tables, columns, and mappings metadata to the proper tables in the BRMetadata database.

Summary

Biml often uses metadata to source data-related objects. In this chapter, you built a relatively simple custom Biml metadata-driven framework. Your solution consisted of a database containing metadata and two Biml files that read and responded to that metadata.

CHAPTER 7

■ ■ ■

Using Biml as an SSIS Design Patterns Engine

The demo for the previous chapter left you with two SSIS packages: Load DimChannel.dtsx and Load DimCurrency.dtsx. Both packages were generated using the same Biml files: LoadBimlRelationalHierarchy.biml and CreatePackages.biml. It might not have been obvious, but your code was implementing a specific SSIS design pattern using your metadata and BimlScripts. With the same metadata and modified BimlScripts, you could implement totally different patterns with altered semantics, performance characteristics, and much more. After implementing multiple such patterns, you might even want to create a mechanism to select the desired pattern for a given transformation through the metadata itself. In fact, let's go ahead and do that right now.

In this chapter, you will decouple the SSIS design pattern from the earlier demo code, persist the pattern name in the BRMetadata database, map target tables to the pattern in the BRMetadata database, add a design pattern for test purposes, update Biml to retrieve and apply said metadata, and test your results.

Identifying the Design Pattern

LoadBimlRelationalHierarchy.biml contains code that retrieves Biml relational hierarchy values from a database named BRMetadata and uses these values to populate the Biml relational hierarchy. CreatePackages.biml contains Biml that builds the SSIS packages from the metadata contained in the Biml relational hierarchy.

More specifically, CreatePackages.biml contains the *design pattern* for constructing the SSIS packages. The pattern builds a data flow task that

1. Loads all rows from a source table;

2. Performs a lookup against a destination table, outputting new rows only;

3. Adds two ETL Instrumentation columns named ETLLoadID and LoadDate; and

4. Writes new rows to a destination table.

© Andy Leonard et al. 2017
A. Leonard et al., *The Biml Book*, https://doi.org/10.1007/978-1-4842-3135-7_7

Let's call this pattern *Instrumented New Only*. Please note the design pattern is hard-coded into the Biml. It longs to be free. Let's set it free.

Decoupling the Design Pattern

Create a new SSIS project in SSDT. Import the `CreatePackages.biml` and `LoadBimlRelationalHierarchy.biml` files from the project you created while working through Chapter 6.

Open the `CreatePackages.biml` file. For your purposes, you are going to define the *design pattern* portion of the Biml in `CreatePackages.biml` as the portion contained within the Package open and closing tags. These are lines 10-54 in Figure 7-1. In order to create a new architecture where your patterns are isolated so that you can easily choose among them, you need to move these lines of code into a new Biml file. The following sections will walk you through the process of refactoring your code do so.

```
1  <#@ template tier="20"#>
2  <Biml xmlns="http://schemas.varigence.com/biml.xsd">
3    <Packages>
4      <#
5      var sourceConnection = "ContosoSource";
6      var targetConnection = "ContosoTarget";
7      foreach(var tgtTable in RootNode.Tables.Where(t => t.Connection.Name == targetConnection)) {
8        var sourceTable = tgtTable.GetTag("MappedTableName");
9        var srcTable = RootNode.Tables[sourceTable];
10       var keyCols = srcTable.Columns.Where(c => c.GetTag("IsBusinessKey").ToLower() == "true");
11       var mappedKeyColNames = keyCols.Select(c => c.GetTag("MappedColumnName"));
12       var lkupSelect = "Select [" + string.Join("],[", mappedKeyColNames) + "] From " + tgtTable.SchemaQualifiedName;
13       var lkupWhere = string.Join("] = ?\nAnd [refTable].[", mappedKeyColNames);
14       #>
15     <Package Name="Load <#=tgtTable.Name#>" ProtectionLevel="EncryptSensitiveWithUserKey">
16       <Tasks>
17         <Dataflow Name="DFT Load <#=tgtTable.Name#>">
18           <Transformations>
19             <OleDbSource Name="OLEDBSrc <#=sourceTable#>" ConnectionName="<#=sourceConnection#>">
20               <DirectInput><#=srcTable.GetSelectSql()#></DirectInput>
21             </OleDbSource>
22             <Lookup Name="LkUp Correlate" OleDbConnectionName="<#=targetConnection#>" NoMatchBehavior="RedirectRowsToNoMatchOutput">
23               <Parameters>
24                 <# foreach(var keyCol in keyCols) { #>
25                 <Parameter SourceColumn="<#=keyCol.Name#>" />
26                 <# } #>
27               </Parameters>
28               <Inputs>
29                 <# foreach(var keyCol in keyCols) { #>
30                 <Column SourceColumn="<#=keyCol.Name#>" TargetColumn="<#=keyCol.GetTag("MappedColumnName")#>" />
31                 <# } #>
32               </Inputs>
33               <DirectInput><#=lkupSelect#></DirectInput>
34               <ParameterizedQuery>select * from (<#=lkupSelect#>) [refTable] where [refTable].[<#=lkupWhere#> = ?</ParameterizedQuery>
35             </Lookup>
36           </Transformations>
37         </Dataflow>
38       </Tasks>
39     </Package>
40     <# } #>
41   </Packages>
42  </Biml>
```

Figure 7-1. The CreatePackages.biml file

■ **Note**   For more information on SSIS design patterns please see the book *SQL Server Integration Services Design Patterns* (`https://smile.amazon.com/Server-Integration-Services-Design-Patterns/dp/1484200837`).

Select these lines of BimlScript code, and then cut them into the clipboard. Create a new Biml file named `InstrumentedNewOnly.biml` and paste the contents of the clipboard into this file, overwriting the opening and closing Biml tags. `CreatePackages.biml` will now appear as shown in Figure 7-2.

```
1   <#@ template tier="20"#>
2 ▾ <Biml xmlns="http://schemas.varigence.com/biml.xsd">
3 ▾   <Packages>
4       <#
5       var sourceConnection = "ContosoSource";
6       var targetConnection = "ContosoTarget";
7       foreach(var tgtTable in RootNode.Tables.Where(t => t.Connection.Name == targetConnection)) {
8         var sourceTable = tgtTable.GetTag("MappedTableName");
9         var srcTable = RootNode.Tables[sourceTable];
10      #>
11      <# } #>
12    </Packages>
13  </Biml>
```

Figure 7-2. CreatePackages.biml after the cut

The new `InstrumentedNewOnly.biml` file appears as shown in Figure 7-3.

```
1   <#
2       var keyCols = srcTable.Columns.Where(c => c.GetTag("IsBusinessKey").ToLower() == "true");
3       var mappedKeyColNames = keyCols.Select(c => c.GetTag("MappedColumnName"));
4       var lkupSelect = "Select [" + string.Join("],[", mappedKeyColNames) + "] From " + tgtTable.SchemaQualifiedName;
5       var lkupWhere = string.Join("] = ?\nAnd [refTable].[", mappedKeyColNames);
6   #>
7 ▾ <Package Name="Load <#=tgtTable.Name#>" ProtectionLevel="EncryptSensitiveWithUserKey">
8 ▾   <Tasks>
9 ▾     <Dataflow Name="DFT Load <#=tgtTable.Name#>">
10 ▾      <Transformations>
11 ▾        <OleDbSource Name="OLEDBSrc <#=sourceTable#>" ConnectionName="<#=sourceConnection#>">
12             <DirectInput><#=srcTable.GetSelectSql()#></DirectInput>
13           </OleDbSource>
14 ▾        <Lookup Name="LkUp Correlate" OleDbConnectionName="<#=targetConnection#>" NoMatchBehavior="RedirectRowsToNoMatchOutput">
15 ▾          <Parameters>
16             <# foreach(var keyCol in keyCols) { #>
17             <Parameter SourceColumn="<#=keyCol.Name#>" />
18             <# } #>
19           </Parameters>
20 ▾         <Inputs>
21             <# foreach(var keyCol in keyCols) { #>
22             <Column SourceColumn="<#=keyCol.Name#>" TargetColumn="<#=keyCol.GetTag("MappedColumnName")#>" />
23             <# } #>
24           </Inputs>
25           <DirectInput><#=lkupSelect#></DirectInput>
26           <ParameterizedQuery>select * from (<#=lkupSelect#>) [refTable] where [refTable].[<#=lkupWhere#> = ?</ParameterizedQuery>
27         </Lookup>
28 ▾       <DerivedColumns Name="DER ETL Instrumentation">
29           <InputPath OutputPathName="LkUp Correlate.NoMatch" />
30 ▾         <Columns>
31             <Column Name="ETLLoadID" DataType="Int32">(DT_I4)@[System::ServerExecutionID]</Column>
32             <Column Name="LoadDate" DataType="Date">@[System::StartTime]</Column>
33           </Columns>
34         </DerivedColumns>
35 ▾       <OleDbDestination Name="OLEDBDest <#=tgtTable.Name#>" ConnectionName="<#=targetConnection#>">
36 ▾         <Columns>
37             <# foreach(var c in srcTable.Columns) { #>
38             <Column SourceColumn="<#=c.Name#>" TargetColumn="<#=c.GetTag("MappedColumnName")#>" />
39             <# } #>
40           </Columns>
41           <ExternalTableOutput Table="<#=tgtTable.SchemaQualifiedName#>" />
42         </OleDbDestination>
43       </Transformations>
44     </Dataflow>
45   </Tasks>
46 </Package>
```

Figure 7-3. The InstrumentedNewOnly.biml file

Since the contents of the InstrumentedNewOnly.biml file were cut from the CreatePackages.biml file, some variable declarations are no longer in scope. The BimlExpress Preview pane shows these errors in InstrumentedNewOnly.biml; they are displayed in Figure 7-4.

```
1  The property 'tgtTable' was not supplied by the caller.
```

Figure 7-4. Errors in InstrumentedNewOnly.biml

To solve this problem, you need to pass these variables from the parent Biml file into your new pattern Biml file. You already know how to do so using CallBimlScript and property directives. Let's go ahead and edit InstrumentedNewOnly.biml for use as a CallBimlScript target.

To ensure that your code editor feature continues to work, begin by adding a template directive to the InstrumentedNewOnly.biml file with the designerbimlpath attribute set to Biml/Packages. Next, add properties for the variables that were declared in CreatePackages.biml but are not declared in InstrumentedNewOnly.biml. The beginning of InstrumentedNewOnly.biml should now read as shown in Listing 7-1, with the added syntax highlighted.

Listing 7-1. Starting the CreatePackages.biml File

```
<#@ template designerbimlpath="Biml/Packages" #>
<#@ property name="sourceConnection" type="String" #>
<#@ property name="targetConnection" type="String" #>
<#@ property name="sourceTable" type="String" #>
<#@ property name="srcTable" type="AstTableNode" #>
<#@ property name="tgtTable" type="AstTableNode" #>
<Package Name="Load <#=tgtTable.Name#>" ProtectionLevel="EncryptSensitive
WithUserKey">
  <Tasks>
```

The error "The property 'tgtTable' was not supplied by the caller" indicates that you have not passed a value to the tgtTable property. How can you? You aren't technically *calling* the InstrumentedNewOnly.biml file at this time; you are merely previewing the code execution. This is a normal and expected error when viewing CallBimlScript targets in the Preview pane.

Next, you will modify the parent package to call your new pattern Biml file. Edit the CreatePackages.biml file to call the InstrumentedNewOnly.biml file by adding the highlighted code in Listing 7-2.

Listing 7-2. Adding Call to InstrumentedNewOnly.biml Pattern Biml

```
<#@ template tier="20"#>
<Biml xmlns="http://schemas.varigence.com/biml.xsd">
  <Packages>
    <#
    var sourceConnection = "ContosoSource";
    var targetConnection = "ContosoTarget";
    foreach(var tgtTable in RootNode.Tables.Where(t => t.Connection.Name ==
    targetConnection)) {
      var sourceTable = tgtTable.GetTag("MappedTableName");
      var srcTable = RootNode.Tables[sourceTable];
    #>
    <#=CallBimlScript("InstrumentedNewOnly.biml", sourceConnection,
    targetConnection, sourceTable, srcTable, tgtTable)#>
    <# } #>
  </Packages>
</Biml>
```

You add a call to the `CallBimlScript` method, passing for the first argument the name of the Biml file you desire to call (`InstrumentedNewOnly.biml`) followed by values for each of the property directives you added to `InstrumentedNewOnly.biml`.

■ **Tip**   Please see Chapter 5 to learn more about the `CallBimlScript` method.

In Solution Explorer, multi-select the `CreatePackages.biml` and `LoadBimlRelationalHierarchy.biml` files. Right-click and click Generate SSIS Packages, as shown in Figure 7-5.

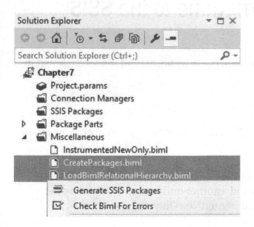

Figure 7-5. *Generating the SSIS packages*

When the Biml expands, you see two SSIS packages generated from metadata, Load DimChannel.dtsx and Load DimCurrency.dtsx, as show in Figure 7-6.

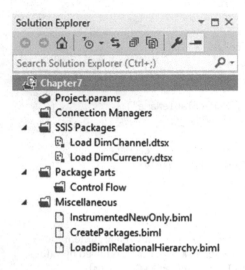

Figure 7-6. *Generated SSIS packages*

At this point, you are generating the same output as in the previous chapter, and you have done so after decoupling your pattern from the CreatePackages.biml file. Success! Let's proceed by editing the names of the SSIS packages to include the name of the design pattern and adding design pattern metadata to your BRMetadata database.

Adding the Design Pattern Name to the SSIS Package Name

Edit the InstrumentedNewOnly.biml file's Package opening tag to read the code shown in Listing 7-3.

Listing 7-3. Building InstrumentedNewOnly.biml File Package Node

```
<Package Name="Load_<#=tgtTable.Name#>_InstrumentedNewOnly" ProtectionLevel=
"EncryptSensitiveWithUserKey">
```

You add an underscore between the word "Load" and the name of the target table contained in the tgtTable variable. You also add another underscore followed by the hard-coded name of the design pattern: InstrumentedNewOnly.

When you regenerate the SSIS packages you will see the updated SSIS package names as shown in Figure 7-7.

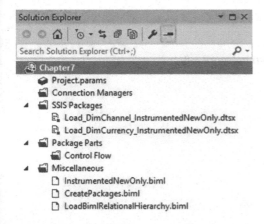

Figure 7-7. Viewing renamed SSIS packages

Adding the Design Pattern Name to the Metadata Database

You need to add two tables to properly store design pattern information in your metadata database named BRMetadata. If you're going to adhere to a normal form, you need one table to hold the list of available design patterns and another table to contain a "mapping" of design pattern to the destination tables described in your metadata database.

Let's first build the design pattern table using the Transact-SQL shown in Listing 7-4.

Listing 7-4. Creating Di.Patterns Table

```
Use BRMetadata
go

Create Table [di].[Patterns]
(PatternID int identity(1,1) Not NULL
,PatternName varchar(255) Not NULL)
```

This Transact-SQL statement creates a table named [di].[Patterns] in the BRMetadata database. Let's populate it with the name of your pattern, InstrumentedNewOnly, using the Transact-SQL statement shown in Listing 7-5.

Listing 7-5. Populating Di.Patterns Table

```
Insert Into [di].[Patterns]
(PatternName)
Values('InstrumentedNewOnly')
```

Before moving forward let's query the [di].[Tables] table using the following Transact-SQL statement:

```
Select *
From [di].[Tables]
```

You'll see results similar to those shown in Figure 7-8.

TableID	SchemaID	TableName
1	1	Channel
2	2	DimChannel
3	1	Currency
4	2	DimCurrency

Figure 7-8. *Viewing the data in the Tables table*

Let's next build and populate a table to hold a "mapping" of tables and patterns using the Transact-SQL statements (or similar, depending on the TableID values returned from your query) in Listing 7-6.

Listing 7-6. Creating Di.TablePatterns Table

```
Create Table [di].[TablePatterns]
(TablePatternID int identity(1,1) Not NULL
,TableID int Not NULL
,PatternID int Not NULL)

Insert Into [di].[TablePatterns]
(TableID, PatternID)
Values
 (2, 1)
,(4, 1)
```

Note that you are only assigning design patterns to destination tables (DimChannel and DimCurrency).

The additions and updates to the BRMetadata database persist the names of available design patterns in the [di].[Patterns] table and map design patterns to tables in the [di].[TablePatterns] table. Let's next update the Biml project to consume this metadata.

Using the Design Pattern Tables

Please recall from the previous chapter that your approach to a metadata-driven Biml solution is to load metadata from the BRMetadata database into the Biml relational hierarchy using the Biml file named LoadBimlRelationalHierarchy.biml, then use the metadata loaded into the Biml relational hierarchy to construct SSIS packages.

You will modify the LoadBimlRelationalHierarchy.biml file to retrieve the name of your pattern. It makes the most sense to modify the query for table metadata, which begins on line 67 as shown in Figure 7-9.

```
28    <!-- Tables -->
29    <# var tableQuery = @"
30    Select distinct mm.SourceDatabaseName + '.' + mm.SourceSchemaName As SourceQualifiedSchemaName
31      , mm.SourceSchemaName, mm.SourceTableName, mm.SourceTableID, mm.SourceTableName
32      , mm.TargetDatabaseName + '.' + mm.TargetSchemaName As TargetQualifiedSchemaName
33      , mm.TargetSchemaName, mm.TargetTableName, mm.TargetTableID
34    From [di].[metadataMappings] As mm;";
```

Figure 7-9. Viewing the current table's BimlScript of LoadBimlRelationalHierarchy.biml

Beginning with the Tables BimlScript that starts at line 28, you modify the BimlScript as shown in Listing 7-7 (new and updated BimlScript is highlighted).

Listing 7-7. Editing Tables BimlScript

```
<!-- Tables -->
<#
var sqlTbl = @"
Select distinct mm.SourceDatabaseName + '.' + mm.SourceSchemaName As
SourceQualifiedSchemaName
, mm.SourceSchemaName, mm.SourceTableName, mm.SourceTableID, mm.SourceTableName
, mm.TargetDatabaseName + '.' + mm.TargetSchemaName As TargetQualifiedSchemaName
, mm.TargetSchemaName, mm.TargetTableName, mm.TargetTableID
, mm.TargetSchemaName, mm.TargetTableName, mm.TargetTableID
, p.PatternName
From [di].[metadataMappings] As mm
Join [di].[TablePatterns] tp On tp.TableID = mm.TargetTableID
Join [di].[Patterns] p On p.PatternID = tp.PatternID;";

var sqlCol = @"
Select mm.SourceTableID, mm.SourceColumnName
, sc.DataType As SourceDataType, sc.[Length] As SourceLength
, sc.IsNullable As SourceIsNullable, mm.TargetTableID, mm.TargetTableName
, mm.TargetColumnName, tc.DataType As TargetDataType
, tc.[Length] As TargetLength, tc.IsNullable As TargetIsNullable
, mm.IsBusinessKey
From [di].[metadataMappings] As mm
Join [di].[Columns] sc
  On sc.ColumnID = mm.SourceColumnID
Join [di].[Columns] tc
  On tc.ColumnID = mm.TargetColumnID";

var tblDataTable = ExternalDataAccess.GetDataTable(connectionString, sqlTbl);
var colDataTable = ExternalDataAccess.GetDataTable(connectionString, sqlCol);
#>
```

```
<Tables>
  <# foreach(DataRow row in tblDataTable.Rows) { #>
  <Table Name="<#=row["SourceTableName"]#>" SchemaName="<#=row["Source
  QualifiedSchemaName"]#>">
    <Columns>
      <# foreach(var scr in colDataTable.Rows.OfType<DataRow>().Where(r => r
      ["SourceTableID"].ToString() == row["SourceTableID"].ToString())) { #>
      <Column Name="<#=scr["SourceColumnName"]#>" DataType="<#=scr["Source
      DataType"]#>" Length="<#=scr["SourceLength"]#> IsNullable="<#=scr["Source
      IsNullable"]#>">
        <Annotations>
          <Annotation AnnotationType="Tag" Tag="IsBusinessKey">
          <#=scr["IsBusinessKey"]#></Annotation>
          <Annotation AnnotationType="Tag" Tag="MappedColumnName">
          <#=scr["TargetColumnName"]#></Annotation>
        </Annotations>
      </Column>
      <# } #>
    </Columns>
    <Annotations>
      <Annotation AnnotationType="Tag" Tag="MappedTableID">
      <#=row["TargetTableID"]#></Annotation>
      <Annotation AnnotationType="Tag" Tag="MappedTableName">
      <#=row["TargetTableName"]#></Annotation>
    </Annotations>
  </Table>
  <Table Name="<#=row["TargetTableName"]#>" SchemaName="<#=row["TargetQualified
  SchemaName"]#>">
    <Columns>
      <# foreach(var tcr in colDataTable.Rows.OfType<DataRow>().Where(r =>
      r["TargetTableID"].ToString() == row["TargetTableID"].ToString())) { #>
      <Column Name="<#=tcr["TargetColumnName"]#>" DataType="<#=tcr["Target
      DataType"]#>" Length="<#=tcr["TargetLength"]#> IsNullable="
      <#=tcr["TargetIsNullable"]#>">
        <Annotations>
          <Annotation AnnotationType="Tag" Tag="IsBusinessKey">
          <#=tcr["IsBusinessKey"]#></Annotation>
          <Annotation AnnotationType="Tag" Tag="MappedColumnName">
          <#=tcr["SourceColumnName"]#></Annotation>
        </Annotations>
      </Column>
      <# } #>
    </Columns>
    <Annotations>
      <Annotation AnnotationType="Tag" Tag="MappedTableID"><#=row["Source
      TableID"]#></Annotation>
      <Annotation AnnotationType="Tag" Tag="MappedTableName"><#=row["Source
      TableName"]#></Annotation>
```

```
      <Annotation AnnotationType="Tag" Tag="PatternName">
      <#=row["PatternName"]#></Annotation>
    </Annotations>
  </Table>
  <# } #>
</Tables>
```

The Tables and Columns BimlScript snippet should now appear as shown in Figure 7-10.

```
28    <!-- Tables -->
29    <# var tableQuery = @"
30    Select distinct mm.SourceDatabaseName + '.' + mm.SourceSchemaName As SourceQualifiedSchemaName
31        , mm.SourceSchemaName, mm.SourceTableName, mm.SourceTableID, mm.SourceTableName
32        , mm.TargetDatabaseName + '.' + mm.TargetSchemaName As TargetQualifiedSchemaName
33        , mm.TargetSchemaName, mm.TargetTableName, mm.TargetTableID
34        , p.PatternName
35    From [di].[metadataMappings] As mm
36    Join [di].[TablePatterns] tp On tp.TableID = mm.TargetTableID
37    Join [di].[Patterns] p On p.PatternID = tp.PatternID;";
38
39    var columnsQuery = @"
40    Select mm.SourceTableID, mm.SourceColumnName
41        , sc.DataType As SourceDataType, sc.[Length] As SourceLength
42        , sc.IsNullable As SourceIsNullable, mm.TargetTableID, mm.TargetTableName
43        , mm.TargetColumnName, tc.DataType As TargetDataType
44        , tc.[Length] As TargetLength, tc.IsNullable As TargetIsNullable
45        , mm.IsBusinessKey
46    From [di].[metadataMappings] As mm
47    Join [di].[Columns] sc
48      On sc.ColumnID = mm.SourceColumnID
49    Join [di].[Columns] tc
50      On tc.ColumnID = mm.TargetColumnID ";
51
52      dataTable = ExternalDataAccess.GetDataTable(connectionString, tableQuery);
53      var colTable = ExternalDataAccess.GetDataTable(connectionString, columnsQuery);#>
54 -      <Tables>
55          <# foreach(DataRow row in dataTable.Rows) { #>
56          <# var sourceTableId = row["SourceTableID"].ToString(); #>
57          <# var targetTableId = row["TargetTableID"].ToString(); #>
58 -        <Table Name="<#=row["SourceTableName"]#>" SchemaName="<#=row["SourceQualifiedSchemaName"]#>">
59 -          <Columns>
60            <# foreach(var scr in colTable.Rows.OfType<DataRow>().Where(r => r["SourceTableID"].ToString()==sourceTableId)) { #>
61 -            <Column Name="<#=scr["SourceColumnName"]#>"
62                    DataType="<#=scr["SourceDataType"]#>"
63                    Length="<#=scr["SourceLength"]#>"
64                    IsNullable="<#=scr["SourceIsNullable"]#>">
65 -              <Annotations>
66                <Annotation Tag="IsBusinessKey"><#=scr["IsBusinessKey"]#></Annotation>
67                <Annotation Tag="MappedColumnName"><#=scr["TargetColumnName"]#></Annotation>
68              </Annotations>
69            </Column>
70            <# } #>
71          </Columns>
72 -        <Annotations>
73            <Annotation Tag="MappedTableID"><#=targetTableId#></Annotation>
74            <Annotation Tag="MappedTableName"><#=row["TargetTableName"]#></Annotation>
75          </Annotations>
76        </Table>
77 -      <Table Name="<#=row["TargetTableName"]#>" SchemaName="<#=row["TargetQualifiedSchemaName"]#>">
78 -        <Columns>
79          <# foreach(var scr in colTable.Rows.OfType<DataRow>().Where(r => r["TargetTableID"].ToString()==targetTableId)) { #>
80 -          <Column Name="<#=scr["TargetColumnName"]#>"
81                  DataType="<#=scr["TargetDataType"]#>"
82                  Length="<#=scr["TargetLength"]#>"
83                  IsNullable="<#=scr["TargetIsNullable"]#>">
84 -            <Annotations>
85              <Annotation Tag="IsBusinessKey"><#=scr["IsBusinessKey"]#></Annotation>
86              <Annotation Tag="MappedColumnName"><#=scr["SourceColumnName"]#></Annotation>
87            </Annotations>
88          </Column>
89          <# } #>
90        </Columns>
91 -      <Annotations>
92          <Annotation Tag="MappedTableID"><#=sourceTableId#></Annotation>
93          <Annotation Tag="MappedTableName"><#=row["SourceTableName"]#></Annotation>
94          <Annotation AnnotationType="Tag" Tag="PatternName"><#=row["PatternName"]#></Annotation>
95        </Annotations>
96      </Table>
97      <# } #>
98    </Tables>
99  </Biml>
```

Figure 7-10. *Updated LoadBimlRelationalHierarchy.biml BimlScript*

When the Biml is updated in the Preview pane, it appears as shown in Figure 7-11.

```xml
<Table Name="DimChannel" SchemaName="ContosoRetailDW.dbo">
  <Columns>
    <Column Name="ChannelLabel"
                DataType="String"
                Length="100"
                IsNullable="false">
      <Annotations>
        <Annotation Tag="IsBusinessKey">true</Annotation>
        <Annotation Tag="MappedColumnName">Label</Annotation>
      </Annotations>
    </Column>
    <Column Name="ChannelName"
                DataType="String"
                Length="20"
                IsNullable="true">
      <Annotations>
        <Annotation Tag="IsBusinessKey">false</Annotation>
        <Annotation Tag="MappedColumnName">Name</Annotation>
      </Annotations>
    </Column>
    <Column Name="ChannelDescription"
                DataType="String"
                Length="50"
                IsNullable="true">
      <Annotations>
        <Annotation Tag="IsBusinessKey">false</Annotation>
        <Annotation Tag="MappedColumnName">Description</Annotation>
      </Annotations>
    </Column>
    <Column Name="UpdateDate"
                DataType="DateTime"
                Length="0"
                IsNullable="true">
      <Annotations>
        <Annotation Tag="IsBusinessKey">false</Annotation>
        <Annotation Tag="MappedColumnName">LastUpdatedDate</Annotation>
      </Annotations>
    </Column>
  </Columns>
  <Annotations>
    <Annotation Tag="MappedTableID">1</Annotation>
    <Annotation Tag="MappedTableName">Channel</Annotation>
    <Annotation AnnotationType="Tag" Tag="PatternName">InstrumentedNewOnly</Annotation>
  </Annotations>
</Table>
```

Figure 7-11. *Viewing the Biml for the DimChannel target table*

As you can see toward the bottom of the code excerpt shown in Figure 7-11, the name of the design pattern is stored in a Biml annotation for the target table.

Let's next update the CreatePackages.biml file to read and use this value as your design pattern value by making the highlighted changes to the BimlScript shown in Listing 7-8.

Listing 7-8. Using CallBimlScript to Call the Pattern BimlScript File

```
<#@ template tier="20"#>
<Biml xmlns="http://schemas.varigence.com/biml.xsd">
  <Packages>
    <#
    var sourceConnection = "ContosoSource";
    var targetConnection = "ContosoTarget";
    foreach(var tgtTable in RootNode.Tables.Where(t => t.Connection.Name ==
    targetConnection)) {
      var sourceTable = tgtTable.GetTag("MappedTableName");
      var srcTable = RootNode.Tables[sourceTable];
      var patternName = tgtTable.GetTag("PatternName");
    #>
    <#=CallBimlScript(patternName + ".biml", sourceConnection,
    targetConnection, sourceTable, srcTable, tgtTable)#>
    <# } #>
  </Packages>
</Biml>
```

With a relatively small code change, you've introduced an almost incredible level of flexibility. Through metadata stored in your BRMetadata database, you can now specify the pattern you want to use to load each destination table. Furthermore, while you presently have implemented just the one pattern from the previous chapter, you can now arbitrarily add many new patterns to accommodate whatever novel data integration scenarios you might encounter.

Let's verify that in making this powerful change, you haven't broken anything. The Preview pane in BimlExpress is truly awesome but you cannot preview Biml generated by multiple files in BimlExpress unless you have all Biml files open and updated. If you have access to a copy of BimlStudio, however, and execute LoadBimlRelationalHierarchy.biml prior to opening CreatePackages.biml in Logical View, the BimlStudio Preview pane will display the Biml. The Biml for the Load_DimCurrency_InstrumentedNewOnly SSIS package appears as shown in Figure 7-12.

```
<Package Name="Load_DimCurrency_InstrumentedNewOnly" ProtectionLevel="EncryptSensitiveWithUserKey">
  <Tasks>
    <DataFlow Name="DFT Load DimCurrency">
      <Transformations>
        <OleDbSource Name="OLEDBSrc Currency" ConnectionName="ContosoSource">
          <DirectInput>SELECT [CurrencyLabel]
,[CurrencyName]
,[CurrencyDescription]
,[UpdateDate]
FROM [dbo].[Currency]
</DirectInput>
        </OleDbSource>
        <Lookup Name="LkUp Correlate" OleDbConnectionName="ContosoTarget" NoMatchBehavior="RedirectRowsToNoMatchOutput">
          <Parameters>
            <Parameter SourceColumn="CurrencyLabel" />
          </Parameters>
          <Inputs>
            <Column SourceColumn="CurrencyLabel" TargetColumn="CurrencyLabel" />
          </Inputs>
          <DirectInput>Select [CurrencyLabel] From [dbo].[DimCurrency]</DirectInput>
          <ParameterizedQuery>select * from (Select [CurrencyLabel] From [dbo].[DimCurrency]) [refTable] where [refTable].[CurrencyLabel] = ?</ParameterizedQuery>
        </Lookup>
        <DerivedColumns Name="DER ETL Instrumentation">
          <InputPath OutputPathName="LkUp Correlate.NoMatch" />
          <Columns>
            <Column Name="ETLLoadID" DataType="Int32">(DT_I4)@[System::ServerExecutionID]</Column>
            <Column Name="LoadDate" DataType="Date">@[System::StartTime]</Column>
          </Columns>
        </DerivedColumns>
        <OleDbDestination Name="OLEDBDest DimCurrency" ConnectionName="ContosoTarget">
          <Columns>
            <Column SourceColumn="CurrencyLabel" TargetColumn="CurrencyLabel" />
            <Column SourceColumn="CurrencyName" TargetColumn="CurrencyName" />
            <Column SourceColumn="CurrencyDescription" TargetColumn="CurrencyDescription" />
            <Column SourceColumn="UpdateDate" TargetColumn="UpdateDate" />
          </Columns>
          <ExternalTableOutput Table="[dbo].[DimCurrency]" />
        </OleDbDestination>
      </Transformations>
    </DataFlow>
  </Tasks>
</Package>
```

Figure 7-12. *Viewing Load_DimCurrency_InstrumentedNewOnly SSIS package Biml*

Perfect! It looks exactly as it did when the pattern was hardcoded. Now you'll verify that your new architecture still works when you have multiple options available for your choice of pattern.

Testing Metadata-Driven Design Pattern Selection

Before you can fully test your new metadata-driven design pattern functionality, you need to add a new design pattern. Rather than walk you through building another pattern Biml file, we're just going to provide you with a new pattern that manages new rows and updates to existing rows. Rather than use an SSIS OLE DB Command transformation to manage the updates, which is the equivalent of an "SSIS cursor," you will implement a set-based update solution. The Biml and BimlScript shown here is complex. For many data integration scenarios, this pattern is Production-ready code.

Adding the IncrementalLoad Pattern

Add the Biml and BimlScript shown in Listing 7-9 to a new file in your project called
IncrementalLoad.biml.

Listing 7-9. Building the IncrementalLoad.biml File

```
<#@ template designerbimlpath="Biml\Packages" #>
<#@ property name="sourceConnection" type="String" #>
<#@ property name="targetConnection" type="String" #>
<#@ property name="sourceTable" type="String" #>
<#@ property name="srcTable" type="AstTableNode" #>
<#@ property name="tgtTable" type="AstTableNode" #>
<#
var bkList = srcTable.Columns.Where(c => c.GetTag("IsBusinessKey").ToLower()
== "true");
var nonBkList = srcTable.Columns.Where(c => c.GetTag("IsBusinessKey").
ToLower() != "true");
var bkListMappedNames = bkList.Select(c => c.GetTag("MappedColumnName"));
#>
<Package Name="Load_<#=tgtTable.Name#>_IncrementalLoad" ProtectionLevel=
"EncryptSensitiveWithUserKey" ConstraintMode="Linear">
  <Tasks>
    <ExecuteSQL Name="Manage stage_<#=tgtTable.Name#>" ConnectionName="
    <#=targetConnection#>">
      <DirectInput>
        <#=tgtTable.GetDropAndCreateDdl().Replace(tgtTable.Name,
        "stage_" + tgtTable.Name)#>
      </DirectInput>
    </ExecuteSQL>
    <Dataflow Name="DFT Load <#=sourceTable#> Source" >
      <Transformations>
        <OleDbSource Name="OLEDBSrc <#=sourceTable#>" ConnectionName=
        "<#=sourceConnection#>">
          <DirectInput>Select <#=srcTable.GetColumnList()#> From
          <#=srcTable.SchemaQualifiedName#></DirectInput>
        </OleDbSource>
        <DerivedColumns Name="DER <#=tgtTable.Name#> ETL Instrumentation">
          <Columns>
            <Column Name="ETLLoadID" DataType="Int32">(DT_I4)@
            [System::ServerExecutionID]</Column>
            <Column Name="LoadDate" DataType="Date">@[System::StartTime]
            </Column>
          </Columns>
        </DerivedColumns>
        <Lookup Name="LkUp <#=tgtTable.Name#> Correlate" OleDbConnectionName="
        <#=targetConnection#>" NoMatchBehavior="RedirectRowsToNoMatchOutput">
          <Parameters>
```

213

```
                    <# foreach(var c in srcTable.Columns) { #>
                    <Parameter SourceColumn="<#=c.Name#>" />
                    <# } #>
                </Parameters>
                <Inputs>
                    <# foreach(var kc in bkList) { #>
                    <Column SourceColumn="<#=kc.Name#>" TargetColumn="Dest_<#=kc.
                    Name#>" />
                    <# } #>
                </Inputs>
                <DirectInput>
Select <#=string.Join(",", srcTable.Columns.Select(c => "[" +
c.GetTag("MappedColumnName") + "] As [Dest_" + c.Name + "]"))#>
From <#=tgtTable.SchemaQualifiedName#>
                </DirectInput>
                <Outputs>
                    <# foreach(var c in srcTable.Columns) { #>
                    <Column SourceColumn="Dest_<#=c.Name#>" TargetColumn="Dest_<#=c.
                    Name#>" />
                    <# } #>
                </Outputs>
            </Lookup>
            <OleDbDestination Name="OLEDBDest <#=tgtTable.Name#>" ConnectionName
            ="<#=targetConnection#>">
                <InputPath OutputPathName="LkUp <#=tgtTable.Name#> Correlate.
                NoMatch" />
                <Columns>
                    <# foreach(var c in srcTable.Columns) { #>
                    <Column SourceColumn="<#=c.Name#>" TargetColumn="<#=c.
                    GetTag("MappedColumnName")#>" />
                    <# } #>
                </Columns>
                <ExternalTableOutput Table="<#=tgtTable.SchemaQualifiedName#>" />
            </OleDbDestination>
            <ConditionalSplit Name="Filter <#=tgtTable.Name#>">
                <InputPath OutputPathName="LkUp <#=tgtTable.Name#> Correlate.
                Match" />
                <OutputPaths>
                    <OutputPath Name="Changed Rows">
                        <Expression><#=string.Join(" || ", nonBkList.
                        Select(GetExpression))#></Expression>
                    </OutputPath>
                </OutputPaths>
            </ConditionalSplit>
            <OleDbDestination Name="OLEDBDest stage_<#=tgtTable.Name #>"
            ConnectionName="<#=targetConnection#>">
                <InputPath OutputPathName="Filter <#=tgtTable.Name#>.Changed Rows" />
                <Columns>
```

```
            <# foreach(var c in srcTable.Columns) { #>
            <Column SourceColumn="<#=c.Name#>" TargetColumn="<#=c.
            GetTag("MappedColumnName")#>" />
            <# } #>
          </Columns>
          <ExternalTableOutput Table="dbo.stage_<#=tgtTable.Name #>" />
        </OleDbDestination>
      </Transformations>
    </Dataflow>
    <ExecuteSQL Name="Apply stage_<#=tgtTable.Name #>" ConnectionName=
    "<#=targetConnection#>">
      <DirectInput>
Update Dest Set
<#=tgtTable.GetColumnAssignmentList(c => c.GetTag("IsBusinessKey").ToLower()
!= "true", "Dest", "Upd")#>
From <#=tgtTable.SchemaQualifiedName#> Dest
Join [dbo].[stage_<#=tgtTable.Name#>] Upd On <#=string.Join(" AND ",
bkListMappedNames.Select(c => "Upd." + c + " = Dest." + c)) #>
      </DirectInput>
    </ExecuteSQL>
  </Tasks>
</Package>

<#@ import namespace="System.Data" #>
<#+
private string GetExpression(AstTableColumnBaseNode col) {
  var name = col.Name;
  switch(col.DataType) {
    case DbType.Guid:
      return "((DT_WSTR,55)" + name + " != (DT_WSTR,55)Dest_" + name + ") || ";
    case DbType.String:
      return "((IsNull(" + name + ") ? \"\" : " + name + ") !=
      (IsNull(Dest_" + name + ") ? \"\" : Dest_" + name + "))";
    case DbType.Int64:
    case DbType.Decimal:
    case DbType.Double:
    case DbType.Int32:
    case DbType.Int16:
    case DbType.Currency:
    case DbType.Single:
    case DbType.Time:
      return "(IsNull(" + name + ") ? 0 : " + name + ") != (IsNull(Dest_" +
      name + ") ? 0 : Dest_" + name + ")";
    case DbType.Boolean:
        return "(IsNull(" + name + ") ? False : " + name + ") !=
        (IsNull(Dest_" + name + ") ? False : Dest_" + name + ")";
    case DbType.Date:
```

```
        case DbType.DateTime:
        case DbType.DateTime2:
        case DbType.DateTimeOffset:
                return "(IsNull(" + name + ") ? (DT_DBTimeStamp)\"1/1/1900\" :
                " + name + ") != (IsNull(Dest_" + name + ") ?
                (DT_DBTimeStamp)\"1/1/1900\" : Dest_" + name + ")";
    }

    return "";
}
#>
```

Be sure to save this code as a new file named IncrementalLoad.biml. The Incremental
Load design pattern is more complex than the Instrumented New Only pattern.

Adding Pattern BimlScript to CreatePackages.biml

Let's next update the CreatePackages.biml file so that it responds to the PatternName
annotation now stored with the target table by adding the highlighted BimlScript shown
in Listing 7-10.

Listing 7-10. Editing the CallBimlScript Logic to Call Pattern Biml Files

```
<#@ template tier="20"#>
<Biml xmlns="http://schemas.varigence.com/biml.xsd">
  <Packages>
    <#
    var sourceConnection = "ContosoSource";
    var targetConnection = "ContosoTarget";
    foreach(var tgtTable in RootNode.Tables.Where(t => t.Connection.Name ==
      targetConnection)) {
      var sourceTable = tgtTable.GetTag("MappedTableName");
      var srcTable = RootNode.Tables[sourceTable];
        string patternName = tgtTable.GetTag("PatternName");
        string scriptName = patternName + ".biml";
        string packagesBiml = "";
        switch(patternName) {
                case "InstrumentedNewOnly":
                        packagesBiml = CallBimlScript(scriptName,
                        sourceConnection, targetConnection, sourceTable,
                        srcTable, tgtTable);
                        break;
                case "IncrementalLoad":
                        packagesBiml = CallBimlScript(scriptName,
                        sourceConnection, targetConnection, sourceTable,
                        srcTable, tgtTable);
                        break;
        }
            #><#=packagesBiml#>
```

```
    <# } #>
  </Packages>
</Biml>
```

Your `CreatePackages.biml` file should appear as shown in Figure 7-13.

```
 1   <#@ template tier="20"#>
 2 - <Biml xmlns="http://schemas.varigence.com/biml.xsd">
 3 -   <Packages>
 4       <#
 5       var sourceConnection = "ContosoSource";
 6       var targetConnection = "ContosoTarget";
 7       foreach(var tgtTable in RootNode.Tables.Where(t => t.Connection.Name == targetConnection)) {
 8         var sourceTable = tgtTable.GetTag("MappedTableName");
 9         var srcTable = RootNode.Tables[sourceTable];
10         string patternName = tgtTable.GetTag("PatternName");
11         string scriptName = patternName + ".biml";
12         string packagesBiml = "";
13         switch(patternName) {
14           case "InstrumentedNewOnly":
15               packagesBiml = CallBimlScript(scriptName, sourceConnection, targetConnection, sourceTable, srcTable, tgtTable);
16               break;
17           case "IncrementalLoad":
18               packagesBiml = CallBimlScript(scriptName, sourceConnection, targetConnection, sourceTable, srcTable, tgtTable);
19               break;
20         }
21         #><#=packagesBiml#>
22       <# } #>
23   </Packages>
24   </Biml>
```

Figure 7-13. CreatePackages.biml file after adding patterns selection BimlScript

Updating the Metadata

Let's add IncrementalLoad metadata to your BRMetadata [di].[Patterns] and
[di].[TablePatterns] tables. The Transact-SQL that follows in Listing 7-11 adds
IncrementalLoad to the list of SSIS design patterns in the [di].[Patterns] table, and
then assigns the IncrementalLoad pattern to the DimChannel table loader.

Listing 7-11. Updating the Metadata in the BRMetadata Database

```
Use BRMetadata
go

Select * From [di].[Patterns]

Insert Into [di].[Patterns]
(PatternName)
Values
('IncrementalLoad')

Select * From [di].[Patterns]

Select t.TableName, p.[PatternName]
From [di].[Tables] t
```

217

```
Join [di].[TablePatterns] tp
  On tp.[TableID] = t.[TableID]
Join [di].[Patterns] p
  On p.[PatternID] = tp.[PatternID]

Update tp
Set tp.PatternID = (Select [PatternID]
                      From [di].[Patterns]
                                    Where [PatternName] = 'IncrementalLoad')
From [di].[Tables] t
Join [di].[TablePatterns] tp
  On tp.[TableID] = t.[TableID]
Join [di].[Patterns] p
  On p.[PatternID] = tp.[PatternID]
Where t.TableName = 'DimChannel'

Select t.TableName, p.[PatternName]
From [di].[Tables] t
Join [di].[TablePatterns] tp
  On tp.[TableID] = t.[TableID]
Join [di].[Patterns] p
  On p.[PatternID] = tp.[PatternID]
```

This Transact-SQL includes before and after queries for the [di].[Patterns] and [di].[TablePatterns] tables, as shown in Figure 7-14.

	PatternID	PatternName
1	1	InstrumentedNewOnly

	PatternID	PatternName
1	1	InstrumentedNewOnly
2	2	IncrementalLoad

	TableName	PatternName
1	DimChannel	InstrumentedNewOnly
2	DimCurrency	InstrumentedNewOnly

	TableName	PatternName
1	DimChannel	IncrementalLoad
2	DimCurrency	InstrumentedNewOnly

Figure 7-14. *Before and after queries of the Patterns and TablePatterns tables*

Building the Packages

To test, multi-select `LoadBimlRelationalHierarchy.biml` and `CreatePackages.biml` in Solution Explorer, then right-click and click Generate SSIS Packages, as shown in Figure 7-15.

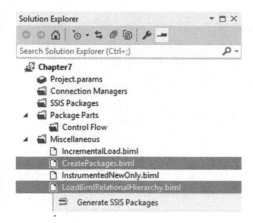

Figure 7-15. *Generating SSIS packages*

When the Biml expands, you see two SSIS packages in Solution Explorer, as shown in Figure 7-16.

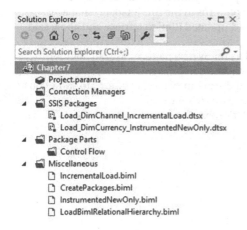

Figure 7-16. *Two new SSIS packages*

Test execute the SSIS packages in SSDT. If all goes as planned, you should see two successful executions, as shown in Figure 7-17.

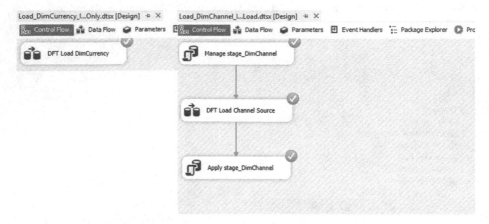

Figure 7-17. *Successful test executions!*

Green circles with white check marks means success!

Summary

In this chapter, you decoupled the SSIS design pattern from an earlier demo, persisted the pattern name and mapped target tables to patterns in the BRMetadata database, added a design pattern (Incremental Load), and updated Biml to retrieve and apply said metadata.

Given this new architecture, you can add as many new patterns as your solution requires, and drive everything through the metadata database you have already configured. In the next chapter, we will dig a bit deeper into design patterns to show you a few options that you might want to add to your pattern library.

Now that you have a flexible framework, let's next orchestrate and manage its execution.

CHAPTER 8

■ ■ ■

Integration with a Custom SSIS Execution Framework

Thus far, you've learned quite a bit about creating "build-time" frameworks with Biml code that govern how your solution is generated and the coding patterns that you enforce. What about frameworks that govern your runtime behaviors such as orchestration and package execution order? The wait is over!

In this chapter, you are going to build a relatively simple solution: a custom metadata-driven SSIS execution framework. We write *relatively* because everyone brings their own experience and comfort level with them to any project. As we wrote in an earlier chapter, some enjoy working with metadata; others type a lot.

■ **Note**   For more information about the SSIS catalog, please see `https://docs.` `microsoft.com/en-us/sql/integration-services/service/ssis-catalog`.

Your solution consists of tables and stored procedures added to the SSIS catalog database (SSISDB). The SSISDB database already contains SSIS package, project, and configuration metadata. You will simply add custom metadata that extends the existing metadata. As with all solutions, this is not the only way to build anything. We're certain there are other ways to provide the same functionality, and we're pretty sure some of those ways are better.

The purpose of this chapter is to discuss and demonstrate one way to integrate with a custom SSIS execution framework.

An SSIS Execution Framework

How does an SSIS execution framework work? You store a minimum amount of metadata about the SSIS applications and SSIS packages in a custom schema you create in the SSISDB database. You then execute stored procedures to execute said SSIS packages in the desired order of execution.

© Andy Leonard et al. 2017
A. Leonard et al., *The Biml Book*, https://doi.org/10.1007/978-1-4842-3135-7_8

Please note it is *not* a best practice to add objects to a third-party database such as SSISDB. I have reasons for adding SSIS Framework Community Edition, though, that are beyond the scope of this book. The demonstration code in this chapter relies on SSIS Framework Community Edition. You do not need SSIS Framework Community Edition to complete the metadata Transact-SQL script creation and execution demos, but you will be unable to execute the SSIS application near the end of the chapter. You may obtain a copy of the free and open-source SSIS Framework Community Edition at https://dilmsuite.com.

Persisting Applications Metadata

Your SSIS execution framework groups SSIS packages into SSIS applications, a construct we invented. The framework begins with a schema added to the SSISDB database, which can be accomplished by executing the Transact-SQL statement shown in Listing 8-1.

Listing 8-1. Creating the Custom Schema

```
Use SSISDB
go

declare @sql varchar(100) = 'Create Schema custom'
exec(@sql)
print ' - Custom schema created'
go
```

This Transact-SQL statement will create a new schema named "custom" in the SSISDB database.

Next, you add some tables to hold application and package metadata. Create a table named Applications in your new custom schema by executing the Transact-SQL statement shown in Listing 8-2.

Listing 8-2. Creating the Custom.Applications Table

```
Create Table custom.Applications
  (ApplicationID int identity(1,1)
  ,ApplicationName nvarchar(130) )
```

Persisting Packages Metadata

Create a table to contain metadata from SSIS packages by executing the Transact-SQL statement shown in Listing 8-3.

Listing 8-3. Creating the Custom.Packages Table

```
Create Table custom.Packages
  (PackageID int identity(1,1)
  ,PackageName nvarchar(130)
  ,ProjectName nvarchar(260)
  ,FolderName nvarchar(260) )
```

Note that the custom.Packages table contains metadata to identify the location of SSIS packages in the SSIS catalog.

Since SSIS applications are made up of SSIS packages, cardinality between the Applications and Packages tables seems at first to be straightforward: one-to-many. One advantage of using an SSIS execution framework is it promotes code (SSIS packages, in this case) reuse. The same SSIS package can be used in multiple SSIS applications. Therefore, the cardinality between the Applications and Packages tables is really *many-to-many.*

Persisting Application Packages Metadata

To resolve the many-to-many cardinality you use a bridge table named ApplicationPackages. Create the ApplicationPackages table by executing the Transact-SQL statement shown in Listing 8-4.

Listing 8-4. Creating the Custom.ApplicationPackages Table

```
Create Table custom.ApplicationPackages
  (ApplicationPackageID int identity(1,1)
  ,ApplicationID int
  ,PackageID int
  ,ExecutionOrder int)
```

The ApplicationPackages *maps* an SSIS package to an SSIS application via the ApplicationID and PackageID columns. The ExecutionOrder column is an attribute of the ApplicationPackage. Why? Consider a common use case for a utility SSIS package, one used to archive a flat file after it has been loaded. The ArchiveFile package may run second in the SSIS application, but it's just as likely to run twenty-second.

These are the fundamental tables used for storing the metadata required to execute SSIS packages in a custom SSIS execution framework. These tables are part of the SSIS Framework Community Edition.

You can read more about the SSIS Framework Community Edition internals in the documentation provided with the download available from https://dilmsuite.com. This chapter is not concerned with the internals of the execution framework; our purpose is to use Biml to populate the metadata tables.

Preparing a Demo SSIS Project

For demonstration purposes let's return to the BimlExpress Contoso example you used in Chapters 6 and 7. You may remember the project. You left it in Chapter 7 with two SSIS packages, Load_DimChannel_IncrementalLoad.dtsx and Load_DimCurrency_ InstrumentedNewOnly.dtsx, as shown in Figure 8-1.

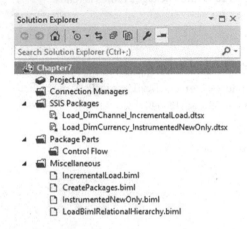

Figure 8-1. *Viewing Solution Explorer for the Chapter7 project*

Before you proceed, let's make a new project named Chapter8. Import the Biml from the Chapter7 project. Multi-select the CreatePackages.biml and LoadBimlRelationalHierarchy.biml files, right-click them, and click Generate SSIS Packages, as shown in Figure 8-2.

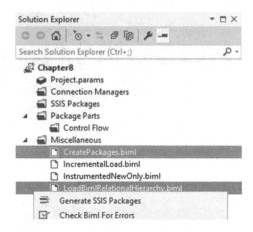

Figure 8-2. *Generating the SSIS packages using Biml*

When the SSIS packages are generated, your Solution Explorer should appear as shown in Figure 8-3.

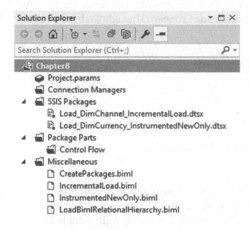

Figure 8-3. *Generated SSIS packages*

The Chapter8 SSIS project is now ready for our demo purposes.

A Biml File to Generate SSIS Framework Metadata

In this section you will add Biml files that will create Transact-SQL to manage SSIS Framework Community Edition metadata.

Add a new Biml file named params.biml to the Chapter8 SSIS project. Replace the Biml in the file with the BimlScript snippet shown in Listing 8-5.

Listing 8-5. Setting the Output File Location

```
<#
var SSISFrameworkMetadataFileName = "E:\\output\\SSISFrameworkMetadata.sql";
#>
```

■ **Note** Please specify a valid path for your SQL file.

Add a new Biml file named FrameworkMetadata.biml to the Chapter8 SSIS project. Add two directives to FrameworkMetadata.biml: a tier, set to 999 to make sure this Biml file is evaluated *after* the other Biml files, and an include directive for an as-yet-not-created Biml file named params.biml. Add two more directives that reference the System. Text and System.IO .Net Framework namespaces. Your FrameworkMetadata.biml should appear as shown in Listing 8-6.

Listing 8-6. Starting the FrameworkMetadata.biml File

```
<#@ template tier="999"#>
<#@ include file="params.biml" #>
<#@ import namespace="System.Text" #>
<#@ import namespace="System.IO" #>
<Biml xmlns="http://schemas.varigence.com/biml.xsd">
</Biml>
```

Let's next add enough BimlScript to test the current design. Declare and initialize a StringBuilder variable named sb. StringBuilder may be new to some readers so let's explain why we use it instead of the more generic string data type. StringBuilder is a bit cleaner for use with strings that include formatting characters, such as "\n" for new line.

Create a foreach loop to iterate the RootNode.Packages collection. Inside the loop, execute the StringBuilder AppendLine method, adding the name of the SSIS package. Use a File object's WriteAllText method to write the StringBuilder contents to the path specified in the SSISFrameworkMetadataFileName variable declared and initialized in the params.biml file. Your BimlScript should appear similar to Listing 8-7 (added code highlighted).

Listing 8-7. Iterating the Packages Collection

```
<#@ template tier="999"#>
<#@ include file="params.biml" #>
<#@ import namespace="System.Text" #>
<#@ import namespace="System.IO" #>
<#
var sb = new StringBuilder();
foreach(var package in RootNode.Packages) {
    sb.AppendLine(package.Name);
}

File.WriteAllText(SSISFrameworkMetadataFileName, sb.ToString());
#>
<Biml xmlns="http://schemas.varigence.com/biml.xsd">
</Biml>
```

Note that the BimlExpress Preview pane will display only the Biml opening and closing tags, as shown in Figure 8-4.

```
<Biml xmlns="http://schemas.varigence.com/biml.xsd">
</Biml>
```

Figure 8-4. *Viewing the BimlExpress Preview Pane*

To test your Biml file, you need to multi-select `CreatePackages.biml`, `FrameworkMetadata.biml`, and `LoadBimlRelationalHierarchy.biml`, right-click, and click Generate SSIS Packages, as shown in Figure 8-5.

Figure 8-5. *Generating SSIS packages and including FrameworkMetadata.biml*

You will be prompted to confirm overwritten items if the SSIS packages exist (they exist and are shown in Figure 8-5). Check the Select All checkbox and click the Commit button.

Browse to the path you specified in the SSISFrameworkMetadataFileName variable initialization in params.biml. You should see your file, similar to that shown in Figure 8-6.

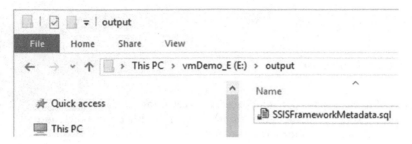

Figure 8-6. *Viewing the SSISFrameworkMetadataFileName file*

Edit the file to view its contents. Your file contents should appear similar to those shown in Figure 8-7.

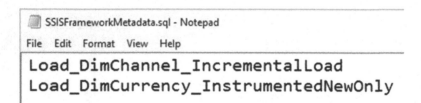

Figure 8-7. *Viewing the SSISFrameworkMetadataFileName file contents*

What does this tell you? It tells you that the SSISFrameworkMetadataFileName variable directs the location of the SQL file. It also tells you that you can successfully iterate the contents of the RootNode.Packages collection *as long as you remember* to multi-select CreatePackages.biml and LoadBimlRelationalHierarchy.biml.

Adding SSIS Framework Application Metadata

Please remember that your SSIS Framework Community Edition metadata tables are custom.Applications, custom.Packages, and custom.ApplicationPackages. You first need to add an SSIS framework application.

Open the params.biml file and add the highlighted BimlScript shown in Listing 8-8.

Listing 8-8. Adding the Framework Application Name

```
<#
var SSISFrameworkMetadataFileName = "E:\\output\\SSISFrameworkMetadata.sql";
var SSISFrameworkApplicationName = "Biml Book Chapter 8";
#>
```

In the FrameworkMetadata.biml file, build a Transact-SQL statement in the StringBuilder to insert the framework application metadata into the custom. Applications table, as shown in the BimlScript in Listing 8-9.

Listing 8-9. Building the Framework Application BimlScript

```
<#@ template tier="999"#>
<#@ include file="params.biml" #>
<#@ import namespace="System.Text" #>
<#@ import namespace="System.IO" #>
<#
var sb = new StringBuilder();

sb.AppendLine("If Not Exists(Select a.ApplicationName");
sb.AppendLine("  From custom.Applications a ");
sb.AppendLine("  Where a.ApplicationName = '" +
                   SSISFrameworkApplicationName + "')");
sb.AppendLine(" begin");
sb.AppendLine("   Insert Into custom.Applications(ApplicationName)");
sb.AppendLine("   Values('" + SSISFrameworkApplicationName + "')");
sb.AppendLine(" end");

foreach(var package in RootNode.Packages) {
    sb.AppendLine(package.Name);
}

File.WriteAllText(SSISFrameworkMetadataFileName, sb.ToString());
#>
<Biml xmlns="http://schemas.varigence.com/biml.xsd">
</Biml>
```

Save FrameworkMetadata.biml and edit your SQL file. The BimlScript you added *just now* should be present in the file, but not the names of the SSIS packages, as shown in Figure 8-8.

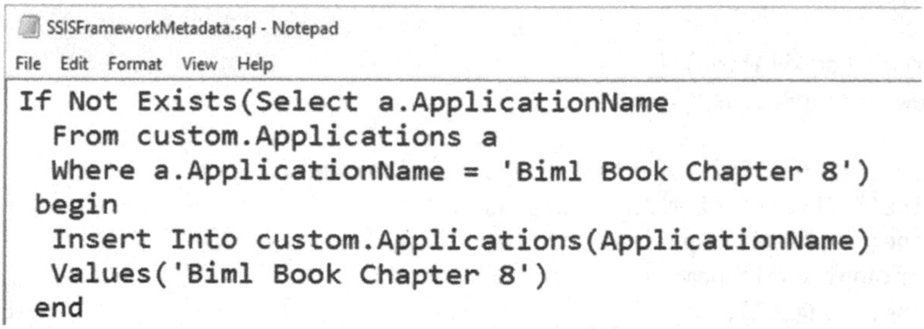

```
SSISFrameworkMetadata.sql - Notepad
File  Edit  Format  View  Help

If Not Exists(Select a.ApplicationName
  From custom.Applications a
  Where a.ApplicationName = 'Biml Book Chapter 8')
 begin
  Insert Into custom.Applications(ApplicationName)
  Values('Biml Book Chapter 8')
 end
```

Figure 8-8. *Viewing the contents of the SQL file*

What just happened? When you saved the `FrameworkMetadata.biml` file, it executed. If you had the Preview pane open and were watching it, you may have noticed, for a few seconds, it appeared as shown in Figure 8-9.

```
1  Compiling Biml...|
```

Figure 8-9. *Compiling Biml*

`FrameworkMetadata.biml` was "running." What happened to the names of the SSIS packages? When the foreach loop executed–standalone, outside the context of the multi-selected `CreatePackages.biml` and `LoadBimlRelationalHierarchy.biml` files–there were *no* SSIS packages found in the RootNode.Packages collection.

Can you alter this behavior? Yes. BimlExpress performs an automatic build in the background on save and to update the preview window. You can wrap your entire script in an `if (!IsBackgroundCompilation)` statement.

Please note the Transact-SQL is safely re-executable, or idempotent. If no rows exist in the `custom.Applications` table with an ApplicationName named "Biml Book Chapter 8," the Insert statement will execute and insert such a row. If that row already exists, the Insert statement will not execute. Regardless of whether the Insert statement executes, the end result is the same: there is a row in the `custom.Applications` table with an ApplicationName named "Biml Book Chapter 8."

Adding SSIS Package Metadata

Let's next add BimlScript to generate metadata for your SSIS packages by adding the highlighted content shown in Listing 8-10 to the `FrameworkMetadata.biml` file.

Listing 8-10. Adding SSIS Package Framework Metadata

```
<#@ template tier="999"#>
<#@ include file="params.biml" #>
<#@ import namespace="System.Text" #>
<#@ import namespace="System.IO" #>
<#
if (!IsBackgroundCompilation) {
  var sb = new StringBuilder();

  sb.AppendLine("If Not Exists(Select a.ApplicationName");
  sb.AppendLine("  From custom.Applications a ");
  sb.AppendLine("  Where a.ApplicationName = '" +
  SSISFrameworkApplicationName + "')");
  sb.AppendLine(" begin");
  sb.AppendLine("  Insert Into custom.Applications(ApplicationName)");
  sb.AppendLine("  Values('" + SSISFrameworkApplicationName + "')");
  sb.AppendLine(" end");
```

```
foreach(var package in RootNode.Packages) {
    sb.AppendLine("If Not Exists(Select p.PackageName");
    sb.AppendLine("  From custom.Packages p ");
    sb.AppendLine("  Where p.PackageName = '" + package.Name + ".dtsx' ");
    sb.AppendLine("    And p.ProjectName = 'Chapter8' ");
    sb.AppendLine("    And p.FolderName = '" + SSISCatalogFolderName + "')");
    sb.AppendLine(" begin");
    sb.AppendLine("  Insert Into custom.Packages ");
    sb.AppendLine("  (PackageName, ProjectName, FolderName)");
    sb.AppendLine("  Values('" + package.Name + ".dtsx' ");
    sb.AppendLine("   , 'Chapter8', '" + SSISCatalogFolderName + "') ");
    sb.AppendLine(" end");
}

    File.WriteAllText(SSISFrameworkMetadataFileName, sb.ToString());
}
#>
<Biml xmlns="http://schemas.varigence.com/biml.xsd">
</Biml>
```

The BimlScript listed here builds Transact-SQL that checks for the existence of an SSIS package that is contained in an SSIS project which is stored in an SSIS catalog folder. If the SSIS package metadata does not exist, the Transact-SQL executes the Insert statement to add it.

Also, be sure to add the highlighted content shown in Listing 8-11 to the params.biml file to persist the name of the SSIS catalog folder.

Listing 8-11. Adding SSIS Catalog Folder Metadata

```
<#
var SSISFrameworkMetadataFileName = "E:\\output\\SSISFrameworkMetadata.sql";
var SSISFrameworkApplicationName = "Biml Book Chapter 8";
var SSISCatalogFolderName = "Test";
#>
```

Note that you declared a new string variable in your params.biml file: SSISCatalogFolderName.

Multi-select CreatePackages.biml, FrameworkMetadata.biml, and LoadBimlRelationalHierarchy.biml, right-click, and click Generate SSIS Packages to test, as shown in Figure 8-10.

Figure 8-10. Generating SSIS packages and the framework metadata file

You will be prompted to confirm overwritten items if the SSIS packages exist. Check the Select All checkbox and click the Commit button.

Browse to the path you specified in the SSISFrameworkMetadataFileName variable initialization in params.biml. Edit the file to view its contents. Your file contents should now contain several Transact-SQL statements. Copy the contents of the file and paste them into SQL Server Management Studio (SSMS), as shown in Figure 8-11.

```
 1 ⊟If Not Exists(Select a.ApplicationName
 2  │   From custom.Applications a
 3  │   Where a.ApplicationName = 'Biml Book Chapter 8')
 4  ⊟ begin
 5  ⊟  Insert Into custom.Applications(ApplicationName)
 6  │    Values('Biml Book Chapter 8')
 7  │  end
 8  ⊟If Not Exists(Select p.PackageName
 9  │   From custom.Packages p
10  │   Where p.PackageName = 'Load_DimChannel_IncrementalLoad.dtsx'
11  │     And p.ProjectName = 'Chapter8'
12  │     And p.FolderName = 'Test')
13  ⊟ begin
14  ⊟  Insert Into custom.Packages
15  │   (PackageName, ProjectName, FolderName)
16  │   Values('Load_DimChannel_IncrementalLoad.dtsx'
17  │   , 'Chapter8', 'Test')
18  │  end
19  ⊟If Not Exists(Select p.PackageName
20  │   From custom.Packages p
21  │   Where p.PackageName = 'Load_DimCurrency_InstrumentedNewOnly.dtsx'
22  │     And p.ProjectName = 'Chapter8'
23  │     And p.FolderName = 'Test')
24  ⊟ begin
25  ⊟  Insert Into custom.Packages
26  │   (PackageName, ProjectName, FolderName)
27  │   Values('Load_DimCurrency_InstrumentedNewOnly.dtsx'
28  │   , 'Chapter8', 'Test')
29  │  end
```

Figure 8-11. *Viewing the Transact-SQL statements*

You now have a file that will manage some of the SSIS Framework Community Edition metadata for your SSIS framework application in an idempotent (safely re-executable) manner.

Adding Framework Application Package Metadata

The final piece of SSIS Framework Community Edition metadata you need to add is application package metadata. Add the highlighted BimlScript shown in Listing 8-12.

Listing 8-12. Adding Framework Application Package Metadata

```
<#@ template tier="999"#>
<#@ include file="params.biml" #>
<#@ import namespace="System.Text" #>
<#@ import namespace="System.IO" #>
<#
if (!IsBackgroundCompilation) {
  var sb = new StringBuilder();
  int executionOrder = 0;
```

```
sb.AppendLine("If Not Exists(Select a.ApplicationName");
sb.AppendLine("  From custom.Applications a ");
sb.AppendLine("  Where a.ApplicationName = '" +
SSISFrameworkApplicationName + "')");
sb.AppendLine(" begin");
sb.AppendLine("  Insert Into custom.Applications(ApplicationName)");
sb.AppendLine("  Values('" + SSISFrameworkApplicationName + "')");
sb.AppendLine(" end");

sb.AppendLine(" declare @applicationID int = (Select a.ApplicationID");
sb.AppendLine("  From custom.Applications a ");
sb.AppendLine("  Where a.ApplicationName = '" +
SSISFrameworkApplicationName + "')");
sb.AppendLine(" declare @packageID int");

foreach(var package in RootNode.Packages) {
  executionOrder += 10;
  sb.AppendLine("If Not Exists(Select p.PackageName");
  sb.AppendLine("  From custom.Packages p ");
  sb.AppendLine("  Where p.PackageName = '" + package.Name + ".dtsx' ");
  sb.AppendLine("    And p.ProjectName = 'Chapter8' ");
  sb.AppendLine("    And p.FolderName = '" + SSISCatalogFolderName + "')");
  sb.AppendLine(" begin");
  sb.AppendLine("  Insert Into custom.Packages ");
  sb.AppendLine(" (PackageName, ProjectName, FolderName)");
  sb.AppendLine("  Values('" + package.Name + ".dtsx' ");
  sb.AppendLine("  , 'Chapter8', '" + SSISCatalogFolderName + "') ");
  sb.AppendLine(" end");
  sb.AppendLine(" Set @packageID = (Select p.PackageID");
  sb.AppendLine("  From custom.Packages p ");
  sb.AppendLine("  Where p.PackageName = '" + package.Name + ".dtsx' ");
  sb.AppendLine("    And p.ProjectName = 'Chapter8' ");
  sb.AppendLine("    And p.FolderName = '" + SSISCatalogFolderName + "')");
  sb.AppendLine("If Not Exists(Select ap.ApplicationPackageID");
  sb.AppendLine("  From custom.ApplicationPackages ap ");
  sb.AppendLine("  Join custom.Packages p On p.PackageID = ap.PackageID ");
  sb.AppendLine("  Join custom.Applications a On a.ApplicationID =
  ap.ApplicationID ");
  sb.AppendLine("  Where p.PackageName = '" + package.Name + ".dtsx' ");
  sb.AppendLine("    And p.ProjectName = 'Chapter8' ");
  sb.AppendLine("    And p.FolderName = '" + SSISCatalogFolderName + "' ");
  sb.AppendLine("    And a.ApplicationID = @applicationID ");
  sb.AppendLine("    And ap.ExecutionOrder = " + executionOrder + ") ");
  sb.AppendLine(" begin");
```

```
    sb.AppendLine("  Insert Into custom.ApplicationPackages ");
    sb.AppendLine("  (ApplicationID, PackageID, ExecutionOrder,
    FailApplicationOnPackageFailure)");
    sb.AppendLine("  Values(@applicationID ");
    sb.AppendLine("  , @packageID, " + executionOrder + ", 1) ");
    sb.AppendLine("  end");
    sb.AppendLine("Set @packageID = -1;");
  }

  File.WriteAllText(SSISFrameworkMetadataFileName, sb.ToString());
}
#>
<Biml xmlns="http://schemas.varigence.com/biml.xsd">
</Biml>
```

You first declare and initialize a variable named executionOrder. You next add BimlScript that builds Transact-SQL that creates and initializes a parameter named @applicationID. The @applicationID parameter is used in the Packages and ApplicationPackages Transact-SQL statements that follow. Inside the RootNode.Packages foreach loop, you add 10 to the value of executionOrder. After the Packages Transact-SQL, your BimlScript builds Transact-SQL that creates and initializes a parameter named @packageID. Lastly, your BimlScript builds Transact-SQL to test for the existence of the application package metadata and executes an Insert statement if the application package metadata is not found in the table.

As before, multi-select CreatePackages.biml, FrameworkMetadata.biml, and LoadBimlRelationalHierarchy.biml, right-click, and click Generate SSIS Packages to test your output. After committing the SSIS package file overwrites, open the file containing your SSIS Framework Community Edition Transact-SQL. Copy and paste the Transact-SQL into SSMS and execute it.

You should be able to view the new SSIS Framework Community Edition metadata by writing three Select statements, shown in Listing 8-13.

Listing 8-13. Viewing Framework Application, Package, and Application Package Metadata

```
Select * From custom.Applications
Select * From custom.Packages
Select * From custom.ApplicationPackages
```

Your results should appear similar to those shown in Figure 8-12.

ApplicationID	ApplicationName
1	Framework Test
3	Biml Book Chapter 8

PackageID	PackageName		ProjectName	FolderName
1	Child1.dtsx		FrameworkTest1	Test
2	Child2.dtsx		FrameworkTest1	Test
3	Child3.dtsx		FrameworkTest2	Test
6	Load_DimChannel_IncrementalLoad.dtsx		Chapter8	Test
7	Load_DimCurrency_InstrumentedNewOnly.dtsx		Chapter8	Test

ApplicationPackageID	ApplicationID	PackageID	ExecutionOrder	FailApplicationOnPackageFailure
1	1	1	10	1
2	1	3	20	1
3	1	2	30	0
6	3	6	10	1
7	3	7	20	1

Figure 8-12. *Viewing the results of SSIS Framework Community Edition metadata queries*

Testing the SSIS Project and SSIS Framework Application

Deploy the SSIS project named Chapter8 to your SSIS catalog that hosts your SSIS Framework Community Edition by right-clicking the SSIS project in Solution Explorer and clicking Deploy, as shown in Figure 8-13.

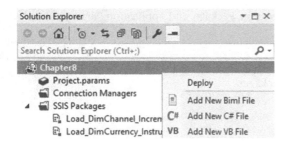

Figure 8-13. *Deploy the SSIS project*

Remember to specify the Test SSIS catalog folder during deployment. Your deployment should appear similar to that shown in Figure 8-14.

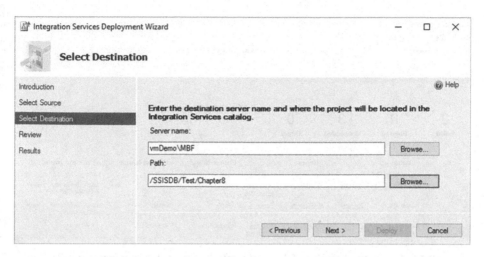

Figure 8-14. *Selecting the Test catalog folder*

The SSIS application named "Biml Book Chapter 8" is now ready for execution in the SSIS Framework Community Edition. Execute the statement shown in Listing 8-14 in the SSISDB database.

Listing 8-14. Executing the Framework Application

```
exec custom.execute_catalog_parent_package @application_name = 'Biml Book
Chapter 8'
```

View the SSIS Catalog All Executions report to examine the execution results. Your report should appear similar to that shown in Figure 8-15.

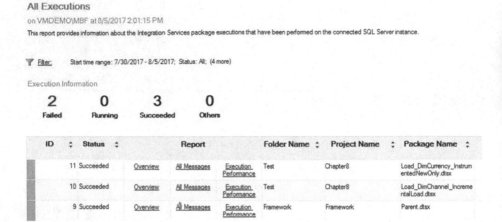

Figure 8-15. *Successful execution of the Biml Book Chapter 8 SSIS framework application*

Success!

In the final code sample, your package execution order is more or less random. It's whatever order the packages showed up in the Biml files. You may manually update the ExecutionOrder column values in the custom.ApplicationPackages table should you desire to change the order of package executions. Why would you want to change the execution order of SSIS packages in an SSIS application? Dependencies, for one. Some tables depend upon other tables being loaded beforehand.

If your tables have foreign key relationships in the data model, you could also use Biml to generate the ordering based on those by starting with all tables that have no foreign key contraints, working your way down to all depending tables and their child, and so on until all tables have been taken care of. More on this can be found in Ben's blog post on that topic: www.solisyon.de/loading-tables-based-on-foreign-key-topology-biml-linear-loads.

Summary

In this chapter we used a relatively simple custom metadata-driven SSIS execution framework, the SSIS Framework Community Edition from https://dilmsuite.com. Your solution consisted of a schema, tables, and stored procedures which you added to the SSISDB database. With a handful of database objects, you were able to build a flexible and functional SSIS execution framework.

CHAPTER 9

■ ■ ■

Metadata Automation

BimlStudio provides the ability to build and maintain a metadata model within your Biml solution. This chapter will start by familiarizing you with what metadata actually is, how it evolves over time, and different types of metadata. Then we introduce the Biml metadata modeling features to implement your metadata model within your Biml solution. We next implement a sample metadata model and demonstrate a metadata model for the framework solution we presented in Chapters 6 and 7. Finally, we take a brief look at another useful type of Biml metadata called offline schemas, which can be used for building SSIS packages and other assets without a live database.

What Is Metadata?

Perhaps the best place to start is with a definition of "metadata." We all know what data is. The adjective "meta" generally means "referring to itself." So when we put them together, we have data that refers to itself. In other words, as Wikipedia summarizes, metadata is "data about data." While correct, that definition is somewhat academic. In terms of an actual data warehouse implementation, what is metadata and how is it used?

Metadata can be descriptions of your database schema, such as tables, columns, constraints, and indexes. It can be descriptions of your execution environment, such as servers, databases, physical machines, and SAN nodes. It can be information about patterns and practices, such as slowly changing dimensions, inferred members, data logs, and data audit reports. It can be operational information about your deployment, such as last execution time, generated errors and warnings, column domains, range assumptions, and profiling statistics.

That's just scratching the surface. Metadata can be literally any information about your solution, except for the actual data you are processing at the moment. Consequently, sometimes the metadata for one application is actually the data for another.

© Andy Leonard et al. 2017
A. Leonard et al., *The Biml Book*, https://doi.org/10.1007/978-1-4842-3135-7_9

The importance of metadata has long been recognized by industry experts. Two of the early thought leaders in data warehouse design had the following to say about metadata:

- The Kimball Group: "Metadata is the DNA of the data warehouse, defining its elements and how they work together."

- William Inmon: "The first image most people have of the data warehouse is a large collection of historical, integrated data. While that image is correct in many regards, there is another very important element of the data warehouse that is vital—metadata."

The benefits of metadata are spread across both technical and non-technical users of your BI platform. Among other benefits,

- Metadata helps resolve ambiguity and inconsistencies within your BI platform.

- Metadata contains information about data that helps reconcile the difference in business terminology, for example "customers" vs. "sales."

- Metadata assists users in understanding and authenticating the origin of the data.

- Metadata establishes an interface between IT developers and business users.

As should be now apparent, metadata is a common, useful feature and critical component of all data warehouse and BI implementations, whether or not you use Biml for automation. So why does it become even more important in context of Biml and other automation technologies? Simple. Metadata IS the data used as an input to Biml.

Biml code without metadata is like an SSIS data flow without any source components. Sure, you can still do some useful things with it, but the really interesting possibilities open up when you start to feed data into the front end.

The Evolution of Metadata

Before discussing how to leverage metadata models within Biml, it is important to understand the different types of metadata that are commonly used in Biml data solutions. In fact, as you may discover in the following sections, your organization likely already has a fair bit of metadata and you may already be using metadata in your Biml solution without even realizing it.

Natural Metadata

You have probably noticed that your organization spends a significant amount of time in schema and process design meetings, entering the conclusions of those meetings into various vendor and internal tools, and modifying them as the business changes and matures. In a nutshell, all of this is natural metadata—the metadata that your organization creates, perhaps unintentionally, as a side effect of some other essential business process. This includes things such as database schemas, flat files with discoverable formats, data dictionaries, business process workflow captured in ERP systems, customer relationship workflows captured in CRM systems, and much more.

We normally refer to these sources as "natural" metadata sources, since they arise naturally from tasks that you and your colleagues have to do anyway to keep the business running. Natural metadata sources can be quite powerful, enabling a significant amount of automation without any manual metadata entry. For example, simple staging environments can be entirely constructed with Biml automation using only natural metadata sources.

Supplemental or Hybrid Metadata

As your Biml solution increases in scale, scope, and complexity, you will eventually need to store some additional metadata to take your automation to the next level. For example, if your metadata sources lack information about slowly changing dimension behaviors (e.g. Column A is SCD Type 1, Column 2 is SCD Type 2, etc.), you may want to supplement your natural metadata with that additional information.

At this point, you only need a few supplemental attributes to be attached to your natural metadata, so it probably won't make sense for you to build a full standalone metadata solution just for those minor enhancements. Furthermore, you likely already have a substantial Biml code base relying on natural metadata that you would like to avoid refactoring. As a result, most developers will seek out a solution to inject these additional values into their existing workflow with minimal impact to the solution.

Before moving forward, we'll be totally clear: There is nothing wrong with taking this approach. Do what is right for your organization. Furthermore, as you'll see later, much of the work you do now will be directly leveraged if and when you eventually decide to shift to a full standalone metadata system using Biml metadata models. However, all supplemental metadata approaches introduce tradeoffs and difficulties that will need to be actively managed until and unless you eventually migrate to a full synthetic metadata solution (as will be described later in this chapter).

Let's explore some of the ways that you can supplement your natural metadata sources with additional attributes. Most natural metadata sources have some mechanism for adding extra attribute values, but those mechanisms vary widely. Consequently, we will consider a few common examples to illustrate the process. If you are using different natural metadata sources, you will need to investigate the extensibility features of those systems.

SQL Server Database: Metadata Schema Tables

Your database provides a variety of mechanisms to store supplemental metadata. Let's focus on two approaches: metadata schema tables and extended properties.

This first approach is probably the most obvious. Within one or more of your databases, you could create an additional "metadata" or "meta" schema. In such cases, you would likely choose a common default for each of the attributes you wish to track, and then store entries only for those database objects that deviate from the default. For example, suppose you'd like to supplement your natural source schema metadata with an additional attribute that indicates the Slowly Changing Dimension (SCD) type of each column of each table. To do this, you could create an SCD table with the definition in Listing 9-1.

Listing 9-1. T-SQL to create a table that holds metadata for SCD type definitions

```
CREATE TABLE [meta].[ColumnScdTypes] (
  [ColumnScdTypeId] [int] IDENTITY(1,1) NOT NULL,
  [ServerName] [nvarchar](256) NOT NULL,
  [DatabaseName] [nvarchar](256) NOT NULL,
  [SchemaName] [nvarchar](256) NOT NULL,
  [TableName] [nvarchar](256) NOT NULL,
  [ColumnName] [nchar](10) NOT NULL,
  [ScdType] [int] NOT NULL DEFAULT((1))
)
```

To improve maintainability and decrease the size of the table, you could just assume that all columns are SCD Type 1 (i.e. overwrite old value), which is the most common column SCD type in most data warehouses. Then you would only need to add rows for columns that required a different SCD type.

Accessing this metadata is then simply a matter of writing a database query to obtain the SCD type for the column of interest. A major downside of this approach is the lack of metadata integrity. There is no built-in way to ensure that columns referenced by the metadata actually exist or that metadata entries are updated when column names change or other schema changes occur. This can be overcome by relatively heavy-weight constraint logic or triggers, but those solutions are expensive, cumbersome, and harm performance.

But there is a way to add this type of metadata attribute while maintaining metadata integrity: extended properties.

SQL Server Database: Extended Properties

SQL Server provides a feature called *extended properties* that enables you to annotate almost any database object with string-based key/value pairs. Using the example from above, you could simply add an SCD extended property to every column in the database indicating its SCD type. Alternatively, you could add extended properties to only those columns with an SCD type other than type 1. To find out more about using extended properties on SQL Server, take a look at the documentation on Microsoft TechNet at https://technet.microsoft.com/en-us/library/ms190243.aspx. If you are using an RDBMS other than SQL Server, check its documentation, as most database products have similar features.

This solution largely solves your data integrity problem, since extended properties maintain their relationship with the database object, regardless of name changes and other schema modifications that might take place. The major downside is that, in SQL Server and most other RDBMSs, you must make a separate stored procedure call for every attribute you want to inspect for every column (or other object). Furthermore, this stored procedure isn't particularly fast given the simplicity of its task. Consequently, this approach might be prohibitively slow for large data warehouses or when storing and retrieving a large number of supplemental attributes.

Excel Spreadsheet

It is quite common to use an Excel spreadsheet to create a data dictionary for your warehouse. These spreadsheets can be targeted either at business users or be used as technical design tools for your data development team. A popular example of the latter is the Kimball Group dimensional data modeling spreadsheet, which is bundled as a resource with the Microsoft Data Warehouse Toolkit.

Furthermore, it is generally quite easy to use a spreadsheet as a metadata source for your Biml solution. If the spreadsheet is structured using a tabular design, you can either export it to a CSV file to be read by Biml with the System.IO.File libraries or use the ACE OLEDB provider to query the spreadsheet tables as if they were database tables. Alternatively, if the spreadsheet has a hierarchical or other non-tabular structure, you can use the VSTO libraries or VBA to directly access the metadata stored in the spreadsheet on a cell-by-cell basis.

In any case, adding supplemental metadata attributes becomes a simple question of adding the appropriate rows, columns, or cells to the metadata spreadsheet.

The major downside of using this approach is its extreme fragility and susceptibility to user error. If a user makes unanticipated changes to the spreadsheet, the script that accesses the metadata may be adversely affected, sometimes producing immediate failure, but worse in other cases, producing subtle changes to the expected behavior. Furthermore, this approach potentially has all of the issues noted for the metadata schema tables approach described above. That is, there is no built-in metadata integrity checking mechanism.

CRM System

The final example that we'll consider here is a customer relationship management (CRM) system such as Microsoft Dynamics CRM or Salesforce. Note that most of what we discuss in this section will also apply to other business process management tools such as accounting, CMS, EAM, ERP, HR, MDM, and SCM tools.

In order to support the widely varying business requirements of their customers, CRM systems provide robust customization capabilities. In fact, many are so customizable that they can be used as a platform for tools that target entirely different use cases from CRM. Generally speaking, your CRM system will provide, among other

243

things, the ability to define or customize your entities with your own attribute values. Consequently, you can add hidden attributes to specify your supplemental metadata. If you are using the CRM system as your metadata source, then accessing these supplemental attributes is normally no different than accessing the attributes that directly drive the business process.

The downside to this approach is that it might require a significant amount of additional development to create a metadata entry and maintenance workflow that works for your organization. Normally, you would hide these supplemental metadata attributes on the end user-facing data entry forms. You would therefore either need to build new metadata entry forms for your data developers to use, or provide them with some other way of reviewing and modifying this metadata.

Why Hybrid Approaches Eventually Break Down

As noted above, there is absolutely nothing wrong with using hybrid approaches. When most Biml projects first begin to outgrow natural metadata sources, it doesn't actually make sense to create a full-blown standalone synthetic metadata store. The cost of doing so could be prohibitively expensive at that point in the project's development. Perhaps even more important, the metadata architect can usually produce a metadata architecture that is better tailored to the business and technical requirements of the solution after they have had some experience learning which additional attributes are most imported using a hybrid approach.

That being said, the hybrid approach will eventually begin to break down and require refactoring into a more formal metadata store. This tends to happen for the following reasons:

1. The number of annotation values grows to a point where they are hard to manage and even remember. Developers will sometimes find themselves adding supplemental metadata for things they have already captured with previous metadata.

2. While key/value pairs that constitute most hybrid metadata are appropriate for simple annotations, any supplemental data that captures complex relationships or multiple related values tends to be difficult to capture with key/value pairs. The workaround is usually to add several key/value pairs for a single relationship or complex value. This aggravates the issue in #1.

3. The large number of small attribute modifications becomes difficult to document and train new developers to use.

4. For very large numbers of supplemental metadata attributes, the performance of accessing those values can become a significant problem, especially if you are using storage techniques such as extended properties that have built-in performance limitations.

5. The BimlScript code that accesses the supplemental values becomes increasingly complex and fragile as the number of supplemental attributes increases.

6. As the solution begins to encapsulate more of the business, stakeholders become involved and requirements are introduced at an accelerating rate. This tends to exacerbate all of the above issues and the issues introduced by the individual hybrid metadata storage mechanisms noted in the previous section.

Synthetic Metadata

Once metadata collection requirements grow large enough—usually in the neighborhood of five or more metadata attributes per entity type (table, column, index, etc.)—the hybrid approach becomes cumbersome and difficult to maintain. At that point, it is usually helpful to shift away from the hybrid approach and move to a synthetic metadata store.

The core reason for this is similar to why relational structures in an RDBMS are often more powerful and descriptive than key/value stores such as Hadoop with equivalent amounts of modeling effort. When using a hybrid approach, the metadata attributes must be key/value pairs attached to existing items. This then limits the types of relationships that metadata attributes can have with each other. Of course, you can hack in support for more complex relationships, but it normally involves a combination of the following:

1. Values that represent encoded or serialized representations of complex objects.

2. A proliferation of related key/value pairs that are associated based on key formats.

In either case, you must write some amount of key/value parsing code and utility code within your BimlScripts to manage and associate your complex and related values. But why would you want to do so when databases and other relational stores have already implemented that for you?

Synthetic metadata stores enable you to build and manage much more complex metadata models to drive your BimlScripts. In Mist 4.0, a comprehensive metadata modeling and metadata entry solution was added directly to the Biml language. This provides a wide variety of benefits to those implementing and managing their own synthetic metadata stores. You don't need to use Biml metadata models to create your own synthetic metadata stores, though.

We have seen Biml users successfully create synthetic metadata stores using plain old databases, Excel files, Microsoft Master Data Services, web service architectures, and even SharePoint lists.

Note that the framework we demonstrated in Chapters 6 and 7 used a synthetic metadata store, and we will extend that solution later in this chapter.

Types of Metadata

Based on the discussion above, you might be thinking that metadata can be almost anything, and you'd be correct. But the breadth and depth of metadata options doesn't prevent us from creating a useful categorization of the most commonly used types of metadata.

Business Metadata

Business metadata includes definitions of data files and attributes in business terms. It may also contain definitions of business rules that apply to these attributes, data owners and stewards, data quality metrics, and similar information.

Technical Metadata

Technical metadata is the most common form of metadata. This type of metadata is created and used by the tools and applications that create, manage, and use data.

- Technical metadata is a key metadata type used to build and maintain the enterprise data environment.

- Technical metadata typically includes database system names, table and column names and sizes, data types and allowed values, and structural information such as primary and foreign key attributes and indices.

Operational Metadata

Operational metadata contains information that is available in operational systems and runtime environments. It may contain data file size, date and time of last load, updates, and backups, names of the operational procedures and scripts that have to be used to create, update, restore, or otherwise access data, etc.

This chapter will mainly focus on technical metadata so, without further ado, onto the Biml metadata models.

Why Metadata Models?

In the previous section, you learned how creating a synthetic metadata store could address many of the issues present with hybrid metadata solutions. Unfortunately, building a synthetic metadata store brings its own challenges, namely the following:

1. Depending on certain architectural decisions that are made early in the design process, it can be difficult to make changes to synthetic metadata stores as the project progresses.

2. It is often required that some type of front-end user interface be developed to support metadata entry and storage.

3. Modifications to the metadata store may require changes in multiple places in your BimlScript. For example, adding a column to a metadata table may require you to change the query for that table, the DataTable access code, and potentially other code locations. If these modifications are not made or are made incorrectly, subtle errors or omissions could be introduced into the code base.

4. It is not uncommon to choose to migrate the metadata store from one storage format to another as the solution matures. For example, you might start by storing it in Excel for convenience but later choose to migrate it to a SQL Server. Consequently, the BimlScript code consuming the metadata must be changed to access the new storage format. This is usually difficult and time-consuming, but shouldn't have to be so.

5. Many developers building their first metadata store have a hard time getting started.

6. Due to all of the above, it can be quite expensive and time-consuming to create synthetic metadata stores.

The Biml metadata modeling functionality solves all of these problems. Let's see how.

Biml Metadata Models and Instances

To make use of metadata in BimlStudio, you will need at least one Biml metadata model and one Biml metadata instance. They can be found and added in BimlStudio within the Metadata group, as shown in Figure 9-1.

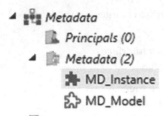

Figure 9-1. *The Metadata group in BimlStudio*

Each instance will reference a model, so it is important to create the model first.

Models

A Biml metadata model will define the structure of your metadata, but it will not hold any actual metadata itself. To use an RDBMS analogy, you can think of metadata models as being like relational schemas. Biml metadata instances, as you will see later, are like the table rows stored in that schema. Metadata models consist of entities that each contain a collection of properties and relationships. As with everything in Biml, these are specified using XML elements and attributes.

Let's explore a very simple model that will store connection metadata, such as connection strings and a Boolean to indicate whether or not the connection is used as a source system in your solution, and the tables that are related to those connections.

Listing 9-2 shows the Biml code to define this model. Note that the metadata model is named MD_Model. It contains both the Connections and the Tables entity. The Connections entity defines both of properties that can be defined on a connection. Additionally, the Tables entity defines a many-to-one relationship with the Connections entity.

Listing 9-2. Defining a Simple Metadata Model

```
<Biml xmlns="http://schemas.varigence.com/biml.xsd">
  <Metadata>
    <MetadataModel Name="MD_Model">
      <Entities>
        <Entity Name="Connections">
          <Properties>
            <Property Name="ConnString" DataType="String" IsRequired="true" />
```

```
            <Property Name="IsSource" DataType="Boolean" />
          </Properties>
        </Entity>
        <Entity Name="Tables">
          <Relationships>
            <Relationship Name="Connection" Cardinality="ManyToOne"
            EntityName="Connections" />
          </Relationships>
        </Entity>
      </Entities>
    </MetadataModel>
  </Metadata>
</Biml>
```

Instances

A Biml metadata instance references a Biml metadata model and includes objects that contain the actual metadata, using the structure defined in the model. Instances reference the relevant entities, properties, and relationships, while storing the metadata values in DataItem elements, one for each metadata record.

Entities and properties reference their equivalent within the model. Relationships reference the data item for the related object, as well as the relationship from the model.

Listing 9-3 shows a connection data item defined against your metadata model. All data items include a Name value. The ConnString and IsSource property values are specified in the Properties collection element.

Listing 9-3. Defining a Metadata Instance Data for Connections

```
<Entity Name="Connections" MetadataModelEntityName="MD_Model.Connections">
  <DataItems>
    <DataItem Name="AW">
      <Properties>
        <Property PropertyName="MD_Model.Connections.ConnString">
          <Value>Provider=SQLNCLI11;Server=.;Initial
            Catalog=AdventureWorks2014;Integrated Security=SSPI;</Value>
        </Property>
        <Property PropertyName="MD_Model.Connections.IsSource">
          <Value>True</Value>
        </Property>
      </Properties>
    </DataItem>
  </DataItems>
</Entity>
```

Listing 9-4 shows a `Tables` data item definition. While tables do not contain properties in your model, they do contain a relationship with a connection, which is specified in a `Relationship` element that references both the relationship in the model and the `Connections.AW` data item defined above.

Listing 9-4. Defining a Metadata Instance Data for Tables

```
<Entity Name="Tables" MetadataModelEntityName="MD_Model.Tables">
  <DataItems>
    <DataItem Name="Person">
      <Relationships>
        <Relationship RelationshipName="MD_Model.Tables.Connection"
          RelatedItemName="Connections.AW" />
      </Relationships>
    </DataItem>
  </DataItems>
</Entity>
```

To complete this example, let's bring both of the data item definitions into the metadata instance definition shown in Listing 9-5.

Listing 9-5. Combined Metadata Instance Definition

```
<Biml xmlns="http://schemas.varigence.com/biml.xsd">
  <Metadata>
    <MetadataInstance Name="MD_Instance" MetadataModelName="MD_Model">
      <Entities>
        <Entity Name="Connections" MetadataModelEntityName="MD_Model.
        Connections">
          <DataItems>
            <DataItem Name="AW">
              <Properties>
                <Property PropertyName="MD_Model.Connections.ConnString">
                  <Value>Provider=SQLNCLI11;Server=.;Initial Catalog=Adventure
                  Works2014;Integrated Security=SSPI;</Value>
                </Property>
                <Property PropertyName="MD_Model.Connections.IsSource">
                  <Value>True</Value>
                </Property>
              </Properties>
            </DataItem>
          </DataItems>
        </Entity>
        <Entity Name="Tables" MetadataModelEntityName="MD_Model.Tables">
          <DataItems>
            <DataItem Name="Person">
              <Relationships>
```

```
            <Relationship RelationshipName="MD_Model.Tables.Connection"
                RelatedItemName="Connections.AW" />
          </Relationships>
        </DataItem>
      </DataItems>
    </Entity>
  </Entities>
  </MetadataInstance>
  </Metadata>
</Biml>
```

Why You Need Them Both

Hopefully, the reason why you need models AND instances has become clear: one will be your definition, and the other one will be the actual data.

Of course, you won't want to maintain those instances manually by writing XML yourself. That would be even more tedious than manually authoring SQL INSERT statements to manage metadata in an underlying database. A preferred approach is to use a proper data entry application to author the metadata instance XML. If you have a way to collect and manage metadata already, an even better choice is to automate the creation of the instance data using BimlScript. In the following sections, we will demonstrate how to do both.

Manually Creating Metadata in BimlStudio

To make use of metadata in Biml, you will need to define a Biml metadata model and a Biml metadata instance. You have already seen how to create both using Biml code. BimlStudio offers the additional option of using visual designers to create the Biml code for you. Recall the layout of the Metadata group of the BimlStudio Logical View, as shown in Figure 9-2.

Figure 9-2. *Visualizing the Logical View inside BimlStudio*

Models

When you double-click a metadata model object (MetadataModel1 in Figure 9-2), BimlStudio launches the metadata model visual designer. The designer enables you to visualize the contents of the model and modify as needed. Accelerator buttons in the Metadata Model Tools contextual ribbon tab enable you to add entities, properties, relationships, and validators to your model, as shown in Figure 9-3.

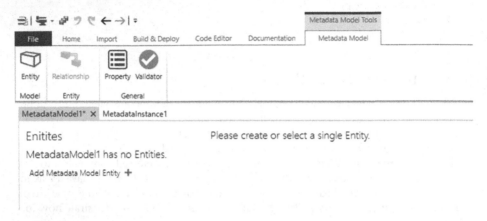

Figure 9-3. *BimlStudio metadata model visual designer*

Instances

When you double-click a metadata instance object (MetadataInstance1 in Figure 9-2), BimlStudio launches the metadata instance visual designer. After selecting a model in the Metadata Model dropdown, you get a user interface that has been customized for the model definition. Selecting entities from the Entity dropdown will enable you to add new data items and configure the properties for each data item in the instance. A partial screenshot of this designer is shown in Figure 9-4.

Figure 9-4. *BimlStudio metadata instance visual designer*

Using these visual designers, you can manage your entire metadata solution, including metadata instance data items. We will show you later in this chapter how to use BimlScript automation to load metadata instance information from a database, if you prefer to use that approach. Before doing so, let's take a look at one of the other features that BimlStudio provides for Biml metadata models: dynamic metadata wrapper objects.

Metadata Model Wrapper Objects

By now, you've seen several examples of using the Biml API object model to access objects that have been defined earlier in the compilation process. For instance, in Chapter 6, you iterated your source tables to create load packages for each. You could use this same approach to iterate the data items in your metadata instance. In the case of metadata instances, this would be rather tedious due to the indirect nature of metadata storage in the Biml API. Listing 9-6 shows the code to create a Biml connection for each connection data item defined in MD_Instance. It requires the following steps:

1. Retrieve the metadata instance.

2. Find the first instance entity that references the Connections entity in the metadata model.

3. Iterate the data items in that instance entity.

4. Find the first data item property that references the ConnString.

5. Retrieve the string value of the ConnString property and convert its type if necessary.

Listing 9-6. Accessing Biml Metadata Instance Information via the Biml API

```
<Biml xmlns="http://schemas.varigence.com/biml.xsd">
  <Connections>
<#
var metadata = RootNode.MetadataInstances["MD_Instance"];
var connectionEntity = metadata.Entities.FirstOrDefault(i =>
i.MetadataModelEntity.Name == "Connections");
if (connectionEntity != null) {
  foreach (var dataItem in connectionEntity.DataItems) {
    var connectionStringProp = dataItem.Properties.FirstOrDefault(i =>
    i.Property.Name == "ConnString");
    if (connectionStringProp != null)
    {
      var connString = connectionStringProp.Value;
      // TODO: If target property is not a string, you might parse it here
#>
```

```
    <Connection Name="<#=dataItem.Name#>" ConnectionString="<#=connString#>" />
<# }
  }
}
#>
  </Connections>
</Biml>
```

This code is cumbersome. Even worse is that you need to repeat this process for every entity and property you wish to use. It would be much better if you had some sort of wrapper object that would expose the entities, properties, and relationships for your metadata in a clean, simple, and customized object model. Of course, you could write such a class for your metadata model using a C# or VB code file, but that represents a significant development and maintenance cost.

Luckily, the Biml engine does this work for you by dynamically generating a wrapper class in the background that makes it exceedingly easy to iterate and access metadata from your Biml metadata instance. Listing 9-7 shows the same code as in Listing 9-6, but uses this dynamically generated wrapper class instead of the standard Biml API.

Listing 9-7. Accessing Biml Metadata Instance Information via the Wrapper Objects

```
<Biml xmlns="http://schemas.varigence.com/biml.xsd">
  <Connections>
<#
var metadata = MD_ModelWrapper.Load(RootNode.MetadataInstances["MD_Instance"]);
foreach (var connection in metadata.Connections) { #>
    <Connection Name="<#=connection.Name#>" ConnectionString="<#=connection.
    ConnString#>" />
<# } #>
  </Connections>
</Biml>
```

This is much cleaner. It also scales well when accessing additional entities, properties, and relationships. In the following sections we show additional examples of using these wrapper classes.

Accessing a Model Using VB.NET

Accessing the metadata with BimlScript and VB.NET is fairly easy. Let's assume you want to create a Table element for each table defined in your metadata instance MD_Instance.

To do that, you will need to

- Declare VB as your language of choice.

- Import the namespace.

  - Attention: This namespace can be customized via the DynamicObjectNamespace property on the metadata model. By default, it is set to Varigence.DynamicObjects.

- Access the instance by loading it into a dynamic wrapper object via the static Load method. The name of the dynamic wrapper class can be customized via the DynamicObjectClassName property on the metadata model. By default, it is set to the name of the metadata model suffixed with Wrapper. For instance, if the model name is MD_Model, then the default wrapper class name is MD_ModelWrapper.

You can make use of everything that you've learned in this book to browse the instance using LINQ. In Listing 9-8, you iterate all connections that have been marked as a source (IsSource = True) and will subsequently loop through all tables that are related to that connection.

Listing 9-8. Accessing Biml Metadata Instance Information with VB

```
<#@ template language="VB" #>
<#@ import namespace="Varigence.DynamicObjects.MD_ModelWrapper" #>
<# Dim Metadata as MD_ModelWrapper = MD_ModelWrapper.Load(RootNode.
Metadata("MD_Instance")) #>
<Biml xmlns="http://schemas.varigence.com/biml.xsd">
  <Tables>
    <# for each conn as ConnectionsWrapper in Metadata.Connections.
    where(function(c) c.IsSource= True)#>
    <# for each tbl as TablesWrapper in  metadata.tables.where(function(t)
    t.Connection.RelatedItem isnot nothing ANDALSO t.Connection.RelatedItem.
    Name = conn.Name) #>
    <Table Name="<#=tbl.Connection.RelatedItem.Name#>_<#=tbl.name#>"
    SchemaName="Target.dbo"/>
    <# next #>
    <# next #>
  </Tables>
</Biml>
```

This sample produces a Table element for each table specified in your metadata instance.

Accessing a Model Using C#

To achieve the same result using C#, use the code in Listing 9-9.

Listing 9-9. Accessing Biml Metadata Instance Information with C#

```
<# MD_ModelWrapper metadata = MD_ModelWrapper.Load(RootNode.Metadata
["MD_Instance"]); #>
<Biml xmlns="http://schemas.varigence.com/biml.xsd">
  <Tables>
    <# foreach (var conn in metadata.Connections.Where(c => c.IsSource=="True")) {
```

```
      foreach (var tbl in metadata.Tables.Where(t => t.Connection.RelatedItem
      != null && t.Connection.RelatedItem.Name == conn.Name)) { #>
   <Table Name="<#=tbl.Connection.RelatedItem.Name#>_<#=tbl.Name#>"
   SchemaName="Target.dbo"/>
   <# }
   }#>
 </Tables>
</Biml>
```

Applying Metadata Models to Your Framework

Recall that in Chapter 7 you loaded the metadata from your BRMetadata database using SQL queries executed via the ExternalDataAccess.GetDataTable utility method. You will actually still do that in your new approach, but instead of loading your metadata into annotations on relational objects, you will instead load it into a metadata instance. Before doing so, you need to define a metadata model that matches the semantics of your BRMetadata database, as shown in Listing 9-10.

Listing 9-10. Metadata Model for BRMetadata

```
<Biml xmlns="http://schemas.varigence.com/biml.xsd">
  <Metadata>
    <MetadataModel Name="BRMetadataModel">
      <Entities>
        <Entity Name="Connections">
          <Properties>
            <Property Name="ConnectionString" DataType="String" Length="255" />
          </Properties>
        </Entity>
        <Entity Name="Databases">
          <Relationships>
            <Relationship Name="Connection" EntityName="Connections"
            Cardinality="ManyToOne" />
          </Relationships>
        </Entity>
        <Entity Name="Schemas">
          <Relationships>
            <Relationship Name="Database" EntityName="Databases"
            Cardinality="ManyToOne" />
          </Relationships>
        </Entity>
        <Entity Name="Tables">
          <Relationships>
            <Relationship Name="Schema" EntityName="Schemas"
            Cardinality="ManyToOne" />
          </Relationships>
          <Properties>
```

```
            <Property Name="PatternName" DataType="String" Length="255" />
          </Properties>
        </Entity>
        <Entity Name="Columns">
          <Relationships>
            <Relationship Name="Table" EntityName="Tables"
            Cardinality="ManyToOne" />
          </Relationships>
          <Properties>
            <Property Name="DataType" DataType="String" Length="255" />
            <Property Name="Length" DataType="Int32" />
            <Property Name="IsNullable" DataType="Boolean" />
            <Property Name="IsIdentity" DataType="Boolean" />
          </Properties>
        </Entity>
        <Entity Name="Mappings">
          <Relationships>
            <Relationship Name="SourceColumn" EntityName="BRMetadataModel.
            Columns" Cardinality="OneToMany" />
            <Relationship Name="TargetColumn" EntityName="BRMetadataModel.
            Columns" Cardinality="OneToMany" />
          </Relationships>
          <Properties>
            <Property Name="IsBusinessKey" DataType="Boolean" />
          </Properties>
        </Entity>
      </Entities>
    </MetadataModel>
  </Metadata>
</Biml>
```

Once you have defined your Biml metadata model, you can now create and load a corresponding Biml metadata instance by reading data out of the BRMetadata database, as shown in Listing 9-11. Note the five separate queries, one for each of the entities you wish to load. These queries are much simpler than the equivalent query used in the view you created in Chapter 6. You simply iterate over the DataRow objects returned when each of these queries is executed to construct Biml DataItem elements with the corresponding properties for your metadata entities. Once metadata instance is created, you can use it in your BimlScript, much as you saw in the previous section by leveraging the dynamically created metadata wrapper object.

Listing 9-11. Metadata Instance for BRMetadata

```
<#@ import namespace="System.Data" #>
<#
var connectionString = @"Provider=SQLNCLI11;Data Source=.;Integrated
Security=SSPI;Initial Catalog=BRMetadata;";

var sqlCon = @"Select ConnectionName, ConnectionString From [di].[Connections]";
var sqlDb = @"Select d.DatabaseName, c.ConnectionName From [di].[Databases]
d JOIN [di].[Connections] c ON d.ConnectionID = c.ConnectionID";
var sqlSch = @"Select s.SchemaName, d.DatabaseName From [di].[Schemas] s
JOIN [di].[Databases] d ON s.DatabaseID = d.DatabaseID";
var sqlTbl = @"Select t.TableName, p.PatternName, s.SchemaName From [di].
[Tables] t JOIN [di].[Schemas] s ON t.SchemaID = s.SchemaID JOIN [di].
[TablePatterns] tp ON t.TableID = tp.TableID JOIN [di].[Patterns]
p ON tp.PatternID = p.PatternID";
var sqlCol = @"Select c.ColumnName, c.DataType, c.Length, c.IsNullable,
c.IsIdentity, t.TableName From [di].[Columns] c JOIN [di].[Tables] t ON
c.TableID = t.TableID";

var conDataTable = ExternalDataAccess.GetDataTable(connectionString,
sqlCon);
var dbDataTable = ExternalDataAccess.GetDataTable(connectionString, sqlDb);
var schDataTable = ExternalDataAccess.GetDataTable(connectionString, sqlSch);
var tblDataTable = ExternalDataAccess.GetDataTable(connectionString, sqlTbl);
var colDataTable = ExternalDataAccess.GetDataTable(connectionString, sqlCol);
#>
<Biml xmlns="http://schemas.varigence.com/biml.xsd">
  <Metadata>
    <MetadataInstance Name="BRMetadataInstance" MetadataModelName=
    "BRMetadataModel">
      <Entities>
        <Entity Name="Connections" MetadataModelEntityName="BRMetadataModel.
        Connections">
          <DataItems>
            <# foreach (DataRow conRow in conDataTable.Rows) { #>
            <DataItem Name="<#=conRow["ConnectionName"]#>">
              <Properties>
                <Property PropertyName="BRMetadataModel.Connections.
                ConnectionString">
                  <Value><#=conRow["ConnectionString"]#></Value>
                </Property>
              </Properties>
            </DataItem>
            <# } #>
          </DataItems>
        </Entity>
```

```xml
<Entity Name="Databases" MetadataModelEntityName="BRMetadataModel.
 Databases">
  <DataItems>
    <# foreach (DataRow dbRow in dbDataTable.Rows) { #>
    <DataItem Name="<#=dbRow["DatabaseName"]#>">
      <Relationships>
        <Relationship RelationshipName="BRMetadataModel.Databases.
        Connection" RelatedItemName="Connections.<#=dbRow
        ["ConnectionName"]#>" />
      </Relationships>
    </DataItem>
    <# } #>
  </DataItems>
</Entity>
<Entity Name="Schemas" MetadataModelEntityName="BRMetadataModel.Schemas">
  <DataItems>
    <# foreach (DataRow schRow in schDataTable.Rows) { #>
    <DataItem Name="<#=schRow["SchemaName"]#>">
      <Relationships>
        <Relationship RelationshipName="BRMetadataModel.Schemas.
        Database" RelatedItemName="Databases.<#=schRow["Database
        Name"]#>" />
      </Relationships>
    </DataItem>
    <# } #>
  </DataItems>
</Entity>
<Entity Name="Tables" MetadataModelEntityName="BRMetadataModel.Tables">
  <DataItems>
    <# foreach (DataRow tblRow in tblDataTable.Rows) { #>
    <DataItem Name="<#=tblRow["TableName"]#>">
      <Relationships>
        <Relationship RelationshipName="BRMetadataModel.Tables.Schema"
        RelatedItemName="Schemas.<#=tblRow["SchemaName"]#>" />
      </Relationships>
      <Properties>
        <Property PropertyName="BRMetadataModel.Columns.DataType">
          <Value><#=tblRow["PatternName"]#></Value>
        </Property>
      </Properties>
    </DataItem>
    <# } #>
  </DataItems>
</Entity>
<Entity Name="Columns" MetadataModelEntityName="BRMetadataModel.Columns">
  <DataItems>
    <# foreach (DataRow colRow in colDataTable.Rows) { #>
    <DataItem Name="<#=colRow["ColumnName"]#>">
```

```
              <Relationships>
                <Relationship RelationshipName="BRMetadataModel.Columns.
                Table" RelatedItemName="Tables.<#=colRow["TableName"]#>" />
              </Relationships>
              <Properties>
                <Property PropertyName="BRMetadataModel.Columns.DataType">
                  <Value><#=colRow["DataType"]#></Value>
                </Property>
                <Property PropertyName="BRMetadataModel.Columns.Length">
                  <Value><#=colRow["Length"]#></Value>
                </Property>
                <Property PropertyName="BRMetadataModel.Columns.IsNullable">
                  <Value><#=colRow["IsNullable"]#></Value>
                </Property>
                <Property PropertyName="BRMetadataModel.Columns.IsIdentity">
                  <Value><#=colRow["IsIdentity"]#></Value>
                </Property>
              </Properties>
            </DataItem>
            <# } #>
          </DataItems>
        </Entity>
      </Entities>
    </MetadataInstance>
  </Metadata>
</Biml>
```

At this point, you might be wondering anew what the advantages of using the metadata instance are. After all, you used SQL queries to load your metadata in both the pure database solution and the Biml metadata solution. Adding this layer of abstraction has several key benefits:

1. You get compile-time checking that your database remains in sync with your model. If the metadata database is modified, you will obtain a clear error early in your build process.

2. Changes to the metadata only need to be managed in the model and instance files. All other locations remain unchanged, except to add new functionality. In complex frameworks using direct metadata access approaches, changes tend to affect many files.

3. This abstraction through the wrapper object simplifies downstream code that leverages the metadata. There is no need for extensive storage of Biml annotations or other mechanisms to pass complex metadata to later BimlScript tiers.

4. While you are using direct database loads for your metadata, you could easily change your storage mechanism in the future. This would result in the need to change only the metadata instance file with its relatively simple code. All other Biml code files would remain unchanged.

5. Over time additional features will be added to Biml metadata models and instances that you will be able to leverage immediately, if you are already using Biml metadata models.

Offline Schemas

Now we're going to cover one of the less-known features of Biml: offline schemas. The offline schema feature was created to allow you to perform offline builds without having to connect to external systems at build time. The offline schema you generate is part of the Biml hierarchy and further information about it can be found at https://varigence.com/Documentation/Language/Element/AstOfflineSchemaNode.

The generated Biml file is comprised of items containing the external metadata used by each query or table.

Due to the way the SSIS execution engine loads and executes pacakges, the Biml compiler must place all external metadata information for data flow components into the package at build time. This means that the external databases, or at least empty versions of them, usually have to exist for a build to succeed. This is true even if you set the SSIS properties DelayValidation or ValidateExternalMedata to false. SSIS will still need to check against the source and destination systems for any queries inside your source, destination, lookup, or other components that need external metadata.

By using offline schemas, you can tell the Biml compiler to skip inspection of the external system metadata and instead use the external metadata specified in your offline schema file. Doing this provides several potential benefits:

1. Quick build times when compiling your Biml files.

2. Simulate pending changes in the source system.

3. Perform builds for environments to which you do not have access.

4. Perform relational and SSIS builds that depend on each other in a single step.

5. Track changes to external metadata for review when the previously created offline schema no longer matches the source system.

Picture the following scenario. You're about to set up work with a client or department where they need to give you access to the source system before you can start working on the proposed solution. Instead of waiting for access, you instead ask the source system owner to create an offline schema file using a BimlScript you provide to them. This way you can start developing Biml code and building SSIS packages without any ability to access the source systems or even obtain a comprehensive DDL for them. Once access is approved, you can go ahead and sync the offline schema against the source system to detect any changes that occurred during offline development.

Generating an Offline Schema File

To make use of offline schemas you will need at least one offline schema file. They can be found in BimlStudio within the Metadata group, as shown in Figure 9-5.

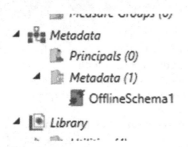

Figure 9-5. *The Logical View inside BimlStudio*

Varigence provides an option to toggle whether the compiler should use the offline schema or not. It also provides accelerator buttons in the Offline Schema ribbon to speed up generating the offline schema, as shown in Figure 9-6.

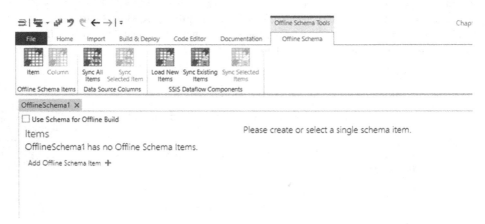

Figure 9-6. *The accelerator buttons inside BimlStudio*

Offline Schema Items

Offline schema items allow you to manually create item and column definitions. You have to write the item queries and the column properties yourself.

SSIS Data Flow Components

SSIS data flow components go through your BimlStudio project and generate the Biml definition for each item used inside SSIS packages and append each to the offline schema for you.

Data Source Columns

Data source columns go through all of the defined items inside your offline schema and generate the Biml definition for each column used in each item and append it to the offline schema for you.

Behind the scenes, the accelerator buttons have updated the Biml file containing your offline schema, as shown in Figure 9-7.

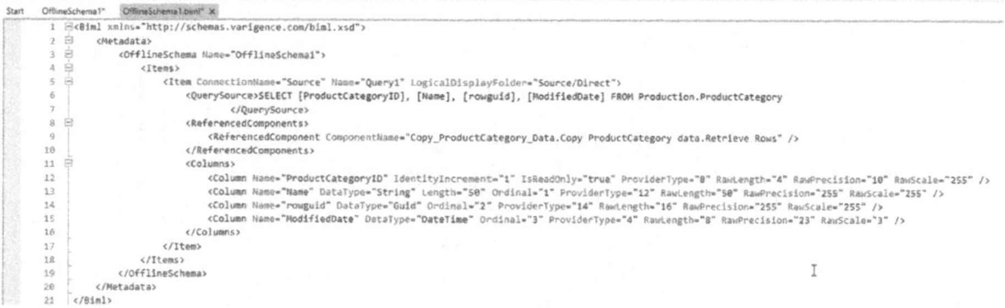

Figure 9-7. *The offline schema definition*

As with everything else in Biml, instead of using the visual designers and accelerators, you could also use BimlScript code nuggets to automate the creation of offline schemas from your metadata store or other locations.

Conclusion

In this chapter, you examined metadata as well as its use within Biml metadata model and instance objects and functionality. You also examined the offline schema feature in BimlStudio.

The next chapter, which will be the last chapter of this part of the book, will show you how to create deployable out-of-the-box solutions with Biml using bundles!

■ ■ ■

CHAPTER 10

Advanced Biml Frameworks and BimlFlex

As with any development technology, your Biml projects will start small and grow over time. At first, all you care about is getting the basics to work, but as you find additional corner cases and incrementally add features, you'll find that the growth of your codebase brings new challenges.

Larger Biml projects will often encounter performance issues due to the additional code that needs to be compiled each time your metadata changes. You may also wish to refactor your code so that it can be reused across projects and is consumable by others as a data integration framework. If your framework contains many Biml files, they can be difficult to deploy and manage across the many developers or customers working on your projects. Providing extensibility to your framework code so that others can seamlessly extend and customize it can also require a substantial amount of additional work to standardize and document your extensibility mechanisms. Perhaps most importantly from a career and business perspective, all of your hard work represents valuable intellectual property that you would like to be able to protect from pirates and license to customers.

Bundles

While there are approaches that can be taken from within a standard BimlStudio or BimlExpress project to address all of the problems that arise in a large and growing codebase, they all require a fair bit of custom work and force each framework to create its own solutions for these issues, even though most of those solutions will be similar or identical. To address these issues in a standard way that can be easily used by framework developers, Varigence has created Biml bundles.

Overview

Biml bundles are a packaging, deployment, and extensibility mechanism for Biml code and other project assets.

© Andy Leonard et al. 2017

A. Leonard et al., *The Biml Book*, https://doi.org/10.1007/978-1-4842-3135-7_10

Consider your large Biml solution. You probably have a metadata model, either using Biml MetadataModels or something you built yourself. You have a large number of reusable BimlScripts that consume metadata stored in an instance of your metadata model to generate code. You probably also have some supplemental SQL and other files that are used for setup, deployment, and other activities. You have some .NET code files and possibly .NET assemblies that are referenced from your BimlScripts. You might have customized documentation templates and schema graph profiles (see Chapter 13 for more information about BimlStudio documentation autogeneration and customization). If you are using build automation or continuous integration, you might also have custom BimlProj build definition files and tests.

In addition to those largely reusable files, you have some assets that are specific to the project you are developing. This will, of course, include the metadata for that project that is loaded into your reusable model. It might include some custom BimlScript files to handle bespoke business logic, unusual data sources, or customized patterns. It might also include BimlScript files that are called via some sort of extensibility mechanism you have defined for your framework.

If you want to reuse your framework for a new project, it becomes necessary to tease out the reusable files and other assets from the project-specific code, copy it into the new solution, and then start filling in the new solution with its own project-specific custom bits.

That model works, more or less, but it has lots of problems. Instantiating a new project is no longer simple because it requires moving a large number of files into the new project–and only those files that are part of the core framework. This is tedious, confusing, and error prone. There is also no formalized mechanism to prevent people from (hopefully inadvertently) editing your framework files, thereby introducing project-specific code into your shared framework files. Finally, there is no way to hide or otherwise protect from prying eyes the contents of these files, which might represent hundreds or thousands of hours of work. After all, even if you have no issues with a customer, client, or employer reading your code, you might not want a subsequent consultant to do so after you have moved on from the project.

Bundles solve all of these problems, and they can be used for frameworks that you use on just a few internal projects or that you package and sell for others to use.

At a high level, you just take all of the files that are part of your shared framework, author a manifest file that describes them, zip it all into a single file, and change the extension to bimlb (for Biml bundle). As you will see in the coming sections, there's a bit more to it than that, but those are the broad strokes.

Bundle Manifest

A bundle manifest describes the contents of the Biml bundle in a way that is machine readable by BimlStudio. It contains bundle version metadata, a list of files included within the bundle, options for those files, extension points, bundle documentation, and much more. For now we will focus on the file descriptions in the manifest.

Listing 10-1 shows a minimal bundle manifest. It contains a list of files. Each file includes a relative path within the bundle zip file, a friendly DisplayName for the UI, an indication of whether or not the file is visible to the end user in the UI, a default build action in BimlStudio (Live or Reference), and an indication of whether or not the user can modify the build action. BimlStudio will automatically read the contents of this manifest to load and display the relevant files in your project.

Listing 10-1. Sample Bundle Manifest with Extension Points

```
<BundleRoot xmlns="http://schemas.varigence.com/Bundle.xsd">
  <Files>
    <File Name="BimlScripts\1-1-Environment.biml" BuildAction="Live"
     Visibility="Public" IsBuildActionEditable="true"
     DisplayName="Environment" />
    <File Name="BimlScripts\1-2-CreateTableMetadata.biml" BuildAction="Live"
     Visibility="Public" IsBuildActionEditable="true" DisplayName="Create
     Table Metadata" />
    <File Name="BimlScripts\1-x-DeployTargetTables.biml" BuildAction="Live"
     Visibility="Public" IsBuildActionEditable="true" DisplayName="Deploy
     Target Tables" />
    <File Name="BimlScripts\x-2-CreateLoadPackages.biml" BuildAction="Live"
     Visibility="Public" IsBuildActionEditable="true" DisplayName="Create
     Load Packages" />
    <File Name="BimlScripts\0-1-CreateTableScript.biml"
     BuildAction="Reference" />
    <File Name="BimlScripts\x-3-CreateLoadBatch.biml" BuildAction="Live" />
    <File Name="BimlScripts\x-9-CreateLoadProject.biml" BuildAction="Live" />
  </Files>
</BundleRoot>
```

Extension Points

Before diving further into manifest authoring and bundle building, let's consider one further problem that bundles solve: extensibility.

As with most features in development tools, there is always a way to do it yourself, but by leveraging built-in capabilities you can save a tremendous amount of time and energy. Nonetheless, to best understand the built-in feature, let's walk through a thought experiment to understand how you might have built the feature if you had chosen to roll your own.

OK, so let's imagine for a moment that bundles were not a Biml feature and that you would still like to somehow create an extensibility system for your Biml framework. Most extensibility scenarios will identify locations within your framework where you support disabling an existing bit of code, modifying a configuration variable to change the functionality of an existing bit of code, adding a new bit of code, or replacing a code segment with a handwritten customization.

Most of the scenarios represented by the first and second category can be achieved strictly through your metadata repository. It's relatively simple to expose a variable in your metadata store to disable a framework feature or configure its functionality.

For the third and fourth categories, you could imagine placing Biml code, including .NET code nuggets, into database table columns in your metadata store to introduce new code into your framework. Anybody who has tried to manage code inside a database field can tell you how troublesome that is. You don't get any good development tools support, versioning and other source control features are non-existent, and any code written into that database will be more difficult to reuse across projects than using a file system-based approach.

267

Luckily, BimlScript already provides a mechanism to call code that exists in another Biml file: CallBimlScript. By invoking CallBimlScript from your framework code on a user Biml file, you can import customized functionality from your users without them ever needing to modify your core framework code. All you need to do as a framework developer is identify the parts of your framework that the user may want to extend or modify, and then place CallBimlScript calls in each of those extensibility locations.

However, CallBimlScript has a limitation. You must supply it with the path to the Biml file that you would like to expand. Since you have to perform the call from within your framework code, and the user of the framework might want to put their extension code in a custom location, or provide no extension at all, there needs to be some discovery mechanism for your extensions. The simplest possible system would look something like Listing 10-2.

Listing 10-2. Using CallBimlScript to Implement Extensibility

```
<#
if (System.IO.File.Exists("Extensions\\OleDbSourceOverride.biml")) { #>
<#=CallBimlScript("Extensions\\OleDbSourceOverride.biml", parameter1,
parameter2) #>
<# } #>
#>
```

This pattern isn't terrible, but it's not great either. It robustly handles the scenario where a user decides not to provide extension code, but it still requires the user to know exactly which relative path you expect for Biml files that extend your framework code. It's also verbose and provides no good error message or other feedback if the user gets something wrong, such as spelling the name of the expected extension file incorrectly.

Can you do better? To do so, you would need to build some sort of registration system. Your framework code would use the registration system to advertise all of the locations in the code base where user-extensible CallBimlScript invocations would reside. To complement that, your framework users would register all of the BimlScript files that would attach to each of the advertised extensibility locations. If you want to maximize the utility of the extension points, you might also want to pass CallBimlScript properties such as objects from your metadata model to the user extensions. Your registration system would also need to ensure that extension points and the user-supplied extensions had matching property expectations.

That sounds like a lot of work to build. What's worse is that every framework developer would need to make the same large investment. Happily, Varigence built exactly this type of registration system and embedded it into the Biml bundle feature set for everyone to use. Let's take a look at how it works.

As you might have guessed, you advertise your framework extension points to the registration system via the Biml bundle manifest file. In Listing 10-3, you supplement your previous manifest file to include advertisements for two extension points. All extension point definitions start with the ExtensionPointCategories element, which contains as many Category elements as you require. As large frameworks can contain hundreds of extension points, the categorization enables you to organize extension points to make them more discoverable for users. BimlStudio automatically uses your defined categories to dynamically generate hierarchical menus for the creation of new extensions. Within each category, you can define any number of ExtensionPoint elements.

Extension points define several useful properties:

- Name: Identifies the extension point when referenced from within the code.

- DisplayName: Used by BimlStudio and other UIs as a friendly name for end users.

- Description: Provides information about the purpose of the extension point and how it should be used.

- NewFileTemplate: Specifies the sample code that will be used in new files created by BimlStudio for this extension point.

- Parameters: As noted earlier, extensions can accept parameters passed by the framework code. The Parameters element allows you to specify any number of such parameters. Each parameter specifies its own Name, Type, and Description. Biml bundles enforce that extensions accept the parameters specified for the extension point.

Listing 10-3. Sample Bundle Manifest with Extension Points

```
<BundleRoot xmlns="http://schemas.varigence.com/Bundle.xsd">
  <Files>
    <File Name="BimlScripts\1-1-Environment.biml" BuildAction="Live"
    Visibility="Public" IsBuildActionEditable="true"
    DisplayName="Environment" />
    <File Name="BimlScripts\1-2-CreateTableMetadata.biml" BuildAction="Live"
    Visibility="Public" IsBuildActionEditable="true" DisplayName="Create
    Table Metadata" />
    <File Name="BimlScripts\1-x-DeployTargetTables.biml" BuildAction="Live"
    Visibility="Public" IsBuildActionEditable="true" DisplayName="Deploy
    Target Tables" />
    <File Name="BimlScripts\x-2-CreateLoadPackages.biml" BuildAction="Live"
    Visibility="Public" IsBuildActionEditable="true" DisplayName="Create
    Load Packages" />

    <File Name="BimlScripts\0-1-CreateTableScript.biml" BuildAction="Reference" />
    <File Name="BimlScripts\x-3-CreateLoadBatch.biml" BuildAction="Live" />
    <File Name="BimlScripts\x-9-CreateLoadProject.biml" BuildAction="Live" />
  </Files>

  <ExtensionPointCategories>
    <Category Name="Table">
      <ExtensionPoints>
        <ExtensionPoint Name="PreProcess" DisplayName="Pre Process">
          <Description>Add prior to the Source DataFlow</Description>
          <Parameters>
            <Parameter Name="table" Type="string">
```

```
                <Description>Table Name</Description>
            </Parameter>
            <Parameter Name="connection" Type="string">
                <Description>Connection Name</Description>
            </Parameter>
        </Parameters>
        <NewFileTemplate>
<![CDATA[<!-- You can add your sample code here. -->
<ExecuteSQL Name="Truncate Staging Table" ConnectionName="<#=connection#>">
  <DirectInput>TRUNCAT TABLE <#=table#></DirectInput>
  <# CustomOutput.OutputPathName = @"SQL - Truncate Staging Table.Output"; #>
</ExecuteSQL>]]>
        </NewFileTemplate>
    </ExtensionPoint>
    <ExtensionPoint Name="SourcePipeline" DisplayName="Source Pipeline">
        <Description>Add into the Source DataFlow</Description>
        <Parameters>
            <Parameter Name="table" Type="string">
                <Description>Table Name</Description>
            </Parameter>
        </Parameters>
        <NewFileTemplate>
<![CDATA[<!-- You can add your sample code here. -->
<DerivedColumns Name="DC - Add Metadata <#=table#>">
  <Columns>
    <Column Name="AuditKey" DataType="Int32">0</Column>
  </Columns>
</DerivedColumns>]]>
        </NewFileTemplate>
    </ExtensionPoint>
  </ExtensionPoints>
    </Category>
  </ExtensionPointCategories>
</BundleRoot>
```

Now that you have advertised your bundle extension points, your end users can author extensions for each of these extension points. Listing 10-4 shows a sample extension for the PreProcess extension point advertised in the manifest file above. Creating an extension is like creating any other CallBimlScript target, with the addition of an extension directive where you specify the bundle name, the name of the extension point, and an optional target parameter.

The target parameter allows you to limit the application of the extension to a filtered list of targets. For instance, if you authored an extension to override an OLEDB source component with a custom component to access data from a CRM system, you would only want that extension to apply to tables whose data source was the CRM system.

Listing 10-4. Sample Extension

```
<#@ extension bundleName="MyBundle.bimlb" extensionPointName="PreProcess" #>
<#@ property name="table" type="string" #>
<#@ property name="connection" type="string" #>
<ExecuteSQL Name="Truncate Staging Table" ConnectionName="<#=connection#>">
  <DirectInput>TRUNCAT TABLE <#=table#></DirectInput>
  <# CustomOutput.OutputPathName = @"SQL - Truncate Staging Table.Output"; #>
</ExecuteSQL>
```

Now that you have advertised your extension points and the user has supplied an extension, the next step is to change your framework code to use any extensions that users might have registered. Listing 10-5 shows how to use the built-in HasExtension and CallExtension methods to check for the existence of user-supplied extensions for the PreProcess extension point and to call the extension if it exists.

Listing 10-5. Calling an Extension from within Your Bundle Code

```
<#
if (HasExtension("PreProcess")) { #>
<#=CallExtension("PreProcess", "connection", "table") #>
<# } #>
#>
```

Using this registration system for Biml bundle extension points, adding user extensibility to your framework becomes technically quite simple. Remember that the challenge of identifying the right extension points within your framework code still exists. This is an unavoidable and difficult design task. For many, it can make the difference between a great framework and one that your users struggle with.

Building the Bundle

Building a Biml bundle is extremely straightforward. All you need to do is to zip up all of the files in the bundle along with the manifest file and then change the file extension to .bimlb. While you can do this with any zip utility or even the Windows zip shell extensions, we have found that using the free and open source tool 7-Zip provides the best experience for automatic builds. After installing 7-Zip from www.7-zip.org, you can run the command line in Listing 10-6 in the folder where your framework code is located, assuming that all of your Biml files are stored in the BimlScripts subfolder.

Listing 10-6. Building a Bundle Using 7-Zip

```
7z.exe a -aoa -tzip Sample.bimlb BimlScripts\*.* bundle.manifest
```

How does this prevent someone from just unzipping your bundle and looking at all of your framework code? The short answer is that it doesn't, but Varigence offers a web service that you can use to upload your bundle and get back an encrypted version that will work with BimlStudio. This isn't a perfect solution. A sufficiently motivated attacker will still be able to access your code using various techniques that we will not detail here. However, this approach significantly increases the cost of accessing your code and invalidates any potential claims that the attacker didn't know they shouldn't access the code.

BimlFlex

If you would prefer to use a preexisting framework or just look at a preexisting framework to better understand what might be possible in your framework, Varigence's BimlFlex framework is worth consideration.

Capabilities

The capabilities of BimlFlex are illustrated in Figure 10-1. BimlFlex users can choose any subset of the capabilities described therein, including staging, ODS, raw DataVault, business DataVault, dimensional data warehouses, data marts, multidimensional cubes, or tabular models. All of these capabilities can be configured strictly through metadata or customized via a large number of available extension points.

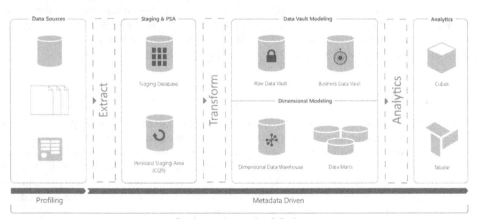

Figure 10-1. BimlFlex capabilities overview

Metadata Entry

The BimlFlex metadata model is defined in Biml code within the BimlFlex bundle, but each instance of this metadata is stored in a database instance. This is a perfectly reasonable and quite common design choice for Biml frameworks, but it creates a potential problem. Direct entry of data into databases is neither convenient nor a particularly sustainable approach. We require some sort of application to manage the entry and maintenance of our metadata. There are tools offered by Microsoft and others to rapidly build a rich data entry UI given a database schema. Microsoft Power Apps is an example of this.

You will always have a better experience with an application that has been custom-designed to work well with your data and user workflow. To that end, Varigence implemented both an Excel add-in and a standalone web and client application to enter and manage metadata for BimlFlex. Figure 10-2 shows a screenshot of the BimlFlex Excel add-in.

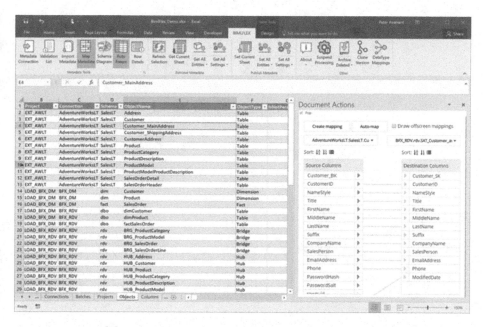

Figure 10-2. BimlFlex metadata entry add-in to Microsoft Excel

Summary

In this chapter, you learned how to create your own Biml bundles and a bit about BimlFlex, which is a great example of a fully featured bundle, and associated tools that have been developed by Varigence. Whether or not BimlFlex is something you might be interested in, it serves as a demonstration of the rich capabilities that bundles offer to framework developers and the possibilities of a comprehensive framework.

Now that you've learned about how to build and package a framework in a bundle, in the next chapter, we'll begin covering a variety of advanced Biml features and topics. This will be useful in expanding the capabilities of your framework.

PART III

■ ■ ■

Biml Topics

CHAPTER 11

■ ■ ■

Biml and Analysis Services

This chapter assumes that you've already familiarized yourself with the basic concepts of Biml. We will focus on the additional elements and attributes needed for Analysis Services projects.

This chapter also requires a basic knowledge of Microsoft SQL Server Analysis Services on at least one of the two project types: multidimensional or tabular. We will provide you with some simple examples of how to use Biml to build SSAS projects as well as how to automate processing of SSAS cubes and dimensions.

■ **Note** Analysis Services projects are only supported in BimlStudio.

The Biml sample for Analysis Services Multidimensional in this chapter will use the SSAS 2014 version. The available options to compile a project can be seen on the Project Properties Versions dropdown for SSAS Multidimensional. This list is displayed in Figure 11-1.

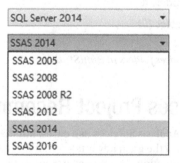

Figure 11-1. Analysis Services Multidimensional versions

© Andy Leonard et al. 2017
A. Leonard et al., *The Biml Book*, https://doi.org/10.1007/978-1-4842-3135-7_11

Biml projects for Analysis Services Tabular are supported only for SSAS 2016 and later. This can be seen in the SSAS Tabular dropdown that is displayed in Figure 11-2.

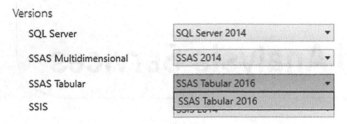

Figure 11-2. Analysis Services Tabular versions

Analysis Services projects are stored in the Analysis Services folder with subfolders to support both project types: Multidimensional and Tabular. See Figure 11-3.

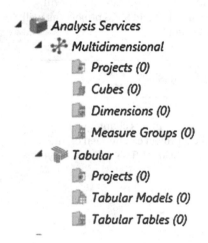

Figure 11-3. Analysis Services folders in BimlStudio

Analysis Services Project Recommendations

Biml can be a great fit for Analysis Services use cases, but there are some exceptions.

Just as with SSIS, one of the great advantages of Biml is that it easily allows scale-out architectures through automation. This makes it a good choice when it comes to multi-tenancy and/or multi-server environments.

Given the ability to automate structures and deployments through metadata, Biml frameworks can also include cube projects that can be driven with some of the same metadata that was used to build data integration frameworks.

Conversely, SSAS multidimensional/tabular can require the specification of additional types of metadata to automate its creation. After all, cubes and tabular models are largely just metadata containers on top of relational structures. If you want to use your own metadata to drive the creation of bespoke SSAS projects that could support any SSAS feature, you essentially need to duplicate the entire SSAS feature set in your metadata store. This will result in complex models that may be very difficult and time-consuming to maintain, potentially leading to longer instead of shorter development and deployment times. In a nutshell, Biml isn't for all SSAS projects, but for the pattern-heavy, scale-out projects where it does fit, it's tremendously valuable.

Multidimensional Biml Projects

This sample will create a simple cube with three dimensions (one of them being a role-playing time dimension), one partition, and one measure group. This example, which is built using AdventureWorks2014DW, will give you a basic understanding of how to create a multidimensional project using Biml.

In the BimlStudio Logical View tool window, multidimensional projects are stored under the Analysis Services top-level folder within the Multidimensional subfolder. Under the Multidimensional folder are Projects, Cubes, Dimensions, and Measure Groups. See Figure 11-4.

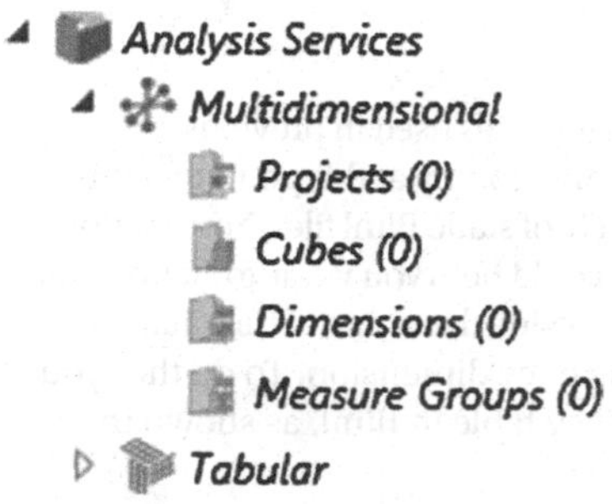

◢ 📦 *Analysis Services*

   ◢ ✳ *Multidimensional*

      📄 *Projects (0)*

      📄 *Cubes (0)*

      📄 *Dimensions (0)*

      📄 *Measure Groups (0)*

  ▷ 📦 *Tabular*

Figure 11-4. Multidimensional logical structure

- Projects **folder**: Contains the Biml objects for the project and multidimensional models that are used in the project.

- Cubes **folder**: Contains the Biml objects for the multidimensional cubes.

- Dimensions **folder**: Contains the Biml objects for the multidimensional dimensions.

- Measure Groups **folder**: Contains the Biml objects for the multidimensional measure groups.

Once the AdventureWorks2014DW database is installed on your SQL instance, you can create a very simple Biml file to provide basic environment configuration such as connection strings. See Listing 11-1.

Listing 11-1. Environment for Your Multidimensional Project Including a SSAS Connection

```
<Biml xmlns="http://schemas.varigence.com/biml.xsd">
  <Connections>
    <AnalysisServicesConnection Name="AW_Cube" Server="localhost"
    Provider="MSOLAP" Database="MyCubeDB" ConnectionString="Data
    Source=localhost;Initial Catalog=MyCubeDB;Provider=MSOLAP;Impersonation
    Level=Impersonate;" />
    <OleDbConnection Name="AdventureWorksDW" ConnectionString="Provider=SQLN
    CLI11;Data Source=localhost;Initial Catalog=AdventureWorksDW2014;
    Integrated Security=SSPI;" />
  </Connections>
  <Databases>
    <Database Name="AdventureWorksDW" ConnectionName="AdventureWorksDW" />
  </Databases>
  <Schemas>
    <Schema Name="dbo" DatabaseName="AdventureWorksDW" />
  </Schemas>
</Biml>
```

As you can see, all of the Biml objects are the same as the ones used in previous examples, except for the SSAS connection. It is also worth mentioning at this point that this and all other code samples in this chapter consist exclusively of static Biml files. You are not using any BimlScript code nuggets. Obviously, BimlScript could help you via automation, but that would require the creation of a metadata store that is outside the scope of this chapter.

Let's start with a very simple example to build a currency dimension. To do this, you start by modeling your relational table for the DimCurrency table in Biml, as shown in Listing 11-2.

■ **Note**   Tables can be easily imported with BimlStudio from the Import ribbon.

Listing 11-2. Currency Table Without SSAS Elements

```
<Biml xmlns="http://schemas.varigence.com/biml.xsd">
  <Tables>
    <Table Name="DimCurrency" SchemaName="AdventureWorksDW.dbo"
    FriendlyName="Source Currency">
      <Columns>
        <Column Name="CurrencyKey" />
        <Column Name="CurrencyName" DataType="String" Length="50" />
      </Columns>
    </Table>
  </Tables>
</Biml>
```

To make an OLAP dimension from the DimCurrency table, you will need to add a primary key as well as some analysis metadata, as shown in Listing 11-3.

Listing 11-3. Currency Table Including SSAS Elements

```
<Biml xmlns="http://schemas.varigence.com/biml.xsd">
  <Tables>
    <Table Name="DimCurrency" SchemaName="AdventureWorksDW.dbo"
    FriendlyName="Source Currency">
      <Columns>
        <Column Name="CurrencyKey" />
        <Column Name="CurrencyName" DataType="String" Length="50" />
      </Columns>
      <Keys>
        <Identity Name="PK_DimCurrency_CurrencyKey">
          <Columns>
            <Column ColumnName="CurrencyKey" />
          </Columns>
        </Identity>
      </Keys>
      <AnalysisMetadata>
        <Dimension Name="Currency" DimensionType="Currency">
          <Attributes>
            <Attribute Name="Currency" Usage="Key"
            AttributeType="CurrencyIsoCode" OrderBy="Name">
              <KeyColumns>
                <KeyColumn ColumnName="CurrencyKey" />
              </KeyColumns>
              <NameColumn ColumnName="CurrencyName" />
            </Attribute>
          </Attributes>
        </Dimension>
      </AnalysisMetadata>
    </Table>
  </Tables>
</Biml>
```

After adding analysis metadata to the `DimCurrency` table, the Logical View will now contain an item in the `Dimensions` folder. See Figure 11-5.

Figure 11-5. *Currency dimension is shown in the Logical View*

Listing 11-3 shows the addition of two elements: `Keys` and `AnalysisMetadata`.

The `Keys` element is used to define the primary key, which you will need to link the fact table to the `Dimension` table.

The `AnalysisMetadata` can hold any number of Dimension, MeasureGroup, or Tabular structure specifications for the parent relational table. This means that you can easily create multiple dimensions with different attribute configurations for the same table. This can also include a table that is a dimension as well as a measure group. Tables can even be used for both a multidimensional cube and a tabular model.

In your case, you have simply added a Dimension specification to `AnalysisMetadata`. This element holds a collection of attributes (just a single element for this example) which is defined by a Name, the KeyColumns collection, and a NameColumn element, as well as potentially additional attributes like `OrderBy` or `AttributeType`.

Most dimensions consist of multiple attributes and at least one hierarchy, as shown for the DimSalesTerritory dimension in Listing 11-4.

Listing 11-4. Biml Code for the Sales Territory Dimension, Including a Hierarchy

```
<Biml xmlns="http://schemas.varigence.com/biml.xsd">
  <Tables>
    <Table Name="DimSalesTerritory" SchemaName="AdventureWorksDW.dbo"
      FriendlyName="Sales Territory" >
      <Columns>
        <Column Name="SalesTerritoryKey" />
        <Column Name="SalesTerritoryRegion" DataType="String" Length="50" />
        <Column Name="SalesTerritoryCountry" DataType="String" Length="50" />
```

```xml
  <Column Name="SalesTerritoryGroup" DataType="String" Length="50"
  IsNullable="true" />
</Columns>
<Keys>
  <Identity Name="PK_DimSalesTerritory_SalesTerritoryKey">
    <Columns>
      <Column ColumnName="SalesTerritoryKey" />
    </Columns>
  </Identity>
</Keys>
<AnalysisMetadata>
  <Dimension Name="Sales Territory"  AttributeAllMemberName="All Sales
  Territories">
    <Attributes>
      <Attribute Name="Sales Territory Region" OrderBy="Name"
      Usage="Key">
        <KeyColumns>
          <KeyColumn ColumnName="SalesTerritoryKey" />
        </KeyColumns>
        <NameColumn ColumnName="SalesTerritoryRegion" />
      </Attribute>
      <Attribute Name="Sales Territory Group" OrderBy="Name">
        <KeyColumns>
          <KeyColumn ColumnName="SalesTerritoryGroup" />
        </KeyColumns>
        <NameColumn ColumnName="SalesTerritoryGroup" />
      </Attribute>
      <Attribute Name="Sales Territory Country" OrderBy="Name">
        <KeyColumns>
          <KeyColumn ColumnName="SalesTerritoryCountry" />
        </KeyColumns>
        <NameColumn ColumnName="SalesTerritoryCountry" />
      </Attribute>
    </Attributes>
    <AttributeHierarchies>
      <Hierarchy Name="Sales Territory">
        <Levels>
          <Level Name="Group" AttributeName="Sales Territory Group" />
          <Level Name="Country" AttributeName="Sales Territory
          Country" />
          <Level Name="Region" AttributeName="Sales Territory Region" />
        </Levels>
      </Hierarchy>
    </AttributeHierarchies>
    <Relationships>
      <Relationship Name="Sales Territory Country"
      ParentAttributeName="Sales Territory Region"
      ChildAttributeName="Sales Territory Country" />
```

```
          <Relationship Name="Sales Territory Group"
          ParentAttributeName="Sales Territory Country"
          ChildAttributeName="Sales Territory Group" />
      </Relationships>
    </Dimension>
  </AnalysisMetadata>
</Table>
</Tables>
</Biml>
```

The Sales Territory dimension has three total attributes. To help organize these attributes for your end users, you add one user hierarchy (using the AttributeHierarchies element) and connect the attributes by defining the relationships. For the user hierarchy, you configure the name and add hierarchy levels that reference your attributes. For the relationships collection, you add one relationship element per hierarchy level. The relationships also specify a name in addition to referencing a parent and a child attribute. Note that, in SSDT for SSAS as well as Biml, these relationships work in the opposite direction of the hierarchy levels. If your hierarchy is Region - Country - Group, your first level relationship element is Group, the second level element is Country, and the third level is Region. While the hierarchy works its way down from the highest aggregation, the relationship will build up from the lowest level.

You will also need a time dimension, as shown in Listing 11-5.

Listing 11-5. Biml Code for the Time Dimension

```
<Biml xmlns="http://schemas.varigence.com/biml.xsd">
  <Tables>
    <Table Name="DimDate" SchemaName="AdventureWorksDW.dbo"
    FriendlyName="Date">
      <Columns>
        <Column Name="DateKey" DataType="Int32" IsNullable="false" />
        <Column Name="FullDateAlternateKey" DataType="Date"
        IsNullable="false" />
        <Column Name="DayNumberOfWeek" DataType="Byte" IsNullable="false" />
        <Column Name="EnglishDayNameOfWeek" DataType="String" Length="10"
        IsNullable="false" />
        <Column Name="SpanishDayNameOfWeek" DataType="String" Length="10"
        IsNullable="false" />
        <Column Name="FrenchDayNameOfWeek" DataType="String" Length="10"
        IsNullable="false" />
        <Column Name="DayNumberOfMonth" DataType="Byte" IsNullable="false" />
        <Column Name="DayNumberOfYear" DataType="Int16" IsNullable="false" />
        <Column Name="WeekNumberOfYear" DataType="Byte" IsNullable="false" />
        <Column Name="EnglishMonthName" DataType="String" Length="10"
        IsNullable="false" />
        <Column Name="SpanishMonthName" DataType="String" Length="10"
        IsNullable="false" />
```

```
  <Column Name="FrenchMonthName" DataType="String" Length="10"
  IsNullable="false" />
  <Column Name="MonthNumberOfYear" DataType="Byte" IsNullable="false" />
  <Column Name="CalendarQuarter" DataType="Byte" IsNullable="false" />
  <Column Name="CalendarYear" DataType="Int16" IsNullable="false" />
  <Column Name="CalendarSemester" DataType="Byte" IsNullable="false" />
  <Column Name="FiscalQuarter" DataType="Byte" IsNullable="false" />
  <Column Name="FiscalYear" DataType="Int16" IsNullable="false" />
  <Column Name="FiscalSemester" DataType="Byte" IsNullable="false" />
</Columns>
<Keys>
  <PrimaryKey Name="PK_DimDate_DateKey">
    <Columns>
      <Column ColumnName="DateKey" />
    </Columns>
  </PrimaryKey>
</Keys>
<AnalysisMetadata>
  <Dimension Name="Date" DimensionType="Time">
    <Attributes>
      <Attribute Usage="Key" Name="Date" AttributeType="Date">
        <KeyColumns>
          <KeyColumn ColumnName="DateKey" />
        </KeyColumns>
        <NameColumn ColumnName="FullDateAlternateKey" />
      </Attribute>
      <Attribute Name="Month Name" AttributeType="Months">
        <KeyColumns>
          <KeyColumn ColumnName="CalendarYear" />
          <KeyColumn ColumnName="MonthNumberOfYear" />
        </KeyColumns>
        <NameColumn ColumnName="EnglishMonthName" />
      </Attribute>
      <Attribute Name="Calendar Year" AttributeType="Years">
        <KeyColumns>
          <KeyColumn ColumnName="CalendarYear" />
        </KeyColumns>
        <NameColumn ColumnName="CalendarYear" />
      </Attribute>
    </Attributes>
    <Relationships>
      <Relationship Name="Month Name" ParentAttributeName="Date"
      ChildAttributeName="Month Name" />
      <Relationship Name="Calendar Year" ParentAttributeName="Month
      Name" ChildAttributeName="Calendar Year" />
    </Relationships>
    <AttributeHierarchies>
      <Hierarchy Name="Calendar">
```

```
            <Levels>
              <Level Name="Year" AttributeName="Calendar Year" />
              <Level Name="Month" AttributeName="Month Name" />
              <Level Name="Date" AttributeName="Date" />
            </Levels>
          </Hierarchy>
        </AttributeHierarchies>
      </Dimension>
    </AnalysisMetadata>
  </Table>
</Tables>
</Biml>
```

Nothing you haven't seen before has been added to the Date dimension, except for `DimensionType` and `AttributeTypes`, which you will need for SSAS to be able to run YTD.

The month element will use multiple key columns, making it obvious why key columns are a collection as opposed to the single `NameColumn` element.

After adding the Biml code for these dimensions, you will see them reflected in the Logical View, as shown in Figure 11-6.

Figure 11-6. All three dimensions visible in the Logical View

Next, you add a measure group for FactInternetSales, as shown in Listing 11-6. As before, you start by defining the relational Biml model for the table and supplement it with AnalysisMetadata. Note in the Biml code sample that columns with foreign key relationships to the dimensions are created using the special TableReference column type.

Listing 11-6. Additional Elements and Attributes for Measure Groups in the Fact Table

```
<Biml xmlns="http://schemas.varigence.com/biml.xsd">
  <Tables>
    <Table Name="FactInternetSales" SchemaName="AdventureWorksDW.dbo">
      <Columns>
        <TableReference Name="OrderDateKey" TableName="AdventureWorksDW.dbo.
        DimDate" />
        <TableReference Name="ShipDateKey" TableName="AdventureWorksDW.dbo.
        DimDate" />
        <TableReference Name="CurrencyKey" TableName="AdventureWorksDW.dbo.
        DimCurrency" />
        <TableReference Name="SalesTerritoryKey"
        TableName="AdventureWorksDW.dbo.DimSalesTerritory" />
        <Column Name="OrderQuantity" DataType="Int16" />
        <Column Name="SalesAmount" DataType="Currency" />
      </Columns>
      <AnalysisMetadata>
        <MeasureGroup Name="Internet Sales">
          <Measures>
            <Measure AggregateColumnName="OrderQuantity" Name="Order
            Quantity" />
            <Measure AggregateColumnName="SalesAmount" Name="Sales Amount" />
          </Measures>
        </MeasureGroup>
      </AnalysisMetadata>
    </Table>
  </Tables>
</Biml>
```

Measure group definitions in AnalysisMetadata contain less metadata than dimensions. For the most part, they are just a collection of measures that reference columns in the parent table and specify a few bits of additional configuration.

After adding the Biml code for this measure group, you will see it reflected in the Logical View, as shown in Figure 11-7.

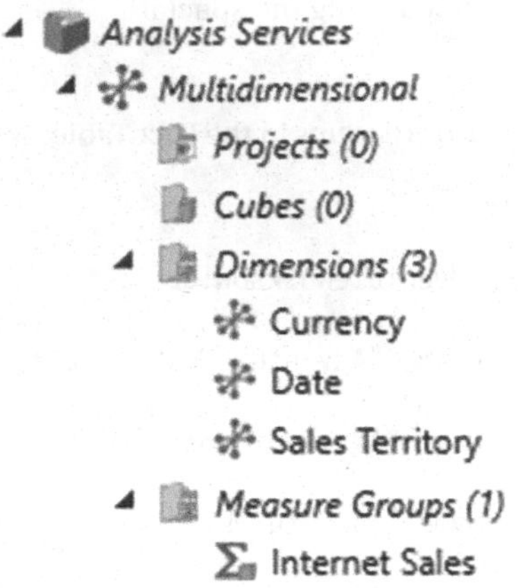

▲ 📦 *Analysis Services*
    ▲ ✳ *Multidimensional*
        📄 *Projects (0)*
        📄 *Cubes (0)*
        ▲ 📄 *Dimensions (3)*
            ✳ Currency
            ✳ Date
            ✳ Sales Territory
        ▲ 📄 *Measure Groups (1)*
            Σ Internet Sales

Figure 11-7. *The measure group also shows up in the Logical View*

Now that you have defined your dimensions and a measure group, all that is missing is a cube. The cube is mainly a collection of references to existing Biml objects, as shown in Listing 11-7.

Listing 11-7. Biml Code for a SSAS Cube

```
<Biml xmlns="http://schemas.varigence.com/biml.xsd">
  <Cubes>
    <Cube Name="MyCube" ConnectionName="AW_Cube">
      <CubeMeasureGroups>
        <CubeMeasureGroup Name="Internet Sales" FactName="AdventureWorksDW.
        dbo.FactInternetSales.Internet Sales">
          <CubeDimensionBindings>
            <CubeDimensionBinding CubeDimensionName="Order Date" FactColumn
            Name="AdventureWorksDW.dbo.FactInternetSales.OrderDateKey" />
            <CubeDimensionBinding CubeDimensionName="Ship Date" FactColumn
            Name="AdventureWorksDW.dbo.FactInternetSales.ShipDateKey" />
            <CubeDimensionBinding CubeDimensionName="Currency" FactColumn
            Name="AdventureWorksDW.dbo.FactInternetSales.CurrencyKey" />
            <CubeDimensionBinding CubeDimensionName="Sales Territory"
            FactColumnName="AdventureWorksDW.dbo.FactInternetSales.
            SalesTerritoryKey" />
          </CubeDimensionBindings>
          <Partitions>
            <Partition Name="Internet Sales Partition">
```

```
            <DsvTableSource ConnectionName="AdventureWorksDW"
            TableName="AdventureWorksDW.dbo.FactInternetSales" />
          </Partition>
        </Partitions>
      </CubeMeasureGroup>
    </CubeMeasureGroups>
    <CubeDimensions>
      <CubeDimension Name="Currency" DimensionName="AdventureWorksDW.dbo.
      DimCurrency.Currency" />
      <CubeDimension Name="Order Date" DimensionName="AdventureWorksDW.
      dbo.DimDate.Date" />
      <CubeDimension Name="Ship Date" DimensionName="AdventureWorksDW.dbo.
      DimDate.Date" />
      <CubeDimension Name="Sales Territory"
      DimensionName="AdventureWorksDW.dbo.DimSalesTerritory.Sales
      Territory" />
    </CubeDimensions>
  </Cube>
  </Cubes>
</Biml>
```

You have defined your CubeDimensions, which reference your previously defined SSAS database dimensions. SSAS does not have the concept of a CubeMeasureGroup, but Biml does provide that abstraction, which references your previously defined measure group. The relationships between the cube dimensions and cube measure group are defined in CubeDimensionBindings, which you're also using here to define a role-playing dimension by linking to the Date dimension twice and potentially multiple partitions. Note that you could provide additional configuration to filter your cube dimension attribute list or your cube measure group measure list, much like the way cube dimensions are defined in SSDT for SSAS.

With that, you have created everything you need for Biml to create your SSAS project, as shown in the Logical View in Figure 11-8.

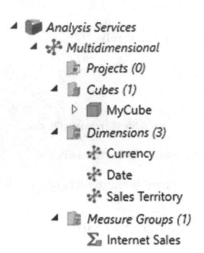

▲ 📦 *Analysis Services*
    ▲ ✴ *Multidimensional*
        📄 *Projects (0)*
        ▲ 📄 *Cubes (1)*
           ▷ 📦 MyCube
        ▲ 📄 *Dimensions (3)*
           ✴ Currency
           ✴ Date
           ✴ Sales Territory
        ▲ 📄 *Measure Groups (1)*
           Σ Internet Sales

Figure 11-8. *Complete SSAS ensemble, consisting of a cube, measure group, and dimensions*

If you build your solution, you will find the SSAS project in the Output\SSAS folder, as shown in Figure 11-9.

📒 Analysis	Analysis Services Database
📒 Analysis	Analysis Services Project file
✦ AW_DWH	Analysis Services Data Source
▦ AW_DWH	Analysis Services Data Source View
∠ Currency	Analysis Services Dimension
∠ Date	Analysis Services Dimension
🖟 MyCube	Analysis Services Cube
🖟 MyCube	Analysis Services Partitions
∠ Sales Territory	Analysis Services Dimension

Figure 11-9. *Content of the Output folder after building the solution*

If you don't define any cube projects within BimlStudio, BimlStudio will always build one default project in the SSAS subfolder of your output path, which will contain all of your cubes and dimensions.

If you want to create separate projects that only contain a subset of those cubes and/ or dimensions, one or multiples cube projects must be defined.

> ■ **Note** Once you define a cube project, BimlStudio will no longer build the default project. If you still need one project to contain all of your multidimensional objects, it has to be defined as a cube project as well.

During the build process, BimlStudio will also take care of all dependencies. Therefore, you do not need to include any connections or dimensions unless they are supplemental. In your current example, you only have one cube, MyCube, which contains all of the dimensions and uses the only existing OLAP connection.

Therefore, the code in Listing 11-8 would also cause BimlStudio to build and include the dimensions and the connection into your output project.

Listing 11-8. Code to Build a Project Called MyCubeProject Containing the Cube Named MyCube and All Dependencies

```
<Biml xmlns="http://schemas.varigence.com/biml.xsd">
  <Projects>
    <CubeProject Name="MyCubeProject">
      <Cubes>
        <Cube CubeName="MyCube" />
      </Cubes>
    </CubeProject>
  </Projects>
</Biml>
```

Listing 11-9 shows how you could define additional connections or dimensions to be built into the project. In this example, the output would be exactly the same because all of those objects are reference by the cube MyCube already.

Listing 11-9. Code to Build a Project Called MyCubeProject Including an Explicit Listing of All Dimensions and Databases to be Included

```
<Biml xmlns="http://schemas.varigence.com/biml.xsd">
  <Projects>
    <CubeProject Name="MyCubeProject">
      <Cubes>
        <Cube CubeName="MyCube" />
      </Cubes>
      <Dimensions>
        <Dimension DimensionName="AdventureWorksDW.dbo.DimCurrency.Currency" />
        <Dimension DimensionName="AdventureWorksDW.dbo.DimDate.Date" />
        <Dimension DimensionName="AdventureWorksDW.dbo.DimSalesTerritory.
        Sales Territory" />
      </Dimensions>
      <Connections>
        <Connection ConnectionName="AW_Cube" />
      </Connections>
```

```
    </CubeProject>
  </Projects>
</Biml>
```

Tabular Biml Projects

Now that you've built a multidimensional cube, let's take a look at how to create an SSAS tabular model using three tables from the same AdventureWorks2014DW database. Remember that BimlStudio will be set to compile the project into Analysis Services 2016 because BimlStudio only supports SQL Server 2016 versions for Analysis Services tabular projects.

Tabular projects are stored under the Analysis Services top-level folder within the Tabular subfolder. Under the Tabular folder are Projects, Tabular Models, and Tabular Tables, as shown in Figure 11-10.

▲ 📦 *Analysis Services*

    ▲ ✳️ *Multidimensional*

    ▲ 📦 *Tabular*

        📄 *Projects*

        📑 *Tabular Models*

        📑 *Tabular Tables*

Figure 11-10. *Tabular logical structure*

- Projects **folder**: Contains the Biml objects for the project and tabular models that are used in the project.

- Tabular Models **folder**: Contains the Biml objects for perspectives, relationships, roles, and tables.

- Tabular Tables **folder**: Contains the Biml objects for Analysis Services metadata for tables.

As with the multidimensional project, let's start with a very simple Biml file to provide the environment configuration for the data sources that will be used for the tabular model. This data is stored in the Relational folder and is shown in Listing 11-10.

Listing 11-10. Tabular Connection Biml

```
<Biml xmlns="http://schemas.varigence.com/biml.xsd">
  <Connections>
    <AnalysisServicesConnection Name="AW_Cube" Server="localhost"
    ConnectionString="provider=MSOLAP;Server=localhost;Database=Analysis;
    Integrated Security=SSPI" />
```

```
<OleDbConnection Name="AdventureWorksDW" ConnectionString=
  "provider=SQLNCLI11;data source=.;integrated security=SSPI;
  Initial Catalog=AdventureWorksDW2014">
    <AnalysisMetadata ImpersonationMode="ImpersonateAccount"
    AccountToImpersonate="Domain\User" />
  </OleDbConnection>
</Connections>
<Databases>
  <Database Name="AdventureWorksDW" ConnectionName="AdventureWorksDW" />
</Databases>
<Schemas>
  <Schema Name="dbo" DatabaseName="AdventureWorksDW" />
</Schemas>
</Biml>
```

Notice the AnalysisMetadata element under the OleDbConnection object. This element supports impersonation credentials that will be used during tabular processing, as shown in Figure 11-11.

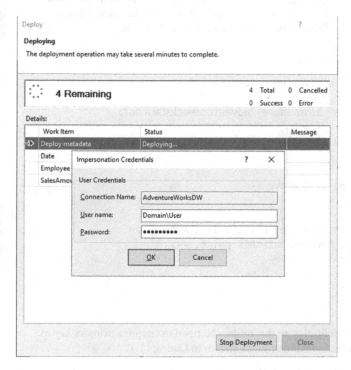

Figure 11-11. *Deploy window with credentials metadata*

After saving the environment Biml file, the objects shown in Figure 11-12 will appear in the Connections, Databases, and Schemas subfolders of your Logical View.

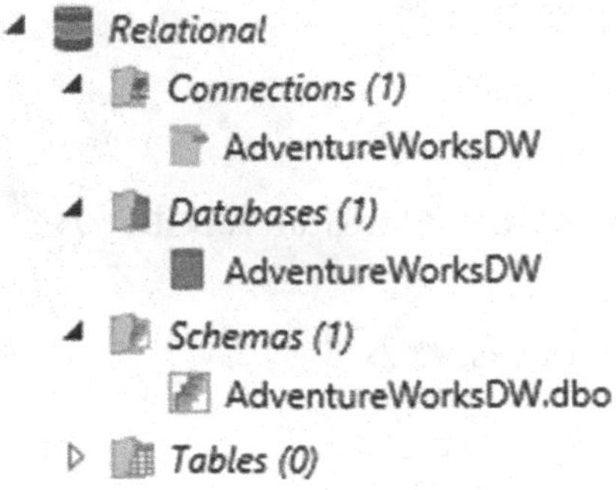

◢ 🗄 *Relational*
    ◢ 📄 *Connections (1)*
        🚩 AdventureWorksDW
    ◢ 📁 *Databases (1)*
        ⬛ AdventureWorksDW
    ◢ 📁 *Schemas (1)*
        🗂 AdventureWorksDW.dbo
    ▷ 🗂 *Tables (0)*

Figure 11-12. *Relational folder after connection file metadata*

Let's start with a very simple example to build a tabular table. As before, you will start by defining a relational table in Biml, either by hand or using the Import Table functionality. Listing 11-11 shows the definition of your DimDate table.

Listing 11-11. DimDate Table Biml

```
<Biml xmlns="http://schemas.varigence.com/biml.xsd">
  <Tables>
    <Table Name="DimDate" SchemaName="AdventureWorksDW.dbo">
      <Columns>
        <!-- See Listing 11-5 Above -->
      </Columns>
      <Keys>
        <!-- See Listing 11-5 Above -->
      </Keys>
      <AnalysisMetadata>
        <!-- Multi Dimensional See Listing 11-5 Above -->
        <!-- No Tabular Metadata at this point. -->
      </AnalysisMetadata>
    </Table>
  </Tables>
</Biml>
```

To add a tabular table definition to this table, you need to ensure a primary key as well as the AnalysisMetadata specification, as shown in Listing 11-12.

The `Tabular` element of `AnalysisMetadata` has four attributes that we will discuss in this chapter: `AutoCreateColumns`, `AutoCreateSinglePartition`, `IsHidden`, and `Name`.

- `AutoCreateColumns`: Creates a complete set of columns for the table/object and eliminates the need to manually specify the AnalysisMetadata/Tabular/Columns collection.

- `AutoCreateSinglePartition`: Creates a complete set of partitions for the tabular table and eliminates the need to define the AnalysisMetadata/Tabular/Partitions collection. You will use this for all of your tables except `SalesAmountQuota`.

- `IsHidden`: Hides the tabular table from client tools.

- `Name` **(Required)**: Name for the tabular table, which can be overridden in later steps if needed.

The `Tabular` element has various subelements that will need to be configured. In this section, we will discuss the Columns collection. In the `Column` element, there are four main attributes that will be discussed: `IsHidden`, `Name`, `SourceColumnName`, and `SortByColumnName`.

- `IsHidden`: Hides tabular column from client tools.

- `Name` **(Required)**: Name for the tabular column.

- `SourceColumnName` **(Required)**: A reference to the relational column that will be used as the source for this tabular column.

- `SortByColumnName`: Sets the sort order of a column values from another column in the same table.

Listing 11-12. DimDate Table AnalysisMetadata Biml

```
<Biml xmlns="http://schemas.varigence.com/biml.xsd">
  <Tables>
    <Table Name="DimDate" SchemaName="AdventureWorksDW.dbo">
      <Columns>
        <!-- See Listing 11-5 Above -->
      </Columns>
      <Keys>
        <!-- See Listing 11-5 Above -->
      </Keys>
      <AnalysisMetadata>
        <!-- Multi Dimensional See Listing 11-5 Above -->
        <Tabular Name="DimDate" AutoCreateSinglePartition="true" >
          <Columns>
            <Column Name="DateKey" SourceColumnName="DateKey"
            IsHidden="true" />
            <Column Name="FullDateAlternateKey" SourceColumnName=
            "FullDateAlternateKey" />
```

```
          <Column Name="DayNumberOfWeek" SourceColumnName=
          "DayNumberOfWeek" />
          <Column Name="EnglishDayNameOfWeek" SourceColumnName=
           "EnglishDayNameOfWeek" SortByColumnName="AdventureWorksDW.dbo.
           DimDate.DayNumberOfWeek" />
          <Column Name="DayNumberOfMonth" SourceColumnName=
           "DayNumberOfMonth" />
          <Column Name="DayNumberOfYear" SourceColumnName=
          "DayNumberOfYear" />
          <Column Name="WeekNumberOfYear" SourceColumnName=
          "WeekNumberOfYear" />
          <Column Name="EnglishMonthName" SourceColumnName=
          "EnglishMonthName" />
          <Column Name="MonthNumberOfYear" SourceColumnName=
          "MonthNumberOfYear" />
          <Column Name="CalendarQuarter" SourceColumnName="CalendarQuarter" />
          <Column Name="CalendarYear" SourceColumnName="CalendarYear" />
          <Column Name="CalendarSemester" SourceColumnName=
          "CalendarSemester" />
          <Column Name="FiscalQuarter" SourceColumnName="FiscalQuarter" />
          <Column Name="FiscalYear" SourceColumnName="FiscalYear" />
          <Column Name="FiscalSemester" SourceColumnName="FiscalSemester" />
        </Columns>
      </Tabular>
    </AnalysisMetadata>
  </Table>
 </Tables>
</Biml>
```

After adding the DimDate Biml file to your project, you will find your new objects in the Relational\Tables folder and the Analysis Services\Tabular\Tabular Tables folder of the Logical View, as shown in Figure 11-13.

▲ 🗄 *Relational*
   ▷ 📇 *Connections (1)*
   ▷ 📔 *Databases (1)*
   ▷ 📑 *Schemas (1)*
   ▲ 🗄 *Tables (1)*
       🗔 dbo.DimDate
▷ 🛢 *Integration Services*
▲ 📦 *Analysis Services*
   ▷ ✻ *Multidimensional*
   ▲ 🗄 *Tabular*
      ▷ 📄 *Projects (0)*
      ▷ 📄 *Tabular Models (0)*
      ▲ 📄 *Tabular Tables (1)*
         🗔 DimDate

Figure 11-13. BimlStudio Logical View of DimDate table

The next table to add to this project is DimEmployee, as shown in Listing 11-13. All of the AnalysisMetadata elements and attributes used in DimEmployee have been discussed in previous listings.

Listing 11-13. DimEmployee Table and AnalysisMetadata Biml

```
<Biml xmlns="http://schemas.varigence.com/biml.xsd">
  <Tables>
    <Table Name="DimEmployee" SchemaName="AdventureWorksDW.dbo">
      <Columns>
        <Column Name="EmployeeKey" DataType="Int32" IsNullable="false" />
        <Column Name="ParentEmployeeKey" DataType="Int32" IsNullable="true" />
        <Column Name="EmployeeNationalIDAlternateKey" DataType="String"
        Length="15" IsNullable="true" />
        <Column Name="ParentEmployeeNationalIDAlternateKey"
        DataType="String" Length="15" IsNullable="true" />
        <Column Name="SalesTerritoryKey" DataType="Int32" IsNullable="true" />
        <Column Name="FirstName" DataType="String" Length="50"
        IsNullable="false" />
        <Column Name="LastName" DataType="String" Length="50"
        IsNullable="false" />
        <Column Name="MiddleName" DataType="String" Length="50"
        IsNullable="true" />
        <Column Name="NameStyle" DataType="Boolean" IsNullable="false" />
```

297

```xml
      <Column Name="Title" DataType="String" Length="50" IsNullable="true" />
      <Column Name="HireDate" DataType="Date" IsNullable="true" />
      <Column Name="BirthDate" DataType="Date" IsNullable="true" />
      <Column Name="LoginID" DataType="String" Length="256"
      IsNullable="true" />
      <Column Name="EmailAddress" DataType="String" Length="50"
      IsNullable="true" />
      <Column Name="Phone" DataType="String" Length="25" IsNullable="true" />
      <Column Name="MaritalStatus" DataType="StringFixedLength" Length="1"
      IsNullable="true" />
      <Column Name="EmergencyContactName" DataType="String" Length="50"
      IsNullable="true" />
      <Column Name="EmergencyContactPhone" DataType="String" Length="25"
      IsNullable="true" />
      <Column Name="SalariedFlag" DataType="Boolean" IsNullable="true" />
      <Column Name="Gender" DataType="StringFixedLength" Length="1"
      IsNullable="true" />
      <Column Name="PayFrequency" DataType="Byte" IsNullable="true" />
      <Column Name="BaseRate" DataType="Currency" IsNullable="true" />
      <Column Name="VacationHours" DataType="Int16" IsNullable="true" />
      <Column Name="SickLeaveHours" DataType="Int16" IsNullable="true" />
      <Column Name="CurrentFlag" DataType="Boolean" IsNullable="false" />
      <Column Name="SalesPersonFlag" DataType="Boolean" IsNullable="false" />
      <Column Name="DepartmentName" DataType="String" Length="50"
      IsNullable="true" />
      <Column Name="StartDate" DataType="Date" IsNullable="true" />
      <Column Name="EndDate" DataType="Date" IsNullable="true" />
      <Column Name="Status" DataType="String" Length="50"
      IsNullable="true" />
      <Column Name="EmployeePhoto" DataType="Binary" Length="-1"
      IsNullable="true" />
    </Columns>
    <AnalysisMetadata>
      <Tabular Name="DimEmployee" AutoCreateSinglePartition="true"
      AutoCreateColumns="true" >
        <Columns>
          <Column Name="EmployeeKey" SourceColumnName="EmployeeKey"
          IsHidden="true"/>
          <Column Name="ParentEmployeeKey" SourceColumnName=
          "ParentEmployeeKey" IsHidden="true" />
          <Column Name="EmployeeNationalIDAlternateKey" SourceColumnName="
          EmployeeNationalIDAlternateKey" IsHidden="true" />
          <Column Name="ParentEmployeeNationalIDAlternateKey" SourceColumn
          Name="ParentEmployeeNationalIDAlternateKey" IsHidden="true" />
          <Column Name="SalesTerritoryKey" SourceColumnName=
          "SalesTerritoryKey" />
          <Column Name="FirstName" SourceColumnName="FirstName" />
```

```
            <Column Name="LastName" SourceColumnName="LastName" />
            <Column Name="MiddleName" SourceColumnName="MiddleName" />
            <Column Name="NameStyle" SourceColumnName="NameStyle" />
            <Column Name="Title" SourceColumnName="Title" />
            <Column Name="HireDate" SourceColumnName="HireDate" />
            <Column Name="BirthDate" SourceColumnName="BirthDate" />
            <Column Name="LoginID" SourceColumnName="LoginID" />
            <Column Name="EmailAddress" SourceColumnName="EmailAddress" />
            <Column Name="Phone" SourceColumnName="Phone" />
            <Column Name="MaritalStatus" SourceColumnName="MaritalStatus" />
            <Column Name="EmergencyContactName" SourceColumnName="Emergency
ContactName" />
            <Column Name="EmergencyContactPhone" SourceColumnName="Emergency
ContactPhone" />
            <Column Name="SalariedFlag" SourceColumnName="SalariedFlag" />
            <Column Name="Gender" SourceColumnName="Gender" />
            <Column Name="PayFrequency" SourceColumnName="PayFrequency" />
            <Column Name="BaseRate" SourceColumnName="BaseRate" />
            <Column Name="VacationHours" SourceColumnName="VacationHours" />
            <Column Name="SickLeaveHours" SourceColumnName="SickLeaveHours" />
            <Column Name="CurrentFlag" SourceColumnName="CurrentFlag" />
            <Column Name="SalesPersonFlag" SourceColumnName="SalesPersonFlag" />
            <Column Name="DepartmentName" SourceColumnName="DepartmentName" />
            <Column Name="StartDate" SourceColumnName="StartDate" />
            <Column Name="EndDate" SourceColumnName="EndDate" />
            <Column Name="Status" SourceColumnName="Status" />
          </Columns>
        </Tabular>
      </AnalysisMetadata>
      <Keys>
        <PrimaryKey Name="PK_DimEmployee">
          <Columns>
            <Column ColumnName="EmployeeKey" />
          </Columns>
        </PrimaryKey>
      </Keys>
    </Table>
  </Tables>
</Biml>
```

The last table to add to your tabular project is FactSalesQuota. This table will relate to your dimension tables and store your single measure. You will also define the partitions manually in the Partitions collection for this tabular table. You create a partition for each year of your sales quota data. This is not needed with the amount of data in this example, but is used to show how to manually create partitions within Biml. See Listing 11-14 for a full set of details. You will also create a measure on the SalesAmountQuota column by summing the amount. This is a contrived example because the sum of a sale quota might not be a true business measure.

Notice that the DAX Calculation must follow the DAX naming conventions for columns: *TableName[ColumnName]*.

Listing 11-14. FactSalesQuota Table and AnalysisMetadata Biml

```
<Biml xmlns="http://schemas.varigence.com/biml.xsd">
  <Tables>
    <Table Name="FactSalesQuota" SchemaName="AdventureWorksDW.dbo">
      <Columns>
        <Column Name="SalesQuotaKey" DataType="Int32" IsNullable="false" />
        <Column Name="EmployeeKey" DataType="Int32" IsNullable="false" />
        <Column Name="DateKey" DataType="Int32" IsNullable="false" />
        <Column Name="CalendarYear" DataType="Int16" IsNullable="false" />
        <Column Name="CalendarQuarter" DataType="Byte" IsNullable="false" />
        <Column Name="SalesAmountQuota" DataType="Currency" IsNullable="false" />
        <Column Name="Date" DataType="DateTime" IsNullable="true" />
      </Columns>
      <Keys>
        <PrimaryKey Name="PK_FactSalesQuota">
          <Columns>
            <Column ColumnName="SalesQuotaKey" SortOrder="Asc" />
          </Columns>
        </PrimaryKey>
      </Keys>
      <AnalysisMetadata>
        <Tabular Name="SalesAmountQuota" >
          <Partitions>
            <Partition Name="2010">
              <SourceQuery>SELECT [SalesQuotaKey], [EmployeeKey], [DateKey],
              [SalesAmountQuota] FROM [dbo].[FactSalesQuota] WHERE
              [CalendarYear] = 2010</SourceQuery>
            </Partition>
            <Partition Name="2011">
              <SourceQuery>SELECT [SalesQuotaKey], [EmployeeKey], [DateKey],
              [SalesAmountQuota] FROM [dbo].[FactSalesQuota] WHERE
              [CalendarYear] = 2011</SourceQuery>
            </Partition>
            <Partition Name="2012">
              <SourceQuery>SELECT [SalesQuotaKey], [EmployeeKey], [DateKey],
              [SalesAmountQuota] FROM [dbo].[FactSalesQuota] WHERE
              [CalendarYear] = 2012</SourceQuery>
            </Partition>
            <Partition Name="2013">
              <SourceQuery>SELECT [SalesQuotaKey], [EmployeeKey], [DateKey],
              [SalesAmountQuota] FROM [dbo].[FactSalesQuota] WHERE
              [CalendarYear] = 2013</SourceQuery>
            </Partition>
          </Partitions>
```

```
      <Columns>
        <Column Name="SalesQuotaKey" SourceColumnName="SalesQuotaKey"  />
        <Column Name="EmployeeKey" SourceColumnName="EmployeeKey" />
        <Column Name="DateKey" SourceColumnName="DateKey" />
        <Column Name="SalesAmountQuota" SourceColumnName="SalesAmountQuota" />
      </Columns>
      <Measures>
        <Measure Name="SalesQuota" DataType="Decimal"
        FormatString="$#,0.00;($#,0.00);$#,0.00">
          <Expression>SUM(SalesAmountQuota[SalesAmountQuota])</Expression>
        </Measure>
      </Measures>
    </Tabular>
  </AnalysisMetadata>
  </Table>
 </Tables>
</Biml>
```

After all of the table Biml files have been added to the project, your Biml objects will
appear in the Relational\Tables folder and the Analysis Services\Tabular\Tabular
Tables folder of the Logical View, as shown in Figure 11-14.

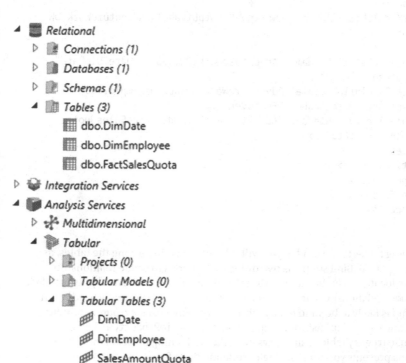

Figure 11-14. BimlStudio Logical View of all tables

Now that you have all of the tabular table objects created, you need to create a tabular model. There are four sub-objects under the TabularModel entity: Perspectives, Relationships, Roles, and Tables. We will discuss the following three in this sample.

- Perspectives: Creates a subset of tabular objects from an original tabular model.

- Relationships: Creates relationships between the tabular tables.

- Tables: Selects the available tabular tables from the current BimlStudio project.

To create a tabular model, you will select tables from the relational folder to be included in the tabular model. If you would like to edit the columns that are available in a tabular table, you can do so by creating a new tabular table definition for the same relational parent table in the AnalysisMetadata of the table. If you would like to change the name of the tabular table in the generated tabular model, you can override the name using the OutputLabel property, as shown for the DimDate and DimEmployee tables in Listing 11-15.

Listing 11-15. TabularModels with Tables Biml

```
<Biml xmlns="http://schemas.varigence.com/biml.xsd">
  <TabularModels>
    <TabularModel Name="AdventureWorksDW" OutputLabel="AdventureWorksDW-
    SalesQuota">
      <Tables>
        <Table TabularTableName="AdventureWorksDW.dbo.DimDate.DimDate"
        OutputLabel="Date" />
        <Table TabularTableName="AdventureWorksDW.dbo.DimEmployee.
        DimEmployee" OutputLabel="Employee" />
        <Table TabularTableName="AdventureWorksDW.dbo.FactSalesQuota.
        SalesAmountQuota" />
      </Tables>
      <Relationships />
      <Perspectives />
    </TabularModel>
  </TabularModels>
</Biml>
```

After adding tables to the model, you will add relationships among the tables, as shown in Listing 11-16. Biml supports two different locations to create relationship metadata. One location is in the TabularModel and the other is in the AnalysisMetadata\Tabular\Column. Relationships defined on the column node are normally used when the relationship is likely to be valid in any tabular model that uses the parent tabular table. For instance, the relationships among DimProduct - DimProductCategory - DimProductSubcategory tables will always be valid, so defining those relationships on the columns prevents you from having to redefine them for each tabular model. Relationships defined on the tabular model are more useful for cases where the tables come from multiple sources.

The Relationship element has the following attributes: Cardinality, FilterDirection, IsActive, TabularColumnName, and TargetTabularColumnName.

- Cardinality: Sets the relationship up as many-to-one or one-to-one.

- FilterDirection: Sets a cross filter of one-way or two-way filtering.

- IsActive: Sets the relationship up as active or inactive.

- SourceTabularColumnName: A reference to the tabular column that defines the foreign key for the relationship.

- TargetTabularColumnName: A reference to the tabular column that defines the primary key for the relationship.

Listing 11-16. TabularModels with Relationships Biml

```
<Biml xmlns="http://schemas.varigence.com/biml.xsd">
  <TabularModels>
    <TabularModel Name="AdventureWorksDW" OutputLabel="AdventureWorks
    DW-SalesQuota">
      <Tables>
        <Table TabularTableName="AdventureWorksDW.dbo.DimDate.DimDate"
        OutputLabel="Date" />
        <Table TabularTableName="AdventureWorksDW.dbo.DimEmployee.
        DimEmployee" OutputLabel="Employee" />
        <Table TabularTableName="AdventureWorksDW.dbo.FactSalesQuota.
        SalesAmountQuota" />
      </Tables>
      <Relationships>
        <Relationship TabularColumnName="AdventureWorksDW.dbo.
        FactSalesQuota.SalesAmountQuota.DateKey" TargetTabularColumnName=
        "AdventureWorksDW.dbo.DimDate.DimDate.DateKey" />
        <Relationship TabularColumnName="AdventureWorksDW.dbo.FactSalesQuota.
        SalesAmountQuota.EmployeeKey" TargetTabularColumnName=
        "AdventureWorksDW.dbo.DimEmployee.DimEmployee.EmployeeKey" />
      </Relationships>
      <Perspectives/>
    </TabularModel>
  </TabularModels>
</Biml>
```

In Listing 11-17, you add perspectives to the tabular model. Perspectives are not used as a security mechanism but as an organizational mechanism. In this code, you use the perspective to limit the tabular columns exposed in the Employee table.

Listing 11-17. TabularModels with Perspectives Biml

```
<Biml xmlns="http://schemas.varigence.com/biml.xsd">
  <TabularModels>
    <TabularModel Name="AdventureWorksDW" OutputLabel="AdventureWorks
    DW-SalesQuota">
      <Tables>
        <!-- See Listing 11-16 Above -->
      </Tables>
      <Relationships>
        <!-- See Listing 11-16 Above  -->
      </Relationships>
      <Perspectives>
        <Perspective Name="Limited Employee Data" >
          <Tables>
            <Table TabularTableName="AdventureWorksDW.dbo.DimDate.DimDate"
            IncludeAllColumns="true" />
            <Table TabularTableName="AdventureWorksDW.dbo.DimEmployee.
            DimEmployee" >
              <Columns>
                <Column TabularColumnName="AdventureWorksDW.dbo.DimEmployee.
                 DimEmployee.EmployeeKey" />
                <Column TabularColumnName="AdventureWorksDW.dbo.DimEmployee.
                DimEmployee.ParentEmployeeKey" />
                <Column TabularColumnName="AdventureWorksDW.dbo.DimEmployee.
                DimEmployee.SalesTerritoryKey" />
                <Column TabularColumnName="AdventureWorksDW.dbo.DimEmployee.
                DimEmployee.DepartmentName" />
              </Columns>
            </Table>
            <Table TabularTableName="AdventureWorksDW.dbo.FactSalesQuota.
            SalesAmountQuota" IncludeAllColumns="true" />
          </Tables>
        </Perspective>
      </Perspectives>
    </TabularModel>
  </TabularModels>
</Biml>
```

The last step in creating a Tabular project is to select a tabular model and choose the tabular server to create the tabular database, as shown in Listing 11-18.

Listing 11-18. Projects Biml

```
<Biml xmlns="http://schemas.varigence.com/biml.xsd">
  <Projects>
    <TabularProject Name="AdventureWorksDW" ServerName="SQL2016\TABULAR"
    Database="AdventureWorksDW" >
      <TabularModels>
        <TabularModel TabularModelName="AdventureWorksDW" />
      </TabularModels>
    </TabularProject>
  </Projects>
</Biml>
```

After adding all of the Biml files, your Logical View should look like Figure 11-15.

Figure 11-15. *BimlStudio Logical View of Tabular project*

■ **Note** Analysis Services tabular projects do not have visual designers for some of the elements and currently require directly editing the Biml.

Build the project and then open the solution from the Output\SSAS folder in Visual Studio to review the tabular project. See Figure 11-16.

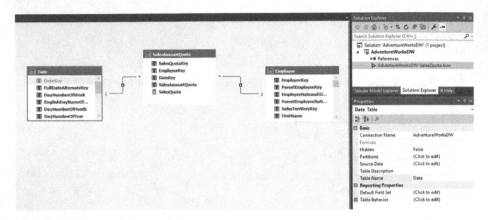

Figure 11-16. *Visual Studio tabular project*

Using Biml to Process Multidimensional Objects in SSIS

In addition to using Biml to define your multidimensional cubes and tabular models, you can also use Biml to create Analysis Services processing scripts that can be executed via SSIS.

Biml Syntax for SSIS Processing

To process your multidimensional cubes and tabular models, you will need to create an Analysis Services processing task and an Analysis Services connection in your Biml solution.

The processing task requires the specification of a name, an Analysis Services connection, and a processing configuration where you will define which objects you want to be processed. In most cases, you will also want to supply a processing order (parallel or sequential) and an error configuration.

A typical AnalysisServicesProcessing task, which would be added to the Tasks collection of an SSIS package or container in your Biml code, is shown in Listing 11-19.

Listing 11-19. Sample Code to Process a SSAS Cube in Biml

```
<Biml xmlns="http://schemas.varigence.com/biml.xsd">
  <Packages>
    <Package Name="Process_MySalesCube">
      <Tasks>
        <AnalysisServicesProcessing Name="Process Cube MySalesCube"
        ConnectionName="AW_Cube" ProcessingOrder="Parallel">
          <ProcessingConfigurations>
            <CubeProcessingConfiguration DatabaseID="MyCubeDB"
            ProcessingOption="ProcessFull" CubeId="MyCube"/>
          </ProcessingConfigurations>
          <ErrorConfiguration KeyDuplicate="IgnoreError" KeyErrorAction=
          "ConvertToUnknown" KeyErrorLimit="0" KeyNotFound="IgnoreError"
          NullKeyNotAllowed="IgnoreError" NullKeyConvertedToUnknown=
          "IgnoreError"/>
        </AnalysisServicesProcessing>
      </Tasks>
    </Package>
  </Packages>
</Biml>
```

Figure 11-17 shows how the AnalysisServicesProcessing task would display within the SSIS control flow design surface in SSDT for a generated package.

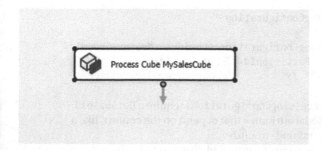

Figure 11-17. *SSAS processing task, created through Biml*

The code in Listing 11-17 creates a task to process the cube MyCube in the MyOLAPDB database using the AW_Cube connection. Since it has an ErrorConfiguration that is set to IgnoreError on all options, all processing errors would be ignored.

Depending on which type of object (Cube, Dimension, etc.) you want to process, you would use different Biml elements, which would be one of the following:

- CubeProcessingConfiguration

  ```
  <CubeProcessingConfiguration CubeId="" CubeName="" DatabaseID=""
  ProcessingOption="ProcessAdd|ProcessClear|ProcessData|Process
  Default|ProcessFull|ProcessIndexes|ProcessStructure"/>
  ```

307

- DimensionProcessingConfiguration

```
<DimensionProcessingConfiguration DimensionId="" DimensionName=""
DatabaseId="" ProcessingOption=""/>
```

- DatabaseProcessingConfiguration

```
<DatabaseProcessingConfiguration DatabaseId=""
ProcessingOption=""/>
```

- MeasureGroupProcessingConfiguration

```
<MeasureGroupProcessingConfiguration CubeId="" MeasureGroupId=""
MeasureGroupName="" DatabaseId="" ProcessingOption=""/>
```

- MiningModelProcessingConfiguration

```
<MiningModelProcessingConfiguration MiningModelId=""
MiningStructureId="" DatabaseId="" ProcessingOption=""/>
```

- MiningStructureProcessingConfiguration

```
<MiningStructureProcessingConfiguration MiningStructureId=""
DatabaseId="" ProcessingOption=""/>
```

- PartitionProcessingConfiguration

```
<PartitionProcessingConfiguration CubeId="" MeasureGroupId=""
ParititionName="" PartitionId="" DatabaseId=""
ProcessingOption="" />
```

As you can see, all of the ProcessingConfigurations require a DatabaseId, a ProcessingOption, and additional attributes that depend on the context, like a MiningStructureId to process a mining structure.

In cases where you can provide a name and an id, like DimensionId and DimensionName on the dimension processing, it is sufficient to provide one of these attributes.

Automated Approach

Processing an entire database sequentially can sometimes present performance problems that can be resolved by processing each cube (and potentially dimension) in parallel using separate processing tasks. Doing this manually would be tedious to implement and difficult to maintain. You can apply what you've learned about Biml to autogenerate this type of dynamic solution.

Analysis Services offers an API to retrieve information about the cubes and dimensions available in an SSAS database. You will use this API (called Analysis Management Objects or AMO) to build a simple package that will first process all dimensions in one processing task (sequential) and then create one processing task for each cube in the OLAP database, as shown in Listing 11-20.

Listing 11-20. Automated Solution to Process All Dimensions in One Task Followed by a Single Task Per Cube in an SSAS Database

```
<#@ template language="VB" #>
<#@ assembly name="C:\Program Files (x86)\Microsoft SQL Server\120\SDK\
Assemblies\Microsoft.AnalysisServices.dll" #>
<#@ import namespace="Microsoft.AnalysisServices" #>
<# Dim OLAPServer as String = "localhost"
   Dim OLAPDB as string = "MyCubeDB"
   Dim OLAPConnection as new Server
   OLAPConnection.connect(OLAPServer)#>
<Biml xmlns="http://schemas.varigence.com/biml.xsd">
  <Packages>
    <Package Name="Process_SSAS" ConstraintMode="Linear">
      <Tasks>
        <AnalysisServicesProcessing Name="Process Dimensions"
        ConnectionName="AW_Cube">
          <ProcessingConfigurations>
            <# for each olapdim as dimension in olapconnection.
            databases(olapdb).dimensions #>
            <DimensionProcessingConfiguration DatabaseId="<#= OLAPDB #>"
            ProcessingOption="ProcessUpdate" DimensionId="<#= olapdim.id #>" />
            <# next #>
          </ProcessingConfigurations>
          <ErrorConfiguration KeyDuplicate="IgnoreError" KeyErrorAction=
          "ConvertToUnknown" KeyErrorLimit="0" KeyNotFound="IgnoreError"
          NullKeyNotAllowed="IgnoreError" NullKeyConvertedToUnknown=
          "IgnoreError"/>
        </AnalysisServicesProcessing>
        <Container Name="Process Cubes" ConstraintMode="Parallel">
          <Tasks>
            <# for each olapcube as cube in olapconnection.
            databases(olapdb).cubes #>
            <AnalysisServicesProcessing Name="Process Cube <#= olapcube.name #>"
            ConnectionName="AW_Cube" ProcessingOrder="Parallel">
              <ProcessingConfigurations>
                <CubeProcessingConfiguration DatabaseID="<#= olapdb #>"
                ProcessingOption="ProcessFull" CubeId="<#= olapcube.id #>"/>
              </ProcessingConfigurations>
```

```
            <ErrorConfiguration KeyDuplicate="IgnoreError" KeyErrorAction=
            "ConvertToUnknown" KeyErrorLimit="0" KeyNotFound="IgnoreError"
            NullKeyNotAllowed="IgnoreError" NullKeyConvertedToUnknown=
            "IgnoreError"/>
          </AnalysisServicesProcessing>
          <# next #>
        </Tasks>
      </Container>
    </Tasks>
  </Package>
 </Packages>
</Biml>
<# OLAPConnection.Disconnect #>
```

If you apply the BimlScript in Listing 11-18 to the database you created earlier in this chapter, the resulting expanded Biml output is shown in Listing 11-21.

Listing 11-21. Result of Automated Processing Package

```
<Biml xmlns="http://schemas.varigence.com/biml.xsd">
  <Packages>
    <Package Name="Process_SSAS" ConstraintMode="Linear">
      <Tasks>
        <AnalysisServicesProcessing Name="Process Dimensions"
        ConnectionName="AW_Cube">
          <ProcessingConfigurations>
            <DimensionProcessingConfiguration DatabaseId="MyCubeDB" Processing
            Option="ProcessUpdate" DimensionId="Sales Territory" />
            <DimensionProcessingConfiguration DatabaseId="MyCubeDB" Processing
            Option="ProcessUpdate" DimensionId="Date" />
            <DimensionProcessingConfiguration DatabaseId="MyCubeDB" Processing
            Option="ProcessUpdate" DimensionId="Currency" />
          </ProcessingConfigurations>
          <ErrorConfiguration KeyDuplicate="IgnoreError" KeyErrorAction=
          "ConvertToUnknown" KeyErrorLimit="0" KeyNotFound="IgnoreError"
          NullKeyNotAllowed="IgnoreError" NullKeyConvertedToUnknown=
          "IgnoreError"/>
        </AnalysisServicesProcessing>
        <Container Name="Process Cubes" ConstraintMode="Parallel">
          <Tasks>
            <AnalysisServicesProcessing Name="Process Cube MyCube"
            ConnectionName="AW_Cube" ProcessingOrder="Parallel">
              <ProcessingConfigurations>
                <CubeProcessingConfiguration DatabaseID="MyCubeDB"
                ProcessingOption="ProcessFull" CubeId="MyCube"/>
              </ProcessingConfigurations>
```

```
            <ErrorConfiguration KeyDuplicate="IgnoreError" KeyErrorAction=
            "ConvertToUnknown" KeyErrorLimit="0" KeyNotFound="IgnoreError"
            NullKeyNotAllowed="IgnoreError" NullKeyConvertedToUnknown=
            "IgnoreError"/>
          </AnalysisServicesProcessing>
        </Tasks>
      </Container>
    </Tasks>
  </Package>
 </Packages>
</Biml>
```

After building, the resulting SSIS control flow is shown in Figure 11-18.

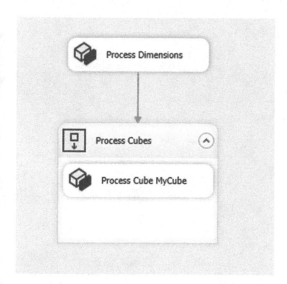

Figure 11-18. *Layout of compiled SSIS package*

By making use of the .NET AMO object model and BimlScript automation capabilities, you have created a package that will process the entire database for you, almost fully in parallel.

Summary

In this chapter, you created SSAS projects for both tabular models and multidimensional cubes. You explored some of the considerations for whether or not to use Biml for your SSAS project, and you learned how to use BimlScript to automatically generate SSAS processing tasks for your SSIS packages.

In the next chapter, we will show you how Biml can help with T-SQL challenges!

CHAPTER 12

■ ■ ■

Biml for T-SQL and Other Little Helpers

Dynamically generating T-SQL statements through functions or stored procedures is an easy task if you are familiar with SQL Server. These routines are subsets of code that may be called once as part of a separate build. Consider the following scenario: you would like to generate data and create or alter statements as part of the same build process. This is doable if you are using continuous integration with Visual Studio but not as easily achieved if you are developing using SSMS. In this chapter, we will show examples of how this can be done with Biml, whether you are using BimlExpress or BimlStudio.

Why Biml?

Many assume BimlScripts only generate expanded Biml, which is compiled into SSIS packages and other Microsoft BI objects. BimlScript is capable of building text based on data in any format, including T-SQL scripts. We can therefore use Biml to generate ad-hoc code such as T-SQL for everyday tasks. The generated T-SQL can be built into Execute SQL tasks in SSIS, saved to a file, or copied and pasted into a database integrated development environment (IDE) such as SQL Server Management Studio (SSMS). In this section, we look at ad-hoc approaches.

How Does Biml Work For T-SQL?

There are four techniques:

- Use the Preview pane.
- Generate SSIS packages.
- Save T-SQL to files.
- Execute T-SQL using SqlCommand.

© Andy Leonard et al. 2017
A. Leonard et al., *The Biml Book*, https://doi.org/10.1007/978-1-4842-3135-7_12

Each technique has strengths and weaknesses. In this section, you'll produce the same sample using each technique to demonstrate the differences. Your first sample generates T-SQL to generate all tables defined in the Biml RootNode.Tables collection.

Using the Preview Pane

Pros:

- Easiest to set up: just execute your script and then copy and paste

Cons:

- A very manual approach

- Does not support automation or continuous integration

The Preview panes in BimlExpress and BimlStudio display any kind of text. The text doesn't necessarily *have* to be Biml code (unless you want the compiler to build the result). This means you can output T-SQL (or JSON, XML, or any format) to the Preview pane, copy and paste, and then run it using SSMS. See Listings 12-1 and 12-2.

Listing 12-1. Foreach Loop Displayed in Preview Pane (C#)

```
<# foreach (var tableNode in RootNode.Tables) { #>
  <#=tableNode.GetDropAndCreateDdl()#>
<# } #>
```

Listing 12-2. Foreach Loop Displayed in Preview Pane (VB)

```
<#@ template language="VB" optionexplicit="False"#>
<#  for each tableNode in RootNode.Tables #>
  <#=tableNode.GetDropAndCreateDdl()#>
<# next #>
```

As you can see, this is a simple approach. You use BimlScript functions and methods that you already know and then copy and paste the result from the Preview pane into SSMS for execution, as shown in Figure 12-1.

```
1  <# foreach (var tableNode in RootNode.Tables) { #>
2      <#=tableNode.GetDropAndCreateDdl()#>
3  <# } #>
4  |
```

```
 1      SET ANSI_NULLS ON
 2  SET QUOTED_IDENTIFIER ON
 3  GO
 4
 5  ---------------------------------------------------------------
 6  IF EXISTS (SELECT * from sys.objects WHERE object_id = OBJECT_ID(N'[myTable]') AND type IN (N'U'))
 7  DROP TABLE [myTable]
 8  GO
 9
10  CREATE TABLE [myTable]
11  (
12  -- Columns Definition
13      [col1] int NOT NULL
14
15  -- Constraints
16
17  )
18  ON "default"
19  WITH (DATA_COMPRESSION = NONE)
20  GO
21
22  ---------------------------------------------------------------
23
24
```
Hide Preview   Preview is up-to-date   Update

Figure 12-1. *Visual Studio and the Preview pane for Biml Express*

Generating SSIS Packages

Pros:

- Easy to set up and deploy

- Supports automation when using BimlStudio

Cons:

- Overhead from SSIS packages

- Continuous automation is limited

Another solution is to generate one or more SSIS packages with Execute SQL tasks using Biml. Since the Execute SQL task is specifically designed to execute T-SQL, generating SSIS packages is a perfect solution for recurring tasks, plus you have the option to schedule SSIS package execution using SQL Agent. See Listings 12-3 and 12-4.

Listing 12-3. Run T-SQL Through SSIS (C#)

```
<Biml xmlns="http://schemas.varigence.com/biml.xsd">
  <Packages>
    <Package Name="Create Tables" ConstraintMode="Parallel">
      <Tasks>
        <# foreach (var tableNode in RootNode.Tables) { #>
        <ExecuteSQL Name="Create <#=tableNode.SchemaQualifiedName#>"
        ConnectionName="targetConnection">
```

```
            <DirectInput><#=tableNode.GetDropAndCreateDdl()#></DirectInput>
          </ExecuteSQL>
          <# } #>
        </Tasks>
      </Package>
    </Packages>
</Biml>
```

Listing 12-4. Run T-SQL Through SSIS (VB)

```
<#@ template language="VB" optionexplicit="False"#>
<Biml xmlns="http://schemas.varigence.com/biml.xsd">
  <Packages>
    <Package Name="Create Tables" ConstraintMode="Parallel">
      <Tasks>
        <# for each tableNode in RootNode.Tables #>
        <ExecuteSQL Name="Create <#=tableNode.SchemaQualifiedName#>"
        ConnectionName="targetConnection">
          <DirectInput><#=tableNode.GetDropAndCreateDdl()#></DirectInput>
        </ExecuteSQL>
        <# next #>
      </Tasks>
    </Package>
  </Packages>
</Biml>
```

The BimlScript in Listings 12-3 and 12-4 calls the GetDropAndCreateDdl() method to create T-SQL statements that drop the table if it already exists, and then create the table.

When generated, the SSIS package may appear similar to that shown in Figure 12-2.

Figure 12-2 shows the resulting DDL in the Enter SQL Query window.

Figure 12-2. *Visual Studio and the Execute SQL task inside SSIS*

Saving T-SQL to Files

Pros:

- Generates .sql files, which can be added to your database solution

- Supports continuous integration when using BimlStudio

Cons:

- Additional overhead due to additional files

Instead of just displaying the T-SQL or creating an SSIS package for it, you can execute the System.IO.File.WriteAllText() method. WriteAllText permits you to save your script to a text file, which can then be distributed and/or executed using common tools.

Something to keep in mind when developing Biml with BimlExpress is the Biml compiler runs when you build your code. BimlExpress code builds when you open the Biml file, update the Preview pane, or manually compile. To manually compile Biml in BimlExpress, select one or more Biml files from the Solution Explorer, right-click, and select Generate SSIS Packages.

In this example, you generate one file per table and write the file to C:\Temp. See Listings 12-5 and 12-6.

■ **Note** To execute the code, you either have to change the path to an already existing folder on your system or manually create the Temp folder under C:.

Listing 12-5. Save Code to Text Files (C#)

```
<#@ import namespace="System.IO" #>
<#
var root = @"C:\Temp\";
foreach (var tableNode in RootNode.Tables) {
  File.WriteAllText
  (
    root + tableNode.SchemaQualifiedName + ".sql",
    tableNode.GetDropAndCreateDdl()
  );
}
#>
```

Listing 12-6. Save Code to Text Files (VB)

```
<#@ template language="VB" optionexplicit="False"#>
<#@ import namespace="System.IO" #>
<#
root = "C:\Temp\"
for each tableNode in RootNode.Tables
  File.WriteAllText (
    root + tableNode.SchemaQualifiedName + ".sql", _
    tableNode.GetDropAndCreateDdl()
  )
Next
#>
```

The BimlScript shown in Listings 12-5 and 12-6 declare and initialize a variable named root. Next, you iterate the RootNode.Tables collection and call the File. WriteAllText method and pass it the value of root plus the SchemaQualifiedName of the Table object plus the .sql file extension as a file name. The contents you write to the file (the "all text" portion of the WriteAllText method) is the T-SQL returned from each table object's GetDropAndCreateDdl() method. The results of this operation are shown in Figure 12-3.

Figure 12-3. *Visual Studio and File Explorer target path*

Consider refactoring this code to employ the `CallBimlScript` function if the generation of your T-SQL becomes complex (in many cases it will be more complex). You can think of `CallBimlScript` as "outsourcing" code execution to a "callee." You may then simply pass the returned result to the text file via `File.WriteAllText`, as shown in Listings 12-7 and 12-8.

Listing 12-7. Make Use of CallBimlScript (C#)

```
<#@ import namespace="System.IO" #>
<#
var root = @"C:\Temp\";
foreach ( var tableNode in RootNode.Tables) {
  File.WriteAllText
  (
    root + tableNode.SchemaQualifiedName + ".sql",
    CallBimlScript("Callee.biml", tableNode)
  );
}
#>
```

Listing 12-8. Make Use of CallBimlScript (VB)

```
<#@ template language="VB" optionexplicit="False"#>
<#@ import namespace="System.IO" #>
<#
root = "C:\Temp\"
for each tableNode in RootNode.Tables
  File.WriteAllText (
    root + tableNode.SchemaQualifiedName + ".sql", _
    CallBimlScript("Callee.biml",tableNode)
  )
next #>
```

The "callee" script for this very basic case would appear similar to that shown in Listing 12-9.

Listing 12-9. Callee

```
<#@ property name="tableNode" type="AstTableNode" #>
<#= tableNode.GetDropAndCreateDdl() #>
```

Instead of calling an extension method directly, you instead call another BimlScript, the "callee," which returns the T-SQL for you. In more complex cases, "outsourcing" a portion of the BimlScript logic improves readability and promotes healthy change management.

Executing T-SQL Using SqlCommand

Pros:

- May be saved as part of your solution
- May be executed before creating SSIS packages
- May be automated

Cons:

- Risks of automation (may cause data loss, or worse)

The last option you'll explore in this chapter is executing T-SQL using SqlCommand, which means you execute T-SQL *directly* during compilation using a .NET method. This is super helpful if you need some steps to run before you generate your objects using Biml. This is also super dangerous and may trigger huge performance impacts. We share this option with caution and highly recommend you *carefully consider* the implications.

SqlCommand does not support "GO," which is a batch separator command used in SSMS. If you auto-generate T-SQL using the Biml GetDropAndCreateDdl method, you need to remove "GO" from the returned string prior to execution. In some cases, you may need to split up your code to run in separate batches.

■ **Note**   The Biml code to create the schemas needed for you in SQL Server is not included. Please create schemas manually to avoid an error.

An example is shown in Listings 12-10 and 12-11.

Listing 12-10. Execute T-SQL with SqlCommand (C#)

```
<#@ import  namespace="System.Data.SqlClient" #>
<#
var ddl = string.Join("", RootNode.Tables.Select(t =>
t.GetDropAndCreateDdl().Replace("GO\n", "")));
using (var conn = new SqlConnection("Data Source=localhost;
Database=MyBiml_Destination;Integrated Security=SSPI"))

{
  conn.Open();
  using (var cmd = new SqlCommand(ddl, conn))
  {
    cmd.ExecuteNonQuery();
  }
}
#>
```

Listing 12-11. Execute T-SQL with SqlCommand (VB)

```
<#@ template language="VB" optionexplicit="False"#>
<#@ import namespace="System.Data.SqlClient" #>
<#
ddl = string.Join("", RootNode.Tables.Select(Function(t)  t.
GetDropAndCreateDdl().Replace("GO" & chr(10), "")))

Using conn as new SqlConnection("Data source=localhost; Database=MyBiml_
Destination;Integrated Security=SSPI")
  conn.Open()
  Using cmd as new SqlCommand(ddl, conn)
    cmd.ExecuteNonQuery()
  End Using
End Using
#>
```

Samples

The following samples all use the Preview pane technique and are designed to inspire ideas for using T-SQL with Biml. Most of what you do here can be achieved using dynamic SQL or third-party products. It's simply amazing how much you can achieve with very few lines of BimlScript!

Truncating and Dropping Tables

A very basic example of an ad-hoc pattern is truncating or dropping tables. Your code iterates the imported collection of tables in RootNode.Tables and creates a SQL script fragment for each table, in this case a Truncate Table statement. You then copy the expanded code from the Preview pane and paste it wherever you might want to use it, as shown in Figure 12-4.

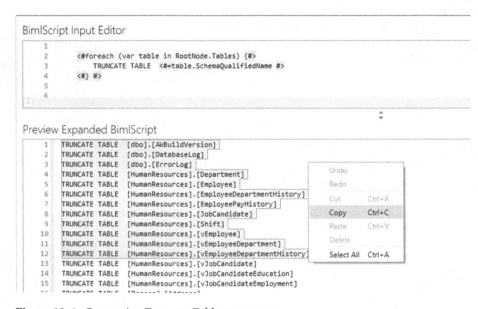

Figure 12-4. *Generating Truncate Table statements*

Building a Clustered Columnstore Index

At the time of this writing, Biml doesn't support Columnstore indexes in its relational model. You can still use these features by writing ad-hoc Biml to generate T-SQL to build the desired indexes. In this example, you create code to drop any existing indexes before creating a non-clustered Columnstore index.

You iterate imported tables, and then iterate table indexes to create the DROP IF EXISTS statements (SQL Server 2016 and above).

You use the GetColumnList method on each table, which returns a comma-separated string of the columns in the current table. GetColumnList accepts an optional lambda function as a predicate to filter out columns of datatypes that aren't supported by columnstores, as shown in Figure 12-5.

```
BimlScript Input Editor
 1  <Biml xmlns="http://schemas.varigence.com/biml.xsd">
 2    <#foreach (var table in RootNode.Tables.Where(x => x.SchemaName == "Person")) {#>
 3      <#foreach (var idx in table.Indexes) { #>
 4        DROP INDEX IF EXISTS <#=idx.Name #> ON <#=table.SchemaQualifiedName #>
 5      <#} #>
 6      CREATE NONCLUSTERED COLUMNSTORE INDEX [NCCI-<#=table.SsisSafeScopedName #>] ON [Person].[Address]
 7      (
 8          <#=table.GetColumnList(x => x.DataType != System.Data.DbType.Object && x.DataType != System.Data.DbType.Guid  ) #>
 9
10      ) WITH (DROP_EXISTING = OFF, COMPRESSION_DELAY = 0)
11      -------------------------------------------------------------------------------------
12    <#} #>
13  </Biml>
14
```

```
Preview Expanded BimlScript
 1  <Biml xmlns="http://schemas.varigence.com/biml.xsd">
 2    DROP INDEX IF EXISTS AK_Address_rowguid ON [Person].[Address]
 3    DROP INDEX IF EXISTS IX_Address_AddressLine1_AddressLine2_City_StateProvinceID_PostalCode ON [Person].[Address]
 4    DROP INDEX IF EXISTS IX_Address_StateProvinceID ON [Person].[Address]
 5    CREATE NONCLUSTERED COLUMNSTORE INDEX [NCCI-AdventureWorks2014_Person_Address] ON [Person].[Address]
 6    (
 7    [AddressID], [AddressLine1], [AddressLine2], [City], [StateProvinceID], [PostalCode], [ModifiedDate]
 8
 9    ) WITH (DROP_EXISTING = OFF, COMPRESSION_DELAY = 0)
10    -------------------------------------------------------------------------------------
```

Figure 12-5. *Building columnstore index statements*

■ **Hint** It might be a good idea to store your information on the desired columnstore index in a Biml annotation. You may later automate the index creation based on the contents of the Biml annotation.

Development Reset

Often when developing a pattern, you want to reset your development environments to a "clean" state. Let's say you want to begin testing but several tables in your environment have Change Data Capture (CDC) enabled. You need to disable CDC in order to proceed. Your code might appear as shown in Figure 12-6.

BimlScript Input Editor

```
1   <#foreach (var table in RootNode.Tables){ #>
2       IF EXISTS (
3           SELECT s.name AS Schema_Name, tb.name AS Table_Name
4           , tb.object_id, tb.type, tb.type_desc, tb.is_tracked_by_cdc
5           FROM sys.tables tb
6           INNER JOIN sys.schemas s on s.schema_id = tb.schema_id
7           WHERE s.name = '<#=table.Schema.Name #>' AND tb.name = '<#=table.Name #>' AND tb.is_tracked_by_cdc = 1
8       )
9       BEGIN
10          EXEC sys.sp_cdc_disable_table
11          @source_schema = N'<#=table.Schema.Name#>',
12          @source_name   = N'<#=table.Name #>',
13          @capture_instance = N'<#=table.Schema.Name#>_<#=table.Name #>'
14      END
15  <#} #>
```

Preview Expanded BimlScript

```
1   IF EXISTS (
2   SELECT s.name AS Schema_Name, tb.name AS Table_Name
3   , tb.object_id, tb.type, tb.type_desc, tb.is_tracked_by_cdc
4   FROM sys.tables tb
5   INNER JOIN sys.schemas s on s.schema_id = tb.schema_id
6   WHERE s.name = 'dbo' AND tb.name = 'AWBuildVersion' AND tb.is_tracked_by_cdc = 1
7   )
8   BEGIN
9   EXEC sys.sp_cdc_disable_table
10  @source_schema = N'dbo',
11  @source_name   = N'AWBuildVersion',
12  @capture_instance = N'dbo_AWBuildVersion'
```

Figure 12-6. *Generating statements to disable CDC*

Comparing Source and Target Tables

A common task is comparing two databases (source and target) and generating scripts that ALTER, CREATE or DROP target tables. You can easily compare them using Biml, as shown in Listing 12-12.

Listing 12-12. Alter Table Statements

```
<# var sourceTables = RootNode.DbConnections["Source"].ImportDB(); #>
<# var targetTables = RootNode.DbConnections["Target"].ImportDB(); #>
<# foreach (var table in sourceTables.TableNodes) { #>
<# var matchingDeployedTable = targetTables.TableNodes.FirstOrDefault
(i => i.SchemaQualifiedName == table.SchemaQualifiedName); #>
<# if (matchingDeployedTable != null) { #>
  <# foreach (var column in table.Columns.Where(i => !matchingDeployedTable.
  Columns.Any(j => j.Name == i.Name))) { #>
  ALTER TABLE <#=table.SchemaQualifiedName#> ADD <#=column.Name#>
<#=Varigence.Biml.CoreLowerer.TSqlEmitter.TSqlTypeTranslator.
Translate(column)#> NULL
  <# } #>
  GO
```

```
<# foreach (var column in matchingDeployedTable.Columns.Where(i => !table.
  Columns.Any(j => j.Name == i.Name))) {#>
    ALTER TABLE <#=table.SchemaQualifiedName#> DROP COLUMN <#=column.Name#>
  <# } #>
  GO
<# } else {#>
  <#=table.GetDropAndCreateDdl()#>
<# } #>
<# } #>
<# foreach (var table in targetTables.TableNodes) { #>
<# var matchingSourceTable = sourceTables.TableNodes.FirstOrDefault
(i => i.SchemaQualifiedName == table.SchemaQualifiedName); #>
<# if (matchingSourceTable == null) { #>
  <#=table.GetDropAndCreateDdl()#>
<# } #>
<# } #>
```

This sample oversimplifies the approach and is therefore *not* production ready; it checks only column names, ignores data types, and doesn't check for additional indexes, extended properties, or other settings. A production-ready solution would compare these settings in the manner demonstrated by this code and adjust the script accordingly.

Detecting Stale Data

Detecting stale data is not an everyday task, but the Biml object model allows you to quickly create SELECT statements that specify data type.

Assume you want to identify the maximum value for each datetime or datetime2 column per table to identify inactive tables. You first need to identify all tables that contain a datetime or datetime2 data type column. Next, query the maximum value for the identified column. Finally, UNION them to get the highest value for each identified table.

Instead of iterating imported tables in RootNode.Tables, this example uses a connection to create Table objects in BimlScript, builds a T-SQL statement based on date data types, and then executes a query against the database to return the maximum date; see Listing 12-13.

Listing 12-13. Stale Data Detection

```
<#@ template language="VB" optionexplicit="False" #>
<# for each tableNode in RootNode.OleDbConnections("Source_2").
GenerateTableNodes()
  Dim dateColumnQueries as new List(of String)
  for each Column in tableNode.Columns.Where(function(c) c.DataType =
  System.Data.DbType.DateTime or c.DataType = System.Data.DbType.DateTime2)
    dateColumnQueries.Add("SELECT MAX(" + column.QualifiedName + ") AS
    DateColumn FROM " + tableNode.SchemaQualifiedName)
  next
```

```
    query = "SELECT MAX(DateColumn) As MaxDate FROM (" + string.Join(" UNION ALL ",
    dateColumnQueries) + ") AS a"
if (dateColumnQueries.Any()) then #>
<#=tableNode.Name#>,<#=ExternalDataAccess.GetDataTable(RootNode.
OleDbConnections("Source_2").ConnectionString, query).Rows(0)(0)#>
<# end if
next #>
```

That's only 10 lines of code and the results are available in the Preview Expanded
BimlScript pane, as also shown in Figure 12-7.

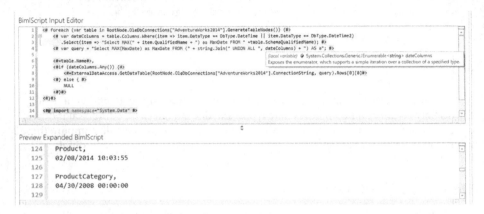

Figure 12-7. *Generating profile statements with the same code from Listing 12-13 but in C#*

The maximum date in the Product table is 02/08/2014. Given this database is
AdventureWorks2014 you might deduce that the Product table is currently active.
The T-SQL query executed against the Product table is shown in Listing 12-14.

Listing 12-14. T-SQL Query Executed Against the Product Table

```
SELECT MAX(MaxDate) AS MaxDate
FROM (
        SELECT MAX([SellStartDate]) AS MaxDate
        FROM [Production].[Product]

        UNION ALL

        SELECT MAX([SellEndDate]) AS MaxDate
        FROM [Production].[Product]

        UNION ALL
```

```
SELECT MAX([DiscontinuedDate]) AS MaxDate
FROM [Production].[Product]

UNION ALL

SELECT MAX([ModifiedDate]) AS MaxDate
FROM [Production].[Product]
) AS a
```

Checking for Duplicate Indexes

Biml generates T-SQL that checks for duplicate indexes. You use GetDatabaseSchema to examine each table with at least two indexes (with less than two indexes the chances are slim that there is a duplicate).

You next iterate indexes and compare them against each other. To compare, you order the columns of the index by name, which shows you indexes that share the same columns. In a second check, you compare column order to flag real duplicates; see Listing 12-15.

Listing 12-15. Duplicate Indexes

```
<#@ template language="VB" optionexplicit="False" #>
<# for each t in Rootnode.connections("CheckDB").GetDatabaseSchema.
tablenodes.where(function(c) c.indexes.count > 1)
Dim visitedList As New List (Of AstTableIndexNode)
  For Each idx In t.indexes
    If Not visitedList.Contains(idx)Then
      visitedList.Add(idx)
      For Each CompareIdx In t.indexes.where(Function(c) Not visitedList.
      Contains(c) and c.Columns.orderby(function(o) o.Column.name).getbiml=
      idx.Columns.orderby(function(o) o.Column.name).getbiml )
        visitedList.Add(CompareIdx)#>
Table: <#= t.name #> / <#= idx.name #> and <#= CompareIdx.name #> reference
the same columns<# if idx.columns.GetBiml = CompareIdx.Columns.GetBiml then #>
in the same order <# end if#>

<# Next
    End If
  Next
next #>
```

Checking for Broken Views

Similar to what you did with the indexes, you can check for broken views. You first get a list of all views. As Biml treats views like tables, you simply look at all table nodes that have the View property set.

Then, you run a SELECT statement on each view within a "try … catch" block. For every statement that comes back with an error message, you output the error. All other views are flagged as OK, as shown in Listing 12-16.

Listing 12-16. Broken Views

```
<#@ template language="VB" optionexplicit="False" #>
<# for each v in Rootnode.connections("CheckDB").GetDatabaseSchema.
tablenodes.where(function(c) c.View IsNot Nothing)
try
  ExternalDataAccess.GetDataTable(Rootnode.dbconnections("CheckDB").
ConnectionString, "SELECT TOP 0 * from (" & v.view.selectsql & ") a")  #>
  <#= v.name #>: OK
<#catch ex as Exception #>
  <#= v.name #>: <#= ex.message.replace(Environment.NewLine,", ") #>
<#end try
next #>
```

Generating Sample Data

You can use Biml to generate data. In this example, you add random data. You could adjust this function to generate data from a catalogue or other sources.

To generate a sample data script, you first define how many rows of data you want per table. Then you loop over each table in your database that has any assignable columns (meaning they don't have identities specified, etc.) and generate just as many INSERT statements as defined in your rowsPerTable variable.

For each INSERT statement, you get a list of all assignable columns and then execute your function to generate the sample data for each column; see Listing 12-17.

Listing 12-17. Sample Data Creation

```
<#@ import namespace="System.Data" #>
<# int rowsPerTable = 10; #>
<# foreach (var table in RootNode.OleDbConnections["Source"].
GenerateTableNodes().Where(i => i.Columns.Any(j => j.IsAssignable))) { #>
<# for (int i = 0; i < rowsPerTable; i ++) { #>
INSERT INTO <#=table.Name#> (<#=table.GetColumnList(j => j.IsAssignable)#>)
VALUES (<#=string.Join(",", table.Columns.Where(j => j.IsAssignable).
Select(j => GetSampleValue(j)))#>)
<# } #>
<# } #>
```

```
<#+
Random Rand = new Random();

string GetSampleValue(AstTableColumnBaseNode column)
{
  switch (column.DataType)
  {
    case DbType.AnsiString:
    case DbType.AnsiStringFixedLength:
    case DbType.String:
    case DbType.StringFixedLength:
      var chars = "ABCDEFGHIJKLMNOPQRSTUVWXYZabcdefghijklmnopqrstuvwxyz
                  0123456789";
      var length = Rand.Next(1, column.Length == -1 ? 10000 : column.Length);
      return "'" + new string(Enumerable.Repeat(chars, length).Select
      (s => s[Rand.Next(s.Length)]).ToArray()) + "'";
    case DbType.Boolean:
      return Rand.Next(0, 1).ToString();
    case DbType.Date:
      return "'" + new DateTime(1970, 1, 1).AddDays(Rand.Next(5000)).
      ToShortDateString() + "'";
    case DbType.DateTime:
      return "'" + new DateTime(1970, 1, 1).AddMilliseconds(Rand.Next
      (int.MaxValue)).ToLongTimeString() + "'";
    case DbType.DateTime2:
      return "'" + new DateTime(1970, 1, 1).AddMilliseconds(Rand.Next
      (int.MaxValue)).ToShortDateString() + "'";
    case DbType.DateTimeOffset:
      return "'01/01/2001'";
    case DbType.Time:
      return "00:00:00";
    case DbType.Decimal:
      return "0.0";
    case DbType.Double:
      return (Rand.NextDouble() * double.MaxValue).ToString();
    case DbType.Single:
      return (Rand.NextDouble() * float.MaxValue).ToString();
    case DbType.Guid:
      return Guid.NewGuid().ToString("N");
    case DbType.Int16:
      return Rand.Next(Int16.MinValue, Int16.MaxValue).ToString();
    case DbType.Int32:
      return Rand.Next(Int32.MinValue, Int32.MaxValue).ToString();
    case DbType.Int64:
      return ((long)(Rand.NextDouble() * Int64.MaxValue)).ToString();
    case DbType.Byte:
      return Rand.Next(byte.MinValue, byte.MaxValue).ToString();
```

```
      case DbType.SByte:
        return Rand.Next(sbyte.MinValue, sbyte.MaxValue).ToString();
      case DbType.Xml:
        return "'<root></root>'";
      default:
        return "NULL";
  }
}
#>
```

Summary

In this chapter, you used Biml for more than just simple SSIS tasks. You created T-SQL code using known extension methods and manually created code that may be automated. You saw various techniques of achieving this goal, which demonstrates the flexibility of Biml.

In the next chapter, you take a look at how you can use Biml to automate your documentation!

CHAPTER 13

■ ■ ■

Documenting Your Biml Solution

Documentation is an important component of any large data project. It provides a high-level view of the database schemas, system architecture, and other important design considerations to all of the stakeholders and users of a data system. It also serves as an important reference for analysts as they work to understand the intricacies of column/attribute values and their relationships.

Why then is documentation so often an afterthought in database development, frequently out of date, incorrect, incomplete, or not implemented at all? There are many reasons for this, but they all revolve around the high cost of developing and maintaining documentation, the prioritization of documentation when project delivery timelines are tight, and the comparatively low value of the documentation that is produced through such efforts.

Biml, along with a bit of automation magic, has the ability to solve all of these problems. Before diving into the many options for automatically documenting your data solutions with Biml, let's first take a deeper look at the reasons documentation is expensive and of low quality today.

Problems with Traditional Approaches

The following sections highlight some of the largest difficulties that face documentation creation and maintenance within your data solution when employing traditional development methodologies.

Requirements and Specifications: A Red Herring

In most data development efforts, stakeholders begin by creating requirements documents that are among the very first written artifacts for the project. These detail the individual metrics, filters, slicers, performance characteristics, data freshness, and other end user-visible attributes of the desired solution. These requirements documents are generally used as the basis for the next artifact, which is a formal specification of a solution that will satisfy those requirements. The specification will usually include

A. Leonard et al., *The Biml Book*, https://doi.org/10.1007/978-1-4842-3135-7_13

global patterns and practices, a description of the logging and auditing implementation, locations of source systems, data refresh windows, important business logic, a variety of technical details targeted at developers, and sometimes even logical and physical data models.

Whether included in the specification or not, data models will be developed and iteratively refined, as they are tested against both business requirements and technical constraints. Finally, data transformation processes will be created to populate those data models. All of the documents and other artifacts that result from this sometimes years-long process have the potential to resemble and function a bit like documentation, but they are not actually documentation in a practical sense.

Of course, they collectively include reasoning for the inclusion of certain database structures and attributes. They also include a description of the schemas that analysts will interact with on their production systems. That makes it appealing to try to reuse these artifacts as *end user* documentation, but that rarely works well in the real world.

The reason for this is that keyword "end user." It is totally appropriate to use requirements, specifications, and models as *developer* documentation; that is, those artifacts that developers will consult to build and maintain a solution that will meet the needs of the business. However, developers and end users are not the same. Their documentation needs are different because they are interacting with the project at different times, while performing different tasks, with different restrictions on their ability to modify the system.

A developer is starting from a blank or partially blank slate and is responsible for building a solution from first principles. This means that the developer has the luxury of taking certain liberties with the interpretation of the specification and requirements artifacts to optimize for performance, development time, and a variety of other factors. However, once that solution is built, those decisions made by the developer (and hopefully approved by the business) are locked in for any future end users. Often, it's those developer decisions that have the largest impact on the day-to-day experience of analysts and end users, but the decisions are almost never encoded back into the previously created requirements and specification documents. Any of the practical nuances that apply to the iterative improvements made to data models are similarly lost to the memories of modelers, developers, and the sands of time.

Consequently, it's not that requirements, specifications, and models aren't useful to end users. It's that from an end user perspective they are incomplete, not current, and are often targeted to a lower or different level of complexity than analysts and end users focus upon. In short, organizations that use their design documents as end-user documentation are almost certainly providing their end users with poor documentation.

Building Documentation Is Hard

The solution must be simple, right? Just take those existing design documents and refactor them to work well for end users. Not so fast. It is often assumed that the specifications and requirements can have the overly technical bits removed while adding a handful of comments targeted at end users. For most projects, however, the modifications required to produce quality documentation are far more extensive.

First, let's consider the requirements documents. These tend to be a listing of prioritized capabilities that business and technical users need to get their jobs done. While that sounds consistent with the type of information an end user might require, in practice these lists tend to include many scenario-specific requests that are later aggregated into schema, business logic, and data transformation features. In many cases a technical solution will be provided that satisfies the business need underlying a given requirement, even though the requirement as stated in the document is left unsatisfied. Once this process of aggregation and reconciliation has been done, the requirements often bear little resemblance to the implemented solution. Consequently, using requirements as a starting place for end-user documentation would save little time and might even be more difficult than starting from scratch.

What about using the specification and/or models as the basis for end-user documentation because that should provide a complete description of what was actually built? Unfortunately, these artifacts have their own issues. Staleness is a significant problem with specifications. After the initial documents are prepared, developers will often encounter technical issues that require modifications to the design, or additional features will be requested by users. Specification documents are very rarely updated to reflect these changes, and there is usually no easy way to obtain a comprehensive listing of all differences between the specification and the implemented solution. Even if that wasn't a problem, there is still the issue of specifications and modelling documents being written for a highly technical audience with a different collection of details than would be relevant to end users.

For these reasons, the best documentation is usually developed from scratch by people who are familiar with the implemented solution and who understand end-user scenarios well enough to write useful documentation. Note that "useful" is the operative word here. When documentation is written by people who are unfamiliar with the end-user scenarios, you often end up with tautological descriptions. For instance, the description for a hypothetical NetRevenue field might read, "Specifies the net revenue for this row." Correct? Yes. Useful? Not at all. A useful description might include the figures that have been removed from gross revenue to produce this net revenue figure, possible usage scenarios, common filters, and much more.

Even if you have the right people who understand both the technology and the business scenarios and even if those people have the time, interest, aptitude, and incentive to write very high-quality documentation, it can still be difficult to manage. In the absence of third-party tools to manage the documentation process, it is exceedingly easy to miss a table or a field or a package or some other asset while you are trying to document thousands of them all at once. Even if you do, keeping it all up-to-date is also a challenge, as you'll see in the next section.

Maintaining Documentation Is Hard

Imagine that your data solution was comprehensively documented on the day that the first version entered production. What happens next? Change.

Once the solution enters production, a broader set of users will find issues that weren't discovered during testing. Some of these issues will be deemed business critical (whether through a formal triage process or more likely because an executive sends an email about a broken report in the wee hours of the morning). Those critical hotfixes are typically made and deployed on an emergency basis. The only priority is to get them done and deployed. Documenting them isn't even an afterthought. Even worse, the critical hotfix wasn't planned for, which means that preparing and deploying the hotfix has put the development team behind on their normally scheduled work. This significantly decreases the chances that they will double-back after the hotfix ships to patch the documentation.

Even without hotfixes, your data solution will almost certainly undergo a variety of changes as your team implements new features across many release cycles. All of the problems associated with the creation of the initial documentation also apply to updates. If the documentation is ever allowed to fall out of date, the staleness tends to compound. After all, you can't add the documentation for a new table column if the parent table wasn't already documented in the previous release. You can think of it like accumulating debt that is difficult to ever fully pay off. Even if you assiduously update the documentation for each new release, the overhead of documentation changes is normally higher than greenfield development. This is usually due to the fact that the individual changes to a data solution are often difficult to capture, as the release criteria for new features tend to be stated in terms of new capabilities as opposed to the schema and other changes that were made to enable those capabilities.

None of this is impossible. It's just tedious and difficult. So many teams have consequently skipped proper documentation that it's become the new normal in many parts of the industry that data solutions aren't documented. With Biml, we can do better because we can leverage our solution metadata to create documentation automatically. This also means that we can generate multiple versions of the documentation for multiple audiences, all having different granularity while at the same time ensuring that they are derived from the same source with consistent and fresh information.

Documentation with Biml

Automation isn't a replacement for human creativity, insight, experience, and know-how. Ultimately, the quality of your project's documentation will depend on the skills and motivation of the people who write the actual documentation text. If they write unhelpful or obvious text, just to fill the space, there is little automation can do to help with that. As we've just explored, however, many of the most painful obstacles to building and maintaining great documentation are largely about process enforcement.

Enforcing processes is something that software automation is very good at. We can build systems that will force developers to enter documentation before their Biml code will successfully build, thereby forcing them to author documentation incrementally. Audits can be performed to ensure that no tables, fields, or other critical assets are missed on later releases. Heuristics can be run on documentation text to ensure that it isn't too short to be useful, doesn't include spelling and grammar errors, isn't following the tautology patterns, and isn't otherwise of little use. Additionally, we can store the documentation local to the Biml objects it describes in plain text. Using automation to generate the actual documentation from this convenient representation significantly cuts down on the cost of initial authorship, since the writer can focus on the content and ignore formatting, styling, and other requirements that the software can handle on the writer's behalf.

Before you explore the approaches used to validate and generate documentation, you first need to understand where and how your documentation text should be stored.

Where to Store Documentation Metadata

As with other types of metadata in your Biml solution, documentation can be stored anywhere: databases, flat files, Biml files, or any other machine-readable location. Regardless of where it is stored, you should be sure to emit the documentation text into a Biml annotation for the documented object. To do this with flat Biml code, consider the simple example in Listing 13-1.

Listing 13-1. Annotations in Flat Biml

```
<Biml xmlns="http://schemas.varigence.com/Biml.xsd">
  <Tables>
    <Table Name="TestTable1" SchemaName="Database1.Schema1">
      <Columns>
        <Column Name="Column1" DataType="Int32" />
      </Columns>
      <Annotations>
        <Annotation AnnotationType="Description">The table 'TestTable1' is
        used for lots of neat stuff in our solution</Annotation>
      </Annotations>
    </Table>
  </Tables>
</Biml>
```

Any annotation with the type of Description can be easily picked up by your own custom documentation generator or by a prebuilt documentation solution. What if you did want to store your documentation in a spreadsheet or some other location that could be more easily managed than source code files by non-developers? No problem! The most common way to handle this is to provide a generic lookup method that accepts a .NET object type and a scoped name and will return the documentation text, if any. Note that objects of different types (such as tables and schemas) can have the same scoped name in Biml, so you will require both parameters. Listing 13-2 contains a condensed sample of this in action.

Listing 13-2. Annotations from a Metadata Store

```
<Biml xmlns="http://schemas.varigence.com/Biml.xsd">
  <Tables>
    <Table Name="TestTable1" SchemaName="Database1.Schema1">
      <Annotations>
        <Annotation AnnotationType="Description"><#=GetDoc(typeof
        (AstTableNode), "Database1.Schema1.TestTable1")#></Annotation>
      </Annotations>
    </Table>
  </Tables>
</Biml>
```

```
<#+
public string GetDoc(System.Type type, string scopedName) {
  string doc = null;
  // Fill in logic to populate doc with an actual value from DB, CSV, etc.
  return doc;
}
#>
```

Now that you have a way to store your documentation text alongside your Biml objects, let's take a look at some strategies to ensure that the documentation is high quality and comprehensive.

Enforcing Documentation Standards

As noted earlier, one of the key challenges to creating and maintaining high-quality documentation is ensuring that nothing slips through the cracks. Especially for hotfixes and updates across multiple versions, writing about a new feature can be overlooked. Additionally, if you leave all documentation tasks until the end of the project, it is common to ship a long-awaited release without it, promising stakeholders that the documentation will be coming soon. The daunting task of writing all of the documentation at once, combined with the competing priorities of hotfixes and new releases, often means that it never gets done.

The ideal situation is to require documentation to be written as each feature is developed and to ensure that the documentation is updated in lockstep with future changes to the solution. Without some sort of tooling or process that enforced these requirements, this would remain an unrealized ideal for the vast majority of projects. Thankfully, there is tooling that can enforce these requirements: the Biml compiler.

There are a variety of logging and diagnostic capabilities built into the Biml compiler. You can learn more about these options in Chapter 14. The most frequently used approach is to create a Biml file on the highest compilation tier that inspects all of the previously defined objects to ensure that they have been documented according to established project standards. Listing 13-3 shows an example of a simple validator file.

Listing 13-3. Simple Validator.biml File

```
<#@ template tier="999999999" #>
<# foreach (var node in RootNode.AllDefinedSuccessors()) {
  var table = node as AstTableNode;
  if (table != null && table.Schema.Name == "dbo") {
    if (table.Annotations.Count == 0) {
      ValidationReporter.Report(Severity.Error, table, "The table '{0}'
      lacks documentation.", table.ScopedName);
    }
  }
} #>
```

There are a few features of this code sample that are worth discussing in further depth. First, note that the file has been placed in a very high-tier level. This ensures that the file will run after everything else in the solution has already been executed. Next, notice the use of the AllDefinedSuccessors method, which provides a list of every Biml object defined underneath the object on which it is called. Since you called it on the RootNode object, it will produce a list of every Biml object defined in the entire solution. You can then test these nodes for the type or types you are interested in, which in this case is relational tables. You additionally check the schema name of the table. This prevents you from having to specify documentation for tables that are not your responsibility or for intermediate tables that are not visible to the end user. In this case, you have checked for the dbo schema, but you could have checked almost any condition.

Before moving on, let's take a look at a somewhat more complicated version of the same validator shown in Listing 13-4.

Listing 13-4. More Complex Validator.biml File

```
<#@ template tier="999999999" #>
<# foreach (var node in RootNode.AllDefinedSuccessors()) {
  var table = node as AstTableNode;
  if (table != null && table.Schema.Name == "dbo") {
    if (table.Annotations.Count == 0) {
      ValidationReporter.Report(Severity.Error, table, "The table '{0}'
      lacks documentation.", table.ScopedName);
    }
    foreach (var column in table.Columns) {
      if (column.Annotations.Count == 0) {
        ValidationReporter.Report(Severity.Error, column, "The column '{0}'
        lacks documentation.", column.ScopedName);
      } else {
        var description = column.Annotations.First(i => i.AnnotationType ==
        AnnotationType.Description);
        if (description.Text.Length < 20) {
          ValidationReporter.Report(Severity.Error, column, "The
          documentation for column '{0}' is too short.", column.ScopedName);
        }
      }
    }
  }
} #>
```

Two significant changes have been made to the validator. First, the child columns of each table are also checked for the presence of annotations. Second, the value of the description annotation is checked to ensure that it is long enough to be non-trivial. In a real-world project, you might use other heuristics to ensure that the documentation is high quality or otherwise follows your standards. A relatively simple addition would be to use the System.Windows.Controls.SpellCheck class or a third-party library to protect against misspellings.

Autogenerating Documentation from Biml

A frequent feature of well-designed developer technologies is that there is often more than one way to accomplish the same task, depending on the tool you use, the effort you wish to expend, the desired output, and even just personal preference. Documentation with Biml is yet another example of this phenomenon. In the following sections, we will walk through several options for autogenerating documentation from your Biml solution.

Getting the Flat XML for a Biml Project

Two of the following documentation solutions require you to pass the flat Biml XML for your project into an XML processing step. This presents an issue because it is almost certain that most of the Biml XML for your project is autogenerated by BimlScripts. How can you conveniently access the flat Biml XML that the Biml compiler uses internally? Simple; you just create a high-tier BimlScript that calls the GetBiml method on RootNode. The result will be a string representation of your entire project. If you are programmatically calling your XML processor from your BimlScript, you can likely parse this string directly, as shown in Listing 13-5.

Listing 13-5. Using Flat Biml XML from a String

```
<#@ template tier="99999999" #>
<#
var bimlXml = RootNode.GetBiml();
var xdocument = System.Xml.Linq.XDocument.Parse(bimlXml);
// ... do your XML processing here ...
#>
```

It's also possible that you might want to write the Biml XML out to a file for later processing. This is also easy to achieve using the approach shown in Listing 13-6.

Listing 13-6. Writing Flat Biml XML to a File

```
<#@ template tier="99999999" #>
<#
var bimlXml = RootNode.GetBiml();
System.File.IO.WriteAllText(@"c:\path_tofile\output.biml", bimlXml);
// ... Optionally, use the file here ...
#>
```

XSLT

Back when XML was all the rage, with some predicting that it was the last format humans would ever need (no, really; a lot of very smart people actually thought that), some very clever tools were developed to process and transform XML documents. The basic idea was that "if everyone everywhere is using XML, then a big chunk of the work that once required custom software could be reduced to simple translations between XML dialects." With that as a guiding principle, a variety of attempts were made to create highly productive programming languages and templating systems so that non-programmers could define complex XML transformations.

Probably the most successful of these was a functional programming language called XML Style Sheets (XSL), which was used to create XSL Templates (XSLTs). Of course, the creators of XSL decided to make the syntax of XSL also XML. XML purists and Xzibit were thrilled with this consistency ("Yo Dawg, I heard you like XML, so I wrote some XML to transform your XML into other XML"). Non-purists found the syntax and functional approach to be confusing, so the language and tools never entered widespread usage outside of dedicated enterprise XML mapping tasks. Some pieces of XSL, such as the XPath query language, found important applications in generic XML processing functions, but XSL itself has become somewhat of a niche technology. Before XSL settled into that niche, however, both the language and the tools surrounding it became mature and freely available.

What does all of this have to do with creating documentation for your data solution? Well, Biml is an XML dialect. HTML, at least for our purposes, can be treated as an XML dialect. That means we can use XSL to automatically convert our Biml code into documentation. Put another way: XSL can make our Biml solutions automatically self-documenting. All that is required is to write an XSL file once, and then many issues surrounding the cost of building and maintaining documentation evaporate. Furthermore, any changes toward improved documentation quality are one-time investments in the XSLT that can be reused for the life of the current and all future projects.

A full XSL tutorial is outside of the scope of this book. As a mature technology, you'll find a wide variety of training and support resources for XSL online. Instead, we will walk you through an example XSLT that is a trimmed-down version of the XSLT that the Varigence team uses to automatically generate documentation for the BimlFlex metadata model directly from the Biml code. (See Chapters 9 and 10 for more information about Biml metadata models and BimlFlex, respectively.) Before highlighting points of particular interest, let's start with a full listing of the XSLT, as shown in Listing 13-7.

Listing 13-7. XSL Stylesheet for Creating HTML Documentation from a Biml Metadata Model

```
<?xml version="1.0" encoding="UTF-8"?>
<xsl:stylesheet version="1.0" xmlns:xsl="http://www.w3.org/1999/XSL/
Transform" xmlns:b="http://schemas.varigence.com/biml.xsd">

<xsl:template name="MetadataEntityDefinitions">
<html>
  <body>
    <div class="title-page">
      <h1>Metadata Entity Definitions</h1>
      <p><xsl:value-of select="format-date(current-date(), '[M01]/[D01]/
      [Y0001]')"/></p>
      <p>Copyright Varigence <xsl:value-of select="format-date(current-
      date(), '[Y0001]')"/></p>
    </div>
```

```
    <xsl:call-template name="MetadataEntityDefinitionsCore" />
  </body>
</html>
</xsl:template>

<xsl:template name="MetadataEntityDefinitionsCore">
  <xsl:for-each select="b:Biml/b:Metadata/b:MetadataModel/b:Entities/b:Entity">
    <h2><xsl:value-of select="@Name" /> Entity</h2>
    <p><xsl:value-of select="b:Annotations/b:Annotation" /></p>

    <h3>Properties</h3>
    <table class="major">
      <tr>
        <th>Attribute</th>
        <th>Description</th>
        <th>DataType</th>
        <th>Required</th>
      </tr>
      <xsl:for-each select="b:Properties/b:Property">
        <tr>
          <td><xsl:value-of select="@Name"/></td>
          <td><xsl:value-of select="b:Annotations/b:Annotation"/></td>
          <td><xsl:value-of select="@DataType"/></td>
          <td>
            <xsl:choose>
              <xsl:when test="@IsRequired = 'true'">True</xsl:when>
              <xsl:otherwise>False</xsl:otherwise>
            </xsl:choose>
          </td>
        </tr>
      </xsl:for-each> <!-- Properties -->
    </table>

    <!-- If there are relationships, emit them -->
    <xsl:if test="b:Relationships/b:Relationship">
      <h3>Relationships</h3>
      <table class="major">
        <tr>
          <th>Attribute</th>
          <th>Description</th>
          <th>Related Entity</th>
          <th>Cardinality</th>
        </tr>
        <xsl:for-each select="b:Relationships/b:Relationship">
          <tr>
            <td><xsl:value-of select="@Name"/></td>
            <td><xsl:value-of select="b:Annotations/b:Annotation"/></td>
```

```
        <td><xsl:value-of select="@EntityName"/></td>
        <td><xsl:value-of select="@Cardinality"/></td>
      </tr>
    </xsl:for-each> <!-- Relationships -->
    </table>
  </xsl:if>
</xsl:for-each> <!-- Entities -->
</xsl:template>
</xsl:stylesheet>
```

This is quite an eyeful, so let's break things down a bit to understand it better. Within the core template, there is some basic information about the date the documentation was generated and a year for the copyright notification, as excerpted in Listing 13-8. Remember that XSL has many built-in operators that let you retrieve and format dates, in addition to a variety of other useful operations. Many XSL tutorials online will give you a comprehensive listing of XSL operators and their usage.

Listing 13-8. Excerpt Using XSL Operators to Create Formatted Date Strings

```
<div class="title-page">
  <h1>Metadata Entity Definitions</h1>
  <p><xsl:value-of select="format-date(current-date(), '[M01]/[D01]/
  [Y0001]')"/></p>
  <p>Copyright Varigence <xsl:value-of select="format-date(current-date(),
  '[Y0001]')"/></p>
</div>
```

The next notable snippet is shown in Listing 13-9 where you use the XSL xsl:for-each element and an XPath query expression to iterate over all of the Entity elements in the Biml metadata model. Notice that you are using the b: namespace prefix as a shorthand for the Biml namespace, which was defined at the beginning of Listing 13-7. Once you are within the xsl:for-each loop, you can easily reference attributes and child elements of the current Entity element. In this example, you reference the name of the entity and emit all the Biml annotations that were applied to the entity.

■ **Tip** The use of Biml annotations is perhaps the most important feature of this and the other documentation generation solutions that you'll consider in this chapter. By including Biml annotations within your tables, columns, metadata models, packages, and other Biml objects, you can expose that documentation to end users.

Listing 13-9. Excerpt Iterating Metadata Entities and Retrieving Biml Annotations Using XSL

```
<xsl:for-each select="b:Biml/b:Metadata/b:MetadataModel/b:Entities/
b:Entity">
    <h2><xsl:value-of select="@Name" /> Entity</h2>
    <p><xsl:value-of select="b:Annotations/b:Annotation" /></p>
```

The last pieces of the XSLT in Listing 13-7 to notice are the `xsl:choose` and `xsl:if` elements. These allow you to provide conditional logic that matches the conditions that might be applied to your Biml elements. For instance, you might want to emit different documentation for tables that serve as Facts rather than Dimensions. XSL provides the capabilities necessary to perform all of that customization and much more.

While XSL has a learning curve and is a bit of a special-purpose technology, it is very good at what it does, and it does play a role in documentation generation for many Biml solutions of varying sizes and scopes around the world.

.NET XML APIs

Perhaps you read the previous section about XSL and thought that it looked like a neat approach, but that your toolbelt has no room for new gadgets, especially XML-based programming languages with a steep learning curve and a single application in your work. That is no problem at all. We're just getting started with the documentation options.

If instead you or someone on your team is a .NET coder who is familiar with the Microsoft XmlDocument, XDocument, or other XML APIs, you can accomplish the same things with .NET code as you can with XSLT. For the most complex transformations, it's likely to even be easier to do.

■ **Note** While we prefer .NET and the XDocument library for this example, all of the XML transformations are equally possible with programs written in Java, Python, node.js, or whichever programming language and XML library is your current favorite.

As with the XSLT example, you have a tremendous amount of control over your output HTML. Listing 13-10 illustrates a simple C# method that uses the XDocument APIs to read the Biml XML and a simple StringBuilder to construct the output HTML. The logic is quite similar to the XSLT, replacing XSL operators and XPath queries with the C# and XDocument equivalents. It creates identical output to the XSLT shown in the previous section.

Listing 13-10. C# Method Using XDocument and StringBuilder to Create HTML

```
public static string GenerateHtml(string bimlXml)
{
  var xdocument = System.Xml.Linq.XDocument.Parse(bimlXml);
  var nsManager = new System.Xml.XmlNamespaceManager(new System.Xml.NameTable());
  nsManager.AddNamespace("b", "http://schemas.varigence.com/Biml.xsd");

  var builder = new System.Text.StringBuilder();
  builder.Append("<html>");
  builder.Append("<body>");
  builder.Append("<div class=\"title-page\">");
  builder.Append("<h1>Metadata Entity Definitions</h1>");
  builder.AppendFormat("<p>{0}</p>", DateTime.Now.ToString("MMddyyyy"));
  builder.AppendFormat("<p>Copyright {0}</p>", DateTime.Now.ToString("yyyy"));
  builder.Append("</div>");
  foreach (var entity in xdocument.XPathSelectElements("b:Biml/b:Metadata/
  b:MetadataModel/b:Entities/b:Entity", nsManager))
  {
    builder.AppendFormat("<h2>{0} Entity</h2>", entity.Attribute("Name").Value);
    var entityDoc = xdocument.XPathSelectElement("b:Annotations/
    b:Annotations", nsManager);
    builder.AppendFormat("<p>{0}</p>", entityDoc == null ? "" : entityDoc.Value);

    builder.Append("<h3>Properties</h3>");
    builder.Append("<table class=\"major\">");
    builder.Append("<tr>");
    builder.Append("<th>Attribute</th>");
    builder.Append("<th>Description</th>");
    builder.Append("<th>DataType</th>");
    builder.Append("<th>Required</th>");
    builder.Append("</tr>");
    foreach (var prop in entity.XPathSelectElements("b:Properties/
    b:Property", nsManager))
    {
      builder.Append("<tr>");
      builder.AppendFormat("<td>{0}</td>", prop.Attribute("Name").Value);
      var propDoc = prop.XPathSelectElement("b:Annotations/
      b:Annotations", nsManager);
      builder.AppendFormat("<td>{0}</td>", propDoc == null ? "" : propDoc.Value);
      builder.AppendFormat("<td>{0}</td>", prop.Attribute("DataType").Value);
      builder.AppendFormat("<td>{0}</td>", prop.Attribute("IsRequired").Value);
      builder.Append ("</tr>");
    }

    builder.Append ("</table>");
```

```
var rels = entity.XPathSelectElements("b:Relationships/b:Relationship",
nsManager);
if (rels.Any())
{
  // If there are relationships, emit them
  builder.Append("<h3>Relationships</h3>");
  builder.Append("<table class=\"major\">");
  builder.Append("<tr>");
  builder.Append("<th>Attribute</th>");
  builder.Append("<th>Description</th>");
  builder.Append("<th>Related Entity</th>");
  builder.Append("<th>Cardinality</th>");
  builder.Append("</tr>");
  foreach (var rel in rels)
  {
    builder.Append("<tr>");
    builder.AppendFormat("<td>{0}</td>", rel.Attribute("Name").Value);
    var relDoc = rel.XPathSelectElement("b:Annotations/b:Annotations",
    nsManager);
    builder.AppendFormat("<td>{0}</td>", relDoc == null ? "" : relDoc.
    Value);
    builder.AppendFormat("<td>{0}</td>", rel.Attribute("EntityName").
    Value);
    builder.AppendFormat("<td>{0}</td>", rel.Attribute("Cardinality").
    Value);
    builder.Append("</tr>");
  }

  builder.Append("</table>");
  }

  builder.Append("</body>");
  builder.Append("</html>");
}

return builder.ToString();
}
```

BimlScripts

The previous approaches assume that you are working from a flat Biml file, parsing the XML source, and using that as a basis for generating HTML documentation. Of course, there's no particular need to compile the Biml solution, emit it as Biml XML, and parse the Biml XML into an XML object model when you could instead work directly from the Biml object model that is already created as part of the Biml compilation process.

Using the same example as with the previous approaches, you will use a BimlScript to create the documentation for your Biml metadata model in Listing 13-11.

Listing 13-11. BimlScript for Creating HTML Documentation from a Biml Metadata Model

```
<html>
  <body>
    <div class="title-page">
      <h1>Metadata Entity Definitions</h1>
      <p><#=System.DateTime.Now.ToString("MMddyyyy")#></p>
      <p>Copyright Varigence <#=System.DateTime.Now.ToString("yyyy")#></p>
    </div>
    <# foreach (var entity in RootNode.MetadataModels.SelectMany(i =>
    i.Entities)) { #>
    <h2><#=entity.Name#> Entity</h2>
    <# var firstEntityDoc = entity.Annotations.FirstOrDefault(); #>
    <p><#= firstEntityDoc == null ? "" : firstEntityDoc.Text#></p>

    <h3>Properties</h3>
    <table class="major">
      <tr>
        <th>Attribute</th>
        <th>Description</th>
        <th>DataType</th>
        <th>Required</th>
      </tr>
      <# foreach (var property in entity.Properties) { #>
      <tr>
        <td><#=property.Name#></td>
        <# var firstPropDoc = property.Annotations.FirstOrDefault(); #>
        <td><#= firstPropDoc == null ? "" : firstPropDoc.Text#></td>
        <td><#=property.DataType#></td>
        <td><#if (property.IsRequired) {#>True<#} else {#>False<#}#></td>
      </tr>
      <# } #>
    </table>

    <# if (entity.Relationships.Any()) {#>
    <!-- If there are relationships, emit them -->
    <h3>Relationships</h3>
    <table class="major">
      <tr>
        <th>Attribute</th>
        <th>Description</th>
        <th>Related Entity</th>
        <th>Cardinality</th>
      </tr>
      <# foreach (var relationship in entity.Relationships) {#>
```

```
        <tr>
          <td><#=relationship.Name#></td>
          <# var firstRelDoc = relationship.Annotations.FirstOrDefault(); #>
          <td><#= firstRelDoc == null ? "" : firstRelDoc.Text#></td>
          <td><#=relationship.Entity.Name#></td>
          <td><#=relationship.Cardinality#></td>
        </tr>
        <#}#>
        </table>
      <#}
}#>
  </body>
</html>
```

The logic for the BimlScript closely mirrors that of the earlier XSLT. Instead of using XPath expressions and XSL elements to iterate and access properties from the Biml XML, you are using C# code nuggets to do the same. How do you write this HTML out to the file system so that it can be presented to users? Assuming that the file in Listing 13-11 is called GenerateHtml.biml, you can use CallBimlScript from a high-tier file to write the output to the file system, as shown in Listing 13-12.

Listing 13-12. Write BimlScript-Generated HTML Documentation to a File

```
<#@ template tier="99999999" #>
<#
System.File.IO.WriteAllText(@"c:\path_tofile\output.html",
CallBimlScript("GenerateDocumentation.biml"));
#>
```

GetJson

The previous methods are great for producing HTML-based documentation using more traditional web development approaches. Specifically, you used a variety of methods to autogenerate static HTML that would then be deployed to the user, hosted directly on a website, or converted to another format such as PDF or Microsoft Word using one of many available conversion tools. That approach has a variety of advantages in terms of deployment and hosting flexibility, but it tends to produce a user experience that feels dated. Page reloads occur with every click. The user interface usually lacks the dynamic interactions that people have come to expect from the modern websites that they use daily for social media and other tasks online.

To match the high standards of modern internet users, it is often better to build your documentation like you would build a customer-facing website. The most common approach for that is a single-page application (SPA). The SPA approach normally uses JavaScript to request a JavaScript Object Notation (JSON) dataset from a webserver, a local file, or from an embedded script block within the page itself. JavaScript code uses this JSON dataset to dynamically create the HTML for the desired view. Navigating within the SPA causes the JavaScript to load additional JSON to render the new HTML within the same page without a reload. This approach, along with all the modern JavaScript libraries that complement it, tends to lead to a much smoother, cleaner, and dynamic browsing experience.

A tutorial on building SPAs is well out of the scope of this book. You can find many free resources online. In all cases of building an SPA to present documentation for your solution, you will likely need a JSON representation of your Biml code. The good news is that Biml natively supports generating JSON, as shown in Listing 13-13.

Listing 13-13. Writing a JSON Representation of Biml to a File

```
<#
var bimlJson = RootNode.GetJson();
System.File.IO.WriteAllText(@"c:\path_tofile\output.json", bimlJson);
// ... Optionally, use the file here ...
#>
```

If you check the online reference documentation for Biml which is published at Varigence.com, you will find a variety of overloads to the GetJson method that allow you to customize the JSON output. Among other options, you can choose the casing (Pascal or camel casing) for your properties, whether or not to emit null and empty properties, whether or not to include a GUID to uniquely identify each object in the JSON, and much more.

Built-in Documentation Function in BimlStudio

■ **Note**   This feature is only available in BimlStudio!

Perhaps the idea of building a SPA to present your documentation, as described in the previous section, sounded like a great idea. If you don't have web development resources on staff or do not have the time to create your own web app, you might want to use one that has already been built. If you are using BimlStudio, you can generate a SPA for your documentation with the click of a button. All of the BimlStudio documentation autogeneration options can be found on the Documentation ribbon tab, shown in Figure 13-1.

Figure 13-1. *BimlStudio Documentation ribbon*

Clicking the Build button will create the SPA and JSON dataset and emit both to the path specified in your project settings.

To see a preview of the application that will be generated, select one of the options from the Preview split button. BimlStudio can produce both reference documentation that is navigated with a treeview and a multiple document interface (MDI) display or it can create a schema graph that shows your tables and their relationships. Examples of both of these displays are shown in Figure 13-2 and Figure 13-3.

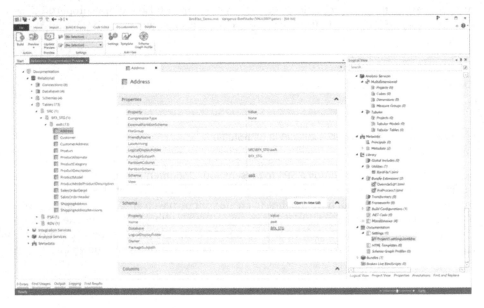

Figure 13-2. *Preview of BimlStudio autogenerated reference documentation*

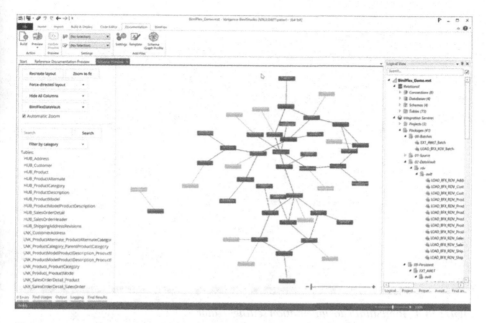

Figure 13-3. *Preview of BimlStudio autogenerated schema graph documentation*

These views will satisfy most users without further modification, but BimlStudio also offers fairly fine-grained control over the documentation process. First, you can create documentation settings files that control which types of objects are included in your documentation, which properties of those objects should be displayed, in which order properties should be displayed, and how properties should be grouped and categorized. All you need to do is to click the Settings button in the Documentation ribbon. BimlStudio will automatically create a new settings file and open the settings editor, as shown in Figure 13-4. Using this editor, you can make any changes you would like to the content of your documentation application.

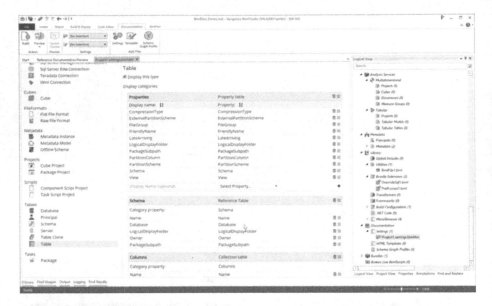

Figure 13-4. *BimlStudio documentation settings editor*

The next customization option is to override the HTML template for the SPA. This is an option that will require some support from a web developer, but it will allow you to customize almost any aspect of the presentation or styling of your documentation. To create a documentation template, click the Template button on the Documentation ribbon. BimlStudio will automatically create a new template file and launch the HTML editor. The most common changes will be to the `navbar-brand` and `navbar-botton` elements where you can add your own project branding. To change styling, you can either edit the emitted `Style-0-1-0.min.css` file or you can create your own CSS file from scratch and reference it in place of `Style-0-1-0.min.css` in your template file.

Finally, if you would like to create a custom schema graph layout, the schema graph view consumes a JSON dataset that defines the nodes and edges to be rendered along with useful metadata. To create one of these JSON datasets, simply click the Schema Graph Profile button in the Documentation ribbon. This will create a new `schemagraph.bimldoc` file and launch the bimlscript editor with a sample dataset. You can use BimlScript code nuggets to automatically generate whichever nodes and edges you would like to display in your schema graph based on inspecting the RootNode of your Biml project.

Perhaps the most useful part of BimlStudio autogenerated documentation is that it can be automated from the command line. To build it as part of your regular BimlStudio build, simply check the Build Documentation toggle on the Build & Deploy ribbon tab, which is highlighted in Figure 13-5. This will cause the compiler to automatically generate documentation as part of the normal solution build process.

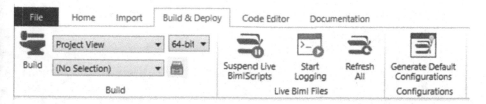

Figure 13-5. BimlStudio documentation settings editor

Summary

There are many options to generate rich and informative documentation for the end users of your Biml solution, and those options eliminate or mitigate many of the issues associated with the documentation of traditional data solutions. While there is some choice involved in choosing an approach and potentially an upfront investment in creating your documentation framework if you choose not to use the built-in BimlStudio documentation solution, there are choices that can fit almost any project requirements and any development skill set.

In the next chapter, you'll learn how to troubleshoot the metadata generated from source systems if the built-in Biml utility methods are not sufficient or do not produce the desired result.

CHAPTER 14

■ ■ ■

Troubleshooting Metadata

In this chapter, we discuss metadata, its location, and how to collect it from source databases. To learn more about metadata and its Biml-related uses, please see Chapters 4, 9, and Appendix C.

Metadata collection enables you to retrieve metadata from databases. The Biml extension method GetDatabaseSchema is one method for retrieving metadata from databases. The reason we discuss metadata collection in this chapter is because GetDatabaseSchema doesn't cover all use cases.

This chapter focuses on the most common sources: SQL Server and flat files. Metadata is used to define database artifacts in Biml. By the end of this chapter you will understand how to collect metadata and be familiar with options for collecting metadata.

Consider the examples shown for SQL Server and .NET Framework as an alternative to collecting metadata if the metadata provided by the extension methods ImportDB or GetDatabaseSchema does not meet your data type mapping expectations. One reason we create an alternative method is to manage data type mappings. Another reason: we can retrieve metadata for stored procedures via custom metadata retrieval.

General Metadata Availability

In most relational databases we have access to the information_schema. The INFORMATION_SCHEMA is an ANSI-standard set of views that most RDBMS application vendors have implemented inside of their database system. The INFORMATION_ SCHEMA is really useful because it provides the same kind of metadata for many relational database engines; see Table 14-1 for details.

© Andy Leonard et al. 2017
A. Leonard et al., *The Biml Book*, https://doi.org/10.1007/978-1-4842-3135-7_14

Table 14-1. *information_schema Availability*

RDBMS	INFORMATION_SCHEMA Availability
Microsoft SQL Server	Yes
MySQL	Yes
PostgreSQL	Yes
InterSystems Caché	Yes
H2 Database	Yes
HSQLDB	Yes
MariaDB	Yes
Oracle Database	No. Proprietary standard.
IBM DB2	No. Proprietary standard.
SQLite	No. Proprietary standard.

Other ways of extracting the data structure of source systems could be through system tables or views similar to INFORMATION_SCHEMA (see Figure 14-1).

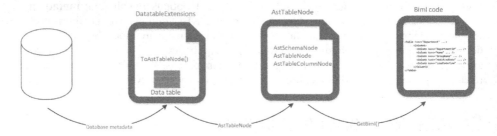

Figure 14-1. *Data extraction process*

We created a class called `DataTableExtensions` containing an extension method, which uses collected metadata and returns a Biml table. This method is used by passing in a data table containing data from a query against a source system's metadata. The data table is used to populate the properties for Biml AstSchemaNode, Biml AstTableNode, and the related AstTableColumnNode; once finished, it returns a Biml table for you. `DataTableExtensions` is shown in Listings 14-1 and 14-2 and is referenced in the following examples. The extension method stays the same but how you use it changes depending on how you've collected the metadata.

Listing 14-1. DataTableExtensions (C#)

```csharp
using System;
using System.Data;
using System.Linq;
using Varigence.Languages.Biml.Table;

public static class DataTableExtensions
{
  public static AstTableNode ToAstTableNode(this DataTable dataTable)
  {
    var schema = new AstSchemaNode(null);
    var table = new AstTableNode(null);
    schema.Name = dataTable.Rows.OfType<DataRow>().Select
    (r => r["TABLE_SCHEMA"].ToString()).First();
    table.Schema = schema;
    table.Name = dataTable.Rows.OfType<DataRow>().Select
    (r => r["TABLE_NAME"].ToString()).First();
    foreach (DataRow row in dataTable.Rows)
    {
      var column = new AstTableColumnNode(table)
      {
        Name = row["COLUMN_NAME"].ToString(),
        DataType = row["DATA_TYPE"].ToString().GetDbType(),
        IsNullable = Convert.ToBoolean(row["IS_NULLABLE"].ToString().
        Replace("YES", "true").Replace("NO", "false"))
      };
      if (!row.IsNull("CHARACTER_MAXIMUM_LENGTH"))
      {
        column.Length = Convert.ToInt32(row["CHARACTER_MAXIMUM_LENGTH"]);
      }

      if (!row.IsNull("NUMERIC_PRECISION"))
      {
        column.Precision = Convert.ToInt32(row["NUMERIC_PRECISION"]);
      }

      if (!row.IsNull("NUMERIC_SCALE"))
      {
        column.Precision = Convert.ToInt32(row["NUMERIC_SCALE"]);
      }

      table.Columns.Add(column);
    }

    return table;
  }
```

```csharp
public static DbType GetDbType(this string type)
{
  switch (type.ToLower())
  {
    case "bigint": return DbType.Int64;
    case "binary": return DbType.Binary;
    case "bit": return DbType.Boolean;
    case "char": return DbType.AnsiStringFixedLength;
    case "date": return DbType.Date;
    case "datetime2": return DbType.DateTime2;
    case "datetime": return DbType.DateTime;
    case "datetimeoffset": return DbType.DateTimeOffset;
    case "decimal": return DbType.Decimal;
    case "float": return DbType.Double;
    case "int": return DbType.Int32;
    case "money": return DbType.Currency;
    case "nchar": return DbType.StringFixedLength;
    case "numeric": return DbType.Decimal;
    case "nvarchar": return DbType.String;
    case "real": return DbType.Single;
    case "smalldatetime": return DbType.DateTime;
    case "smallint": return DbType.Int16;
    case "smallmoney": return DbType.Currency;
    case "time": return DbType.Time;
    case "timestamp": return DbType.Binary;
    case "tinyint": return DbType.Byte;
    case "uniqueidentifier": return DbType.Guid;
    case "varbinary": return DbType.Binary;
    case "varchar": return DbType.AnsiString;
    case "xml": return DbType.Xml;
    default: return DbType.Object;
  }
}
}
```

Listing 14-2. DataTableExtensions (VB)

```vb
Imports Varigence.Languages.Biml.Table
Imports System
Imports System.Data
Imports System.Linq
Imports System.Runtime.CompilerServices

Module DataTableExtensionsVb
  <Extension()>
  Public Function ToAstTableNode(dataTable As DataTable) As AstTableNode
    Dim table As New AstTableNode(Nothing)
```

```vbnet
    Dim schema As New AstSchemaNode(Nothing) With {
         .Name = dataTable.Rows.OfType (Of DataRow)().Select(Function(row)
         row("TABLE_SCHEMA").ToString).First()
         }
    table.Schema = schema
    table.Name = dataTable.Rows.OfType (Of DataRow)().Select(Function(row)
    row("TABLE_NAME").ToString).First()
    For Each row In dataTable.Rows
      Dim column As New AstTableColumnNode(table)
      column.Name = row("COLUMN_NAME")
      column.IsNullable = Convert.ToBoolean(row("IS_NULLABLE").ToString().
      Replace("YES", "true").Replace("NO", "false"))
      If Not row.IsNull("CHARACTER_MAXIMUM_LENGTH") Then _
        column.Length = Convert.ToInt32(row("CHARACTER_MAXIMUM_LENGTH"))
      column.DataType = row("DATA_TYPE").ToString().GetDbType()
      If Not row.IsNull("NUMERIC_PRECISION") Then column.Precision =
      Convert.ToInt32(row("NUMERIC_PRECISION"))
      If Not row.IsNull("NUMERIC_SCALE") Then column.Precision = Convert.
      ToInt32(row("NUMERIC_SCALE"))
      table.Columns.Add(column)
    Next
    Return table
End Function


<Extension()>
Public Function GetDbType(type As String) As DbType
  Select Case type
    Case "bigint" : Return DbType.Int64
    Case "binary" : Return DbType.Binary
    Case "bit" : Return DbType.Boolean
    Case "char" : Return DbType.AnsiStringFixedLength
    Case "date" : Return DbType.Date
    Case "datetime2" : Return DbType.DateTime2
    Case "datetime" : Return DbType.DateTime
    Case "datetimeoffset" : Return DbType.DateTimeOffset
    Case "decimal" : Return DbType.Decimal
    Case "float" : Return DbType.Double
    Case "int" : Return DbType.Int32
    Case "money" : Return DbType.Currency
    Case "nchar" : Return DbType.StringFixedLength
    Case "numeric" : Return DbType.Decimal
    Case "nvarchar" : Return DbType.String
    Case "real" : Return DbType.Single
    Case "smalldatetime" : Return DbType.DateTime
    Case "smallint" : Return DbType.Int16
    Case "smallmoney" : Return DbType.Currency
    Case "time" : Return DbType.Time
    Case "timestamp" : Return DbType.Binary
```

357

```
      Case "tinyint" : Return DbType.Byte
      Case "uniqueidentifier" : Return DbType.Guid
      Case "varbinary" : Return DbType.Binary
      Case "varchar" : Return DbType.AnsiString
      Case "xml" : Return DbType.Xml
      Case Else : Return DbType.Object
    End Select
  End Function
End Module
```

Note that the data collected from information_schema may differ across the database engines because database engines are not developed by the same people or in the same way. Our focus is SQL Server. You can execute these examples against other sources like PostgreSQL, but you will likely have to add or change the data type mappings.

Collecting Database Metadata Using SQL Server

SQL Server provides several methods to collect metadata. One method is information_schema views.

Using INFORMATION_SCHEMA

SQL Server supports a three-part naming convention so you can view metadata from one database when connected to another database:

```
SELECT * FROM [msdb].[INFORMATION_SCHEMA].[TABLES]
```

```
SELECT * FROM [AdventureWorks2014].[INFORMATION_SCHEMA].[TABLES]
```

In these examples you'll focus on the INFORMATION_SCHEMA.TABLES and INFORMATION_SCHEMA.COLUMNS views.

If you've never worked with the INFORMATION_SCHEMA.TABLES and INFORMATION_SCHEMA.COLUMNS views, query them to get a better understanding of the data returned by these views. You can learn more at https://docs.microsoft.com/en-us/sql/relational-databases/system-information-schema-views/system-information-schema-views-transact-sql.

Note that INFORMATION_SCHEMA acts as a layer over SQL Server's system tables like sys.objects or sys.tables.

The BimlScripts in Listings 14-3 and 14-4 use the GetDataTable method to query INFORMATION_SCHEMA.COLUMNS and return a data table populated with metadata for the Person table. The data table is then passed into extension method DatatableExtensions, which returns a Biml table for you.

Listing 14-3. Using INFORMATION_SCHEMA (C#)

```
<#@ code file="DataTableExtensions.cs" #>
<#@ import namespace="System.Data" #>
<Biml xmlns="http://schemas.varigence.com/biml.xsd">
<#
var table = "Person";
var connection = "Provider=SQLNCLI11;Server=localhost;Initial
Catalog=AdventureWorks2014;Integrated Security=SSPI";
var dataTable = ExternalDataAccess.GetDataTable(connection, @"
SELECT c.TABLE_SCHEMA
      ,c.TABLE_NAME
      ,c.COLUMN_NAME
      ,c.IS_NULLABLE
      ,c.DATA_TYPE
      ,c.CHARACTER_MAXIMUM_LENGTH
      ,c.NUMERIC_PRECISION
      ,c.NUMERIC_SCALE
FROM INFORMATION_SCHEMA.COLUMNS c
LEFT OUTER JOIN INFORMATION_SCHEMA.TABLES t
        ON c.TABLE_CATALOG = t.TABLE_CATALOG
        AND c.TABLE_SCHEMA = t.TABLE_SCHEMA
        AND c.TABLE_NAME = t.TABLE_NAME
WHERE t.TABLE_NAME IN ('" + table + @"')
ORDER BY c.TABLE_SCHEMA ASC,
        c.TABLE_NAME ASC
");
#>
  <Tables>
        <#=dataTable.ToAstTableNode().GetBiml()#>
  </Tables>
</Biml>
```

Listing 14-4. Using INFORMATION_SCHEMA (VB)

```
<#@ template language="VB" optionexplicit="False"#>
<#@ code file="DataTableExtensionsVb.vb" #>
<#@ import namespace="System.Data" #>
<Biml xmlns="http://schemas.varigence.com/biml.xsd">
<#
Dim table = "Person"
Dim connection = "Provider=SQLNCLI11;Server=localhost;Initial
Catalog=AdventureWorks2014;Integrated Security=SSPI"
Dim dataTable as DataTable = ExternalDataAccess.GetDataTable(connection, "
SELECT c.TABLE_SCHEMA
      ,c.TABLE_NAME
      ,c.COLUMN_NAME
      ,c.IS_NULLABLE
```

```
        ,c.DATA_TYPE
        ,c.CHARACTER_MAXIMUM_LENGTH
        ,c.NUMERIC_PRECISION
        ,c.NUMERIC_SCALE
FROM INFORMATION_SCHEMA.COLUMNS c
LEFT OUTER JOIN INFORMATION_SCHEMA.TABLES t
        ON c.TABLE_CATALOG = t.TABLE_CATALOG
        AND c.TABLE_SCHEMA = t.TABLE_SCHEMA
        AND c.TABLE_NAME = t.TABLE_NAME
WHERE t.TABLE_NAME = '" + table + "'
ORDER BY c.TABLE_SCHEMA ASC,
        c.TABLE_NAME ASC
")
#>
    <Tables>
        <#=dataTable.ToAstTableNode().GetBiml()#>
    </Tables>
</Biml>
```

Using dm_exec_describe_first_result_set

Another way to collect metadata is to use the system function provided by Microsoft called sys.dm_exec_describe_first_result_set. One drawback when using this function is that it only retrieves the metadata for the first result set of the statement. One benefit is that you can collect metadata from a stored procedure. This metadata can be used to represent a table or a schema structure for the source system.

If you'd like to learn more about the sys.dm_exec_describe_first_result_set function, visit https://docs.microsoft.com/en-us/sql/relational-databases/system-dynamic-management-views/sys-dm-exec-describe-first-result-set-transact-sql.

This is quite similar to the previous example where you used information_schema to collect your metadata; the only thing that has changed is your source query and that you map the column names to the ones used by your DataTableExtensions method.

The BimlScripts in Listings 14-5 and 14-6 use the GetDataTable method to query the sys.dm_exec_describe_first_result_set function. A data table is returned, populated with metadata for the stored procedure uspGetEmployeeManagers. The data table is then passed into extension method DatatableExtensions, which returns a Biml table.

Listing 14-5. Using dm_exec_describe_first_result_set (C#)

```
<#@ code file="DataTableExtensions.cs" #>
<#@ import namespace="System.Data" #>
<Biml xmlns="http://schemas.varigence.com/biml.xsd">
<#
var storedProcedure = "[dbo].[uspGetEmployeeManagers]";
var connection = "Provider=SQLNCLI11;Server=localhost;Initial
Catalog=AdventureWorks2014;Integrated Security=SSPI";
var dataTable = ExternalDataAccess.GetDataTable(connection, @"
```

```
SELECT 'dbo' AS TABLE_SCHEMA
      ,'EmployeeManagers'AS TABLE_NAME
      ,f.name AS COLUMN_NAME
      ,f.is_nullable AS IS_NULLABLE
      ,t.name AS DATA_TYPE
      ,f.max_length AS CHARACTER_MAXIMUM_LENGTH
      ,f.precision AS NUMERIC_PRECISION
      ,f.scale AS NUMERIC_SCALE
FROM sys.dm_exec_describe_first_result_set('EXEC " + storedProcedure + @" 30',
null, 0) AS f
LEFT OUTER JOIN sys.types AS t
ON t.user_type_id = f.system_type_id
");
#>
  <Tables>
       <#=dataTable.ToAstTableNode().GetBiml()#>
  </Tables>
</Biml>
```

Listing 14-6. Using dm_exec_describe_first_result_set (VB)

```
<#@ template language="VB" optionexplicit="False"#>
<#@ code file="DataTableExtensionsVb.vb" #>
<#@ import namespace="System.Data" #>
<Biml xmlns="http://schemas.varigence.com/biml.xsd">
<#
Dim storedProcedure = "[dbo].[uspGetEmployeeManagers]"
Dim connection = "Provider=SQLNCLI11;Server=localhost;Initial
Catalog=AdventureWorks2014;Integrated Security=SSPI"
Dim dataTable as DataTable = ExternalDataAccess.GetDataTable(connection, "
SELECT 'dbo'AS TABLE_SCHEMA
      ,'EmployeeManagers'AS TABLE_NAME
      ,f.name AS COLUMN_NAME
      ,f.is_nullable AS IS_NULLABLE
      ,t.name AS DATA_TYPE
      ,f.max_length AS CHARACTER_MAXIMUM_LENGTH
      ,f.precision AS NUMERIC_PRECISION
      ,f.scale AS NUMERIC_SCALE
FROM sys.dm_exec_describe_first_result_set('EXEC " + storedProcedure + " 30',
null, 0) AS f
LEFT OUTER JOIN sys.types AS t
ON t.user_type_id = f.system_type_id
")
#>
    <Tables>
        <#=dataTable.ToAstTableNode().GetBiml()#>
    </Tables>
</Biml>
```

Collecting Database Metadata Using the .NET Framework

Using C# or VB, you have access to the rich features and class libraries included in the .NET Framework. If you can't find a solution or method suited for your use case, you can create your own solution or method. We next show you how to collect metadata in two ways using the SqlConnection class, the GetSchema method, the SqlDataReader class, and the GetSchemaTable method.

Using SqlConnection.GetSchema

In the next example, you connect to a database and retrieve metadata for a table or view using the SqlConnection.GetSchema method. The metadata is then passed into a data table and then into an AstTableNode extension method before returning a Biml table. Learn more about this method at https://msdn.microsoft.com/en-us/library/ms136366(v=vs.110).aspx.

The BimlScripts in Listings 14-7 and 14-8 use the GetSchema method. You pass the GetSchema method two arguments: columns, which indicates that you want metadata for the columns collection; and restrictions, which is an array of strings used to filter the metadata returned. The array consists of four strings that you can use and filter the metadata returned. In the following order, they are TABLE_CATALOG, TABLE_SCHEMA, TABLE_NAME, and COLUMN_NAME. This data table is then passed into extension method DatatableExtensions, which returns a Biml table for you.

Listing 14-7. Using SqlConnection.GetSchema (C#)

```
<#@ code file="DataTableExtensions.cs" #>
<#@ import namespace="System.Data" #>
<#@ import namespace="System.Data.SqlClient" #>
<Biml xmlns="http://schemas.varigence.com/biml.xsd">
<#
var dataTable = new DataTable(null);
using (var connection = new SqlConnection("Server=localhost;Initial Catalog=
AdventureWorks2014;Integrated Security=SSPI;"))
{
  connection.Open();
  var restrictions = new string[] { null, null, "Person", null };
  dataTable = connection.GetSchema("Columns", restrictions);
  dataTable.DefaultView.Sort = "ORDINAL_POSITION ASC";
}
#>
<# if (dataTable != null) { #>
  <Tables>
        <#=dataTable.ToAstTableNode().GetBiml()#>
  </Tables>
<# } #>
</Biml>
```

Listing 14-8. Using SqlConnection.GetSchema (VB)

```
<#@ template language="VB" optionexplicit="False"#>
<#@ code file="DataTableExtensions.vb" #>
<#@ import namespace="System.Data" #>
<#@ import namespace="System.Data.SqlClient" #>
<Biml xmlns="http://schemas.varigence.com/biml.xsd">
<#
Dim dataTable As New DataTable(Nothing)
Using connection as new SqlConnection("Server=localhost;Initial Catalog=Adve
ntureWorks2014;Integrated Security=SSPI;")
  connection.Open()
  Dim restrictions() as String =  { Nothing, Nothing, "Person", Nothing }
  dataTable = connection.GetSchema("Columns", restrictions)
  dataTable.DefaultView.Sort = "ORDINAL_POSITION ASC"
End Using
#>
<# If Not IsNothing(dataTable) #>
    <Tables>
        <#=dataTable.ToAstTableNode().GetBiml()#>
    </Tables>
<# End If #>
</Biml>
```

Using SqlDataReader.GetSchemaTable

The SqlDataReader.GetSchemaTable method connects to a database and retrieves metadata. You have defined two queries for the SqlCommand. You then pass each result set inside SqlDataReader with the CommandBehavior set to KeyInfo. Next, you call upon GetSchemaTable and collect the metadata for your current result set. Then you use NextResult and go to the next result set and go through the same process again.

Note that this could even be used to describe stored procedures with multiple result sets. Learn more at https://msdn.microsoft.com/en-us/library/system.data. sqlclient.sqldatareader.getschematable(v=vs.110).aspx.

The BimlScripts in Listings 14-9 and 14-10 use the GetSchemaTable method. Each result set returned by ExecuteReader goes and collects metadata for the result set into a data table. The major difference from the previous scripts is that you do change the data tables' column names to fit into what you are going to process using the DataTableExtensions class. This table will then be converted to a Biml table using the ToAstTableNode extension method.

Listing 14-9. Using SqlDataReader.GetSchemaTable (C#)

```
<#@ code file="DataTableExtensions.cs" #>
<#@ import namespace="System.Data" #>
<#@ import namespace="System.Data.SqlClient" #>
<Biml xmlns="http://schemas.varigence.com/biml.xsd">
```

```
  <Tables>
<#
using (var connection = new SqlConnection("Data Source=.;Integrated
Security=SSPI;Initial Catalog=AdventureWorks2014"))
{
  connection.Open();
  var command = new SqlCommand(@"SELECT TOP(1) * FROM [Person].[Person]
    SELECT TOP(1) * FROM [Person].[Address]", connection);
  var reader = command.ExecuteReader(CommandBehavior.KeyInfo);
  while (reader.Read())
  {
    var dataTable = reader.GetSchemaTable();
    dataTable.Columns["BaseSchemaName"].ColumnName = "TABLE_SCHEMA";
    dataTable.Columns["BaseTableName"].ColumnName = "TABLE_NAME";
    dataTable.Columns["ColumnName"].ColumnName = "COLUMN_NAME";
    dataTable.Columns["AllowDBNull"].ColumnName = "IS_NULLABLE";
    dataTable.Columns["DataTypeName"].ColumnName = "DATA_TYPE";
    dataTable.Columns["ColumnSize"].ColumnName = "CHARACTER_MAXIMUM_LENGTH";
    dataTable.Columns["NumericPrecision"].ColumnName = "NUMERIC_PRECISION";
    dataTable.Columns["NumericScale"].ColumnName = "NUMERIC_SCALE";
#>
    <#=dataTable.ToAstTableNode().GetBiml()#>
<#  reader.NextResult();
  }
}
#>
  </Tables>
</Biml>
```

Listing 14-10. Using SqlDataReader.GetSchemaTable (VB)

```
<#@ template language="VB" optionexplicit="False"#>
<#@ code file="DataTableExtensions.vb" #>
<#@ import namespace="System.Data" #>
<#@ import namespace="System.Data.SqlClient" #>
<Biml xmlns="http://schemas.varigence.com/biml.xsd">
  <Tables>
<#
Using connection as new SqlConnection("Data Source=.;Integrated
Security=SSPI;Initial Catalog=AdventureWorks2014")
  connection.Open()
  Dim command as new SqlCommand("SELECT TOP(1) * FROM [Person].[Person]
    SELECT TOP(1) * FROM [Person].[Address]", connection)
  Dim reader = command.ExecuteReader(CommandBehavior.KeyInfo)
  While (reader.Read())
    Dim dataTable = reader.GetSchemaTable()
    dataTable.Columns("BaseSchemaName").ColumnName = "TABLE_SCHEMA"
    dataTable.Columns("BaseTableName").ColumnName = "TABLE_NAME"
```

```
      dataTable.Columns("ColumnName").ColumnName = "COLUMN_NAME"
      dataTable.Columns("AllowDBNull").ColumnName = "IS_NULLABLE"
      dataTable.Columns("DataTypeName").ColumnName = "DATA_TYPE"
      dataTable.Columns("ColumnSize").ColumnName = "CHARACTER_MAXIMUM_LENGTH"
      dataTable.Columns("NumericPrecision").ColumnName = "NUMERIC_PRECISION"
      dataTable.Columns("NumericScale").ColumnName = "NUMERIC_SCALE"
#>
      <#=dataTable.ToAstTableNode().GetBiml()#>
  <# reader.NextResult()
    End While
End Using
#>
  </Tables>
</Biml>
```

Collecting Flat File Metadata

Given their nature and structure, you cannot use any of the previous methods to collect metadata from flat files. For flat files, you must identify a way to obtain metadata, figure out a way to programmatically determine the structure of the file, or (if none of the other ways is achievable or if the files are simple) define metadata manually.

Using a BCP-Generated XML Format Definition

One popular way of describing the contents of a flat file is an XML flat file definition. If your data resides in a SQL Server database, you may use the bcp command line tool (see https://docs.microsoft.com/en-us/sql/tools/bcp-utility) to generate such a file.

The two command lines that follow generate a CSV and format definition for the Person.PersonPhone table in AdventureWorks 2014:

```
bcp adventureworks2014.person.personphone out Data\PersonPhone.csv -T -t, -c
bcp adventureworks2014.person.personphone format nul -f Format\PersonPhone.
xml -T -t, -c -x
```

The contents of the CSV should be obvious, but let's take a brief look at the XML format, shown in Listing 14-11.

Listing 14-11. The XML Format

```
<?xml version="1.0"?>
<BCPFORMAT xmlns="http://schemas.microsoft.com/sqlserver/2004/bulkload/
format" xmlns:xsi="http://www.w3.org/2001/XMLSchema-instance">
  <RECORD>
    <FIELD ID="1" xsi:type="CharTerm" TERMINATOR="," MAX_LENGTH="12"/>
    <FIELD ID="2" xsi:type="CharTerm" TERMINATOR="," MAX_LENGTH="50"
     COLLATION="SQL_Latin1_General_CP1_CI_AS"/>
```

365

```
  <FIELD ID="3" xsi:type="CharTerm" TERMINATOR="," MAX_LENGTH="12"/>
  <FIELD ID="4" xsi:type="CharTerm" TERMINATOR="\r\n" MAX_LENGTH="24"/>
 </RECORD>
 <ROW>
  <COLUMN SOURCE="1" NAME="BusinessEntityID" xsi:type="SQLINT"/>
  <COLUMN SOURCE="2" NAME="PhoneNumber" xsi:type="SQLNVARCHAR"/>
  <COLUMN SOURCE="3" NAME="PhoneNumberTypeID" xsi:type="SQLINT"/>
  <COLUMN SOURCE="4" NAME="ModifiedDate" xsi:type="SQLDATETIME"/>
 </ROW>
</BCPFORMAT>
```

XML is a completely different format but it still follows a similar logic to describe the contents of the file. You need an easy way of converting XML into Biml. The ideal way to achieve this conversion is a custom extension method. For more information about extension methods, please see Chapter 5.

Let's assume you have a folder full of flat file definitions and just want a flat file format in Biml for each of them; see Listings 14-12 and 14-13.

Listing 14-12. Get One Flat File Format Per Definition File (C#)

```
<#@ code file="FlatFileExtension.cs" #>
<#@ import namespace="System.IO" #>
<Biml xmlns="http://schemas.varigence.com/biml.xsd">
  <FileFormats>
    <# foreach(var file in Directory.GetFiles(@"C:\FlatFiles\Format")) { #>
    <#= file.GetFlatFileFormatFromXml().GetBiml() #>
    <# } #>
  </FileFormats>
</Biml>
```

Listing 14-13. Get One Flat File Format Per Definition File (VB)

```
<#@ template language="VB" optionexplicit="False"#>
<#@ code file="FlatFileExtensionsVb.vb" #>
<#@ import namespace="System.IO" #>
<Biml xmlns="http://schemas.varigence.com/biml.xsd">
  <FileFormats>
    <# for each file in Directory.Getfiles("C:\FlatFiles\Format") #>
    <#= file.GetFlatFileFormatfromXml().GetBiml() #>
    <# next #>
  </FileFormats>
</Biml>
```

By referring to the System.IO namespace, you can easily loop through all files in a folder and then call the extension method GetFlatFileFormatfromXML on each of those strings. And since this extension method will return an AstFlatFileFormatNode, you can also just use the built-in extension method GetBiml on it, so this is also a great example on how you can actually combine custom build and built-in extension methods.

Of course, GetFlatFileFormatfromXML doesn't exist by default so you must declare and define it. It will sit in the code file referenced in your Biml file; see Listings 14-14 and 14-15.

Listing 14-14. Flat File Extensions (C#)

```
using System;
using System.Data;
using System.IO;
using System.Xml;
using Varigence.Biml.Extensions;
using Varigence.Languages.Biml.Cube;
using Varigence.Languages.Biml;
using Varigence.Languages.Biml.FileFormat;
using Varigence.Languages.Biml.Table;

static class FlatFileExtensions
{
  public static AstFlatFileFormatNode GetFlatFileFormatFromXml
  (this string xmlFile)
  {
    var xmldoc = new XmlDocument();
    xmldoc.Load(xmlFile);
    var records = xmldoc.GetElementsByTagName("RECORD").Item(0).ChildNodes;
    var rows = xmldoc.GetElementsByTagName("ROW").Item(0).ChildNodes;
    var flatFileFormat = new AstFlatFileFormatNode(null)
    {
      Locale = Language.Lcid1033,
      Name = Path.GetFileNameWithoutExtension(xmlFile),
      RowDelimiter = ConvertDelimiter(records[records.Count - 1].Attributes
      ["TERMINATOR"].Value),
      ColumnNamesInFirstDataRow = false,
      IsUnicode = false,
      TextQualifier = "_x0022_"
    };
    foreach (XmlNode record in records)
    {
      if (record.Attributes == null) continue;
      var nuID = Convert.ToInt32(record.Attributes["ID"].Value) - 1;
      var row = rows.Item(nuID);
      var csvDataType = row.Attributes["xsi:type"].Value;
      var dataTypeID = ConvertDataType(csvDataType);
      var column = new AstFlatFileColumnNode(flatFileFormat)
      {
        Name = row.Attributes["NAME"].Value,
        Delimiter = ConvertDelimiter(record.Attributes["TERMINATOR"].Value),
        DataType = dataTypeID ?? DbType.String
      };
```

```
   if (dataTypeID == null)
   {
     // By default, we want out strings to be 1000 Characters
     column.Length = 1000;
   }
   else if (dataTypeID == DbType.AnsiString | dataTypeID == DbType.String)
   {
     column.Length = Convert.ToInt32(record.Attributes["MAX_LENGTH"].Value);
   }
   else if (dataTypeID == DbType.VarNumeric)
   {
     column.Precision = 32;
     column.Scale = 16;
   }

   if (dataTypeID == null)
   {
     var columnannotation = new AstAnnotationNode(null) {Tag = "Original
     Datatype", Text = csvDataType};
     column.Annotations.Add(columnannotation);
   }
   flatFileFormat.Columns.Add(column);
  }
  return flatFileFormat;
}

public static DbType? ConvertDataType(string csvType)
{
  switch (csvType)
  {
    case "SQLINT": return DbType.Int32;
    case "SQLSMALLINT": return DbType.Int16;
    case "SQLVARCHAR": return DbType.AnsiString;
    case "SQLDATETIME": return DbType.DateTime;
    case "SQLMONEY": return DbType.Currency;
    case "SQLNUMERIC": return DbType.Double;
    case "SQLNVARCHAR": return DbType.String;
    case "SQLUNIQUEID": return DbType.String;
    default: return null;
  }
}

public static string ConvertDelimiter(string csvDelimiter)
{
  return csvDelimiter == "\\r\\n" ? "CRLF" : csvDelimiter;
}
}
```

Listing 14-15. Flat File Extensions (VB)

```vb
Imports Varigence.Biml.Extensions
Imports Varigence.Languages.Biml
Imports Varigence.Languages.Biml.FileFormat
Imports Varigence.Languages.Biml.Table
Imports System.IO
Imports System.Xml
Imports System.Data
Imports System.Runtime.CompilerServices

Module FlatFileExtension
    Public Locale As Varigence.Languages.Biml.Cube.Language = Varigence.
    Languages.Biml.Cube.Language.Lcid1033

    <Extension()>
    Public Function GetFlatFileFormatfromXml(xmlFile As String)
    As AstFlatFileFormatNode
        Dim flatFileFormat As New AstFlatFileFormatNode(Nothing)
        Dim xmldoc As New XmlDocument
        xmldoc.Load(XmlFile)
        Dim records As XmlNodeList = xmldoc.GetElementsByTagName("RECORD").
        item(0).childnodes
        Dim rows As XmlNodeList = xmldoc.GetElementsByTagName("ROW").item(0).
        childnodes
        Dim row As xmlnode
        flatFileFormat.Locale = Locale
        flatFileFormat.Name = path.GetFileNameWithoutExtension(XmlFile)
        flatFileFormat.RowDelimiter = ConvertDelimiter(records.item(records.
        count - 1).attributes("TERMINATOR").value)
        flatFileFormat.ColumnNamesInFirstDataRow = False
        flatFileFormat.isunicode = False
        flatFileFormat.TextQualifier = "_x0022_"
        For Each record As xmlnode In records
            row = rows.item(record.attributes("ID").value - 1)
            Dim dataType As String = row.attributes("xsi:type").value
            Dim datatypeId As Integer = ConvertDatatype(dataType)
            Dim column As New AstFlatFileColumnNode(flatFileFormat)
            column.name = row.attributes("NAME").value
            column.Delimiter = ConvertDelimiter(record.attributes("TERMINATOR").value)
            If datatypeId = Nothing Then
                ' By default, we will make this a string!
                column.DataType = DbType.String
            Else
                column.DataType = datatypeId
            End If
```

```vb
      If datatypeId = Nothing Then
        ' By default, we want out strings to be 1000 Characters
        column.Length = 1000
      ElseIf datatypeId = dbtype.AnsiString Or datatypeId = DbType.String Then
        column.Length = record.attributes("MAX_LENGTH").value
      End If
      If ConvertDatatype(dataType) = dbtype.VarNumeric Then
        column.Precision = 32
        column.Scale = 16
      End If
      If datatypeId = Nothing Then
        Dim columnannotation As New AstAnnotationNode(Nothing)
        columnannotation.Tag = "Original Datatype"
        columnannotation.Text = dataType
        column.Annotations.Add(columnannotation)
      End If
      flatFileFormat.Columns.Add(column)
    Next
    Return flatFileFormat
  End Function

  Public Function ConvertDatatype(csvType As String) As String
    Select Case csvType
      Case "SQLINT"
        Return dbtype.Int32
      Case "SQLSMALLINT"
        Return dbtype.int16
      Case "SQLVARCHAR"
        Return dbtype.AnsiString
      Case "SQLDATETIME"
        Return dbtype.DateTime
      Case "SQLMONEY"
        Return dbtype.Currency
      Case "SQLNUMERIC"
        Return dbtype.Double
      Case "SQLNVARCHAR"
        Return DbType.String
      Case "SQLUNIQUEID"
        ' GUIDs should be interpreted as strings
        Return DbType.String
      Case Else
        Return Nothing
    End Select
  End Function
```

```
Public Function ConvertDelimiter(csvDelimiter As String) As String
  Select Case csvDelimiter
    Case "\r\n"
      Return "CRLF"
    Case Else
      Return csvDelimiter
  End Select
End Function
End Module
```

The extension method loops through the XML file, parses it, and creates an AstFlatFileNode, which is returned by the function. The method calls two other functions, ConvertDelimiter and ConvertDatatype, which you may modify if necessary.

Programmatically Identifying Flat File Structures

Another approach is to programmatically interpret the file contents. First, you need to determine the column structure which is not difficult, especially if you know text qualifiers and delimiters.

The challenging part is identifying data types. Without going into details, you must find a way to iterate every row or a representative set of sample rows, try to cast every value to multiple different data types, and then determine the "lowest common denominator" data type (which would probably be a string). For example, the iteration would check whether every row in a column can be cast as a datetime and, if so, set it to the datetime data type; otherwise, try the next data type.

We highly recommend you check out Shannon Lowder's Interrogator. Shannon presents an interesting approach; see http://shannonlowder.com/2017/06/ bimlexpress-directions-for-the-interrogator/.

Summary

In this chapter, you learned new ways to extract and work with metadata from your data source. You also learned that you can modify the way Biml uses .NET code to increase agility and flexibility. You can now troubleshoot issues with metadata generated from source systems.

In the next chapter, you'll examine troubleshooting issues with Biml code!

■ ■ ■

CHAPTER 15

Troubleshooting Biml

Writing Biml code provides you with unprecedented power to create and customize large and complex data solutions. The power to create value brings with it the power to create bugs and other issues, both at build time and runtime, that can be difficult to diagnose. For many development technologies, this issue is managed by using an interactive debugger that allows you to set breakpoints, step through code, and inspect intermediate values. Biml does not yet have an option for interactive debugging, but there are many strategies you can use to quickly find, fix, and avoid issues.

Logging

The first approach to finding and avoiding issues is to enable logging on your Biml solution. For most people, logging in a data solution is limited to the type of runtime logging that might occur in your SSIS packages or SQL stored procedures. For Biml solutions, we can extend the notion of logging to include the Biml compilation process itself. This allows us to identify issues before they become a problem and also to identify performance and other bottlenecks.

The following sections provide three tiers of options for logging within your Biml project. For most people, the logging capabilities included with the Biml engine will be sufficient. If you have special needs, you always have the option to implement your own logging infrastructure and even to hook into the very lowest level of the Biml infrastructure to capture change events as they occur.

Biml Engine Logging

Built-in Biml engine logging is based on the `Varigence.Utility.Logging.LoggingManager` class. This class has static methods that allow you to configure log storage to a text buffer, a file, a list object, or to fire an event each time a new log entry is created.

© Andy Leonard et al. 2017
A. Leonard et al., *The Biml Book*, https://doi.org/10.1007/978-1-4842-3135-7_15

In BimlStudio, the simplest way to interact with the LoggingManager is by clicking the Start Logging toggle button on the Build & Deploy ribbon tab, as shown in Figure 15-1. This will launch the Logging tool window and display new log entries as they occur, as shown in Figure 15-2.

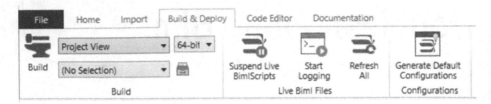

Figure 15-1. *Enable logging in BimlStudio with the Start Logging button*

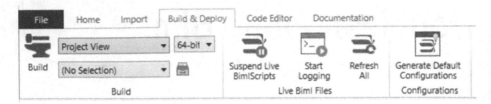

Figure 15-2. *Logging tool window in BimlStudio*

How do you customize the logging behavior and use it from BimlExpress? To do that, you need to write a bit of code. The first major consideration for configuring your LoggingManager through code is to select where your logs will be stored. The standard logging capability provides four separate, distinct persistence modes:

1. **None**: Used exclusively in cases where you are extending the LoggingManager with your own persistence mode. We'll show you how to do that later in this chapter.

2. **EventDriven**: Primarily used to display output in the BimlStudio Logging window, but can also be used by your own code that subscribes to the LogMessage event on the LoggingManager class.

3. **FullText**: Used when you would like to print the contents of the log to a text window or file output. At any time you can access the contents of the log through the FullLog property on the LoggingManager class.

4. **List**: Used when you would like to store the log entries as objects in a list that you can iterate and manipulate. At any time you can access the list of log event objects through the LogEvents property on the LoggingManager class.

5. **File**: Used when you would like an external text file to store the contents of the log. To use this mode, you must also set the LogFilePath property on the LoggingManager class to indicate the path where the log file should be written.

Each of these logging modes can be used individually or concurrently. If used concurrently, the log entries will be written to multiple locations based on which modes have been selected. For example, if you would like to configure the log to just a file, you could use the code in Listing 15-1.

Listing 15-1. Configuring the LoggingManager to Log to a File

```
<#@ import namespace="Varigence.Utility.Logging" #>
<#
var loggingManager = new LoggingManager(Logging.LoggingMode.File) {
IsEnabled = true, LogFilePath = @"c:\path_to_log\log.txt" };
LoggingManager.RegisterDefaultLoggingManager(loggingManager);
#>
```

Note that since LoggingManagers can be enabled and disabled, you must be sure to set IsEnabled to true if you want the LoggingManager to be active for your project. If you would like to log simultaneously to a file, the BimlStudio output window, and a list, you can do that using the code in Listing 15-2.

Listing 15-2. Configuring the LoggingManager to Log to Multiple Targets

```
<#@ import namespace="Varigence.Utility.Logging" #>
<#
var loggingManager = new LoggingManager(Logging.LoggingMode.File | Logging.
LoggingMode.List | Logging.LoggingMode.EventDriven) { IsEnabled = true,
LogFilePath = @"c:\path_to_log\log.txt" };
LoggingManager.RegisterDefaultLoggingManager(loggingManager);
#>
```

Note that the only change required to log to additional targets is to supply the desired LoggingMode enum values to the LoggingManager constructor. The call to RegisterDefaultLoggingManager only needs to be called once per process, since a static property is used to cache that LoggingManager for all future uses. If you ever need to clear the LoggingManager entirely, you can do so by registering a null manager as shown in Listing 15-3.

Listing 15-3. Clearing the LoggingManager

```
<#@ import namespace="Varigence.Utility.Logging" #>
<#
LoggingManager.RegisterDefaultLoggingManager(null);
```

The LoggingManager collects a wealth of data about the compilation process, including file expansion start and end events, all queries executed against external databases, and more. Listing 15-4 shows a small excerpt of a log file.

Listing 15-4. Log File Excerpt

```
9:08:08 PM        7d5b638b-0a0c-4c1f-b2f0-ee95a836c8a2      None
GetProjectTargetVersion   Assigning SsisVersion.2014
9:08:08 PM        1eef7bef-dfb9-4246-9c48-68d94927705a      Start    Expansion
C:\StagingLoader\StagingLoader\1-2-CreateTableMetadata.biml
9:08:13 PM        1683080b-962e-45b4-bb70-57d644626cbd      Start    Compile
C:\StagingLoader\StagingLoader\1-2-CreateTableMetadata.biml
9:08:13 PM        1dce5ef2-c784-427f-a3da-a570afab71bb      Start    Query Execute
Data Source=localhost;Initial Catalog=DataPatterns;Integrated Security=True;
Persist Security Info=False       SELECT \t  con.CONSTRAINT_NAME       ,
con.CONSTRAINT_SCHEMA \t, con.CONSTRAINT_TYPE       , con.TABLE_SCHEMA       ,
con.TABLE_NAME \t, usage.COLUMN_NAME \t, COALESCE(ref_con.UNIQUE_
CONSTRAINT_SCHEMA, '') AS UNIQUE_CONSTRAINT_SCHEMA \t, COALESCE(ref_con.
UNIQUE_CONSTRAINT_NAME, '') AS UNIQUE_CONSTRAINT_NAME \t, COALESCE(usage.
ORDINAL_POSITION, -1) AS ORDINAL_POSITION FROM \tINFORMATION_SCHEMA.TABLE_
CONSTRAINTS con \tLEFT JOIN INFORMATION_SCHEMA.KEY_COLUMN_USAGE usage \t\tON
(con.CONSTRAINT_SCHEMA = usage.CONSTRAINT_SCHEMA \t\t\tAND con.CONSTRAINT_
NAME = usage.CONSTRAINT_NAME)    LEFT OUTER JOIN INFORMATION_SCHEMA.
REFERENTIAL_CONSTRAINTS ref_con        ON (con.CONSTRAINT_SCHEMA = ref_con.
CONSTRAINT_SCHEMA        AND con.CONSTRAINT_NAME = ref_con.CONSTRAINT_
NAME) ORDER BY \t con.CONSTRAINT_NAME \t, usage.ORDINAL_POSITION
9:08:13 PM        1dce5ef2-c784-427f-a3da-a570afab71bb      End
Query Execute   00:00:00.2492151
9:08:14 PM        1683080b-962e-45b4-bb70-
57d644626cbd      End      Compile        C:\StagingLoader\StagingLoader\
1-2-CreateTableMetadata.biml
9:08:14 PM        1eef7bef-dfb9-4246-9c48-
68d94927705a      End      Expansion        C:\StagingLoader\StagingLoader\
1-2-CreateTableMetadata.biml
```

With all of this information being logged, the size of the log file can grow quickly for larger projects. This can make it difficult to find points of interest in the data. You can instruct the LoggingManager to log only a subset of event categories using the LoggingDetail property and the LoggingBimlFileFilter property of the LoggingManager.

LoggingDetail provides four detail filter options:

1. **None**: Used exclusively in cases where you are extending the LoggingManager with your own filtering capabilities.

2. **Files**: Used to log all events related to the starting and stopping of the compilation of Biml and other code files.

3. **Objects**: Used to log all events related to individual Biml objects and dynamically generated objects (e.g. metadata model wrapper classes).

4. **Queries**: Used to log all queries along with their target connection strings and elapsed runtimes. This tends to produce a large amount of logging data.

As with the logging persistence modes, you can select multiple logging detail options by separating all of your choices with a pipe operator, as shown in Listing 15-5.

You can also supply a semicolon-separated list of file names that you would like to use to filter the Biml files that will be logged. Note that this setting interacts with the detail filter options. For instance, if you limit the LoggingManager to a specific Biml file, it will only log the queries executed during the compilation and execution of that Biml file if you have specified the Queries detail filter. This is also demonstrated in Listing 15-5.

Listing 15-5. Configuring Filters on the LoggingManager

```
<#@ import namespace="Varigence.Utility.Logging" #>
<#
var loggingManager = new LoggingManager(Logging.LoggingMode.File) {
IsEnabled = true, LogFilePath = @"c:\path_to_log\log.txt" };
loggingManager.LoggingDetail = LoggingDetail.Files | LoggingDetail.Queries;
loggingManager.LoggingBimlFileFilter = @"c:\path\foo.biml;c:\path\bar.biml";
LoggingManager.RegisterDefaultLoggingManager(loggingManager);
#>
```

You may also want to create your own log entries throughout your BimlScript code. This will enable you to keep track of key events in the execution of your code, track the execution time of long-running operations, and capture intermediate values that may be of interest for troubleshooting.

To do this, you can access the same logging methods that the Biml engine calls internally. The simplest approach is to register a standalone log entry; see Listing 15-6.

Listing 15-6. Writing a Standalone Entry to the Log

```
<#@ import namespace="Varigence.Utility.Logging" #>
<# LoggingManager.TryDefaultLog("Category", BimlFile.FilePath,
"HelloWorld"); #>
```

As Listing 15-6 demonstrates, you can access the LoggingManager that you've already registered using RegisterDefaultLoggingManager by just calling the TryDefaultLog method on the LoggingManager class. This approach is safe in any context because the logging call will be ignored if no LoggingManager has been registered. The TryDefaultLog method takes a category as its first parameter. This is a free-form entry, and you can choose whichever category you prefer. Additionally, you can provide zero or more messages to be associated with that log entry. Messages often include the name of the Biml file, diagnostic values of interest, exception details, or other information. In Listing 15-6, we have logged the Biml file path and a fun message.

In the log excerpt shown in Listing 15-4, you might have also noticed log entries that tracked start, end, and elapsed times for some events. While you could create your own solution for tracking event start and end times, the LoggingManager has this functionality built in. The simplest way to leverage this capability is illustrated in Listing 15-7. The TryDefaultLogStart method will return a log event object that can have the LogEnd method called after the logged operation has completed. The LoggingManager will automatically create start and end entries along with timestamps and elapsed time calculations when this pattern is used.

Listing 15-7. Writing Start and End Entries to the Log

```
<#@ import namespace="Varigence.Utility.Logging" #>
<#
var logEvent = LoggingManager.TryDefaultLogStart(false, "Category",
"Message");
// ... Do Stuff ...
logEvent.LogEnd();
#>
```

In some rare instances, your coding pattern will make it difficult to store the log event object returned by the TryDefaultLogStart method. The most commonly affected scenario is when you need to begin a logged operation in one Biml file and conclude the logged operation in a different file. While you could pass the log event object between the Biml files using CallBimlScript or another mechanism, it would be more convenient if the LoggingManager could cache the log event object for us. The first Boolean parameter in TryDefaultLogStart tells the LoggingManager whether or not the log event object should be cached. If so, you can call TryDefaultLogEnd with the same category and message as the call to TryDefaultLogStart. Using this pattern, the LoggingManager will automatically match the start and end calls and produce the appropriate log entries, as illustrated in Listing 15-8.

Listing 15-8. Writing Start and End Entries to the Log with Caching

```
<#@ import namespace="Varigence.Utility.Logging" #>
<#
var logEvent = LoggingManager.TryDefaultLogStart(true, "Category", "Exact");
// ... Do Stuff ...
LoggingManager.TryDefaultLogEnd(true, "Category", "Exact");#>
```

There is one additional logging scenario for which the LoggingManager infrastructure provides special treatment: database commands. When passing a DbCommand to TryDefaultLogStart, the LoggingManager will automatically write the associated connection string and query text information into the log entries for that command. While you could certainly do this manually, it is a common operation and a welcome time saver, as shown in Listing 15-9 for C# and Listing 15-10 for VB.

Listing 15-9. Logging a Database Command in C#

```
var connection = new SqlConnection("Data Source=.;Initial
Catalog=TestDB;Integrated Security=SSPI;");
connection.Open();
using (var command = connection.CreateCommand())
{
  command.CommandText = "SELECT * FROM TestTable";
  var startLogEvent = LoggingManager.TryDefaultLogStart(command);
  using (var resultSet = command.ExecuteReader())
  {
    // ... Do Stuff ...
  }
  startLogEvent.LogEnd();

}
Connection.Close();
```

Listing 15-10. Logging a Database Command in VB

```
Dim connection = New SqlConnection("Data Source=.;Initial
Catalog=TestDB;Integrated Security=SSPI;")
connection.Open
Using command = Connection.CreateCommand()
  command.CommandText = "SELECT * FROM TestTable"
  Dim startLogEvent = LoggingManager.TryDefaultLogStart(command)
  Using resultSet = command.ExecuteReader()
    ' ... Do Stuff ...
  End Using
  startLogEvent.LogEnd()
End Using
Connection.Close
```

Writing a Custom Logger

If the LoggingManager functionality built into the Biml engine is not capable of meeting your needs, you can still continue using the LoggingManager infrastructure, but with some custom persistence or other functionality. To do that, you need to extend the LoggingManager class with your own class and override the methods you would like to change. A very simple example of this, which creates a WinForms dialog for each log entry (a very bad idea in practice, by the way, due to the volume of log entries), is shown in Listing 15-11.

Listing 15-11. Simple Customization of LoggingManager

```
public class MessageBoxLoggingManager : LoggingManager
{
  public MessageBoxLoggingManager() : base(LoggingMode.None) {}

  protected override void Log(LogEvent logEvent)
  {
    System.Windows.Forms.MessageBox.Show(logEvent.Category);
  }
}
```

Once you have defined this customized LoggingManager, you can register it as your default by using the code in Listing 15-12.

Listing 15-12. Registering the MessageBoxLoggingManager as the Default

```
<#@ import namespace="Varigence.Utility.Logging" #>
<#
var loggingManager = new MessageBoxLoggingManager() { IsEnabled = true };
LoggingManager.RegisterDefaultLoggingManager(loggingManager);
#>
```

While the MessageBoxLoggingManager is somewhat contrived and intentionally simple for the purposes of brevity, there are reasonable scenarios where you might want to implement you own LoggingManager to persist log entries to a custom location (e.g. a logging database) or where you might want to add custom filtering logic to the logging methods to reduce the size of the logs and target only entries of interest.

Diagnostics

Logging is a powerful tool for creating large amounts of information about your build process. It is most useful when previously captured logging information can be employed to figure out what went wrong after a failure or when you are uncertain of the cause of an issue. There is an entirely different class of issues where you know the root cause, you can anticipate the conditions under which the issue will occur, and you would like to create helpful diagnostics that surface errors or warnings to yourself or other developers to prevent the issue before it occurs. In the following sections, you'll learn how to leverage the built-in Biml validation list to do just that.

Creating Validation Items

Every BimlScript file has access to the object responsible for managing and reporting all errors, warnings, and notifications associated with your project build. You can use this object to create your own validation items that will be reported alongside those generated by the Biml engine. Doing so is perhaps surprisingly simple. Just call the Report method on the ValidationReporter property that is available to your BimlScript code nugget, as shown in Listing 15-13.

Listing 15-13. Creating a New Warning in the Validation List

```
<# ValidationReporter.Report(Severity.Warning, "This is custom warning!"); #>
```

This is the simplest version of the Report method where you need only specify a severity and a message. Warnings are used when you would like to raise a diagnostic but the build should still succeed. If you would like to instead generate an error that causes the build to fail, you should instead use Severity.Error as shown in Listing 15-14.

Listing 15-14. Creating a Fatal Error in the Validation List

```
<# ValidationReporter.Report(Severity.Error, "This is custom error!"); #>
```

Generating an error will cause the build to fail, but not immediately. The compiler will continue trying to compile code and may encounter many additional warnings and errors. This is the appropriate and expected behavior in most cases. Errors tend to be local and won't necessarily create spurious or false-positive errors in other areas of the code. The benefit of continuing compilation is that, in situations where there are many errors, you can work on a consolidated list of issues rather than needing to recompile after each fix to see the next issue. In other cases, an error is so fundamental that you know all or most future errors are likely to be noise. This would occur, for instance, in cases where critical source connections were not properly configured or required metadata attributes were not supplied. To immediately terminate a Biml build with failure, you should use Severity.Fatal as shown in Listing 15-15.

Listing 15-15. Creating a New Error in the Validation List

```
<# ValidationReporter.Report(Severity.Fatal, "This is custom error!"); #>
```

When you create an error or warning, it will be added to the same validation list that is used by the Biml engine. Figures 15-3 and 15-4 show what this looks like in BimlStudio and BimlExpress, respectively.

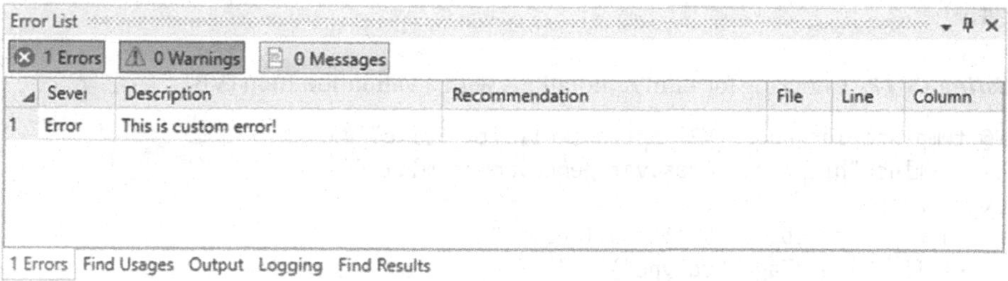

Error List						▾ ⏷ ✕
⊗ 1 Errors	⚠ 0 Warnings	🗎 0 Messages				
⊿ Sevei	Description		Recommendation	File	Line	Column
1 Error	This is custom error!					

1 Errors   Find Usages   Output   Logging   Find Results

Figure 15-3. The validation list in BimlStudio

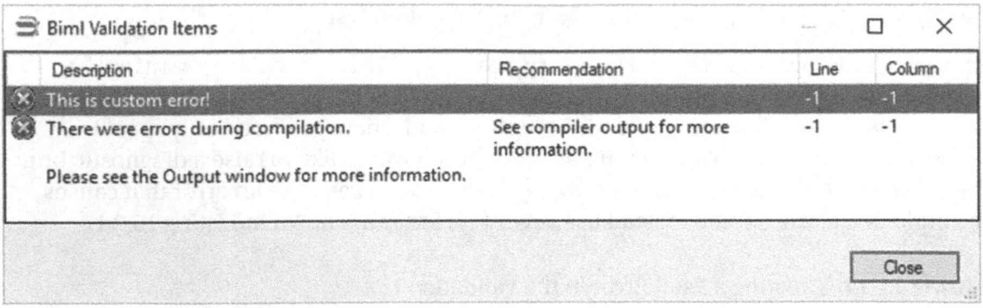

Figure 15-4. *The validation list in BimlExpress*

Of course, the validation reports we've shown thus far are very simple. In real world situations, we would normally have some logic in a BimlScript code nugget that would check for an error condition before generating the validation item. In Listing 15-16 for C# and Listing 15-17 for VB, you can see an example of this. In this hypothetical framework, the ScdType annotation tag is required to indicate which slowly changing dimension (SCD) processing type you should use for the table. If the annotation is not present, then the code generation cannot proceed for that table.

Listing 15-16. Checking for Biml Annotations with a Validation Item (C#)

```
<Biml xmlns="http://schemas.varigence.com/biml.xsd">
  <Packages>
    <# foreach (var table in RootNode.Tables) { #>
    <# if (table.GetTag("ScdType") == "") {
      ValidationReporter.Report(Severity.Error, "Please specify the
      'ScdType' Biml annotation tag for table '{0}'", table.Name);
    } #>
    <Package Name="Package for <#=table.Name#>" />
    <# } #>
  </Packages>
</Biml>
```

Listing 15-17. Checking for Biml Annotations with a Validation Item (VB)

```
<#@ template language="VB" optionexplicit="False" #>
<Biml xmlns="http://schemas.varigence.com/biml.xsd">
  <Packages>
    <# For Each tbl In RootNode.Tables #>
    <# If tbl.GetTag("ScdType") = "" Then
      ValidationReporter.Report(Severity.Error, "Please specify the
      'ScdType' Biml annotation tag for table '{0}'", tbl.Name)
    End If #>
    <Package Name="Package for <#= tbl.Name#>" />
    <# Next #>
  </Packages>
</Biml>
```

One thing you will note if you try the code sample in Listing 15-16 or Listing 15-17 is that, like the first validation examples in this chapter, there is no line or offset information associated with the error. While there are overloads to pass line and offset information to the Report method, the easiest way to handle this is just to pass the Biml object into the Report method. The Report method will automatically determine the line and offset information to include with the error, as shown in Listing 15-18.

Listing 15-18. Automatic Line/Offset Information for a Biml Object in a Validation Item

```
<Biml xmlns="http://schemas.varigence.com/biml.xsd">
  <Packages>
    <# foreach (var table in RootNode.Tables) { #>
    <# if (table.GetTag("ScdType") == "") {
      ValidationReporter.Report(table, Severity.Error, "Please specify the
      'ScdType' Biml annotation tag for table {0}", table.Name);
    } #>
    <Package Name="Package for <#=table.Name #>" />
    <# } #>
  </Packages>
</Biml>
```

There are many additional overloads of the Report method that will allow you to customize every aspect of the reported issue, but most of them are used for internal purposes within the Biml engine. If you are curious, all of the overloads are documented in the reference documentation for the ValidationReporter class at http://varigence.com.

Manipulating the Validation List

While adding your own errors and warnings to the validation list is very useful for diagnostic purposes, in some cases you may want to inspect, modify, or remove items that have already been added to the validation list, either by you or by the Biml engine. This is also possible through the ValidationReporter object. It is easy to check if there are errors or warnings in the validation list by using the HasErrors and HasWarnings properties, as shown in Listing 15-19.

Listing 15-19. Checking for Errors and Warnings

```
<# if (ValidationReporter.HasErrors || ValidationReporter.HasWarnings) {
  // ... Do Stuff ...
} #s>
```

You might want to perform this type of check to avoid issuing your own errors if you know that the build is already in an error state. This approach is not very granular, though. You might instead want to inspect the errors and warnings to see if a certain type of issue has been encountered. There are three collection properties on the ValidationReporter object that allow us to do that: Errors, Warnings, and ValidationItems. ValidationItems includes both errors and warnings, in addition to any notifications (which are the informational messages issued by the compiler when it starts a new phase or generates an object).

In Listing 15-20, you can see how to iterate over these collections. In this example, you iterate over Errors to remove an unwanted item, but you can choose the collection that is most appropriate to your needs. Note that the call to ToList() is not necessary if you do not modify the contents of the collection within the foreach loop. Since you are potentially removing an error item, you need to iterate over a copy of the original Errors collection (which ToList effectively does) so that you avoid any .NET errors related to modifying a collection while it is being enumerated.

Listing 15-20. Removing a Specific Error from the ValidationReporter

```
<# foreach (var error in ValidationReporter.Errors.ToList()) {
    if (error.Message.Contains("MyTable")) {
      ValidationReporter.Errors.Remove(error);
    }
  } #>
```

In some cases while you are troubleshooting an issue, there might be a need to clear out the validation list entirely; either because there are too many distracting warnings or so that you can continue the build past a failure location. To do so, you can use the Reset method as shown in Listing 15-21.

Listing 15-21. Clearing All Validation Items

```
<# ValidationReporter.Reset(); #>
```

Logging and Diagnostics Together

One of the capabilities that was discussed briefly in the earlier section about the LoggingManager was its ability to be enabled and disabled via the IsEnabled property. Since logging can generate a large amount of data, it can be helpful to only enable logging during those times when the issue under investigation is about to occur. In Listing 15-22, you enable logging if the ScdType annotation is not discovered on a table, rather than raising an error. At the end of the foreach loop iteration for that table, you disable logging. Using this approach, your log will contain only the information you need, making it much faster to sift through the log entries to discover the root cause of our issue.

Listing 15-22. Enabling Logging Conditionally

```
<Biml xmlns="http://schemas.varigence.com/biml.xsd">
  <Packages>
    <# foreach (var table in RootNode.Tables) { #>
    <# if (table.GetTag("ScdType") == "") {
      LoggingManager.GetDefaultLoggingManager().IsEnabled = true;
    } #>
    <Package Name="Package for <#=table.Name #>" />
    <#
```

```
        LoggingManager.GetDefaultLoggingManager().IsEnabled = false;
    } #>
  </Packages>
</Biml>
```

Troubleshooting

Logging and diagnostics are powerful tools for locating and preventing issues in code that already works or nearly works. In many cases, your issue is more fundamental and requires a workflow more akin to interactive debugging. In the following sections, we look at three approaches for working through these types of issues.

Preview Pane

Both BimlStudio and BimlExpress allow you to view the expanded version of any BimlScript. All of the code nuggets will be executed and the flat Biml is shown. Figure 15-5 shows the BimlScript designer in BimlStudio and Figure 15-6 shows the Preview pane in BimlExpress.

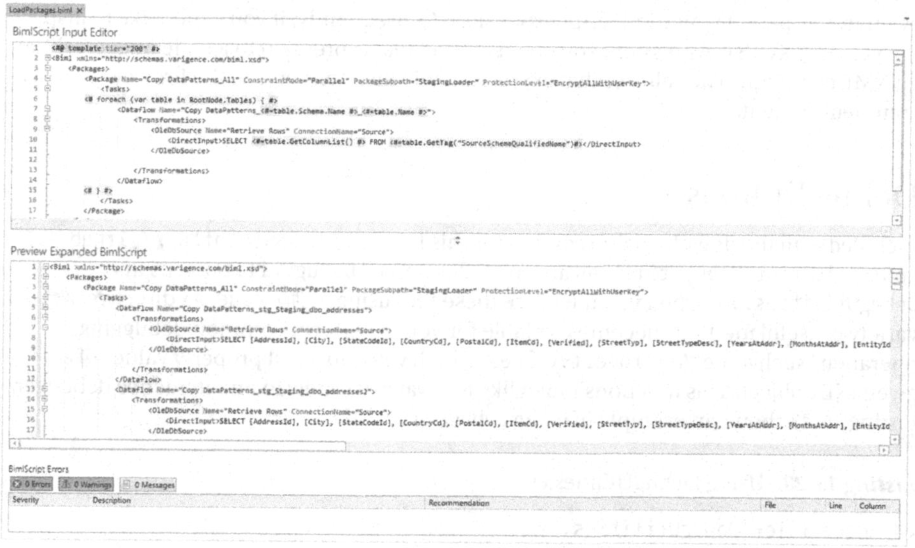

Figure 15-5. *BimlScript designer in BimlStudio*

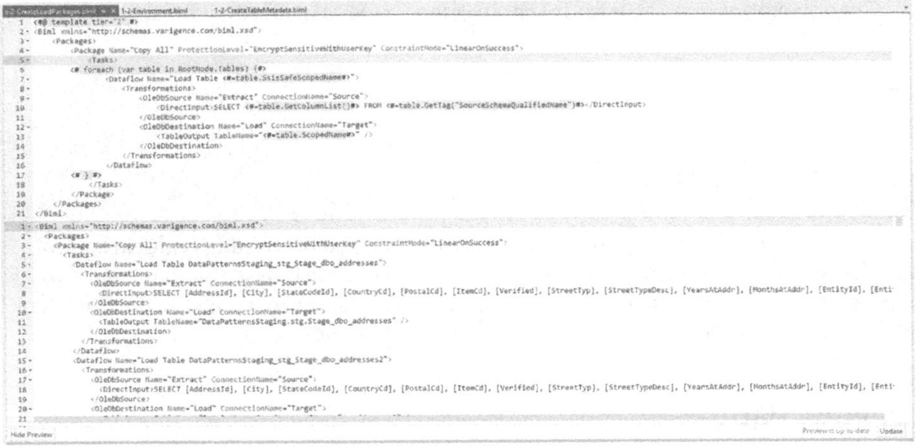

Figure 15-6. *Preview pane in BimlExpress*

The Preview pane is a critically important feature for designing your BimlScripts and debugging issues. A commonly used debugging strategy is to add comments to your Biml output. Recall that in Biml, the contents of XML comments (`<!-- Comment -->`) are evaluated as part of your BimlScript expansion. Consequently, if you would like to inspect the values of a .NET expression, you could embed that expression in a code nugget within an XML comment. The value of that expression will then render into the Preview pane as comment content.

Debug Utilities

Included with the downloadable content for this book and hosted at `http://github.com/bimlscript/DebugUtilities` are code files named `DebugUtilities.cs` and `DebugUtilities.vb`. When you reference these files using a `<#@ code #>` directive, a variety of useful methods become available for you to perform common debugging operations such as `GetAllPropertyValues`, which will output all property values of a given .NET object. This functions much like the watch window in an interactive debugger. Listing 15-23 shows an example of using `DebugUtilities`.

Listing 15-23. Using DebugUtilities.cs

```
<#@ code file="DebugUtilities.cs" #>
<Biml xmlns="http://schemas.varigence.com/biml.xsd">
  <Packages>
    <# foreach (var table in RootNode.Tables) { #>
    <# if (table.GetTag("ScdType") == "") { #>
      <!--<#=table.GetAllPropertyValues()#>-->
    } #> #>
```

```
  <Package Name="Package for <#=table.Name #>" />
  <# } #>
  </Packages>
</Biml>
```

In the Preview pane, this code would produce a comment prior to each table that lacked a ScdType annotation with a listing of all of the property values of that table.

There is much more to explore in DebugUtilities, and it is a moving target that is actively developed on GitHub to add new functionality regularly. Check the readme documents on GitHub for a full accounting of what is available and file issues with feature requests for additional functionality if there is something you think might improve the utility.

Code Files and Visual Studio

When you first start a Biml solution, most of your C# and VB code will be written inline within standard code nuggets. Over time, some of these code nuggets will become increasingly complex or you'll find that you are repeating the same bit of code in multiple places. To enhance readability and maintainability, you will usually start to rearrange your code so that the complex .NET bits are relocated into <#+ ... #> class code nuggets. Even these nuggets have downsides, because they are restricted to a single file and don't offer all the code editing features that you will find in a standalone C# or VB code editor. Consequently, as your solution continues to grow, you will likely move the code within the class code nuggets into their own code files and then reference those files from your BimlScripts using a <#@ code #> directive.

Getting to this point is key because it provides you with a variety of additional options for debugging these code segments. In addition to referencing your code files from your BimlScripts, you can additionally create a Visual Studio C# or VB command line project. Reference those same code files from your C#/VB project and then call the code from your helper methods with suitable test inputs. Then you can use Visual Studio's excellent .NET interactive debugger to figure out any issues you might have with the code.

Summary

In this chapter, you learned more about some of the techniques available to troubleshoot issues with your code, create and manage diagnostics, and log information about your BimlScript builds. As troubleshooting code will always be closely bound to the features and patterns used in that code, much of the heavy lifting of logging, diagnostics, and troubleshooting will be specific to your solution. Take the techniques and strategies outlined in them as a starting point and apply the guidance to your unique situation.

PART IV

■ ■ ■

Appendices

APPENDIX A

■ ■ ■

Source Control

Source control (or version control) is a management system that tracks and controls changes to files in a project (code files, text files, config files, biml files, resources, etc.). Source control systems are becoming ubiquitous in development teams across the world, and much has been written about their benefits. In this chapter, we quickly touch on a couple of said benefits, and dive into using source control with your Biml projects.

One of the main reasons for source control's popularity is **versioning**. Source control enables you to maintain a history of changes that have been implemented in your source code, and it provides access to these historical "states" of the project. For example, say you've introduced a bug into some formerly working code. With the help of source control you can go through each previous "state" (often referred to as a commit or a changeset) and determine the precise moment the bug was introduced.

Another big benefit of source control is the opportunity for collaboration between developers. Without a source control system in place, teams resort to using a shared folder of a single set of files, constantly in fear of overwriting each other's work. Source control frees each team member to work independently on any file at any time. Source control systems have a built-in mechanism that allows changes to be merged together into a common version for the entire team to use. Collaboration is further enhanced by source control's ability to view a "diff" (or difference) between two file states. This allows developers to see exactly what code was edited, without cluttering the file with notes or guessing to determine which changes were made. Each "commit" is accompanied by a commit message. Commit messages are invaluable in a team setting because they enable everyone to remain on the same page without having to sift through pages of source code or hassle developers to determine the status of their work.

Now that we have briefly touched on why source control is beneficial to all software development teams, let's

- Explain some common terminology.

- Discuss how to use source control with Biml Express.

- Mention the various source control clients that are, as of this writing, compatible with BimlStudio.

- Show you how to set up your first repository in the three source control systems currently supported in BimlStudio.

© Andy Leonard et al. 2017
A. Leonard et al., *The Biml Book*, https://doi.org/10.1007/978-1-4842-3135-7_16

- Create a Biml project that is tracked by source control.

- Navigate the user interface while touching on some of the cool features BimlStudio has to offer.

If you are new to source control and would like to learn more, Microsoft has a great article that goes into more detail about the benefits of source control: www.visualstudio. com/en-us/docs/tfvc/overview.

Common Terminology

This section quickly touches on a few terms we use throughout the chapter. Even if you are well-versed in the world of source control, many clients use different terminology. This section provides common definitions for the remainder of the chapter.

Repository: The collection of files and folders under source control (and each file or folder's revision history). Similar to a project folder or a master folder. Also called a workspace.

Commit: A commit (also called a revision or a changeset) is an individual change to a file (or a number of files). It is essentially a way of saving your work in source control. Each commit is associated with its own ID number, author, and commit message.

Check-out status: In BimlStudio, the check-out status describes a file that has been edited and changed since the last revision in the local repository.

Check-in status: In BimlStudio, files that have a check-in status are up to date and have not been edited since the last revision.

Revert: Revert is essentially an undo that will erase all changes from a checked out file and return it to check-in status.

Add: Add takes an untracked file and adds it to source control tracking. This can be a brand new file or a file that was previously not being tracked.

Can I Use Source Control with Biml?

Yes! Just about any file is capable of being tracked with source control. Due to Biml's readability, it makes *more* sense to track Biml files in source control than to manually track .dtsx files. When comparing the text of a .dtsx file to its previous state, it is hard to determine exactly what the changes are accomplishing. Because of Biml's readable nature, file comparison is easier, more intuitive, and stress-free.

Using Source Control for Biml with BimlExpress

BimlExpress supports whatever version control software you are already using within Visual Studio. BimlExpress works as a plugin for Visual Studio so the files are added inside the BI solution you have created. If your solution is checked into your repository, you only need to add your BimlScript files and any helper methods you've created.

Which Source Control Clients Are Compatible with BimlStudio?

The BimlStudio integrated development environment (IDE) has its own built-in source control interface that is sleek and easy to use. Three source control clients are currently supported by BimlStudio:

- **Git**

- **Subversion** (SVN)

- **Team Foundation Version Control** (TFVC)

Setting up a Source Control Repository

If you already have a repository or workspace set up on your machine, feel free to jump to the next section. If this is your first foray into source control, this section briefly covers how to set up a repository from scratch. Each version control client comes with its own quirks, so we will quickly touch on each one.

Team Foundation Version Control

Team Foundation Server (TFS) and Visual Studio Team Services (VSTS) (formerly known as Team Foundation Service) serve as Microsoft's one-stop-shop for *application lifecycle management* solutions. TFS is installed on an on-premises server (or servers) and VSTS serves as the cloud-based equivalent. Both solutions have two native options for source control. The first–and the one we will be discussing here–is Team Foundation Version Control (TFVC). In order to use TFVC, you first need Team Foundation Server or Visual Studio Team Services.

■ **Note** There is a third way outside of TFS and VSTS: an eclipse plugin called Team Explorer Everywhere. For the sake of brevity, we focus on the two used by Visual Studio.

To proceed,

1. You must have your favorite version of Visual Studio installed on your machine.

2. If you do not already have TFS, then you need to

   a. Set up Team Foundation Server on your local server, which can be found by following this link: www.visualstudio.com/tfs/.

   b. Set up a cloud-based server with Visual Studio Team Services by following the steps at www.visualstudio.com/vso/.

■ Note   You need to install the version of Team Foundation Server that matches your version of Visual Studio. For example, if you are using Visual Studio 2012, you need the 2012 version of the TFS client.

Creating the Team Project

Create the team project by opening Visual Studio and then opening the Team Explorer tab. Next, connect to the instance of TFS (or VSTS) that you just set up, as shown in Figure A-1.

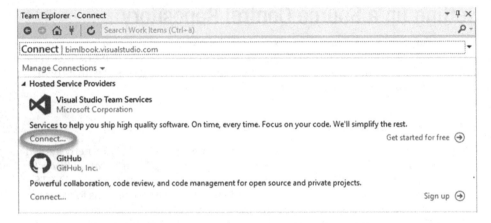

Figure A-1. *The Connect button in the Team Explorer window in Visual Studio 2015*

After you connect, select "New Team Project" to launch the New Project Wizard, as shown in Figure A-2.

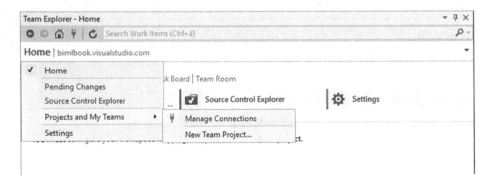

Figure A-2. *Where to create a new team project in Visual Studio 2015*

Once your project is set up, click "Source Control Explorer," as shown in Figure A-3.

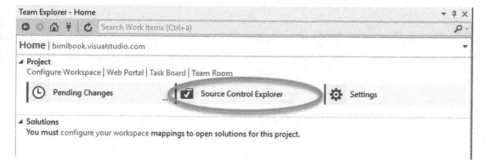

Figure A-3. *How to navigate to Source Control Explorer*

If your project has not been set up with source control, there will be a link that says "Not Mapped" (Figure A-4).

Figure A-4. *A workspace that is not yet mapped to a local folder*

Click the "Not Mapped" link and select a local folder to map to your server folder. This local folder will be your **workspace**, or repository. You are now ready to rock and roll! We will show you how to use source control with a Biml project in the next section.

Subversion

Subversion (SVN) is a free and open source version control system. Subversion was started by CollabNet around the turn of the millennium, and was one of the first widely adopted source control systems. There are many options for setting up SVN. For the sake of simplicity, we suggest you use https://riouxsvn.com/ for hosting and TortoiseSvn as a shell extension (although there are many other shell extension and hosting options available). To proceed, follow these steps:

1. Create a RiouxSvn account and repository at https://riouxsvn.com.

2. Install TortoiseSVN from http://tortoisesvn.net/downloads.html.

■ **Note** TortoiseSVN is a shell extension; it is integrated into Windows Explorer. You may use TortoiseSVN source control through either the BimlStudio UI or Windows Explorer.

Select or create a folder to serve as your Subversion Workspace. Right-click the folder and select SVN Checkout, as shown in Figure A-5.

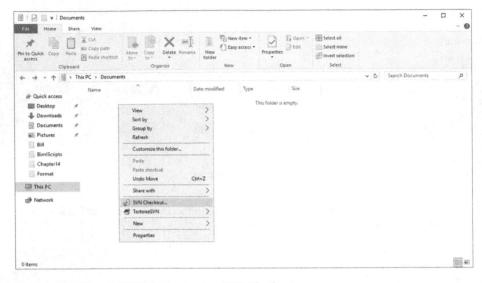

Figure A-5. *TortoiseSVN shell extension SVN Checkout*

You will be asked for your Subversion URL. This is the URL that links to your newly created repository, as shown in Figure A-6.

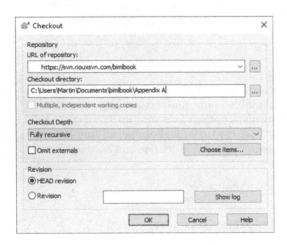

Figure A-6. *TortoiseSVN Checkout dialog box*

After you select the OK button you will be prompted for the username and password you registered when setting up your online repository. You have now set up your first Subversion repository!

Git

Git, originally created by Linus Torvalds in 2005 for Linux, is a *distributed* source control management system. Git behaves differently from the previously discussed source control clients, which are considered *centralized systems*. Unlike centralized systems that synchronize with one central repository, distributed version control takes a peer-to-peer approach. In Git, each user's working copy of the codebase is its own complete repository. This distinction leads to some interesting differences between Git and its counterparts. Git makes use of a separate set of Sync commands (you will learn more about them later in the chapter). Sync commands compensate for the lack of one central repository. However, Git is often much faster than SVN and TFVC when performing basic tasks because it is unnecessary to communicate with a server. Why? Your complete repository is local! The only time you take the performance hit of communicating to the server is during the special set of Sync commands, as these commands enable your repository to stay up to date with the remote one and vice versa.

■ **Note**   Basic tasks include performing commits, viewing a file history, and reverting changes.

Like Subversion, Git is a free, open source project. There are plenty of hosting clients for Git, many of which are free (i.e. BitBucket, GitHub, GitLab). The simplest and perhaps most popular hosting client is GitHub. In this demo we will use GitHub.

There are many clients that you can use to set up a Git repository on your computer. We have found the GitHub Desktop application to be the most intuitive and beginner-friendly.

To set up the GitHub Desktop application,

1. Go to www.github.com/ and sign up, and create a new project.

2. Download the GitHub Desktop application at https://
    desktop.github.com/.

3. Launch the GitHub Desktop application and select the "Clone
    Repository" option from the file menu.

4. Enter the link to your GitHub project in the "Enter a repository
    URL or GitHub username and repository" textbox, and then
    choose the local directory to set up as your local repository
    (see Figure A-7). Select "Clone." You have now set up your
    local repository and linked it to the remote github.com
    repository.

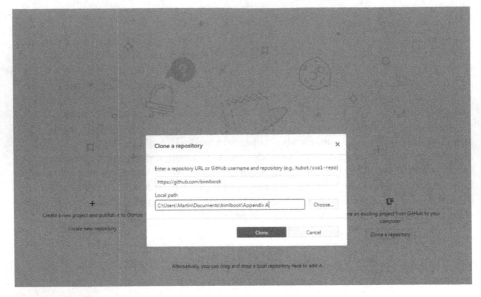

Figure A-7. *A screenshot of the Clone screen in the GitHub Desktop app*

Now let's set up a Biml Project under source control.

Tracking a BimlStudio Project in Source Control

Now that you are completely set up and raring to go, it's time to dive in and create your first Biml project that is tracked by source control. Both Git and Svn work pretty much out of the box, whereas TFVC requires a small amount of configuration for each new project. I can feel your excitement from here, so without any further ado, let's jump in!

Git and Subversion

First, open BimlStudio and create a new project inside your directory that you just linked to your repository (or move an existing project into said directory), as shown in Figure A-8.

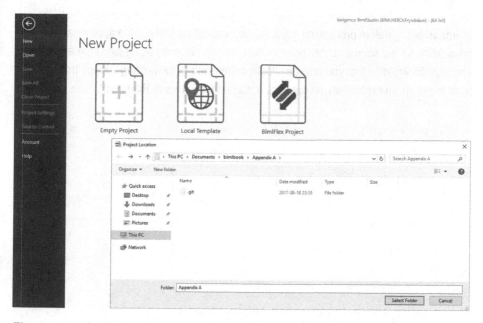

Figure A-8. *File selection for a new project in BimlStudio*

Under the File menu, select "Source Control." You should see a screen similar to Figure A-9.

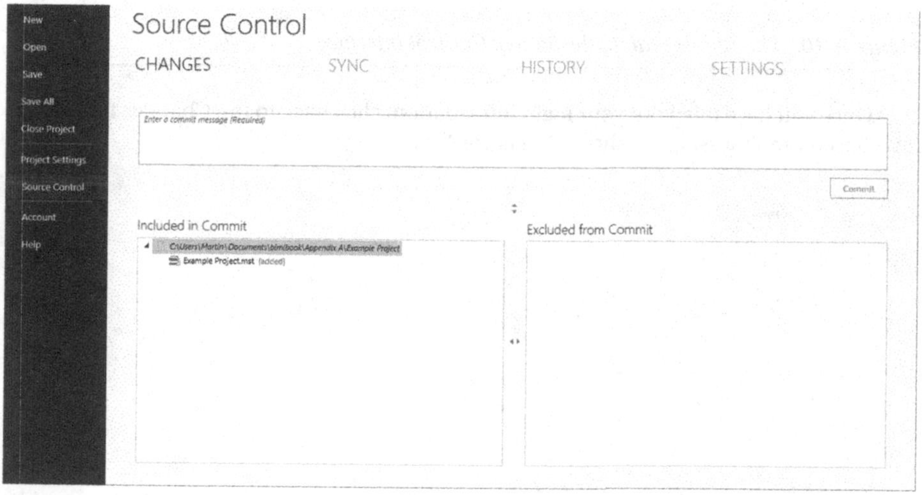

Figure A-9. *The Changes tab of the Source Control interface*

■ **Important**   Before proceeding, click the Settings tab and fill out the appropriate information for the source control provider that you are currently using (see Figure A-10). The login information that you provide should correspond to the hosting service that you used to set up your repository (in our case it was either GitHub or RiouxSvn).

Source Control

CHANGES	SYNC	HISTORY	SETTINGS

Git

Username:	bimlbook
Password:	********
Name:	Optional for signing commits
Email:	Optional for signing commits
	☑ Remember Me

Subversion

Username:	
Password:	
	☐ Remember Me

Team Foundation Services (TFS)

TFS Path:	[...] [Reload]
	☐ Lock On Checkout
	☐ Use Visual Studio Online (VSO) Authentication
Username:	
Password:	
	☑ Remember Me

Figure A-10. *The Settings tab of the Source Control interface*

Once you have filled out your login information, click back to the Changes tab and fill out a commit message, as shown in Figure A-11.

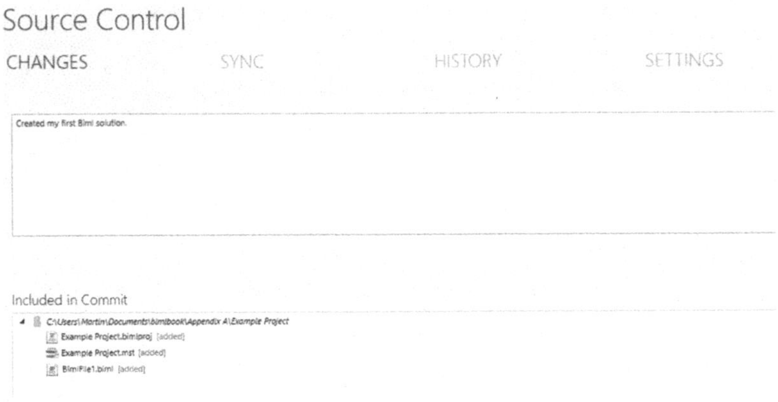

Source Control

CHANGES	SYNC	HISTORY	SETTINGS

Created my first Biml solution.

Included in Commit

▲ 🗎 C:\Users\Martin\Documents\bimlbook\Appendix A\Example Project
  📄 Example Project.bimlproj [added]
  🔷 Example Project.mst [added]
  📄 BimlFile1.biml [added]

Figure A-11. *A closer look at a commit message in the Changes tab*

■ **Tip** You can see which files have changes that are being tracked. These will be included in the commit. In order to exclude a file from a commit, simply right-click and choose the Exclude option.

Practice the art of the Commit message; they can be invaluable resources when going through past work. Also, it is best to keep in mind that, in a team environment, other people will likely be reading your commit messages. Keep commit messages clean, concise, and informative.

Once you have reviewed the files that are to be committed and are content with your commit message, press the Commit button. If the operation was successful, the "Included in Commit" file list will clear out and you will see the success message, shown in Figure A-12.

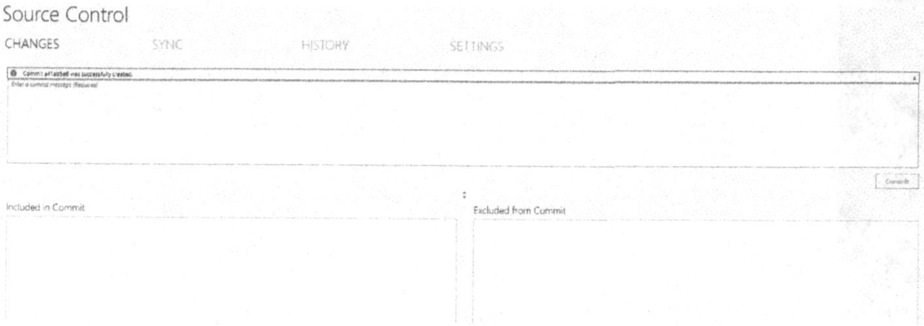

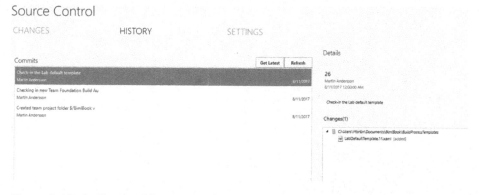

Figure A-12. The state of the Changes tab after a successful commit

You can further verify that your commit was successful by heading to the History tab. Your most recent commit should be at the top of the list, as shown in Figure A-13.

Figure A-13. A glimpse of the History tab

That is all there is to it for your first Svn or Git commit. Now let's talk about TFVC.

Team Foundation Version Control

There is a little bit more to do in order to get TFVC configured. However, with the guidance provided in this section, you will be operational in no time. To begin, create a new project inside your mapped TF directory (Figure A-8). In the File menu, select the Source Control option, and you will see the Getting Started page shown in Figure A-14.

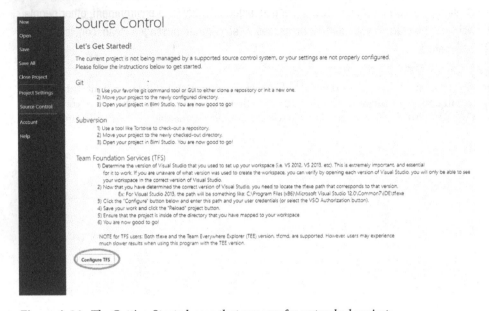

Figure A-14. *The Getting Started page that appears for untracked projects*

Press the Configure TFS button and a new window will pop up, as shown in Figure A-15.

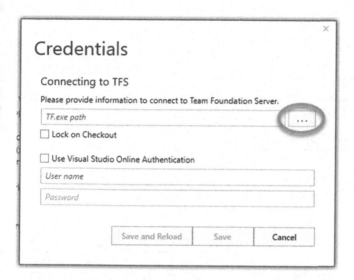

Figure A-15. *The Credentials window for configuring TFS, with the file picker highlighted*

First, locate your tf.exe path. Tf.exe is installed by default with all Visual Studio installations after 2010. In order to locate your version of tf.exe, simply launch the file picker (shown in Figure A-15), locate the address bar, and enter the Environment variable from Table A-1 that corresponds to the version of Visual Studio that you used to set up the workspace. Locate the tf.exe path inside this folder, as shown in Figure A-16.

Table A-1. *Environment Variables for the IDE Folder of Visual Studio*

Version	Path
Visual Studio 2012	%VS110COMNTOOLS%..\IDE
Visual Studio 2013	%VS120COMNTOOLS%..\IDE
Visual Studio 2015	%VS140COMNTOOLS%..\IDE

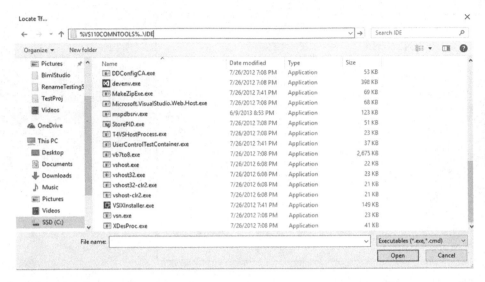

Figure A-16. *File options*

■ **Note** Once again, it is imperative that you use the `tf.exe` path that corresponds to the version of Visual Studio that you used to set up your workspace. This can be confusing if you have multiple versions of Visual Studio on your machine. In order to verify your version, open the version of Visual Studio that you used to configure your workspace and open the About dialog from the Help menu.

Once you locate `tf.exe` you can click the Open button to return to the Credentials window. If you are using an on-premises version of Team Foundation Server, you need to enter your credentials. If you are using the cloud-based version, check the "Use Visual Studio Online Authentication" checkbox.

Once your credentials have been entered, click the Save and Reload button. It is necessary that the BimlStudio project is reloaded in order to enable Source Control tracking. Once the project has reloaded, navigate back to the Source Control screen. The Getting Started screen is replaced with the Source Control interface.

Enter a commit message and commit your changes, as shown in Figure A-17.

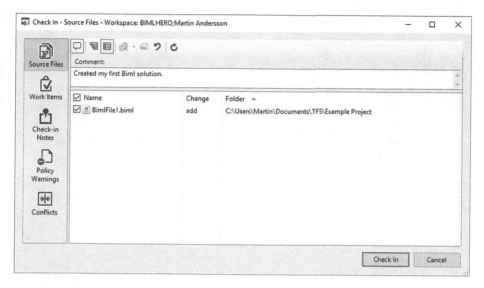

Figure A-17. *TF.exe UI*

Once the commit button is pressed in TFVC, BimlStudio hands off operation to the tf.exe UI. This provides a familiar face and gives the user one last opportunity to verify the commit before proceeding.

Wasn't that easy? Now let's really level up by checking out how to use some of the source control features that BimlStudio offers.

Source Control Features in BimlStudio

In this section, we take a look at some of the cool source control features that have been integrated into BimlStudio.

Project View Status

Project View now displays icons next to the files. The icons reflect the state of each file in relation to your repository, as shown in Figure A-18.

Figure A-18. *An example of the different status icons inside of the project view*

Viewing Figure A-18, note the following:

- CodeFile.cs shows an Add status, meaning that it is a new file or one that was not previously tracked by source control.

- SourceControlTest.biml shows a Checked-out status. This signifies that the file has been changed since the last revision, meaning that the content of the file was edited or the file itself was renamed.

- TransformerTest.bimlt shows a Checked-in status, meaning that the file is unchanged and is in the same state as the last commit.

- If a folder shows Checked-in status, none of its children have been changed. The addedBiml folder's children are not all checked in, so it shows Checked-out status.

Project View Context Menu

When you right-click on a file in the project view, you are presented with a variety of options relating to source control, as shown in Figure A-19.

Figure A-19. *An example of the context menu in the Project View.*

- **Add:** Takes files that are not currently being tracked and adds them to source control.

- **Rename:** Allows you to change the name of your file (or folder).

- **Revert:** Allows you to undo any changes that have occurred since the last commit. Be careful because Revert will override any local saves and return the file to the state it was in during the last successful commit.

- **Update:** Communicates with the server and retrieves the most recent iteration of the file.

- **Commit:** Takes you to the Changes tab of the source control interface, allowing you to commit any changes to your project.

File Comparison

An important facet of source control is being able to view differences (diffs) between states of files. BimlStudio makes viewing diffs easy with your favorite file comparison tool. In order to get this feature working correctly, head over to the Project Settings menu and locate the Diff Viewer options, as shown in Figure A-20.

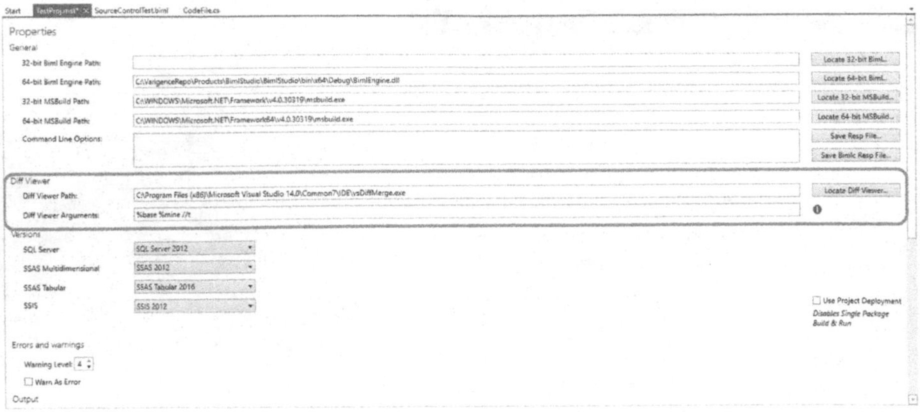

![Figure A-20 screenshot of Project Settings tab showing Diff Viewer settings]

Figure A-20. The location of the Diff Viewer settings inside the Project Settings tab

Click the Locate Diff Viewer button to locate your favorite comparison tool and configure command line arguments in the "Diff Viewer Arguments" property. For help with configuring the arguments for your specific compare tool, click the information icon.

Once Diff Viewer is configured, open the Source Control interface and select the Changes tab. Right-click the file that you would like to compare and select the "Compare with Unmodified" to see what changes have been made since the last commit, as shown in Figure A-21.

Figure A-21. The context menu of a file in the Changes tab

Your favorite file-comparison utility tool will now launch with the unmodified file on the left and the modified one on the right, as shown in Figure A-22.

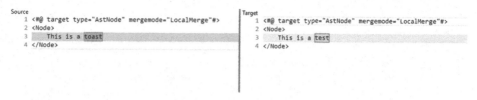

```
Source
  1 <#@ target type="AstNode" mergemode="LocalMerge"#>
  2 <Node>
  3     This is a toast
  4 </Node>
```

```
Target
  1 <#@ target type="AstNode" mergemode="LocalMerge"#>
  2 <Node>
  3     This is a test
  4 </Node>
```

Figure A-22. *A comparison of two files*

In the History tab, you can use this feature to compare any file to its state in the previous commit.

Sync Tab

As mentioned earlier, Git (and all other distributed source control providers) operate differently than centralized source control providers. If you are using Git, you will see an option to select the Sync tab inside the Source Control interface, as shown in Figure A-23.

Source Control

CHANGES   SYNC   HISTORY   SETTINGS

Incoming Commits   Outgoing Commits

Create RemoteFileAdd.txt   Added two new files.
Rin-Bork   4/18/2017   Default   5/18/2017

                                              My First Commit
                                              Default   5/18/2017

                         Fetch   Pull   Push   Sync

Figure A-23. *An overview of the Sync tab*

Inside the Sync tab (Figure A-23), you will see an **Incoming Commit** list on your left. These are commits that have been synchronized with the remote repository, but have not yet been merged with your local repository. Essentially, they are other developers' commits. On the right you will see **Outgoing Commits**, which (you guessed it) are your local commits that have yet to be synchronized with the remote repository.

The **Fetch** button queries the remote repository to determine which commits your local repository are missing, but does not actually do any synchronizing. In order to obtain these remote commits, you need to press the **Pull** button, as shown in Figure A-24.

Incoming Commits

Create RemoteFileAdd.txt	
BimlBook	8/18/2017

Fetch   Pull

Figure A-24. *A closer look at the Incoming Commits list and its associated commands*

In order to send your commits to the remote repository, there cannot be any outstanding incoming commits. You must always pull before you *push*, as show in Figure A-25.

Outgoing Commits

Added two new files.	
Default	8/18/2017
My First Commit	
Default	8/18/2017

Push   Sync

Figure A-25. *A closer look at the Outgoing Commits list and its associated commands*

Once you have "pulled" any remote commits, you are free to "push" your commits to the remote, thus achieving complete synchronization between the remote repository and the local repository on your machine.

The **Sync** button attempts to save you one click and performs a pull before pushing any outgoing commits. On a successful sync, both lists will clear out and a success banner will be displayed, as shown in Figure A-26.

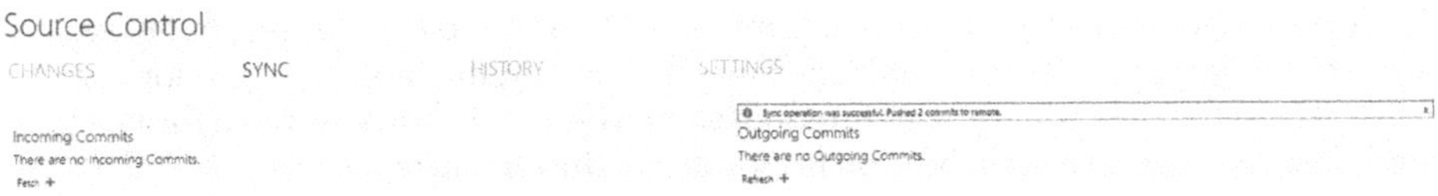

Source Control

CHANGES   SYNC   HISTORY   SETTINGS

Incoming Commits
There are no Incoming Commits.
Fetch +

Sync operation was successful. Pushed 2 commits to remote.
Outgoing Commits
There are no Outgoing Commits.
Refresh +

Figure A-26. *After a successful sync, both lists are cleared and the success banner is displayed*

History Tab

One of the coolest features in BimlStudio is the History tab, located inside of the Source Control menu. You can see a list of all previous commits and view the commit Id, author, date, and commit message. You can also see which files changed from one commit to the next and view the historical state of said files, as shown in Figure A-27.

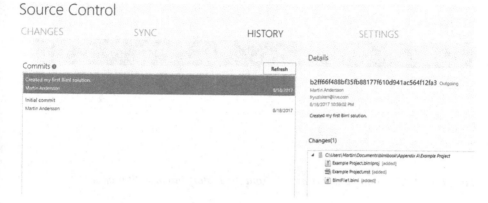

Figure A-27. *A closer look at the History tab*

Figure A-27 displays a quick overview of the History. The Commit list on the left displays a list of previous commits. Under the Details header on the right you see information regarding the selected commit.

The Refresh button updates the commit list. If you created a commit in Windows File Explorer (why you would want to do it outside of this beautiful UI is beyond me, but for the sake of this example let's say it happened), the Refresh button detects this and updates the commit list accordingly, even though the commit occurred outside of BimlStudio.

■ **Note**   One difference between the Svn/TFVC History tab and the one that you see when using Git is the presence of the Get Latest button. The Get Latest button updates all files in the local repository to the newest state. Git's Sync tab manages similar functionality.

The missing Get Latest button is not the only difference exhibited by the History tab when using Git. Another difference is that commits in the historical commit list are color-coded based on their current state, as shown in Figure A-28.

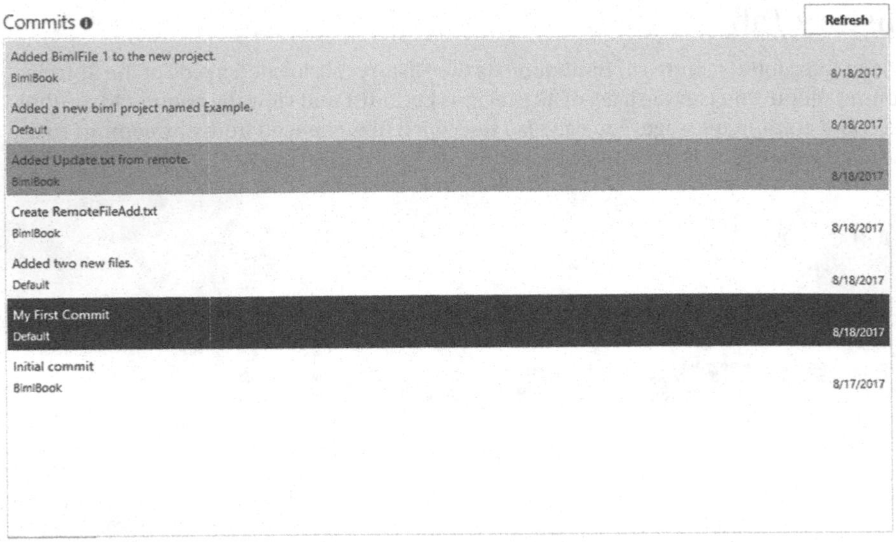

Commits ❶		Refresh
Added BimlFile 1 to the new project.		
BimlBook		8/18/2017
Added a new biml project named Example.		
Default		8/18/2017
Added Update.txt from remote.		
BimlBook		8/18/2017
Create RemoteFileAdd.txt		
BimlBook		8/18/2017
Added two new files.		
Default		8/18/2017
My First Commit		
Default		8/18/2017
Initial commit		
BimlBook		8/17/2017

Figure A-28. *The commit history as seen from the History tab in a Git project*

Light yellow signifies outgoing commits that have not yet been pushed to the remote repository. Orange signifies incoming commits that have been synchronized remotely but are missing from your local repository. Blue signifies selected commits (details are displayed on the right, as shown in Figure A-27). The remainder of the commits are fully synchronized between the remote repository and the local one.

Conclusion

After reading this appendix, you should have a greater understanding of the value of source control and why its usage is widespread.

We have also touched on a number of common terms and demonstrated how to build your first repository from scratch. We put your new knowledge to the test and created your first Biml project tracked in source control. We also looked at some of the cool features BimlStudio offers source control users.

In the next appendix, you'll build on what you learned in Chapter 7 by exploring two additional data load patterns that could prove useful with custom Biml frameworks.

Parallel Load Patterns in Biml

In Chapter 7, we demonstrated an approach for modularizing data load patterns within a metadata-driven Biml framework so that we could easily select which pattern to use on a table-by-table basis. As our focus was on the modular pattern architecture, we presented only two interchangeable patterns for loading data. Of course, there are countless other patterns that you could choose to author and customize for your organization. Ultimately, you will need to decide which pattern or patterns will work best for your organization and either write new or customize existing Biml code to implement your solution.

In this appendix, we attempt to give you a head start on that process by presenting additional data load patterns that you might find useful to customize within your own frameworks. Specifically, we will consider multiple approaches for parallelizing the execution of dataflow tasks.

Parallelizing Dataflows

Note When there are independent sections of an SSIS data flow, SSIS can distribute the work over multiple threads. To relieve bottlenecks in your SSIS packages, you can take advantage of the multiple cores found in modern CPUs to achieve greater levels of throughput.

Transformations like script components and fuzzy lookups can be a performance bottleneck, especially when performing complex operations. Creating a pattern to multi-thread these components with Biml is simple but can produce dramatic performance improvements. If, for instance, you have a script component that retrieves data from a web service or API, then parallelizing these calls can make a huge positive impact to the performance of your packages. Hand coding this parallelization can be time consuming, prone to error, and you're less likely to have the time to fine tune the number of threads and other variables that would optimize performance.

© Andy Leonard et al. 2017
A. Leonard et al., *The Biml Book*, https://doi.org/10.1007/978-1-4842-3135-7_17

Using Balanced Data Distributor (BDD)

The SSIS Balanced Data Distributor (BDD) has been available as a free downloadable custom component since 2011, and it was included in SSIS as a standard component with the release of SQL Server 2016.

Figure B-1 is a screenshot from a dataflow that has four threads that are managed by the BDD.

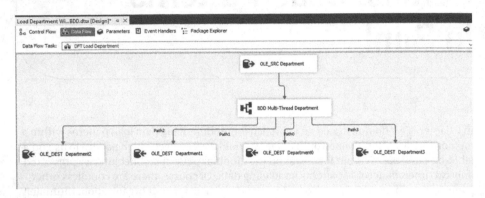

Figure B-1. *An SSIS data flow task with four threads*

The Biml to generate the data flow task, using the same modular pattern architecture described in Chapter 8, is shown in Listing B-1.

Listing B-1. BDD Load Pattern

```
<#@ template designerbimlpath="Biml\Packages" #>
<#@ property name="sourceConnection" type="String" #>
<#@ property name="targetConnection" type="String" #>
<#@ property name="sourceTable" type="String" #>
<#@ property name="srcTable" type="AstTableNode" #>
<#@ property name="tgtTable" type="AstTableNode" #>

<#int numberOfThreads = 4; #>
<Package Name="Load <#=package.Name #> With BDD">
  <Tasks>
    <Dataflow Name="DFT Load <#=package.Name #>">
      <Transformations>
        <OleDbSource Name="OLE_SRC" ConnectionName="<#=sourceConnection#>">
          <ExternalTableInput Table="<#=srcTable.SchemaQualifiedName#>" />
        </OleDbSource>
        <BalancedDataDistributor Name="BDD Multi-Thread <#=package.Name#>">
```

```
        <OutputPaths>
          <# for (int i = 0; i < numberOfThreads; i++) { #>
          <OutputPath Name="Path<#=i#>"/>
          <# } #>
        </OutputPaths>
      </BalancedDataDistributor>
      <# for (int i = 0; i < numberOfThreads; i++) {#>
      <OleDbDestination Name="OLE_DEST <#=package.Name#><#=i#>" Connection
      Name="<#=targetConnection#>">
        <InputPath OutputPathName="BDD Multi-Thread <#=package.Name #>
        .Path<#=i#>" />
        <ExternalTableOutput Table="<#=tgtTable.SchemaQualifiedName #>" />
      </OleDbDestination>
      <# } #>
    </Transformations>
  </Dataflow>
 </Tasks>
</Package>
```

An excerpt from the SQL Server Customer Advisory Teams (SQLCAT) e-book (*SQL CAT's Guide to BI and Analytics*) states

> *Whatever you put behind the Balanced Data Distributor (BDD), be sure the same work is being done on all paths. It doesn't make logical sense to have the paths be different, and from a performance point of view, you want them all to be the same speed. Remember, the "B" in BDD stands for "Balanced."*

Of course, using Biml guarantees that this best practice is fully satisfied. A second excerpt:

> *When working on the Extract, Transform, and Load (ETL) World Record a while ago, we used a heap for a side experiment and found that loading 56 streams concurrently into a single heap was almost as fast as loading 56 streams into 56 independent tables.*

While 56 may be the magic number for the hardware the SQLCAT team used for the ETL world record, it is likely that some other number will produce the best results in your environment. Using Biml, you can easily test different levels of multi-threading to find your optimal value. In Listing B-1, you just change the value of the numberOfThreads variable, rebuild, and time the load.

Using a Row Counter and Conditional Split

Some organizations forbid the installation of custom SSIS components, and BDD did not ship with SSIS until 2016. If you can't use the BDD, then the next pattern will produce similar results. Note that performance won't be exactly the same, as the BDD distributes buffers of data and this pattern distributes rows into new buffers using a script component to increment a variable and a conditional split component to distribute rows across output paths based on the value of that variable. This works best with file sources where you don't have the option of using SQL to generate your row counter. Figure B-2 shows what the pattern looks like in SSIS.

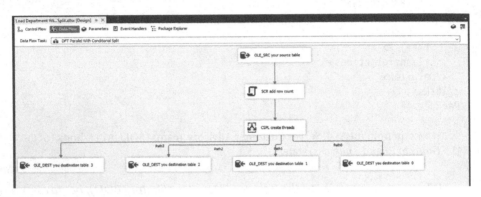

Figure B-2. *An alternative parallelization pattern*

In the Biml code in Listing B-2, notice the use of the for loop to generate the Conditional Split output paths based on the numberOfThreads variable at the start of the script. Simple yet powerful.

Listing B-2. Biml Code for the Alternative Parallelization Pattern

```
<#@ template designerbimlpath="Biml\Packages" #>
<#@ property name="sourceConnection" type="String" #>
<#@ property name="targetConnection" type="String" #>
<#@ property name="sourceTable" type="String" #>
<#@ property name="srcTable" type="AstTableNode" #>
<#@ property name="tgtTable" type="AstTableNode" #>

<#int numberOfThreads = 4;#>
<Package Name="Load <#=package.Name #> With Conditional Split">
  <Tasks>
    <Dataflow Name="DFT Parallel With Conditional Split">
      <Transformations>
        <OleDbSource Name="OLE_SRC" ConnectionName="<#=sourceConnection#>">
          <ExternalTableInput Table="[Person].[Person]" />
        </OleDbSource>
```

```
        <ScriptComponentTransformation ProjectCoreName="SC_92efa7fa8bd14486b
        2a0b02c00f6246e" Name="SCR add row count">
          <ScriptComponentProjectReference ScriptComponentProjectName=
          "SC_RowCounter" />
        </ScriptComponentTransformation>
        <ConditionalSplit Name="CSPL create threads">
          <InputPath OutputPathName="SCR add row count.Output 0" />
          <OutputPaths>
            <# for (int i = 0; i < numberOfThreads; i++) { #>
            <OutputPath Name="Path<#=i #>">
              <Expression>rowCounter % <#=numberOfThreads#> == <#=i#>
              </Expression>
            </OutputPath>
            <# } #>
          </OutputPaths>
        </ConditionalSplit>
        <#for (int i = 0; i < numberOfThreads; i++) {#>
        <OleDbDestination Name="OLE_DEST <#=i#>" ConnectionName="
        <#=targetConnection#>">
          <InputPath OutputPathName="CSPL create threads.Path<#=i #>" />
          <ExternalTableOutput Table="[Person].[PersonDest]" />
        </OleDbDestination>
        <# } #>
      </Transformations>
    </Dataflow>
  </Tasks>
</Package>
```

If your source is a SQL Server table, you could remove the script component that adds the row counter and replace it with a windowing function such as ROW_NUMBER that will act as a row counter. Notice how you've used Biml to auto-generate your ROW_NUMBER query code. If you have IDENTITY column in your source table, you could also use that to achieve a similar result. See Listing B-3.

Listing B-3. Yet Another Alternative Parallelization Pattern

```
<#@ template designerbimlpath="Biml\Packages" #>
<#@ property name="sourceConnection" type="String" #>
<#@ property name="targetConnection" type="String" #>
<#@ property name="sourceTable" type="String" #>
<#@ property name="srcTable" type="AstTableNode" #>
<#@ property name="tgtTable" type="AstTableNode" #>

<#int numberOfThreads = 4; #>
<Package Name="Load <#=srcTable.Name #> With Conditional Split and Window
Function">
  <Tasks>
    <Dataflow Name="DFT Parallel With Conditional Split">
      <Transformations>
```

```
          <OleDbSource Name="OLE_SRC <#=srcTable.Name #>" ConnectionName=
       "<#=sourceConnection#>">
          <DirectInput>
SELECT <#=srcTable.GetColumnList()#>,ROW_NUMBER() OVER(ORDER BY <#=srcTable.
GetColumnList() #>) as rowCounter FROM <#=srcTable.SchemaQualifiedName #>
</DirectInput>
          </OleDbSource>
          <ConditionalSplit Name="CSPL Multi-Thread <#=srcTable.Name #>">
             <InputPath OutputPathName="OLE_SRC <#=srcTable.Name #>.Output" />
             <OutputPaths>
                <# for (int i = 0; i < numberOfThreads; i++) { #>
                <OutputPath Name="Path<#=i #>">
                  <Expression>rowCounter % <#=numberOfThreads#> == <#=i#>
                  </Expression>
                </OutputPath>
                <# } #>
             </OutputPaths>
          </ConditionalSplit>
          <# for (int i = 0; i < numberOfThreads; i++) {#>
          <OleDbDestination Name="OLE_DEST <#=tgtTable.Name #> Path <#=i #>"
          ConnectionName="<#=targetConnection#>">
             <InputPath OutputPathName="CSPL Multi-Thread <#=srcTable.Name #>
             .Path<#=i #>" />
             <ExternalTableOutput Table<#=tgtTable.SchemaQualifiedName#>" />
          </OleDbDestination>
          <# } #>
        </Transformations>
      </Dataflow>
   </Tasks>
</Package>
```

Conclusion

In this appendix, you saw the implementation of additional patterns that help to parallelize the execution of your dataflow tasks in SSIS. Given the level of complexity of code in some of these patterns, if you choose to include them in your own frameworks, you will likely need to customize them a bit for your needs. Regardless, this appendix should provide a solid starting point for that process.

APPENDIX C

■ ■ ■

Metadata Persistence

You may desire to manage Biml metadata instance data in a database. Biml developers can copy, delete, and manipulate metadata values stored in a database using Transact-SQL. Metadata persisted in a database may be retrieved by one or more Biml projects.

Persisting Biml Metadata in a Database

Before you can persist metadata to a database you must first create tables to host your Biml metadata instance.

Creating Metadata Instance Tables

You will use a database named BimlBook for persisting Biml metadata instance data. There are two approaches to persisting Biml metadata instance data:

1. A custom schema design

2. A generic schema design

We will examine both options but first, why choose one option over the other? A custom schema design is built around the data you wish to persist. The tables and columns reflect the natural structure of the data itself. A generic schema design is built around the Biml metadata instance object. The tables and columns reflect the structure of the Biml metadata instance.

First, you create the BimlBook database by executing the Transact-SQL script in Listing C-1.

Listing C-1. Creating the BimlBook Database

```
Use master
Go

Create Database [BimlBook]
```

© Andy Leonard et al. 2017
A. Leonard et al., *The Biml Book*, https://doi.org/10.1007/978-1-4842-3135-7_18

Designing a Custom Schema for Biml Metadata Instances

Let's create a schema named di (an abbreviation for data integration) for your custom design using the Transact-SQL statement shown in Listing C-2.

Listing C-2. Creating the Di Schema

```
Use BimlBook
Go

Create Schema [di]
```

A Biml project can contain multiple Biml metadata instances, so let's first create a table to contain Biml metadata instance data by executing the Transact-SQL statement shown in Listing C-3.

Listing C-3. Creating the Di.Instance Table

```
Create Table [di].[Instance]
(InstanceID int identity(1,1) Constraint PK_Instance Primary Key
, InstanceName varchar(255) Not NULL)
```

The tables and columns in your custom design are built to represent the metadata you will be persisting. In this case, you are persisting connections and tables, so you build Connection and Table tables.

To properly design the Connection table you need to look at the Biml metadata model design. Recall the definition of the Connections object in your Biml metadata model design shown in Listing C-4.

Listing C-4. Viewing the Connections Entity Metadata

```
<Entity Name="Connections">
  <Properties>
    <Property Name="ConnString" DataType="String" IsRequired="true" />
    <Property Name="IsSource" DataType="Boolean" />
  </Properties>
</Entity>
```

Note the properties:

- ConnString is a String data type with the IsRequired flag set to true. ConnString represents the connection string.

- IsSource is a Boolean data type with no specification for the IsRequired flag. IsSource is a flag that indicates the connection is a source.

IsRequired defaults to False and you can create a default constraint in your table to reflect this object default.

There is an additional implied property: Name is a String that represents the connection name. Since a connection is a child of a Biml metadata instance, you include a foreign-key-enforced reference to the di.Instance.InstanceID column. Create one design for the Connection table by executing the Transact-SQL statement shown in Listing C-5.

Listing C-5. Creating the Di.Connection Table

```
Create Table [di].[Connection]
(ConnectionID int identity(1,1) Constraint PK_Connection Primary Key
, InstanceID int Constraint FK_Connection_Instance Foreign Key References
[di].[Instance](InstanceID)
, ConnectionName varchar(255) Not NULL
, ConnString varchar(1024) Not NULL
, IsSource bit NULL Constraint DF_Connection_IsSource Default(0))
```

Similarly, let's examine the Biml metadata model's Tables object to learn how you should persist tables metadata; see Listing C-6.

Listing C-6. Viewing the Tables Entity Metadata

```
<Entity Name="Tables">
  <Relationships>
    <Relationship Name="Connection" Cardinality="ManyToOne"
    EntityName="Connections" />
  </Relationships>
</Entity>
```

Note the absence of properties but the presence of a many-to-one relationship to the Connections object. The relationship implies foreign key in the database table design. As before, the Name implied property is a String that represents the table name.

You create the Table table by executing the Transact-SQL statement shown in Listing C-7.

Listing C-7. Creating the Di.Table Table

```
Create Table [di].[Table]
(TableID int identity(1,1) Constraint PK_Table Primary Key
, TableName varchar(255) Not NULL
, ConnectionID int Constraint FK_Table_Connection Foreign Key References
[di].[Connection](ConnectionID))
```

Your custom Biml metadata instance database design is now complete. You can use Biml to load the metadata from the Biml metadata instance. You begin by iterating the Biml metadata instance.

Iterating and Persisting the Biml Metadata Instance

To iterate the Biml metadata instance, create a new BimlScript in BimlStudio. You can name your BimlScript file whatever you want; we named ours MetadataInstancePersistCustom. biml. Creative name, yes?

This approach to persisting Biml metadata instance metadata in the custom database design is to iterate the object hierarchy starting at the top (the metadata instance) and drill down into the individual objects. In a BimlScript code block, begin a foreach loop to retrieve all Biml metadata instances. (Did you know your Biml solution can contain multiple Biml metadata instances? It can.). If you're using C#, you can inject similar code between your begin and end <Biml> tags; see Listing C-8.

Listing C-8. Displaying the Metadata Instance Name

```
<Annotations>
  <# foreach(var m in RootNode.MetadataInstances) { #>
  <Annotation Tag="MetadataInstance.Name"><#=m.Name#></Annotation>
  <# } #>
</Annotations>
```

Believe it or not, this small snippet of BimlScript will search RootNode.Metadata for MetadataInstance objects and return the name of each one it finds. Let's add some code to store a Biml metadata instance in the custom database design.

You add BimlScript to MetadataInstancePersistCustom.biml to persist instance metadata to the BimlBook database, as shown in Listing C-9.

Listing C-9. Persisting the Metadata Instance Name

```
<Biml xmlns="http://schemas.varigence.com/biml.xsd">
<Annotations>
<#
var cs = @"data source=vmDemo\Demo;initial catalog=BimlBook;provider=
SQLNCLI11;integrated security=SSPI;";
var sqlMi = @"
If Not Exists(Select InstanceName From [di].[Instance] Where InstanceName =
'{0}')
  begin
    Insert Into [di].[Instance] (InstanceName)
    Output inserted.InstanceID As InstanceID
    Values('{0}')
  end
Else
  begin
    Select InstanceID From [di].[Instance] Where InstanceName = '{0}'
  end";
foreach(var mi in RootNode.MetadataInstances) {
  var query = string.Format(sqlMi, mi.Name);
  var dt = ExternalDataAccess.GetDataTable(cs, query);
```

```
var instanceID = Convert.ToInt32(dt.Rows[0][0].ToString());
#>
<Annotation Tag="MetadataInstance.Name"><#=mi.Name#></Annotation>
<Annotation Tag="InstanceID"><#=instanceID#></Annotation>
<# } #>
</Annotations>
</Biml>
```

This code uses the Biml extension method ExternalDataAccess.GetDataTable that executes dynamic Transact-SQL, built using the query string variable. GetDataTable returns the InstanceID variable value using the Transact-SQL OUTPUT clause in the INSERT statement if the instance metadata is not already present in the di.Instance table; otherwise the InstanceID value is selected and returned. Either way, this Transact-SQL statement returns the value of InstanceID that you need to proceed with your metadata persistence.

To iterate and view Biml metadata instance entities, add the BimlScript from Listing C-10 just inside the closing curly brace for the foreach MetadataInstances loop.

Listing C-10. Displaying the Metadata Instance Entity Name

```
// Connection
<# foreach(var mie in mi.Entities) { #>
  <Annotation Tag="MetadataInstanceEntity.Name"><#=mie.Name#></Annotation>
<# } #>
```

This code loops through the Entities collection of the metadata instance object and writes Biml annotations containing the name of each entity.

From the perspective of the Biml metadata instance, Connections and Tables are *both* entity objects. In the Biml metadata model, you established a relationship between Connections and Tables, relating Table entities to Connection entities with a relationship named Connection, as seen in the section of the MD_Model Biml metadata model shown in Listing C-11.

Listing C-11. Viewing the Table-to-Connection Relationship

```
<Entity Name="Tables">
  <Relationships>
    <Relationship Name="Connection" Cardinality="ManyToOne"
    EntityName="Connections" />
  </Relationships>
</Entity>
```

The cardinality of the Connection relationship, many-to-one, effectively creates a parent-child relationship between Connections and Tables in the MD_Instance Biml metadata instance.

Persisting Connections

To build the BimlScript snippet that iterates Biml metadata instance entities named Connections, you begin with a foreach loop that employs Language-Integrated Query (Linq) to select only Connections entities, as shown in Listing C-12.

Listing C-12. Displaying the Connections Metadata Instance Entity Name

```
// Connections
foreach(var mie in mi.Entities.Where(c => c.Name == "Connections")) { #>
  <Annotation Tag="MetadataInstanceEntity.Name"><#=mie.Name#></Annotation><#
```

This foreach loop will enumerate the Biml metadata instance entities named Connections contained in the Biml metadata instance object. A Biml annotation provides visibility by writing the name of the metadata instance entity to a tag named MetadataInstanceEntity.Name as shown in Figure C-1.

```
<Biml xmlns="http://schemas.varigence.com/biml.xsd">
    <Annotations>
        <Annotation Tag="MetadataInstance.Name">MD_Instance</Annotation>
        <Annotation Tag="Connection.InstanceID">1</Annotation>
        <Annotation Tag="MetadataInstanceEntity.Name">Connections</Annotation>
    </Annotations>
</Biml>
```

Figure C-1. *A custom Biml metadata instance entity*

When you enumerate the Entities collection in this loop you only encounter connections that you persist to the di.Connection table. You enumerate the *instances* of connection entities in a nested foreach loop:

```
foreach(var connection in mie.DataItems) {
    ...
```

The code snippet that persists each connection replaces the "...". You persist the Connection entity by enumerating its DataItems collection. You use a var data type enumerator named connection for the foreach loop. From the DataItems collection you obtain the name of the connection entity by reading the connection.Name property. To read the values of the ConnString and IsSource properties, you read connection.Properties[0].Value and connection.Properties[1].Value, respectively. The BimlScript to persist the Connections entity appears as shown in Listing C-13.

Listing C-13. Persisting the Connections Metadata Instance Entity Name

```
// Connections
 var sqlConn = @"
 If Not Exists(Select ConnectionName From [di].[Connection] Where
 ConnectionName = '{1}')
  begin
   Insert Into [di].[Connection] (InstanceID, ConnectionName, ConnString,
   IsSource)
   Output inserted.ConnectionID As ConnectionID
   Values({0},'{1}','{2}',{3})
  end
 Else
  begin
   Select ConnectionID From [di].[Connection] Where ConnectionName = '{1}'
  end";
 foreach(var mie in mi.Entities.Where(c => c.Name == "Connections")) {
  #><Annotation Tag="MetadataInstanceEntity.Name"><#=mie.Name #></
  Annotation><#
  foreach(var connection in mie.DataItems) {
   var connectionString = connection.Properties[0].Value;
   var isSource = (Convert.ToBoolean(connection.Properties[1].Value)) ==
   true ? 1 : 0;
   query = string.Format(sqlConn, instanceID, mi.Name, connectionString,
   isSource);
   dt = ExternalDataAccess.GetDataTable(cs, query);
   var connectionID = Convert.ToInt32(dt.Rows[0][0].ToString());
  #><Annotation Tag="Connection.Name"><#=connection.Name #></Annotation>
   <Annotation Tag="Connection.ConnString"><#=connectionString #>
   </Annotation>
   <Annotation Tag="Connection.IsSource"><#=isSource #></Annotation><#
  }
}
```

When added to the MetadataInstancePersistCustom.biml file, the complete
(to this point) file appears as shown in Listing C-14, with the added Biml and BimlScript
highlighted.

Listing C-14. Persisting the Metadata Instance and Connections Metadata Instance
Entity Name

```
<Biml xmlns="http://schemas.varigence.com/biml.xsd">
<Annotations>
<#
var cs = @"data source=vmDemo\Demo;initial catalog=BimlBook;provider=
SQLNCLI11;integrated security=SSPI;";
var sqlMi = @"
```

425

```
If Not Exists(Select InstanceName From [di].[Instance] Where InstanceName =
'{0}')
  begin
    Insert Into [di].[Instance] (InstanceName)
    Output inserted.InstanceID As InstanceID
    Values('{0}')
  end
Else
  begin
    Select InstanceID From [di].[Instance] Where InstanceName = '{0}'
  end";
foreach(var mi in RootNode.MetadataInstances) {
  var query = string.Format(sqlMi, mi.Name);
  var dt = ExternalDataAccess.GetDataTable(cs, query);

  var instanceID = Convert.ToInt32(dt.Rows[0][0].ToString());
  #><Annotation Tag="MetadataInstance.Name"><#=mi.Name #></Annotation>
  <Annotation Tag="Connection.InstanceID"><#=instanceID #></Annotation><#

        // Connections
        var sqlConn = @"
        If Not Exists(Select ConnectionName From [di].[Connection] Where
        ConnectionName = '{1}')
        begin
                Insert Into [di].[Connection] (InstanceID, ConnectionName,
                ConnString, IsSource)
                Output inserted.ConnectionID As ConnectionID
                        Values({0},'{1}','{2}',{3})
                end
        Else
                begin
                        Select ConnectionID From [di].[Connection] Where
                        ConnectionName = '{1}'
                end";
        foreach(var mie in mi.Entities.Where(c => c.Name == "Connections")) {
  #><Annotation Tag="MetadataInstanceEntity.Name"><#=mie.Name #>
  </Annotation><#
                foreach(var connection in mie.DataItems) {
                        var connectionString = connection.Properties[0].
                        Value;
                        var isSource = (Convert.ToBoolean(connection.
                        Properties[1].Value)) == true ? 1 : 0;
                        query = string.Format(sqlConn, instanceID,
                        connection.Name, connectionString, isSource);
                        dt = ExternalDataAccess.GetDataTable(cs, query);
                        var connectionID = Convert.ToInt32(dt.Rows[0][0].
                        ToString());
```

```
#><Annotation Tag="Connection.Name"><#=connection.Name #></Annotation>
    <Annotation Tag="Connection.ConnString"><#=connectionString #>
    </Annotation>
        <Annotation Tag="Connection.IsSource"><#=isSource #></Annotation><#
            }
        }
} #>
</Annotations>
</Biml>
```

If you view this file in the BimlScript designer, the preview expanded BimlScript window should display something similar to the Biml shown in Figure C-2.

```
<Biml xmlns="http://schemas.varigence.com/biml.xsd">
    <Annotations>
        <Annotation Tag="MetadataInstance.Name">MD_Instance</Annotation>
        <Annotation Tag="Connection.InstanceID">1</Annotation>
        <Annotation Tag="MetadataInstanceEntity.Name">Connections</Annotation>
        <Annotation Tag="Connection.Name">AW</Annotation>
        <Annotation Tag="Connection.ConnString">Provider=SQLNCLI11;Server=.;Initial Catalog=AdventureWorks2014;Integrated Security=SSPI;</Annotation>
        <Annotation Tag="Connection.IsSource">1</Annotation>
    </Annotations>
</Biml>
```

Figure C-2. *The connection Biml metadata instance entity*

If you query the BimlBook database, you will find one instance and one connection persisted. Use the Transact-SQL query shown in Listing C-15 to read data from the di. Instance and di.Connection tables.

Listing C-15. Reading the Metadata Instance and Connection Metadata

```
Use BimlBook
go
Select * From [di].[Instance]
Select * From [di].[Connection]
```

Your results should appear similar to ours, shown in Figure C-3.

	InstanceID	InstanceName
1	1	MD_Instance

	ConnectionID	InstanceID	ConnectionName	ConnString	IsSource
1	1	1	AW	Provider=SQLNCLI11;Server=.;Initial Catalog=Adve...	1

Figure C-3. *Viewing persisted instance and connection metadata*

Let's now look at persisting table metadata.

Persisting Tables

Since Tables and Connections are both Biml metadata instance entities, they are persisted in much the same way. The relationship between Tables and Connections, however, throws a wrinkle into the BimlScript and Transact-SQL you use to persist table metadata.

Because the Biml and BimlScript are similar to the Connection persist logic, let's examine the Table persist logic in one pass; see Listing C-16.

Listing C-16. Persisting the Tables Metadata Instance Entity Name

```
// Tables
var sqlTbl = @"declare @connectionID int = (Select ConnectionID
From [di].[Connection] Where ConnectionName = '{0}')
If Not Exists(Select TableName From [di].[Table] Where TableName = '{1}')
        begin
                Insert Into [di].[Table] (ConnectionID, TableName)
                Output inserted.TableID As TableID
                Values(@connectionID,'{1}')
        end
Else
        begin
                Select TableID From [di].[Table] Where TableName = '{1}'
        end";
foreach(var mie in mi.Entities.Where(t => t.Name == "Tables")) {
  #><Annotation AnnotationType="CodeComment" Tag="MetadataInstanceEntity.
  Name"><#=mie.Name #></Annotation><#
        foreach(var table in mie.DataItems) {
                var relatedConnectionName = table.Relationships[0].
                RelatedItem.Name;
                query = string.Format(sqlTbl, relatedConnectionName, table.Name);
                dt = ExternalDataAccess.GetDataTable(cs, query);
                //tableID = Convert.ToInt32(dt.Rows[0][0].ToString());
  #><Annotation Tag="Table.Name"><#=table.Name #></Annotation>
    <Annotation Tag="RelatedConnectionName"><#=relatedConnectionName #>
    </Annotation><#
            }
        }
```

The first difference between the Connections and Tables entities persistence code is found in the foreach statement's Linq. You now use a Linq WHERE function to filter for Biml metadata instance entities named Tables. The second difference is related to relationships; you read the table entity's related item name into a variable named relatedConnectionName by reading table.Relationships[0].RelatedItem.Name. The third difference lies with the Transact-SQL statement used to persist the Table object. You first declare a parameter, @connectionID, and set the value to a subquery that returns the ConnectionID value from the di.Connection table based on the value in the relatedConnectionName variable. The remainder of the Transact-SQL statement mirrors the functionality found in the Connection-persistence logic.

With the Table-persistence Biml and BimlScript added (plus refactoring the repeated BimlBook database connection string), your MetadataInstancePersistCustom.biml file should read as shown in Listing C-17 (added code highlighted).

Listing C-17. Persisting the Metadata Instance, Connections and Tables Metadata Instance Entity Name

```
<Biml xmlns="http://schemas.varigence.com/biml.xsd">
<Annotations>
<#
var cs = @"data source=vmDemo\Demo;initial catalog=BimlBook;provider=
SQLNCLI11;integrated security=SSPI;";
var sqlMi = @"
If Not Exists(Select InstanceName From [di].[Instance] Where InstanceName = '{0}')
  begin
    Insert Into [di].[Instance] (InstanceName)
    Output inserted.InstanceID As InstanceID
    Values('{0}')
  end
Else
  begin
    Select InstanceID From [di].[Instance] Where InstanceName = '{0}'
  end";
foreach(var mi in RootNode.MetadataInstances) {
  var query = string.Format(sqlMi, mi.Name);
  var dt = ExternalDataAccess.GetDataTable(cs, query);

  var instanceID = Convert.ToInt32(dt.Rows[0][0].ToString());
#><Annotation Tag="MetadataInstance.Name"><#=mi.Name #></Annotation>
<Annotation Tag="Connection.InstanceID"><#=instanceID #></Annotation><#

        // Connections
        var sqlConn = @"
        If Not Exists(Select ConnectionName From [di].[Connection] Where
        ConnectionName = '{1}')
        begin
                Insert Into [di].[Connection] (InstanceID, ConnectionName,
                ConnString, IsSource)
                Output inserted.ConnectionID As ConnectionID
                        Values({0},'{1}','{2}',{3})
                end
        Else
                begin
                        Select ConnectionID From [di].[Connection] Where
                        ConnectionName = '{1}'
                end";
        foreach(var mie in mi.Entities.Where(c => c.Name == "Connections")) {
          #><Annotation Tag="MetadataInstanceEntity.Name"><#=mie.Name #>
          </Annotation><#
```

429

```
                foreach(var connection in mie.DataItems) {
                        var connectionString = connection.Properties[0].Value;
                        var isSource = (Convert.ToBoolean(connection.
                        Properties[1].Value)) == true ? 1 : 0;
                        query = string.Format(sqlConn, instanceID,
                        connection.Name, connectionString, isSource);
                        dt = ExternalDataAccess.GetDataTable(cs, query);
                        var connectionID = Convert.ToInt32(dt.Rows[0][0].
                        ToString());
  #><Annotation Tag="Connection.Name"><#=connection.Name #></Annotation>
    <Annotation Tag="Connection.ConnString"><#=connectionString #>
    </Annotation>
        <Annotation Tag="Connection.IsSource"><#=isSource #></Annotation><#
            }
        }


        // Tables
        var sqlTbl = @"declare @connectionID int = (Select ConnectionID From
        [di].[Connection] Where ConnectionName = '{0}')
        If Not Exists(Select TableName From [di].[Table] Where TableName = '{1}')
                begin
                        Insert Into [di].[Table] (ConnectionID, TableName)
                        Output inserted.TableID As TableID
                        Values(@connectionID,'{1}')
                end
        Else
                begin
                        Select TableID From [di].[Table] Where TableName = '{1}'
                end";
        foreach(var mie in mi.Entities.Where(t => t.Name == "Tables")) {
          #><Annotation Tag="MetadataInstanceEntity.Name"><#=mie.Name #>
          </Annotation><#
                foreach(var table in mie.DataItems) {
                        var relatedConnectionName = table.Relationships[0].
                        RelatedItem.Name;
                        query = string.Format(sqlTbl, relatedConnectionName,
                        table.Name);
                        dt = ExternalDataAccess.GetDataTable(cs, query);
          tableID = Convert.ToInt32(dt.Rows[0][0].ToString());
          #><Annotation Tag="Table.Name"><#=table.Name #></Annotation>
        <Annotation Tag="RelatedConnectionName"><#=relatedConnectionName #>
        </Annotation><#
            }
        }
} #>
</Annotations>
</Biml>
```

The expanded Biml appears as shown in Figure C-4.

```
<Biml xmlns="http://schemas.varigence.com/biml.xsd">
    <Annotations>
        <Annotation Tag="MetadataInstance.Name">MD_Instance</Annotation>
        <Annotation Tag="Connection.InstanceID">1</Annotation>
        <Annotation Tag="MetadataInstanceEntity.Name">Connections</Annotation>
        <Annotation Tag="Connection.Name">AW</Annotation>
        <Annotation Tag="Connection.ConnString">Provider=SQLNCLI11;Server=.;Initial Catalog=AdventureWorks2014;Integrated Security=SSPI;</Annotation>
        <Annotation Tag="Connection.IsSource">1</Annotation>
        <Annotation Tag="MetadataInstanceEntity.Name">Tables</Annotation>
        <Annotation Tag="Table.Name">Person</Annotation>
        <Annotation Tag="RelatedConnectionName">AW</Annotation>
    </Annotations>
</Biml>
```

Figure C-4. *The Table Biml metadata instance entity*

If you query the BimlBook database, you will find one instance and one connection persisted. Use the Transact-SQL query in Listing C-18 to read data from the di.Instance and di.Connection tables.

Listing C-18. Reading the Metadata Instance, Connection, and Table Metadata

```
Use BimlBook
go
Select * From [di].[Instance]
Select * From [di].[Connection]
Select * From [di].[Table]
```

Your results should appear similar to ours, which are shown in Figure C-5.

	InstanceID	InstanceName
1	1	MD_Instance

	ConnectionID	InstanceID	ConnectionName	ConnString	IsSource
1	1	1	AW	Provider=SQLNCLI11;Server=.;Initial Catalog=AdventureWorks2014;Integrated Security=SSPI;	1

	TableID	TableName	ConnectionID
1	1	Person	1

Figure C-5. *Viewing persisted instance, connection, and table metadata*

This is a fair example of custom metadata persistence that uses the Biml metadata instance object. Is this demonstration exhaustive? Goodness, no. Is it real-world? Absolutely.

There are limitations to this approach, and some are serious. What happens when you want to add a new entity, such as Columns entity? You have to create a new table in your persistence database (BimlBook in this case). You also have to hand-code BimlScript and Transact-SQL for persisting property values and relationships.

In the next example, you build a generic metadata persistence solution. The generic solution is more complex but, as is often the case, more flexible.

Designing a Generic Schema for Biml Metadata Instances

A generic metadata persistence solution may be described as a "meta-metadata" solution. As you work through this section and the accompanying demo code, I hope the reasons why become apparent. The impetus for this statement, however, lies with the Biml metadata solution, which is essentially a "meta-metadata" engine.

How to Fish

There's an old adage: "*Give* someone a fish and you feed them for a day. *Teach* someone to fish and you feed them for a lifetime." In this section, we teach you how to fish.

Let's return to the MD_Instance metadata instance Biml, shown in Listing C-19.

Listing C-19. Viewing the MD_Instance Metadata

```
<Biml xmlns="http://schemas.varigence.com/biml.xsd">
  <Metadata>
    <MetadataInstance Name="MD_Instance" MetadataModelName="MD_Model">
      <Entities>
        <Entity Name="Connections" MetadataModelEntityName="MD_Model.
        Connections">
          <DataItems>
            <DataItem Name="AW">
              <Properties>
                <Property PropertyName="MD_Model.Connections.ConnString">
                  <Value>Provider=SQLNCLI11;Server=.;Initial Catalog=
                  AdventureWorks2014;Integrated Security=SSPI;</Value>
                </Property>
                <Property PropertyName="MD_Model.Connections.IsSource">
                  <Value>True</Value>
                </Property>
              </Properties>
            </DataItem>
          </DataItems>
        </Entity>
        <Entity Name="Tables" MetadataModelEntityName="MD_Model.Tables">
          <DataItems>
            <DataItem Name="Person">
              <Relationships>
                <Relationship RelationshipName="MD_Model.Tables.Connection"
                RelatedItemName="Connections.AW" />
              </Relationships>
            </DataItem>
          </DataItems>
        </Entity>
      </Entities>
```

```
    </MetadataInstance>
  </Metadata>
</Biml>
```

What do you see? As with all Biml files, the MD_Instance begins and ends with the Biml tag. Just inside the Biml tags you find the starting and ending Metadata tags. So far, not too much in the way of complexity. The file gets interesting with the MetadataInstance tag, which includes attributes for Name and MetadataModelName. MetadataInstance includes the Entities tag which includes Entity tags, one entry each for Connections and Tables.

The Connections entity contains one DataItem named AW. The AW connection contains two properties: ConnString and IsSource. Each property contains a Value.

The Table entity contains one DataItem named Person. The Person entity contains no properties, but contains a relationship named MD_Model.Tables.Connection. The MD_Model.Tables.Connection relationship is related to the Connections entity named AW.

If you put on your "abstraction glasses," you will notice patterns of object design. You see aspects of object-oriented design in the hierarchy of the nodes in the MD_Instance.biml file. To what do we refer? Consider the following (beginning with the MetadataInstance node):

- MetadataInstance
  - Entity
    - DataItem
      - Property
      - Relationship

Do you see this pattern in MD_Instance.biml? How might you persist this metadata (or meta-metadata)? We propose to use this abstraction to store Biml metadata instance data generically.

In the BimlBook database, create a new schema named meta using the Transact-SQL statement shown in Listing C-20.

Listing C-20. Creating the Meta Schema

```
Use BimlBook
go

Create Schema meta
```

Let's next create a table in which to persist the MetadataInstance data using the Transact-SQL statement shown in Listing C-21.

Listing C-21. Creating the Meta.MetadataInstance Table

```
Use BimlBook
go

Create Table [meta].[MetadataInstance]
(MetadataInstanceID int identity(1,1) Constraint PK_MetadataInstance Primary Key
, MetadataModelName varchar(255) Not NULL
, MetadataInstanceName varchar(255) Not NULL)
```

You need to be sure to create columns for MetadataInstance attributes, such as the MetadataModelName attribute.

There isn't much difference in the di.Instance and meta.MetadataInstance table designs. With the design of the meta.MetadataInstanceEntity table, you begin to diverge from the design for a custom persistence solution.

The next type of object you want to persist is Entity. The Transact-SQL statement shown in Listing C-22 creates the MetadataInstanceEntity table.

Listing C-22. Creating the Meta.MetadataInstanceEntity Table

```
Create Table [meta].[MetadataInstanceEntity]
(MetadataInstanceEntityID int identity(1,1) Constraint PK_MetadataInstanceEntity
Primary Key
, MetadataInstanceID int Constraint FK_MetadataInstanceEntity_MetadataInstance
Foreign Key References [meta].[MetadataInstance](MetadataInstanceID)
, MetadataInstanceEntityName varchar(255) Not NULL)
```

MetadataInstanceEntity is a child of MetadataInstance in your hierarchy, so you require a foreign key to the MetadataInstance.MetadataInstanceID column.

Similarly, MetadataInstanceEntityDataItem is a child of MetadataInstanceEntity. Create the MetadataInstanceEntityDataItem table by executing the Transact-SQL shown in Listing C-23.

Listing C-23. Creating the Meta.MetadataInstanceDataItem Table

```
Create Table [meta].[MetadataInstanceEntityDataItem]
(MetadataInstanceEntityDataItemID int identity(1,1) Constraint
PK_MetadataInstanceEntityDataItem Primary Key
, MetadataInstanceEntityID int Constraint FK_MetadataInstanceEntityDataItem_
MetadataInstanceEntity Foreign Key References [meta].
[MetadataInstanceEntity](MetadataInstanceEntityID)
, MetadataInstanceEntityDataItemName varchar(255) Not NULL)
```

Proceeding "down" your hierarchy, your next table is MetadataInstanceEntityDataItem, which is created using the Transact-SQL statement shown in Listing C-24.

Listing C-24. Creating the Meta.MetadataInstanceDataItemProperty Table

```
Create Table [meta].[MetadataInstanceEntityDataItemProperty]
(MetadataInstanceEntityDataItemPropertyID int identity(1,1) Constraint
PK_MetadataInstanceEntityDataItemProperty Primary Key
, MetadataInstanceEntityDataItemID int Constraint FK_
MetadataInstanceEntityDataItemProperty_MetadataInstanceEntityDataItem
Foreign Key References [meta].[MetadataInstanceEntityDataItem]
(MetadataInstanceEntityDataItemID)
, MetadataInstanceEntityDataItemPropertyName varchar(255) Not NULL
, MetadataInstanceEntityDataItemPropertyValue varchar(255))
```

Note that you combine Property and PropertyValue into a single table, rather than create another table called MetadataInstanceEntityDataItemPropertyValue. You repeat this pattern with MetadataInstanceEntityDataItemRelationship, which you create using the Transact-SQL shown in Listing C-25.

Listing C-25. Creating the Meta.MetadataInstanceDataItemRelationship Table

```
Create Table [meta].[MetadataInstanceEntityDataItemRelationship]
(MetadataInstanceEntityDataItemRelationshipID int identity(1,1) Constraint
PK_MetadataInstanceEntityDataItemRelationship Primary Key
, MetadataInstanceEntityDataItemID int Constraint FK_
MetadataInstanceEntityDataItemRelationship_MetadataInstanceEntityDataItem
Foreign Key References [meta].[MetadataInstanceEntityDataItem]
(MetadataInstanceEntityDataItemID)
, MetadataInstanceEntityDataItemRelationshipName varchar(255) Not NULL
, MetadataInstanceEntityDataItemRelatedItemName varchar(255) Not NULL)
```

If you create a database diagram of the tables in the BimlBook.meta schema, it will look similar to Figure C-6.

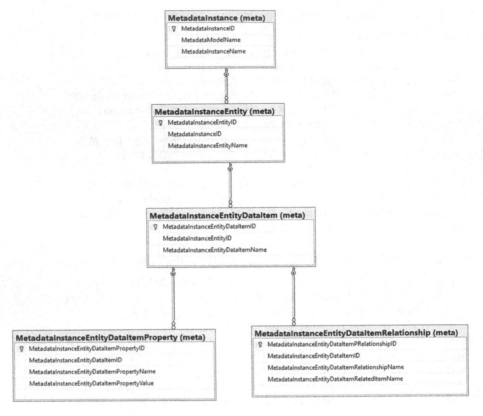

Figure C-6. *The data diagram for the BimlBook.meta schema*

We hope you are able to discern from the diagram that this design captures the "meta-metadata-ness" of the Biml metadata instance object. This particular design includes tables and columns for only the Biml metadata instance objects you consume in the demonstration code in this chapter. This is by no means exhaustive!

Populating the Meta Schema

In BimlStudio, create a new Biml file named `MetadataInstancePersistGeneric.biml`. As before, let's use Biml annotations to help visualize the Biml metadata objects you are persisting. Also as before, let's build dynamic Transact-SQL statements in BimlScript and execute them to persist Biml metadata instance data to the `meta` schema.

Persist the metadata instance by adding the Biml and BimlScript shown in Listing C-26 to `MetadataInstancePersistGeneric.biml`.

Listing C-26. Persisting the Metadata Instance

```
<Biml xmlns="http://schemas.varigence.com/biml.xsd">
        <Annotations>
<#
var cs = @"data source=vmDemo\Demo;initial catalog=BimlBook;provider=
SQLNCLI11;integrated security=SSPI;";
var sqlMi = @"
If Not Exists(Select MetadataInstanceName From [meta].[MetadataInstance]
Where MetadataInstanceName = '{0}')
  begin
    Insert Into [meta].[MetadataInstance]
    (MetadataInstanceName, MetadataModelName)
    Output inserted.MetadataInstanceID  As MetadataInstanceID
    Values('{0}','{1}')
  end
Else
  begin
    Select MetadataInstanceID From [meta].[MetadataInstance]
    Where MetadataInstanceName = '{0}'
  end";
foreach(var mi in RootNode.MetadataInstances) {
  var query = string.Format(sqlMi, mi.Name, mi.MetadataModel.Name);
  var dt = ExternalDataAccess.GetDataTable(cs, query);
  var instanceID = Convert.ToInt32(dt.Rows[0][0].ToString());
  #><Annotation Tag="MetadataInstance.Name"><#=mi.Name #></Annotation>
  <Annotation Tag="MetadataModel.Name"><#=mi.MetadataModel.Name #>
  </Annotation>
  <Annotation Tag="MetadataInstanceID"><#=instanceID #></Annotation><#
}#>
    </Annotations>
</Biml>
```

Note that this code is remarkably similar to the BimlScript you used earlier to persist Biml metadata instance data to the di schema. The name of the table is different, as are the column names. If all has gone according to plan, your BimlScript preview should appear similar to that shown in Figure C-7.

```
<Biml xmlns="http://schemas.varigence.com/biml.xsd">
    <Annotations>
        <Annotation Tag="MetadataInstance.Name">MD_Instance</Annotation>
        <Annotation Tag="MetadataModel.Name">MD_Model</Annotation>
        <Annotation Tag="MetadataInstanceID">1</Annotation>
    </Annotations>
</Biml>
```

Figure C-7. Persisting metadata instance to the meta schema

Query the BimlBook database to view Biml metadata instance data in the meta.MetadataInstance table using the Transact-SQL statement shown in Listing C-27.

Listing C-27. Viewing the Metadata Instance

```
Use BimlBook
go
Select *
From [meta].[MetadataInstance]
```

Your results should appear similar to those shown in Figure C-8.

	MetadataInstanceID	MetadataModelName	MetadataInstanceName
1	1	MD_Model	MD_Instance

Figure C-8. Biml metadata instance in the Meta.MetadataInstance table

As you populate the meta.MetadataInstanceEntity table, we remind you that this is where you begin to diverge from the design for a custom schema. Instead of persisting specific Biml metadata instance entities such as Connections and Tables, you persist *generic* Biml metadata instance entities.

A good way to visualize is to add the generic foreach loop and Biml annotations for Biml metadata instance entity (the highlighted code shown in Listing C-28).

Listing C-28. Persisting the Metadata Instance and Metadata Instance Entity

```
<Biml xmlns="http://schemas.varigence.com/biml.xsd">
        <Annotations>
<#
var cs = @"data source=vmDemo\Demo;initial catalog=BimlBook;provider=
SQLNCLI11;integrated security=SSPI;";
var sqlMi = @"
If Not Exists(Select MetadataInstanceName From [meta].[MetadataInstance]
Where MetadataInstanceName = '{0}')
  begin
    Insert Into [meta].[MetadataInstance]
    (MetadataInstanceName, MetadataModelName)
    Output inserted.MetadataInstanceID  As MetadataInstanceID
    Values('{0}','{1}')
  end
Else
  begin
    Select MetadataInstanceID From [meta].[MetadataInstance] Where
    MetadataInstanceName = '{0}'
  end";
```

```
foreach(var mi in RootNode.MetadataInstances) {
  var query = string.Format(sqlMi, mi.Name, mi.MetadataModel.Name);
  var dt = ExternalDataAccess.GetDataTable(cs, query);
  var instanceID = Convert.ToInt32(dt.Rows[0][0].ToString());
  #><Annotation Tag="MetadataInstance.Name"><#=mi.Name #></Annotation>
  <Annotation Tag="MetadataModel.Name"><#=mi.MetadataModel.Name #>
  </Annotation>
  <Annotation Tag="MetadataInstanceID"><#=instanceID #></Annotation><#

// Entities
  int entityID = -1;
  foreach(var mie in mi.Entities) {
  #><Annotation Tag="MetadataInstanceEntity.Name"><#=mie.Name#>
  </Annotation><#
  }
}
#>
    </Annotations>
</Biml>
```

Viewing the expanded BimlScript reveals the name of the entities shown in Figure C-9.

```
<Biml xmlns="http://schemas.varigence.com/biml.xsd">
    <Annotations>
        <Annotation Tag="MetadataInstance.Name">MD_Instance</Annotation>
        <Annotation Tag="MetadataModel.Name">MD_Model</Annotation>
        <Annotation Tag="MetadataInstanceID">1</Annotation>
        <Annotation Tag="MetadataInstanceEntity.Name">Connections</Annotation>
        <Annotation Tag="MetadataInstanceEntity.Name">Tables</Annotation>
    </Annotations>
</Biml>
```

Figure C-9. *The metadata instance and metadata instance entity objects*

Let's build out the remainder of the Biml metadata instance entity generic persist code by completing the foreach loop BimlScript as shown in Listing C-29.

Listing C-29. Persisting the Metadata Instance Entity Metadata

```
// Entities
string sqlMie = @"If Not Exists(Select MetadataInstanceEntityName
  From [meta].[MetadataInstanceEntity]
  Where MetadataInstanceEntityName = '{0}'
    And MetadataInstanceID = {1})
  begin
```

```
  Insert Into [meta].[MetadataInstanceEntity]
  (MetadataInstanceEntityName, MetadataInstanceID)
  Output inserted.MetadataInstanceEntityID As MetadataInstanceEntityID
  Values('{0}',{1})
 end
Else
 begin
  Select MetadataInstanceEntityID
  From [meta].[MetadataInstanceEntity]
  Where MetadataInstanceEntityName = '{0}'
 end";
  foreach(var mie in mi.Entities) {
    query = string.Format(sqlMie, mie.Name, instanceID);
    var dte = ExternalDataAccess.GetDataTable(cs, query);
        var metadataInstanceEntityId = Convert.ToInt32(dte.Rows[0][0].
        ToString());
  #><Annotation Tag="MetadataInstanceEntity.Name"><#=mie.Name#></Annotation>
    <Annotation Tag="MetadataInstanceEntityId"><#=metadataInstanceEntityId#>
    </Annotation><#
}
```

Your MetadataInstancePersistGeneric.biml file should now appear as shown in
Listing C-30 (added code highlighted).

Listing C-30. Persisting the Metadata Instance and Metadata Instance Entities in the
MetadataInstancePersistGeneric.biml File

```
<Biml xmlns="http://schemas.varigence.com/biml.xsd">
        <Annotations>
<#
var cs = @"data source=vmDemo\Demo;initial catalog=BimlBook;provider=
SQLNCLI11;integrated security=SSPI;";
var sqlMi = @"
If Not Exists(Select MetadataInstanceName From [meta].[MetadataInstance]
Where MetadataInstanceName = '{0}')
  begin
    Insert Into [meta].[MetadataInstance]
    (MetadataInstanceName, MetadataModelName)
    Output inserted.MetadataInstanceID  As MetadataInstanceID
    Values('{0}','{1}')
  end
Else
  begin
    Select MetadataInstanceID From [meta].[MetadataInstance]
    Where MetadataInstanceName = '{0}'
  end";
foreach(var mi in RootNode.MetadataInstances) {
  var query = string.Format(sqlMi, mi.Name, mi.MetadataModel.Name);
  var dt = ExternalDataAccess.GetDataTable(cs, query);
```

```
    var instanceID = Convert.ToInt32(dt.Rows[0][0].ToString());
#><Annotation Tag="MetadataInstance.Name"><#=mi.Name #></Annotation>
<Annotation Tag="MetadataModel.Name"><#=mi.MetadataModel.Name #>
</Annotation>
<Annotation Tag="MetadataInstanceID"><#=instanceID #></Annotation><#

    // Entities
    string sqlMie = @"If Not Exists(Select MetadataInstanceEntityName
    From [meta].[MetadataInstanceEntity]
    Where MetadataInstanceEntityName = '{0}'
      And MetadataInstanceID = {1})
  begin
   Insert Into [meta].[MetadataInstanceEntity]
   (MetadataInstanceEntityName, MetadataInstanceID)
   Output inserted.MetadataInstanceEntityID As MetadataInstanceEntityID
   Values('{0}',{1})
   end
 Else
  begin
   Select MetadataInstanceEntityID
   From [meta].[MetadataInstanceEntity]
   Where MetadataInstanceEntityName = '{0}'
   end";
    foreach(var mie in mi.Entities) {
      query = string.Format(sqlMie, mie.Name, instanceID);
      var dte = ExternalDataAccess.GetDataTable(cs, query);
          var metadataInstanceEntityId = Convert.ToInt32(dte.Rows[0][0].
          ToString());
   #><Annotation Tag="MetadataInstanceEntity.Name"><#=mie.Name#></Annotation>
      <Annotation Tag="MetadataInstanceEntityId">
      <#=metadataInstanceEntityId#></Annotation><#
  }
}#>
    </Annotations>
</Biml>
```

Next, let's code for the Biml metadata instance entity data items. As before, you begin with a minimal BimlScript code snippet to display data items, just inside the foreach loop for the entity logic, in Biml annotations to make sure you're on the right track; see Listing C-31.

Listing C-31. Viewing Metadata Instance Entity Data Items

```
// Data Items
foreach(var mied in mie.DataItems) {
  #><Annotation Tag="MetadataInstanceEntityDataItem.Name"><#=mied.Name #>
  </Annotation><#
}
```

If you save `MetadataInstancePersistGeneric.biml` and update the BimlScript preview, your preview expanded BimlScript should appear as shown in Figure C-10.

```
<Biml xmlns="http://schemas.varigence.com/biml.xsd">
    <Annotations>
        <Annotation Tag="MetadataInstance.Name">MD_Instance</Annotation>
        <Annotation Tag="MetadataModel.Name">MD_Model</Annotation>
        <Annotation Tag="MetadataInstanceID">1</Annotation>
        <Annotation Tag="MetadataInstanceEntity.Name">Connections</Annotation>
        <Annotation Tag="MetadataInstanceEntityId">1</Annotation>
        <Annotation Tag="MetadataInstanceEntityDataItem.Name">AW</Annotation>
        <Annotation Tag="MetadataInstanceEntity.Name">Tables</Annotation>
        <Annotation Tag="MetadataInstanceEntityId">2</Annotation>
        <Annotation Tag="MetadataInstanceEntityDataItem.Name">Person</Annotation>
    </Annotations>
</Biml>
```

Figure C-10. *The Biml metadata instance entity data items*

Let's build out the Biml metadata instance entity data item persistence logic in BimlScript. When completed, the data item BimlScript should appear as shown in Listing C-32.

Listing C-32. Persisting Metadata Instance Entity Data Items

```
// Data Items
string sqlMied = @"If Not Exists(Select MetadataInstanceEntityDataItemName
From [meta].[MetadataInstanceEntityDataItem]
Where MetadataInstanceEntityDataItemName = '{0}'
And MetadataInstanceEntityID = {1})
 begin
  Insert Into [meta].[MetadataInstanceEntityDataItem]
  (MetadataInstanceEntityDataItemName, MetadataInstanceEntityID)
  Output inserted.MetadataInstanceEntityDataItemID As
  MetadataInstanceEntityDataItemID
  Values('{0}',{1})
 end
Else
 begin
 Select MetadataInstanceEntityDataItemID
 From [meta].[MetadataInstanceEntityDataItem]
 Where MetadataInstanceEntityDataItemName = '{0}'
   And MetadataInstanceEntityID = {1}
 end";
foreach(var mied in mie.DataItems) {
        query = string.Format(sqlMied, mied.Name, metadataInstanceEntityId);
        var dted = ExternalDataAccess.GetDataTable(cs, query);
        var metadataInstanceEntityDataItemId = Convert.ToInt32(dted.Rows[0]
        [0].ToString());
```

```
#><Annotation Tag="MetadataInstanceEntityDataItem.Name"><#=mied.Name #>
</Annotation>
    <Annotation Tag="MetadataInstanceEntityDataItemId">
    <#=metadataInstanceEntityDataItemId #></Annotation><#
}
```

After adding the Biml metadata instance entity data item persist BimlScript, your
MetadataInstancePersistGeneric.biml file should now appear as shown in Listing C-33
(added code highlighted).

Listing C-33. Persisting Metadata Instance, Metadata Instance Entities, and Metadata
Instance Entity Data Items

```
<Biml xmlns="http://schemas.varigence.com/biml.xsd">
        <Annotations>
<#
var cs = @"data source=vmDemo\Demo;initial catalog=BimlBook;provider=
SQLNCLI11;integrated security=SSPI;";
var sqlMi = @"
If Not Exists(Select MetadataInstanceName From [meta].[MetadataInstance]
Where MetadataInstanceName = '{0}')
  begin
    Insert Into [meta].[MetadataInstance]
    (MetadataInstanceName, MetadataModelName)
    Output inserted.MetadataInstanceID  As MetadataInstanceID
    Values('{0}','{1}')
  end
Else
  begin
    Select MetadataInstanceID From [meta].[MetadataInstance]
    Where MetadataInstanceName = '{0}'
  end";
foreach(var mi in RootNode.MetadataInstances) {
  var query = string.Format(sqlMi, mi.Name, mi.MetadataModel.Name);
  var dt = ExternalDataAccess.GetDataTable(cs, query);
  var instanceID = Convert.ToInt32(dt.Rows[0][0].ToString());
  #><Annotation Tag="MetadataInstance.Name"><#=mi.Name #></Annotation>
  <Annotation Tag="MetadataModel.Name"><#=mi.MetadataModel.Name #>
  </Annotation>
  <Annotation Tag="MetadataInstanceID"><#=instanceID #></Annotation><#

  // Entities
  string sqlMie = @"If Not Exists(Select MetadataInstanceEntityName
  From [meta].[MetadataInstanceEntity]
  Where MetadataInstanceEntityName = '{0}'
    And MetadataInstanceID = {1})
```

```
begin
 Insert Into [meta].[MetadataInstanceEntity]
 (MetadataInstanceEntityName, MetadataInstanceID)
 Output inserted.MetadataInstanceEntityID As MetadataInstanceEntityID
 Values('{0}',{1})
end
Else
 begin
  Select MetadataInstanceEntityID
  From [meta].[MetadataInstanceEntity]
  Where MetadataInstanceEntityName = '{0}'
 end";
  foreach(var mie in mi.Entities) {
    query = string.Format(sqlMie, mie.Name, instanceID);
    var dte = ExternalDataAccess.GetDataTable(cs, query);
        var metadataInstanceEntityId = Convert.ToInt32(dte.Rows[0][0].
        ToString());
  #><Annotation Tag="MetadataInstanceEntity.Name"><#=mie.Name#></Annotation>
    <Annotation Tag="MetadataInstanceEntityId"><#=metadataInstanceEntityId#>
    </Annotation><#

  // Data Items
string sqlMied = @"If Not Exists(Select MetadataInstanceEntityDataItemName
From [meta].[MetadataInstanceEntityDataItem]
Where MetadataInstanceEntityDataItemName = '{0}'
And MetadataInstanceEntityID = {1})
 begin
  Insert Into [meta].[MetadataInstanceEntityDataItem]
  (MetadataInstanceEntityDataItemName, MetadataInstanceEntityID)
  Output inserted.MetadataInstanceEntityDataItemID As
  MetadataInstanceEntityDataItemID
  Values('{0}',{1})
 end
Else
 begin
 Select MetadataInstanceEntityDataItemID
 From [meta].[MetadataInstanceEntityDataItem]
 Where MetadataInstanceEntityDataItemName = '{0}'
   And MetadataInstanceEntityID = {1}
 end";
foreach(var mied in mie.DataItems) {
        query = string.Format(sqlMied, mied.Name, metadataInstanceEntityId);
        var dted = ExternalDataAccess.GetDataTable(cs, query);
        var metadataInstanceEntityDataItemId = Convert.ToInt32(dted.Rows[0]
        [0].ToString());
  #><Annotation Tag="MetadataInstanceEntityDataItem.Name"><#=mied.Name #>
    </Annotation>
```

```
    <Annotation Tag="MetadataInstanceEntityDataItemId">
    <#=metadataInstanceEntityDataItemId #></Annotation><#
  }
  }
}#>
    </Annotations>
</Biml>
```

Querying the BimlBook database tables loaded thus far reveals the results shown in Figure C-11.

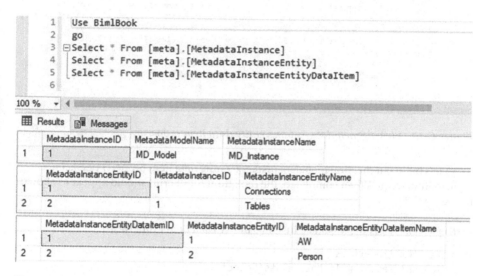

Figure C-11. *Viewing the results loaded thus far*

You're almost done loading your generic schema. As before, let's begin by adding minimal code, just enough to enumerate the Biml metadata instance entity data item property object. Add the BimlScript and Biml annotation in Listing C-34 just inside the foreach loop for the data item.

Listing C-34. Viewing Metadata Instance Entity Data Item Properties

```
// Data Item Properties
        foreach(var miedp in mied.Properties) {
  #><Annotation Tag="MetadataInstanceEntityDataItemProperty.Name">
  <#=miedp.Property.Name #></Annotation>
    <Annotation Tag="MetadataInstanceEntityDataItemProperty.Value">
    <#=miedp.Value #></Annotation><#
        }
```

If you save `MetadataInstancePersistGeneric.biml` and update the BimlScript preview, your preview expanded BimlScript should appear as shown in Figure C-12.

```
<Biml xmlns="http://schemas.varigence.com/biml.xsd">
    <Annotations>
        <Annotation Tag="MetadataInstance.Name">MD_Instance</Annotation>
        <Annotation Tag="MetadataModel.Name">MD_Model</Annotation>
        <Annotation Tag="MetadataInstanceID">1</Annotation>
        <Annotation Tag="MetadataInstanceEntity.Name">Connections</Annotation>
        <Annotation Tag="MetadataInstanceEntityId">1</Annotation>
        <Annotation Tag="MetadataInstanceEntityDataItem.Name">AW</Annotation>
        <Annotation Tag="MetadataInstanceEntityDataItemID">1</Annotation>
        <Annotation Tag="MetadataInstanceEntityDataItemProperty.Name">ConnString</Annotation>
        <Annotation Tag="MetadataInstanceEntityDataItemProperty.Value">Provider=SQLNCLI11;Server=.;
        <Annotation Tag="MetadataInstanceEntityDataItemProperty.Name">IsSource</Annotation>
        <Annotation Tag="MetadataInstanceEntityDataItemProperty.Value">True</Annotation>
        <Annotation Tag="MetadataInstanceEntity.Name">Tables</Annotation>
        <Annotation Tag="MetadataInstanceEntityId">2</Annotation>
        <Annotation Tag="MetadataInstanceEntityDataItem.Name">Person</Annotation>
        <Annotation Tag="MetadataInstanceEntityDataItemId">2</Annotation>
    </Annotations>
</Biml>
```

Figure C-12. *Viewing metadata instance entity data item properties*

Let's build out the Biml metadata instance entity data item property persistence logic in BimlScript. When completed, the data item BimlScript should appear as shown in Listing C-35.

Listing C-35. Persisting Metadata Instance Entity Data Item Properties

```
// Data Item Properties
  string sqlMiedp = @"If Not Exists(Select
  MetadataInstanceEntityDataItemPropertyName
  From [meta].[MetadataInstanceEntityDataItemProperty]
  Where MetadataInstanceEntityDataItemPropertyName = '{0}'
  And MetadataInstanceEntityDataItemID = {1})
 begin
  Insert Into [meta].[MetadataInstanceEntityDataItemProperty]
  (MetadataInstanceEntityDataItemPropertyName,
  MetadataInstanceEntityDataItemID,
  MetadataInstanceEntityDataItemPropertyValue)
  Output inserted.MetadataInstanceEntityDataItemPropertyID As
  MetadataInstanceEntityDataItemPropertyID
  Values('{0}',{1},'{2}')
  end
Else
 begin
  Select MetadataInstanceEntityDataItemPropertyID
  From [meta].[MetadataInstanceEntityDataItemProperty]
  Where MetadataInstanceEntityDataItemPropertyName = '{0}'
  And MetadataInstanceEntityDataItemID = {1}
  end";
```

```
foreach(var miedp in mied.Properties) {
query = string.Format(sqlMiedp, miedp.Property.Name,
metadataInstanceEntityDataItemId, miedp.Value);
var dtedp = ExternalDataAccess.GetDataTable(cs, query);
var metadataInstanceEntityDataItemPropertyId = Convert.
ToInt32(dtedp.Rows[0][0].ToString());

#><Annotation Tag="MetadataInstanceEntityDataItemProperty.Name">
<#=miedp.Property.Name #></Annotation>
    <Annotation Tag="MetadataInstanceEntityDataItemProperty.Value">
    <#=miedp.Value #></Annotation><#
    }
```

After adding the Biml metadata instance entity data item property persist BimlScript, your `MetadataInstancePersistGeneric.biml` file should now appear as shown in Listing C-36 (added code highlighted).

Listing C-36. Persisting Metadata Instance, Metadata Instance Entities, Metadata Instance Entity Data Item, and Metadata Instance Entity Data Item Properties

```
<Biml xmlns="http://schemas.varigence.com/biml.xsd">
        <Annotations>
<#
var cs = @"data source=vmDemo\Demo;initial catalog=BimlBook;provider=
SQLNCLI11;integrated security=SSPI;";
var sqlMi = @"
If Not Exists(Select MetadataInstanceName From [meta].[MetadataInstance]
Where MetadataInstanceName = '{0}')
  begin
    Insert Into [meta].[MetadataInstance]
    (MetadataInstanceName, MetadataModelName)
    Output inserted.MetadataInstanceID  As MetadataInstanceID
    Values('{0}','{1}')
  end
Else
  begin
    Select MetadataInstanceID From [meta].[MetadataInstance]
    Where MetadataInstanceName = '{0}'
  end";
foreach(var mi in RootNode.MetadataInstances) {
  var query = string.Format(sqlMi, mi.Name, mi.MetadataModel.Name);
  var dt = ExternalDataAccess.GetDataTable(cs, query);
  var instanceID = Convert.ToInt32(dt.Rows[0][0].ToString());
#><Annotation Tag="MetadataInstance.Name"><#=mi.Name #></Annotation>
<Annotation Tag="MetadataModel.Name"><#=mi.MetadataModel.Name #>
</Annotation>
<Annotation Tag="MetadataInstanceID"><#=instanceID #></Annotation><#
```

447

```
  // Entities
  string sqlMie = @"If Not Exists(Select MetadataInstanceEntityName
  From [meta].[MetadataInstanceEntity]
  Where MetadataInstanceEntityName = '{0}'
    And MetadataInstanceID = {1})
 begin
  Insert Into [meta].[MetadataInstanceEntity]
  (MetadataInstanceEntityName, MetadataInstanceID)
  Output inserted.MetadataInstanceEntityID As MetadataInstanceEntityID
  Values('{0}',{1})
 end
Else
 begin
  Select MetadataInstanceEntityID
  From [meta].[MetadataInstanceEntity]
  Where MetadataInstanceEntityName = '{0}'
 end";
  foreach(var mie in mi.Entities) {
    query = string.Format(sqlMie, mie.Name, instanceID);
    var dte = ExternalDataAccess.GetDataTable(cs, query);
        var metadataInstanceEntityId = Convert.ToInt32(dte.Rows[0][0].
        ToString());
  #><Annotation Tag="MetadataInstanceEntity.Name"><#=mie.Name#></Annotation>
    <Annotation Tag="MetadataInstanceEntityId"><#=metadataInstanceEntityId#>
    </Annotation><#


        // Data Items
string sqlMied = @"If Not Exists(Select MetadataInstanceEntityDataItemName
From [meta].[MetadataInstanceEntityDataItem]
Where MetadataInstanceEntityDataItemName = '{0}'
And MetadataInstanceEntityID = {1})
 begin
  Insert Into [meta].[MetadataInstanceEntityDataItem]
  (MetadataInstanceEntityDataItemName, MetadataInstanceEntityID)
  Output inserted.MetadataInstanceEntityDataItemID As
  MetadataInstanceEntityDataItemID
  Values('{0}',{1})
 end
Else
 begin
 Select MetadataInstanceEntityDataItemID
 From [meta].[MetadataInstanceEntityDataItem]
 Where MetadataInstanceEntityDataItemName = '{0}'
   And MetadataInstanceEntityID = {1}
 end";
 foreach(var mied in mie.DataItems) {
        query = string.Format(sqlMied, mied.Name, metadataInstanceEntityId);
        var dted = ExternalDataAccess.GetDataTable(cs, query);
```

```
      var metadataInstanceEntityDataItemId = Convert.ToInt32(dted.Rows[0]
      [0].ToString());
  #><Annotation Tag="MetadataInstanceEntityDataItem.Name"><#=mied.Name #>
  </Annotation>
    <Annotation Tag="MetadataInstanceEntityDataItemId">
    <#=metadataInstanceEntityDataItemId #></Annotation><#

  // Data Item Properties
  string sqlMiedp = @"If Not Exists(Select
MetadataInstanceEntityDataItemPropertyName
From [meta].[MetadataInstanceEntityDataItemProperty]
Where MetadataInstanceEntityDataItemPropertyName = '{0}'
  And MetadataInstanceEntityDataItemID = {1})
 begin
  Insert Into [meta].[MetadataInstanceEntityDataItemProperty]
  (MetadataInstanceEntityDataItemPropertyName,
  MetadataInstanceEntityDataItemID,
  MetadataInstanceEntityDataItemPropertyValue)
  Output inserted.MetadataInstanceEntityDataItemPropertyID As
  MetadataInstanceEntityDataItemPropertyID
  Values('{0}',{1},'{2}')
 end
Else
 begin
  Select MetadataInstanceEntityDataItemPropertyID
  From [meta].[MetadataInstanceEntityDataItemProperty]
  Where MetadataInstanceEntityDataItemPropertyName = '{0}'
  And MetadataInstanceEntityDataItemID = {1}
 end";
        foreach(var miedp in mied.Properties) {
        query = string.Format(sqlMiedp, miedp.Property.Name,
        metadataInstanceEntityDataItemId, miedp.Value);
        var dtedp = ExternalDataAccess.GetDataTable(cs, query);
        var metadataInstanceEntityDataItemPropertyId = Convert.
        ToInt32(dtedp.Rows[0][0].ToString());

  #><Annotation Tag="MetadataInstanceEntityDataItemProperty.Name">
  <#=miedp.Property.Name #></Annotation>
    <Annotation Tag="MetadataInstanceEntityDataItemProperty.Value">
    <#=miedp.Value #></Annotation><#
  }
 }
}
}#>
    </Annotations>
</Biml>
```

449

A query of the `BimlBook.meta.MetadataInstanceEntityDataItemProperty` table returns results similar to those shown in Figure C-13.

	MetadataInstanceEntityDataItemPropertyID	MetadataInstanceEntityDataItemID	MetadataInstanceEntityDataItemPropertyName	MetadataInstanceEntityDataItemPropertyValue
1	1	1	ConnString	Provider=SQLNCLI11;Server=.;Initial Catalog=Adve...
2	2	1	IsSource	True

Figure C-13. Viewing metadata instance entity data item properties and values

Loading metadata instance entity data item relationships is the last step for loading your generic schema. As before, let's add enough BimlScript code to enumerate the Biml metadata instance entity data item relationship object. Add the BimlScript and Biml annotation shown in Listing C-37 just inside the foreach loop for the data item but *after* the foreach loop for metadata instance entity data item property.

Listing C-37. Viewing Metadata Instance Entity Data Item Relationships

```
// Data Item Relationships
foreach(var miedr in mied.Relationships) {
 #><Annotation Tag="MetadataInstanceEntityDataItemRelationship.Name">
<#=miedr.Relationship.Name #></Annotation>
 <Annotation Tag="MetadataInstanceEntityDataItemRelationship.
 RelatedItemName"><#=miedr.RelatedItem #></Annotation><#
}
```

If you save `MetadataInstancePersistGeneric.biml` and update the BimlScript preview, your preview expanded BimlScript should appear as shown in Figure C-14.

```
<Biml xmlns="http://schemas.varigence.com/biml.xsd">
    <Annotations>
        <Annotation Tag="MetadataInstance.Name">MD_Instance</Annotation>
        <Annotation Tag="MetadataModel.Name">MD_Model</Annotation>
        <Annotation Tag="MetadataInstanceID">1</Annotation>
        <Annotation Tag="MetadataInstanceEntity.Name">Connections</Annotation>
        <Annotation Tag="MetadataInstanceEntityId">1</Annotation>
        <Annotation Tag="MetadataInstanceEntityDataItem.Name">AW</Annotation>
        <Annotation Tag="MetadataInstanceEntityDataItemId">1</Annotation>
        <Annotation Tag="MetadataInstanceEntityDataItemProperty.Name">ConnString</Annotation>
        <Annotation Tag="MetadataInstanceEntityDataItemProperty.Value">Provider=SQLNCLI11;Server=.;In
        <Annotation Tag="MetadataInstanceEntityDataItemProperty.Name">IsSource</Annotation>
        <Annotation Tag="MetadataInstanceEntityDataItemProperty.Value">True</Annotation>
        <Annotation Tag="MetadataInstanceEntity.Name">Tables</Annotation>
        <Annotation Tag="MetadataInstanceEntityId">2</Annotation>
        <Annotation Tag="MetadataInstanceEntityDataItem.Name">Person</Annotation>
        <Annotation Tag="MetadataInstanceEntityDataItemId">2</Annotation>
        <Annotation Tag="MetadataInstanceEntityDataItemRelationship.Name">Connection</Annotation>
        <Annotation Tag="MetadataInstanceEntityDataItemRelationship.RelatedItemName">AW</Annotation>
    </Annotations>
</Biml>
```

Figure C-14. Viewing metadata instance entity data item relationships

Let's build out the Biml metadata instance entity data item relationship persistence logic in BimlScript. When completed, the data item BimlScript should appear as shown in Listing C-38.

Listing C-38. Persisting Metadata Instance Entity Data Item Relationships

```
// Data Item Relationships
string sqlMiedr = @"If Not Exists(Select
MetadataInstanceEntityDataItemRelationshipName
        From [meta].[MetadataInstanceEntityDataItemRelationship]
        Where MetadataInstanceEntityDataItemRelationshipName = '{0}'
         And MetadataInstanceEntityDataItemID = {1})
 begin
  Insert Into [meta].[MetadataInstanceEntityDataItemRelationship]
  (MetadataInstanceEntityDataItemRelationshipName,
  MetadataInstanceEntityDataItemID,
  MetadataInstanceEntityDataItemRelatedItemName)
  Output inserted.MetadataInstanceEntityDataItemRelationshipID As
  MetadataInstanceEntityDataItemRelationshipID
  Values('{0}',{1},'{2}')
 end
Else
 begin
  Select MetadataInstanceEntityDataItemRelationshipID
  From [meta].[MetadataInstanceEntityDataItemRelationship]
  Where MetadataInstanceEntityDataItemRelationshipName = '{0}'
   And MetadataInstanceEntityDataItemID = {1}
 end";
        foreach(var miedr in mied.Relationships) {
                query = string.Format(sqlMiedr, miedr.Relationship.Name,
                metadataInstanceEntityDataItemId, miedr.RelatedItem);
                var dtedr = ExternalDataAccess.GetDataTable(cs, query);
                var metadataInstanceEntityDataItemRelationshipId =
                Convert.ToInt32(dtedr.Rows[0][0].ToString());
 #><Annotation Tag="MetadataInstanceEntityDataItemRelationship.Name">
 <#=miedr.Relationship.Name #></Annotation>
  <Annotation Tag="MetadataInstanceEntityDataItemRelationship.
  RelatedItemName"><#=miedr.RelatedItem #></Annotation><#
 }
```

After adding the Biml metadata instance entity data item relationship persist BimlScript, your `MetadataInstancePersistGeneric.biml` file should now appear as shown in Listing C-39 (added code highlighted).

Listing C-39. Persisting Metadata Instance, Metadata Instance Entity, Metadata Instance
Entity Data Item, Metadata Instance Entity Data Item Properties, and Metadata Instance
Entity Data Item Relationships

```
<Biml xmlns="http://schemas.varigence.com/biml.xsd">
        <Annotations>
<#
var cs = @"data source=vmDemo\Demo;initial catalog=BimlBook;provider=
SQLNCLI11;integrated security=SSPI;";
var sqlMi = @"
If Not Exists(Select MetadataInstanceName From [meta].[MetadataInstance]
Where MetadataInstanceName = '{0}')
  begin
    Insert Into [meta].[MetadataInstance]
    (MetadataInstanceName, MetadataModelName)
    Output inserted.MetadataInstanceID  As MetadataInstanceID
    Values('{0}','{1}')
  end
Else
  begin
    Select MetadataInstanceID From [meta].[MetadataInstance]
    Where MetadataInstanceName = '{0}'
  end";
foreach(var mi in RootNode.MetadataInstances) {
  var query = string.Format(sqlMi, mi.Name, mi.MetadataModel.Name);
  var dt = ExternalDataAccess.GetDataTable(cs, query);
  var instanceID = Convert.ToInt32(dt.Rows[0][0].ToString());
  #><Annotation Tag="MetadataInstance.Name"><#=mi.Name #></Annotation>
  <Annotation Tag="MetadataModel.Name"><#=mi.MetadataModel.Name #>
  </Annotation>
  <Annotation Tag="MetadataInstanceID"><#=instanceID #></Annotation><#

  // Entities
  string sqlMie = @"If Not Exists(Select MetadataInstanceEntityName
  From [meta].[MetadataInstanceEntity]
  Where MetadataInstanceEntityName = '{0}'
    And MetadataInstanceID = {1})
 begin
  Insert Into [meta].[MetadataInstanceEntity]
  (MetadataInstanceEntityName, MetadataInstanceID)
  Output inserted.MetadataInstanceEntityID As MetadataInstanceEntityID
  Values('{0}',{1})
 end
Else
 begin
  Select MetadataInstanceEntityID
  From [meta].[MetadataInstanceEntity]
  Where MetadataInstanceEntityName = '{0}'
 end";
```

```
foreach(var mie in mi.Entities) {
    query = string.Format(sqlMie, mie.Name, instanceID);
    var dte = ExternalDataAccess.GetDataTable(cs, query);
        var metadataInstanceEntityId = Convert.ToInt32(dte.Rows[0][0].
        ToString());
#><Annotation Tag="MetadataInstanceEntity.Name"><#=mie.Name#></Annotation>
    <Annotation Tag="MetadataInstanceEntityId"><#=metadataInstanceEntityId#>
    </Annotation><#


        // Data Items
string sqlMied = @"If Not Exists(Select MetadataInstanceEntityDataItemName
From [meta].[MetadataInstanceEntityDataItem]
Where MetadataInstanceEntityDataItemName = '{0}'
And MetadataInstanceEntityID = {1})
 begin
  Insert Into [meta].[MetadataInstanceEntityDataItem]
  (MetadataInstanceEntityDataItemName, MetadataInstanceEntityID)
  Output inserted.MetadataInstanceEntityDataItemID As
MetadataInstanceEntityDataItemID
  Values('{0}',{1})
 end
Else
 begin
 Select MetadataInstanceEntityDataItemID
 From [meta].[MetadataInstanceEntityDataItem]
 Where MetadataInstanceEntityDataItemName = '{0}'
   And MetadataInstanceEntityID = {1}
 end";
foreach(var mied in mie.DataItems) {
        query = string.Format(sqlMied, mied.Name, metadataInstanceEntityId);
        var dted = ExternalDataAccess.GetDataTable(cs, query);
        var metadataInstanceEntityDataItemId = Convert.ToInt32(dted.Rows[0]
        [0].ToString());
#><Annotation Tag="MetadataInstanceEntityDataItem.Name"><#=mied.Name #>
</Annotation>
    <Annotation Tag="MetadataInstanceEntityDataItemId">
    <#=metadataInstanceEntityDataItemId #></Annotation><#

// Data Item Properties
string sqlMiedp = @"If Not Exists(Select
MetadataInstanceEntityDataItemPropertyName
From [meta].[MetadataInstanceEntityDataItemProperty]
Where MetadataInstanceEntityDataItemPropertyName = '{0}'
  And MetadataInstanceEntityDataItemID = {1})
begin
```

```
  Insert Into [meta].[MetadataInstanceEntityDataItemProperty]
  (MetadataInstanceEntityDataItemPropertyName,
  MetadataInstanceEntityDataItemID,
  MetadataInstanceEntityDataItemPropertyValue)
  Output inserted.MetadataInstanceEntityDataItemPropertyID As
  MetadataInstanceEntityDataItemPropertyID
  Values('{0}',{1},'{2}')
 end
Else
 begin
  Select MetadataInstanceEntityDataItemPropertyID
  From [meta].[MetadataInstanceEntityDataItemProperty]
  Where MetadataInstanceEntityDataItemPropertyName = '{0}'
  And MetadataInstanceEntityDataItemID = {1}
 end";
        foreach(var miedp in mied.Properties) {
                query = string.Format(sqlMiedp, miedp.Property.Name,
                metadataInstanceEntityDataItemId, miedp.Value);
                var dtedp = ExternalDataAccess.GetDataTable(cs, query);
                var metadataInstanceEntityDataItemPropertyId =
                Convert.ToInt32(dtedp.Rows[0][0].ToString());
 #><Annotation Tag="MetadataInstanceEntityDataItemProperty.Name">
 <#=miedp.Property.Name #></Annotation>
   <Annotation Tag="MetadataInstanceEntityDataItemProperty.Value">
    <#=miedp.Value #></Annotation><#
  }

        // Data Item Relationships
        string sqlMiedr = @"If Not Exists(Select
        MetadataInstanceEntityDataItemRelationshipName
        From [meta].[MetadataInstanceEntityDataItemRelationship]
        Where MetadataInstanceEntityDataItemRelationshipName = '{0}'
         And MetadataInstanceEntityDataItemID = {1})
 begin
  Insert Into [meta].[MetadataInstanceEntityDataItemRelationship]
  (MetadataInstanceEntityDataItemRelationshipName,
  MetadataInstanceEntityDataItemID,
  MetadataInstanceEntityDataItemRelatedItemName)
  Output inserted.MetadataInstanceEntityDataItemRelationshipID As
  MetadataInstanceEntityDataItemRelationshipID
  Values('{0}',{1},'{2}')
 end
Else
 begin
  Select MetadataInstanceEntityDataItemRelationshipID
  From [meta].[MetadataInstanceEntityDataItemRelationship]
  Where MetadataInstanceEntityDataItemRelationshipName = '{0}'
    And MetadataInstanceEntityDataItemID = {1}
 end";
```

```
    foreach(var miedr in mied.Relationships) {
            query = string.Format(sqlMiedr, miedr.Relationship.Name,
            metadataInstanceEntityDataItemId, miedr.RelatedItem);
            var dtedr = ExternalDataAccess.GetDataTable(cs, query);
            var metadataInstanceEntityDataItemRelationshipId =
            Convert.ToInt32(dtedr.Rows[0][0].ToString());
  #><Annotation Tag="MetadataInstanceEntityDataItemRelationship.Name">
  <#=miedr.Relationship.Name #></Annotation>
    <Annotation Tag="MetadataInstanceEntityDataItemRelationship.
    RelatedItemName"><#=miedr.RelatedItem #></Annotation><#
  }
 }
 }
}#>
    </Annotations>
</Biml>
```

A query of the `BimlBook.meta.MetadataInstanceEntityDataItemRelationship` table returns results similar to those shown in Figure C-15.

MetadataInstanceEntityDataItemRelationshipID	MetadataInstanceEntityDataItemID	MetadataInstanceEntityDataItemRelationshipName	MetadataInstanceEntityDataItemRelatedItemName
1	2	Connection	AW

Figure C-15. *Viewing metadata instance entity data item relationships*

Retrieving Biml Metadata from a Database

In the previous section, we discussed and demonstrated persisting Biml metadata instance data to a database named BimlBook. Storing metadata in a database presents options such as manipulating sets of metadata using Transact-SQL and building a custom application to manage the metadata stored in the BimlBook database.

Once the data has been created, updated, and/or deleted, you need to read it back into your Biml project. You now turn your attention to retrieving Biml metadata instance data *from* the BimlBook database. In this section, you will build a Biml file to do just that: retrieve the data you stored in the BimlBook database and use it to build a Biml metadata instance file.

Retrieving a Biml Metadata Instance from a Custom Schema

Let's build a Biml file to retrieve the custom schema data you persisted in the previous section. Begin by creating a new Biml file named MetadataInstanceRetrieveCustom. biml. Add an import directive to the System.Data .Net Framework namespace and a BimlScript string variable to contain the connection string so that your code appears as shown in Listing C-40.

Listing C-40. Starting the MetadataInstanceRetrieveCustom.biml File

```
<#@ import namespace="System.Data" #>
<Biml xmlns="http://schemas.varigence.com/biml.xsd">
<#
var cs = @"data source=vmDemo\Demo;initial catalog=BimlBook;provider=
SQLNCLI11;integrated security=SSPI;";
#>
</Biml>
```

Retrieving the Biml Metadata Instance

Let's next add some BimlScript to retrieve instance data from your custom schema, di, in the BimlBook database. Since you are adding so much BimlScript to a relatively few lines of existing BimlScript, let's view the MetadataInstanceRetrieveCustom.biml file in its entirety after adding the code in Listing C-41 (added code highlighted).

Listing C-41. Retrieving the Instance

```
<#@ import namespace="System.Data" #>
<Biml xmlns="http://schemas.varigence.com/biml.xsd">
        <Metadata>
<#
var cs = @"data source=vmDemo\Demo;initial catalog=BimlBook;provider=
SQLNCLI11;integrated security=SSPI;";
// Metadata Instance
string sqlMi = @"Select InstanceID, InstanceName
From [di].[Instance]";
var dt = ExternalDataAccess.GetDataTable(cs, sqlMi);
foreach(DataRow i in dt.Rows) {
  var instanceId = Convert.ToInt32(i["InstanceID"]);
  #><MetadataInstance Name="<#=i["InstanceName"] #>"
  MetadataModelName="MD_Model"><#
}
#>
                </MetadataInstance>
    </Metadata>
</Biml>
```

Let's walk through this pattern because you will repeat it throughout the MetadataInstanceRetrieveCustom.biml file. To do so, you'll make use of the BimlScript code shown in Figure C-16.

```
1    <#@ import namespace="System.Data" #>
2    <Biml xmlns="http://schemas.varigence.com/biml.xsd">
3        <Metadata>
4    <#
5    var cs = @"data source=vmDemo\Demo;initial catalog=BimlBook;provider=SQLNCLI11;integrated security=SSPI;";
6    // Metadata Instance
7    string sqlMi = @"Select InstanceID, InstanceName
8    From [di].[Instance]";
9    var dt = ExternalDataAccess.GetDataTable(cs, sqlMi);
10   foreach(DataRow i in dt.Rows) {
11       var instanceId = Convert.ToInt32(i["InstanceID"]);
12   #><MetadataInstance Name="<#=i["InstanceName"] #>" MetadataModelName="MD_Model"><#
13   }
14   #>
15           </MetadataInstance>
16       </Metadata>
17   </Biml>
```

Figure C-16. *Viewing MetadataInstanceRetrieveCustom.biml*

Lines 2 and 15 contain the opening and closing Biml tags. Lines 3 and 14 contain the opening and closing Metadata tags, and Line 5 contains a string variable named cs that holds the connection string to the BimlBook database.

On Line 7 you populate a string variable named sqlMi that contains the Transact-SQL query you use to retrieve values from the BimlBook database. On Line 9 you call the ExternalDataAccess.GetDataTable extension method to populate the variable dt with the results returned from executing the Transact-SQL statement in the sqlMi variable. Lines 10-13 contain a foreach loop that iterates the rows in the dt results. On Line 11 you instantiate and initialize a variable named instanceId that contains the instanceID value for the persisted metadata instance. instanceId is used in subsequent queries.

Your expanded Biml should appear similar to that shown in Figure C-17.

```
<Biml xmlns="http://schemas.varigence.com/biml.xsd">
    <Metadata>
        <MetadataInstance Name="MD_Instance" MetadataModelName="MD_Model">
        </MetadataInstance>
    </Metadata>
</Biml>
```

Figure C-17. *Viewing the instance name*

Retrieving the Connection Entity

You now turn your attention to retrieving the Connections and Tables metadata instance entities from the BimlBook database. You will leverage the pattern you used for retrieving data from the [di].[Instance] table and, because the metadata XML is nested, you will nest queries. Once updated, your version of MetadataInstanceRetrieveCustom.biml file should appear as shown in Listing C-42 (added code highlighted).

457

Listing C-42. Retrieving Connections

```
<#@ import namespace="System.Data" #>
<Biml xmlns="http://schemas.varigence.com/biml.xsd">
        <Metadata>
<#
var cs = @"data source=vmDemo\Demo;initial catalog=BimlBook;provider=
SQLNCLI11;integrated security=SSPI;";
// Metadata Instance
string sqlMi = @"Select InstanceID, InstanceName
From [di].[Instance]";
var dt = ExternalDataAccess.GetDataTable(cs, sqlMi);
foreach(DataRow i in dt.Rows) {
  var instanceId = Convert.ToInt32(i["InstanceID"]);
  #><MetadataInstance Name="<#=i["InstanceName"] #>"
  MetadataModelName="MD_Model">
          <Entities><#
  string sqlConn = @"Select ConnectionName, ConnString, IsSource
  From [di].[Connection]
  Where InstanceID = {0}";
  var query = string.Format(sqlConn, instanceId);
  var dtc = ExternalDataAccess.GetDataTable(cs, query);
  foreach(DataRow c in dtc.Rows) {
  #><Entity Name="Connections" MetadataModelEntityName=
  "MD_Model.Connections">
                <DataItems>
                        <DataItem Name="<#=c["ConnectionName"] #>">
                                <Properties>
                                        <Property PropertyName="MD_Model.
                                        Connections.ConnString">
                                                <Value><#=c["ConnString"] #>
                                                </Value>
                </Property>
                                        <Property PropertyName="MD_Model.
                                        Connections.IsSource">
                                                <Value><#=c["IsSource"] #>
                                                </Value>
                </Property>
                                </Properties>
                        </DataItem>
                </DataItems>
        </Entity><#
  }
}
#>                      </Entities>
                </MetadataInstance>
    </Metadata>
  </Biml>
```

As before, let's walk through the BimlScript by line number, as shown in Figure C-18.

```
1   <#@ import namespace="System.Data" #>
2   <Biml xmlns="http://schemas.varigence.com/biml.xsd">
3       <Metadata>
4   <#
5   var cs = @"data source=vmDemo\Demo;initial catalog=BimlBook;provider=SQLNCLI11;integrated security=SSPI;";
6   // Metadata Instance
7   string sqlMi = @"Select InstanceID, InstanceName
8   From [di].[Instance]";
9   var dt = ExternalDataAccess.GetDataTable(cs, sqlMi);
10  foreach(DataRow i in dt.Rows) {
11      var instanceId = Convert.ToInt32(i["InstanceID"]);
12  #><MetadataInstance Name="<#=i["InstanceName"] #>" MetadataModelName="MD_Model">
13      <Entities><#
14  string sqlConn = @"Select ConnectionName, ConnString, IsSource
15  From [di].[Connection]
16  Where InstanceID = {0}";
17  var query = string.Format(sqlConn, instanceId);
18  var dtc = ExternalDataAccess.GetDataTable(cs, query);
19  foreach(DataRow c in dtc.Rows) {
20  #><Entity Name="Connections" MetadataModelEntityName="MD_Model.Connections">
21          <DataItems>
22              <DataItem Name="<#=c["ConnectionName"] #>">
23                  <Properties>
24                      <Property PropertyName="MD_Model.Connections.ConnString">
25                          <Value><#=c["ConnString"] #></Value>
26                      </Property>
27                      <Property PropertyName="MD_Model.Connections.IsSource">
28                          <Value><#=c["IsSource"] #></Value>
29                      </Property>
30                  </Properties>
31              </DataItem>
32          </DataItems>
33      </Entity><#
34      }
35  }
36  #>      </Entities>
37      </MetadataInstance>
38      </Metadata>
39  </Biml>
```

Figure C-18. *Viewing MetadataInstanceRetrieveCustom.biml after loading entity metadata*

The Connections entity logic spans lines 13-36. Lines 13 and 36 contain the opening and closing Entities tags. On lines 14-16 you populate a string variable named sqlConn that contains the Transact-SQL to retrieve InstanceID, ConnectionName, ConnString, and IsSource properties from the [di].[Connection] table. On Lines 17 and 18 you configure the query and populate the dtc data table. On Lines 19-34 you loop through the data returned by executing the query and read the results to populate Connections entities.

You retrieve the Tables entity in a manner much the same as you retrieve the Connections entity.

Your expanded Biml should appear similar to that shown in Figure C-19.

```
<Biml xmlns="http://schemas.varigence.com/biml.xsd">
    <Metadata>
        <MetadataInstance Name="MD_Instance" MetadataModelName="MD_Model">
            <Entities>
                <Entity Name="Connections" MetadataModelEntityName="MD_Model.Connections">
                    <DataItems>
                        <DataItem Name="MD_Instance">
                            <Properties>
                                <Property PropertyName="MD_Model.Connections.ConnString">
                                    <Value>Provider=SQLNCLI11;Server=.;Initial Catalog=AdventureWorks2014;Integrated Security=SSPI;</Value>
                                </Property>
                                <Property PropertyName="MD_Model.Connections.IsSource">
                                    <Value>true</Value>
                                </Property>
                            </Properties>
                        </DataItem>
                    </DataItems>
                </Entity>
            </Entities>
        </MetadataInstance>
    </Metadata>
</Biml>
```

Figure C-19. *Viewing the Connections entity*

Retrieving the Table Entity

Once the Tables entity Biml and BimlScript are added, the
MetadataInstanceRetrieveCustom.biml file is complete as shown in Listing C-43 (added
code highlighted).

Listing C-43. Retrieving Tables

```
<#@ import namespace="System.Data" #>
<Biml xmlns="http://schemas.varigence.com/biml.xsd">
        <Metadata>
<#
var cs = @"data source=vmDemo\Demo;initial catalog=BimlBook;provider=
SQLNCLI11;integrated security=SSPI;";
// Metadata Instance
string sqlMi = @"Select InstanceID, InstanceName
From [di].[Instance]";
var dt = ExternalDataAccess.GetDataTable(cs, sqlMi);
foreach(DataRow i in dt.Rows) {
  var instanceId = Convert.ToInt32(i["InstanceID"]);
  #><MetadataInstance Name="<#=i["InstanceName"] #>"
  MetadataModelName="MD_Model">
        <Entities><#
  string sqlConn = @"Select ConnectionName, ConnString, IsSource
From [di].[Connection]
Where InstanceID = {0}";
  var query = string.Format(sqlConn, instanceId);
  var dtc = ExternalDataAccess.GetDataTable(cs, query);
  foreach(DataRow c in dtc.Rows) {
  #><Entity Name="Connections" MetadataModelEntityName=
  "MD_Model.Connections">
```

```
                <DataItems>
                    <DataItem Name="<#=c["ConnectionName"] #>">
                        <Properties>
                            <Property PropertyName="MD_Model.
                            Connections.ConnString">
                                <Value><#=c["ConnString"] #>
                                </Value>
                </Property>
                            <Property PropertyName="MD_Model.
                            Connections.IsSource">
                                <Value><#=c["IsSource"] #>
                                </Value>
                </Property>
                        </Properties>
                    </DataItem>
                </DataItems>
        </Entity><#
    }
    string sqlTbl = @"Select c.ConnectionName, t.TableName
    , i.InstanceName + '.Connections.' + c.ConnectionName As RelatedItemName
    From [di].[Table] t
    Join [di].[Connection] c On c.ConnectionID = t.ConnectionID
    Join [di].[Instance] i On i.InstanceID = c.InstanceID
    Where c.InstanceID = {0}";
    query = string.Format(sqlTbl, instanceId);
    var dtt = ExternalDataAccess.GetDataTable(cs, query);
    foreach(DataRow t in dtt.Rows) {
    #><Entity Name="Tables" MetadataModelEntityName="MD_Model.Tables">
                <DataItems>
                    <DataItem Name="<#=t["TableName"] #>">
                        <Relationships>
                            <Relationship RelationshipName=
                            "MD_Model.Tables.Connection"
                            RelatedItemName="<#=t["RelatedItem
                            Name"] #>" />
                        </Relationships>
                    </DataItem>
                </DataItems>
        </Entity><#
    }
}
#>                      </Entities>
            </MetadataInstance>
    </Metadata>
</Biml>
```

MetadataInstanceRetrieveCustom.biml expands into the Biml displayed in
Figure C-20, which represents the complete MD_Instance Biml metadata instance.

Preview Expanded BimlScript

```
 1  <Biml xmlns="http://schemas.varigence.com/biml.xsd">
 2      <Metadata>
 3          <MetadataInstance Name="MD_Instance" MetadataModelName="MD_Model">
 4              <Entities>
 5                  <Entity Name="Connections" MetadataModelEntityName="MD_Model.Connections">
 6                      <DataItems>
 7                          <DataItem Name="AW">
 8                              <Properties>
 9                                  <Property PropertyName="MD_Model.Connections.ConnString">
10                                      <Value>Provider=SQLNCLI11;Server=.;Initial Catalog=AdventureWorks2014;I
11                                  </Property>
12                                  <Property PropertyName="MD_Model.Connections.IsSource">
13                                      <Value>True</Value>
14                                  </Property>
15                              </Properties>
16                          </DataItem>
17                      </DataItems>
18                  </Entity>
19                  <Entity Name="Tables" MetadataModelEntityName="MD_Model.Tables">
20                      <DataItems>
21                          <DataItem Name="Person">
22                              <Relationships>
23                                  <Relationship RelationshipName="Person" RelatedItemName="Connections.AW" />
24                              </Relationships>
25                          </DataItem>
26                      </DataItems>
27                  </Entity>
28              </Entities>
29          </MetadataInstance>
30      </Metadata>
31  </Biml>
```

Figure C-20. *Viewing the complete MD_Instance Biml metadata instance in expanded
BimlScript preview*

Your Biml and BimlScript appear as shown in Figure C-21.

```
1   <#@ import namespace="System.Data" #>
2   <Biml xmlns="http://schemas.varigence.com/biml.xsd">
3       <Metadata>
4   <#
5   var cs = @"data source=vmDemo\Demo;initial catalog=BimlBook;provider=SQLNCLI11;integrated security=SSPI;";
6   // Metadata Instance
7   string sqlMi = @"Select InstanceID, InstanceName
8   From [di].[Instance]";
9   var dt = ExternalDataAccess.GetDataTable(cs, sqlMi);
10  foreach(DataRow i in dt.Rows) {
11      var instanceId = Convert.ToInt32(i["InstanceID"]);
12      #><MetadataInstance Name="<#=i["InstanceName"] #>" MetadataModelName="MD_Model">
13          <Entities><#
14      string sqlConn = @"Select ConnectionName, ConnString, IsSource
15      From [di].[Connection]
16      Where InstanceID = {0}";
17      var query = string.Format(sqlConn, instanceId);
18      var dtc = ExternalDataAccess.GetDataTable(cs, query);
19      foreach(DataRow c in dtc.Rows) {
20          #><Entity Name="Connections" MetadataModelEntityName="MD_Model.Connections">
21              <DataItems>
22                  <DataItem Name="<#=c["ConnectionName"] #>">
23                      <Properties>
24                          <Property PropertyName="MD_Model.Connections.ConnString">
25                              <Value><#=c["ConnString"] #></Value>
26                          </Property>
27                          <Property PropertyName="MD_Model.Connections.IsSource">
28                              <Value><#=c["IsSource"] #></Value>
29                          </Property>
30                      </Properties>
31                  </DataItem>
32              </DataItems>
33          </Entity><#
34      }
35      string sqlTbl = @"Select c.ConnectionName, t.TableName
36      , i.InstanceName + '.Connections.' + c.ConnectionName As RelatedItemName
37      From [di].[Table] t
38      Join [di].[Connection] c On c.ConnectionID = t.ConnectionID
39      Join [di].[Instance] i On i.InstanceID = c.InstanceID
40      Where c.InstanceID = {0}";
41      query = string.Format(sqlTbl, instanceId);
42      var dtt = ExternalDataAccess.GetDataTable(cs, query);
43      foreach(DataRow t in dtt.Rows) {
44          #><Entity Name="Tables" MetadataModelEntityName="MD_Model.Tables">
45              <DataItems>
46                  <DataItem Name="<#=t["TableName"] #>">
47                      <Relationships>
48                          <Relationship RelationshipName="MD_Model.Tables.Connection" RelatedItemName="<#=t["RelatedItemName"] #>" />
49                      </Relationships>
50                  </DataItem>
51              </DataItems>
52          </Entity><#
53      }
54  }
55  #>      </Entities>
56      </MetadataInstance>
57      </Metadata>
58  </Biml>
```

Figure C-21. *Full Biml and BimlScript for MetadataInstanceRetrieveCustom.biml*

The Tables entity logic spans lines 35-53. On Lines 35-40, you populate a string variable named sqlTbl that contains the Transact-SQL to retrieve Table properties from the [di].[Table] table. Lines 41-42 configure and execute the query to return data to the dtt data table. On Lines 43-53 you iterate the data returned the dtt data table.

MetadataInstanceRetrieveCustom.biml represents *one* way to retrieve Biml metadata instance data stored in a custom schema. This is not the *only* way to accomplish retrieving this data (or to accomplish storing it, for that matter).

463

Retrieving a Biml Metadata Instance from a Generic Schema

Let's now build a Biml file to retrieve the generic schema data you persisted in the previous section. Begin by creating a new Biml file named MetadataInstanceRetrieveGeneric.biml. Add a BimlScript string variable to contain the connection string so that your code appears as shown in Listing C-44.

Listing C-44. Starting the MetadataInstanceRetrieveGeneric.biml File

```
<#@ import namespace="System.Data" #>
<Biml xmlns="http://schemas.varigence.com/biml.xsd">
<#
var cs = @"data source=vmDemo\Demo;initial catalog=BimlBook;provider=
SQLNCLI11;integrated security=SSPI;";
#>
</Biml>
```

Retrieving the Biml Metadata Instance

Let's next add some BimlScript to retrieve instance data from your generic meta schema in the BimlBook database. Since you are adding so much BimlScript to a relatively few lines of existing BimlScript, let's view the MetadataInstanceRetrieveGeneric.biml file in its entirety after adding the code in Listing C-45 (added code highlighted).

Listing C-45. Retrieving the Metadata Instance

```
<#@ import namespace="System.Data" #>
<Biml xmlns="http://schemas.varigence.com/biml.xsd">
 <Metadata>
<#
var cs = @"data source=vmDemo\Demo;initial catalog=BimlBook;provider=
SQLNCLI11;integrated security=SSPI;";
// Metadata Instance
string sqlMi = @"Select MetadataInstanceID, MetadataModelName,
MetadataInstanceName
From [meta].[MetadataInstance]";
var dt = ExternalDataAccess.GetDataTable(cs, sqlMi);
foreach(DataRow row in dt.Rows) {
  var metadataInstanceId = Convert.ToInt32(row["MetadataInstanceID"]);
  #><MetadataInstance Name="<#=row["MetadataInstanceName"] #>"
  MetadataModelName="<#=row["MetadataModelName"] #>">
        </MetadataInstance><#
}
#>
 </Metadata>
 </Biml>
```

As with the custom schema code, let's walk through this pattern because you will repeat it throughout the MetadataInstanceRetrieveGeneric.biml file. To do so, you'll make use of the BimlScript code shown in Figure C-22.

```
1  <#@ import namespace="System.Data" #>
2  <Biml xmlns="http://schemas.varigence.com/biml.xsd">
3    <Metadata>
4  <#
5    var cs = @"data source=vmDemo\Demo;initial catalog=BimlBook;provider=SQLNCLI11;integrated security=SSPI;";
6    // Metadata Instance
7    string sqlMi = @"Select MetadataInstanceID, MetadataModelName, MetadataInstanceName
8    From [meta].[MetadataInstance]";
9    var dt = ExternalDataAccess.GetDataTable(cs, sqlMi);
10   foreach(DataRow row in dt.Rows) {
11     var metadataInstanceId = Convert.ToInt32(row["MetadataInstanceID"]);
12     #><MetadataInstance Name="<#=row["MetadataInstanceName"] #>" MetadataModelName="<#=row["MetadataModelName"] #>">
13     </MetadataInstance><#
14   }
15   #>
16   </Metadata>
17  </Biml>
```

Figure C-22. *Viewing MetadataInstanceRetrieveGeneric.biml*

Lines 2 and 17 contain the opening and closing Biml tags. Lines 3 and 16 contain the opening and closing Metadata tags and Line 5 contains a variable named cs that contains the connection string to the BimlBook database.

On Lines 7-8 you populate a string variable named sqlMi that contains the Transact-SQL query you use to retrieve values from the BimlBook database's meta schema. On Line 9 you execute the query via the ExternalDataAccess.GetDataTable extension method. On lines 10-14 you iterate rows returned to data table dt, placing the MetadataInstanceID data into the variable metadataInstanceId and populating the MetadataInstance tag.

The expanded Biml appears as shown in Figure C-23.

```
<Biml xmlns="http://schemas.varigence.com/biml.xsd">
    <Metadata>
        <MetadataInstance Name="MD_Model" MetadataModelName="MD_Model">
        </MetadataInstance>
    </Metadata>
</Biml>
```

Figure C-23. *Metadata instance, expanded*

Retrieving the Metadata Instance Entities

This is where the custom and generic approaches deviate. In the custom approach, you retrieved the Connections and Tables metadata instance entities from the BimlBook database's [di] schema. In the generic approach, you query the (generically-named) meta.MetadataInstanceEntity table to retrieve data at a similar level of the hierarchy. As with the custom approach, you will leverage the pattern you used for retrieving data from the meta.MetadataInstance table and, because the metadata XML is nested, you

465

will nest query executions. Examine the MetadataInstanceRetrieveCustom.biml file. Note that the metadata instance entity code is wedged between the MetadataInstance opening and closing tags on Line 12 in Figure C-22, with new code highlighted in Listing C-46.

Listing C-46. Retrieving the Metadata Instance Entities

```
<#@ import namespace="System.Data" #>
<Biml xmlns="http://schemas.varigence.com/biml.xsd">
 <Metadata>
<#
var cs = @"data source=vmDemo\Demo;initial catalog=BimlBook;provider=
SQLNCLI11;integrated security=SSPI;";
// Metadata Instance
string sqlMi = @"Select MetadataInstanceID, MetadataModelName,
MetadataInstanceName
From [meta].[MetadataInstance]";
var dt = ExternalDataAccess.GetDataTable(cs, sqlMi);
foreach(DataRow row in dt.Rows) {
  var metadataInstanceId = Convert.ToInt32(row["MetadataInstanceID"]);
  #><MetadataInstance Name="<#=row["MetadataInstanceName"] #>"
  MetadataModelName="<#=row["MetadataModelName"] #>">
          <Entities><#
// Metadata Instance Entity
  string sqlMie = @"Select mie.MetadataInstanceEntityID
  , mi.MetadataModelName + '.' + mie.MetadataInstanceEntityName As
  MetadataModelEntityName
  , mie.MetadataInstanceEntityName
  From [meta].MetadataInstanceEntity mie
  Join [meta].MetadataInstance mi On mi.MetadataInstanceID =
  mie.MetadataInstanceID
  Where mie.MetadataInstanceID = {0}";
  var query = string.Format(sqlMie, metadataInstanceId);
  var dte = ExternalDataAccess.GetDataTable(cs, query);
  foreach(DataRow e in dte.Rows) {
    int instanceEntityID = Convert.ToInt32(e["MetadataInstanceEntityID"]);
#>
        <Entity Name="<#=e["MetadataInstanceEntityName"] #>" MetadataModel
        EntityName="<#=e["MetadataModelEntityName"] #>">
        </Entity>
<# } #>
        </Entities>
        </MetadataInstance><#
}
#>
 </Metadata>
</Biml>
```

As before, let's walk through the BimlScript by the line numbers shown in Figure C-24.

```
1    <#@ import namespace="System.Data" #>
2    <Biml xmlns="http://schemas.varigence.com/biml.xsd">
3      <Metadata>
4        <#
5        var cs = @"data source=vmDemo\Demo;initial catalog=BimlBook;provider=SQLNCLI11;integrated security=SSPI;";
6        // Metadata Instance
7        string sqlMi = @"Select MetadataInstanceID, MetadataModelName, MetadataInstanceName
8        From [meta].[MetadataInstance]";
9        var dt = ExternalDataAccess.GetDataTable(cs, sqlMi);
10       foreach(DataRow row in dt.Rows) {
11           var metadataInstanceId = Convert.ToInt32(row["MetadataInstanceID"]);
12           #><MetadataInstance Name="<#=row["MetadataInstanceName"] #>" MetadataModelName="<#=row["MetadataModelName"] #>">
13             <Entities><#
14       // Metadata Instance Entity
15       string sqlMie = @"Select mie.MetadataInstanceEntityID
16       , mi.MetadataModelName + '.' + mie.MetadataInstanceEntityName As MetadataModelEntityName
17       , mie.MetadataInstanceEntityName
18       From [meta].MetadataInstanceEntity mie
19       Join [meta].MetadataInstance mi On mi.MetadataInstanceID = mie.MetadataInstanceID
20       Where mie.MetadataInstanceID = {0}";
21       var query = string.Format(sqlMie, metadataInstanceId);
22       var dte = ExternalDataAccess.GetDataTable(cs, query);
23       foreach(DataRow e in dte.Rows) {
24           int instanceEntityID = Convert.ToInt32(e["MetadataInstanceEntityID"]);
25       #>
26           <Entity Name="<#=e["MetadataInstanceEntityName"] #>" MetadataModelEntityName="<#=e["MetadataModelEntityName"] #>">
27           </Entity>
28       <# } #>
29           </Entities>
30       </MetadataInstance><#
31       }
32       #>
33      </Metadata>
34    </Biml>
```

Figure C-24. *Viewing MetadataInstanceRetrieveGeneric.biml after loading entity metadata*

The entity logic spans lines 13-29. On Lines 15-20 you populate a string variable named sqlMie that contains the Transact-SQL to retrieve MetadataInstanceInstanceID, MetadataModelEntityName, and MetadataInstanceEntityName properties from the meta. MetadataInstanceEntity and meta.MetadataInstance tables. Lines 21-22 configure and execute the query via the ExternalDataAccess.GetDataTable extension method, sending the results to the dte variable. On lines 23-28 you iterate the data returned to the dte variable by executing the query, populating the instanceEntityID variable and the Entity tag attributes.

Please note that Connections *and* Tables metadata instance entities are returned by this generic design. The generic approach is more succinct for returning values from the BimlBook database's meta schema. View the results returned by previewing the expanded BimlScript, shown in Figure C-25.

Preview Expanded BimlScript

```
1  ⊟<Biml xmlns="http://schemas.varigence.com/biml.xsd">
2  ├   <Metadata>
3  ├      <MetadataInstance Name="MD_Instance" MetadataModelName="MD_Model">
4  ├         <Entities>
5            <Entity Name="Connections" MetadataModelEntityName="MD_Model.Connections">
6            </Entity>
7            <Entity Name="Tables" MetadataModelEntityName="MD_Model.Tables">
8            </Entity>
9         </Entities>
10        </MetadataInstance>
11     </Metadata>
12 └</Biml>
```

Figure C-25. *Connections and Tables entities loaded by MetadataInstanceRetrieveGeneric.biml*

In Figure C-25 you see the MetadataInstance open and close tags on lines 3 and 10 in the expanded BimlScript preview, respectively. The open and close tags for Entities appear on lines 4 and 9. The entities, Connections and Tables, appear on lines 5-8.

Let's now retrieve data items.

Retrieving the Metadata Instance Entity Data Items

You continue to expand and extend the pattern used thus far, this time to retrieve metadata instance entity data items. The additional code is highlighted in the MetadataInstanceRetrieveGeneric.biml file (to date) in Listing C-47.

Listing C-47. Retrieving the Metadata Instance Entity Data Items

```
<#@ import namespace="System.Data" #>
<Biml xmlns="http://schemas.varigence.com/biml.xsd">
 <Metadata>
<#
var cs = @"data source=vmDemo\Demo;initial catalog=BimlBook;provider=
SQLNCLI11;integrated security=SSPI;";
// Metadata Instance
string sqlMi = @"Select MetadataInstanceID, MetadataModelName,
MetadataInstanceName
From [meta].[MetadataInstance]";
var dt = ExternalDataAccess.GetDataTable(cs, sqlMi);
foreach(DataRow row in dt.Rows) {
  var metadataInstanceId = Convert.ToInt32(row["MetadataInstanceID"]);
  #><MetadataInstance Name="<#=row["MetadataInstanceName"] #>"
  MetadataModelName="<#=row["MetadataModelName"] #>">
          <Entities><#
// Metadata Instance Entity
  string sqlMie = @"Select mie.MetadataInstanceEntityID
  , mi.MetadataModelName + '.' + mie.MetadataInstanceEntityName As
  MetadataModelEntityName
  , mie.MetadataInstanceEntityName
```

```
    From [meta].MetadataInstanceEntity mie
    Join [meta].MetadataInstance mi On mi.MetadataInstanceID =
    mie.MetadataInstanceID
    Where mie.MetadataInstanceID = {0}";
    var query = string.Format(sqlMie, metadataInstanceId);
    var dte = ExternalDataAccess.GetDataTable(cs, query);
    foreach(DataRow e in dte.Rows) {
      int instanceEntityID = Convert.ToInt32(e["MetadataInstanceEntityID"]);
#>
        <Entity Name="<#=e["MetadataInstanceEntityName"] #>"
        MetadataModelEntityName="<#=e["MetadataModelEntityName"] #>">
            <DataItems>
<#
        // Metadata Instance Entity Data Item
      string sqlMied = @"Select mied.MetadataInstanceEntityDataItemName,
      mied.MetadataInstanceEntityDataItemID
        From [meta].MetadataInstanceEntityDataItem mied
        Where mied.MetadataInstanceEntityID = {0}";
        query = string.Format(sqlMied, instanceEntityID);
        var dtd = ExternalDataAccess.GetDataTable(cs, query);
      foreach(DataRow d in dtd.Rows) {
        int instanceEntityDataItemID = Convert.ToInt32(d["MetadataInstance
        EntityDataItemID"]);
#>
          <DataItem Name="<#=d["MetadataInstanceEntityDataItemName"] #>">
          </DataItem>
<# } #>
        </DataItems>
        </Entity>
<# } #>
        </Entities>
        </MetadataInstance>
<# } #>
 </Metadata>
</Biml>
```

This is the same pattern you've used thus far in this Biml file. You begin by building a variable that contains a Transact-SQL statement that retrieves data item metadata. You create a DataItems tag and nested DataItem tags for each metadata instance entity data item returned for the given metadata instance entity.

Since the Biml + BimlScript pattern is identical to the previous listings, you can examine the output shown in Figure C-26.

Preview Expanded BimlScript

```
 1  <Biml xmlns="http://schemas.varigence.com/biml.xsd">
 2      <Metadata>
 3          <MetadataInstance Name="MD_Instance" MetadataModelName="MD_Model">
 4              <Entities>
 5                  <Entity Name="Connections" MetadataModelEntityName="MD_Model.Connections">
 6                      <DataItems>
 7                          <DataItem Name="AW">
 8                          </DataItem>
 9                      </DataItems>
10                  </Entity>
11                  <Entity Name="Tables" MetadataModelEntityName="MD_Model.Tables">
12                      <DataItems>
13                          <DataItem Name="Person">
14                          </DataItem>
15                      </DataItems>
16                  </Entity>
17              </Entities>
18          </MetadataInstance>
19      </Metadata>
20  </Biml>
```

Figure C-26. *Entity data items loaded by MetadataInstanceRetrieveGeneric.biml*

You can see the DataItems on lines 7 and 13 in Figure C-26.

Retrieving the Metadata Instance Entity Data Item Properties

Next, let's expand and extend the pattern, this time to retrieve metadata instance entity data item properties. The additional code is highlighted in the MetadataInstanceRetrieveGeneric.biml file (to date) in Listing C-48.

Listing C-48. Retrieving the Metadata Instance Entity Data Item Properties

```
<#@ import namespace="System.Data" #>
<Biml xmlns="http://schemas.varigence.com/biml.xsd">
 <Metadata>
<#
var cs = @"data source=vmDemo\Demo;initial catalog=BimlBook;provider=
SQLNCLI11;integrated security=SSPI;";
// Metadata Instance
string sqlMi = @"Select MetadataInstanceID, MetadataModelName,
MetadataInstanceName
From [meta].[MetadataInstance]";
var dt = ExternalDataAccess.GetDataTable(cs, sqlMi);
foreach(DataRow row in dt.Rows) {
   var metadataInstanceId = Convert.ToInt32(row["MetadataInstanceID"]);
   #><MetadataInstance Name="<#=row["MetadataInstanceName"] #>"
   MetadataModelName="<#=row["MetadataModelName"] #>">
```

```
        <Entities><#
// Metadata Instance Entity
  string sqlMie = @"Select mie.MetadataInstanceEntityID
  , mi.MetadataModelName + '.' + mie.MetadataInstanceEntityName As
  MetadataModelEntityName
  , mie.MetadataInstanceEntityName
  From [meta].MetadataInstanceEntity mie
  Join [meta].MetadataInstance mi On mi.MetadataInstanceID =
  mie.MetadataInstanceID
  Where mie.MetadataInstanceID = {0}";
  var query = string.Format(sqlMie, metadataInstanceId);
  var dte = ExternalDataAccess.GetDataTable(cs, query);
  foreach(DataRow e in dte.Rows) {
    int instanceEntityID = Convert.ToInt32(e["MetadataInstanceEntityID"]);
#>
      <Entity Name="<#=e["MetadataInstanceEntityName"] #>"
      MetadataModelEntityName="<#=e["MetadataModelEntityName"] #>">
          <DataItems>
<#
        // Metadata Instance Entity Data Item
    string sqlMied = @"Select mied.MetadataInstanceEntityDataItemName,
    mied.MetadataInstanceEntityDataItemID
      From [meta].MetadataInstanceEntityDataItem mied
      Where mied.MetadataInstanceEntityID = {0}";
      query = string.Format(sqlMied, instanceEntityID);
      var dtd = ExternalDataAccess.GetDataTable(cs, query);
    foreach(DataRow d in dtd.Rows) {
      int instanceEntityDataItemID = Convert.ToInt32(d["MetadataInstance
      EntityDataItemID"]);
#>
        <DataItem Name="<#=d["MetadataInstanceEntityDataItemName"] #>">
<#
              // Metadata Instance Entity Data Item Property
              bool hasProperties = false;
              string sqlMiedp = @"Select mi.MetadataModelName
                + '.' + mie.MetadataInstanceEntityName
                + '.' + miedp.MetadataInstanceEntityDataItemPropertyName
                As MetadataInstanceEntityDataItemPropertyName
              , miedp.MetadataInstanceEntityDataItemPropertyValue
              , miedp.MetadataInstanceEntityDataItemPropertyID
              From [meta].MetadataInstanceEntityDataItemProperty miedp
              Join [meta].MetadataInstanceEntityDataItem mied
                On mied.MetadataInstanceEntityDataItemID =
                miedp.MetadataInstanceEntityDataItemID
              Join [meta].MetadataInstanceEntity mie
                On mie.MetadataInstanceEntityID =
                mied.MetadataInstanceEntityID
```

471

```
              Join [meta].MetadataInstance mi
                On mi.MetadataInstanceID = mie.MetadataInstanceID
              Where miedp.MetadataInstanceEntityDataItemID = {0}";
              query = string.Format(sqlMiedp, instanceEntityDataItemID);
              var dtp = ExternalDataAccess.GetDataTable(cs, query);
              if(dtp.Rows.Count > 0) {
                      hasProperties = true;
#>                                            <Properties>
<#

                      foreach(DataRow p in dtp.Rows) {
                              int instanceEntityDataItemPropertyID =
                              Convert.ToInt32(p["MetadataInstanceEntity
                              DataItemPropertyID"]);
#>
                              <Property PropertyName="<#=p["Metadata
                              InstanceEntityDataItemPropertyName"] #>">
                                      <Value><#=p["MetadataInstanceEntity
                                      DataItemPropertyValue"] #></Value>
                              </Property>
<#
                      }
              }
              if(hasProperties) {
#>                            </Properties>
<# } #>
          </DataItem>
<# } #>
        </DataItems>
        </Entity>
<# } #>
          </Entities>
        </MetadataInstance>
<# } #>
  </Metadata>
</Biml>
```

You are repeating yourself here: this is *almost* the same pattern you've used thus far in this Biml file. The difference is the hasProperties Boolean variable you add to manage the display of the Properties tags. You declare hasProperties as initialize the value to false. This is followed by building a string that contains a Transact-SQL statement that retrieves data item property metadata. The data table, named dtp, is then initialized populated. If dtp contains rows, you set hasProperties to true and create a Property tag. You iterate dtp.Rows and populate nested Property and Value tags for each metadata instance entity data item property returned for the given metadata instance entity data item. Finally, if hasProperties is true, you output a Properties closing tag.

Since the Biml + BimlScript pattern is nearly identical to the previous listings, let's examine the output shown in Figure C-27.

Preview Expanded BimlScript

```
 1  ⊟<Biml xmlns="http://schemas.varigence.com/biml.xsd">
 2  ⊟   <Metadata>
 3  ⊟      <MetadataInstance Name="MD_Instance" MetadataModelName="MD_Model">
 4  ⊟         <Entities>
 5  ⊟            <Entity Name="Connections" MetadataModelEntityName="MD_Model.Connections">
 6  ⊟               <DataItems>
 7  ⊟                  <DataItem Name="AW">
 8  ⊟                     <Properties>
 9  ⊟                        <Property PropertyName="MD_Model.Connections.ConnString">
10                             <Value>Provider=SQLNCLI11;Server=.;Initial Catalog=AdventureWorks2014;Integrated Security=SSPI;</Value>
11                          </Property>
12  ⊟                        <Property PropertyName="MD_Model.Connections.IsSource">
13                             <Value>True</Value>
14                          </Property>
15                        </Properties>
16                     </DataItem>
17                  </DataItems>
18               </Entity>
19               <Entity Name="Tables" MetadataModelEntityName="MD_Model.Tables">
20  ⊟               <DataItems>
21                     <DataItem Name="Person">
22                     </DataItem>
23                  </DataItems>
24               </Entity>
25            </Entities>
26         </MetadataInstance>
27      </Metadata>
28  └ </Biml>
```

Figure C-27. *Entity data item properties loaded by MetadataInstanceRetrieveGeneric.biml*

Retrieving the Metadata Instance Entity Data Item Relationships

You next copy and edit the pattern used for metadata instance entity data item properties, this time to retrieve metadata instance entity data item relationships. The additional code is highlighted in the MetadataInstanceRetrieveGeneric.biml file (to date) in Listing C-49.

Listing C-49. Retrieving the Metadata Instance Entity Data Item Relationships

```
<#@ import namespace="System.Data" #>
<Biml xmlns="http://schemas.varigence.com/biml.xsd">
 <Metadata>
<#
var cs = @"data source=vmDemo\Demo;initial catalog=BimlBook;provider=
SQLNCLI11;integrated security=SSPI;";
// Metadata Instance
string sqlMi = @"Select MetadataInstanceID, MetadataModelName,
MetadataInstanceName
From [meta].[MetadataInstance]";
var dt = ExternalDataAccess.GetDataTable(cs, sqlMi);
foreach(DataRow row in dt.Rows) {
  var metadataInstanceId = Convert.ToInt32(row["MetadataInstanceID"]);
  #><MetadataInstance Name="<#=row["MetadataInstanceName"] #>"
  MetadataModelName="<#=row["MetadataModelName"] #>">
          <Entities><#
// Metadata Instance Entity
  string sqlMie = @"Select mie.MetadataInstanceEntityID
, mi.MetadataModelName + '.' + mie.MetadataInstanceEntityName As
MetadataModelEntityName
, mie.MetadataInstanceEntityName
  From [meta].MetadataInstanceEntity mie
```

473

```
Join [meta].MetadataInstance mi On mi.MetadataInstanceID =
mie.MetadataInstanceID
Where mie.MetadataInstanceID = {0}";
var query = string.Format(sqlMie, metadataInstanceId);
var dte = ExternalDataAccess.GetDataTable(cs, query);
foreach(DataRow e in dte.Rows) {
  int instanceEntityID = Convert.ToInt32(e["MetadataInstanceEntityID"]);
#>
    <Entity Name="<#=e["MetadataInstanceEntityName"] #>"
    MetadataModelEntityName="<#=e["MetadataModelEntityName"] #>">
        <DataItems>
<#
      // Metadata Instance Entity Data Item
    string sqlMied = @"Select mied.MetadataInstanceEntityDataItemName,
    mied.MetadataInstanceEntityDataItemID
        From [meta].MetadataInstanceEntityDataItem mied
        Where mied.MetadataInstanceEntityID = {0}";
        query = string.Format(sqlMied, instanceEntityID);
        var dtd = ExternalDataAccess.GetDataTable(cs, query);
    foreach(DataRow d in dtd.Rows) {
      int instanceEntityDataItemID = Convert.ToInt32(d["MetadataInstance
      EntityDataItemID"]);
#>
        <DataItem Name="<#=d["MetadataInstanceEntityDataItemName"] #>">
<#
            // Metadata Instance Entity Data Item Property
            bool hasProperties = false;
            string sqlMiedp = @"Select mi.MetadataModelName
              + '.' + mie.MetadataInstanceEntityName
              + '.' + miedp.MetadataInstanceEntityDataItemPropertyName
              As MetadataInstanceEntityDataItemPropertyName
            , miedp.MetadataInstanceEntityDataItemPropertyValue
            , miedp.MetadataInstanceEntityDataItemPropertyID
            From [meta].MetadataInstanceEntityDataItemProperty miedp
            Join [meta].MetadataInstanceEntityDataItem mied
              On mied.MetadataInstanceEntityDataItemID =
              miedp.MetadataInstanceEntityDataItemID
            Join [meta].MetadataInstanceEntity mie
              On mie.MetadataInstanceEntityID =
              mied.MetadataInstanceEntityID
            Join [meta].MetadataInstance mi
              On mi.MetadataInstanceID = mie.MetadataInstanceID
            Where miedp.MetadataInstanceEntityDataItemID = {0}";
            query = string.Format(sqlMiedp, instanceEntityDataItemID);
            var dtp = ExternalDataAccess.GetDataTable(cs, query);
```

```
        if(dtp.Rows.Count > 0) {
            hasProperties = true;
#>                              <Properties>
<#

            foreach(DataRow p in dtp.Rows) {
                int instanceEntityDataItemPropertyID =
                Convert.ToInt32(p["MetadataInstanceEntity
                DataItemPropertyID"]);
#>

                <Property PropertyName="<#=p["Metadata
                InstanceEntityDataItemPropertyName"] #>">
                    <Value><#=p["MetadataInstanceEntity
                        DataItemPropertyValue"] #></Value>
                </Property>
<#

            }
        }
        if(hasProperties) {
#>                  </Properties>
<# } #>
<#

        // Metadata Instance Entity Data Item Relationship
        bool hasRelationships = false;
        string sqlMiedr = @"Select mi.MetadataInstanceName
          + '.' + mie.MetadataInstanceEntityName
          + '.' + mied.MetadataInstanceEntityDataItemName As
          MetadataInstanceEntityDataItemRelatedItemName
        , mi.MetadataModelName
          + '.' + mie.MetadataInstanceEntityName
          + '.' + miedr.
          MetadataInstanceEntityDataItemRelationshipName As
          MetadataInstanceEntityDataItemRelationshipName
        , miedr.MetadataInstanceEntityDataItemRelationshipID
        From [meta].MetadataInstanceEntityDataItemRelationship miedr
        Join [meta].MetadataInstanceEntityDataItem mied
          On mied.MetadataInstanceEntityDataItemID = miedr.
          MetadataInstanceEntityDataItemID
        Join [meta].MetadataInstanceEntity mie
          On mie.MetadataInstanceEntityID =
          mied.MetadataInstanceEntityID
        Join [meta].MetadataInstance mi
          On mi.MetadataInstanceID = mie.MetadataInstanceID
        Where mied.MetadataInstanceEntityDataItemID = {0}";
        query = string.Format(sqlMiedr, instanceEntityDataItemID);
        var dtr = ExternalDataAccess.GetDataTable(cs, query);
```

```
                    if(dtr.Rows.Count > 0) {
                         hasRelationships = true;
#>                       <Relationships>
<#

                         foreach(DataRow r in dtr.Rows) {
                             int instanceEntityDataItemRelationshipID =
                             Convert.ToInt32(r["MetadataInstanceEntity
                             DataItemRelationshipID"]);
#>
                                       <Relationship RelationshipName="
                                       <#=r["MetadataInstanceEntity
                                       DataItemRelationshipName"] #>"
                                       RelatedItemName="<#=r
                                       ["MetadataInstanceEntity
                                       DataItemRelatedItemName"] #>" />
<#                       }
                     }
                         if(hasRelationships) {
#>                               </Relationships>
<#   } #>
        </DataItem>
<# } #>
      </DataItems>
      </Entity>
<# } #>
        </Entities>
      </MetadataInstance>
<# } #>
 </Metadata>
</Biml>
```

As with metadata instance entity data item properties, the pattern for
metadata instance entity data item relationships begins with the declaration of the
hasRelationships Boolean variable, initialized to false. You next use a using block for
the SqlConnection. Nested just inside is another using block for a SqlCommand. This is
followed by building a string that contains a Transact-SQL statement that retrieves data
item relationship metadata. The SqlCommand named cmdMiedr is then initialized before
being executed to populate a SqlDataReader named rdrMiedr. If rdrMiedr contains
rows, you set hasRelationships to true and create a Relationships tag. You enumerate
the rdrMiedr SqlDataReader and populate nested Relationship tags for each metadata
instance entity data item relationship returned for the given metadata instance entity
data item. Finally, if hasRelationships is true, you output a Relationships closing tag.

Since the Biml + BimlScript pattern is nearly identical to the previous listings, let's examine the output shown in Figure C-28.

Preview Expanded BimlScript

```
 1  <Biml xmlns="http://schemas.varigence.com/biml.xsd">
 2    <Metadata>
 3      <MetadataInstance Name="MD_Instance" MetadataModelName="MD_Model">
 4        <Entities>
 5          <Entity Name="Connections" MetadataModelEntityName="MD_Model.Connections">
 6            <DataItems>
 7              <DataItem Name="AW">
 8                <Properties>
 9                  <Property PropertyName="MD_Model.Connections.ConnString">
10                    <Value>Provider=SQLNCLI11;Server=.;Initial Catalog=AdventureWorks2014;Integrated Security=SSPI;</Value>
11                  </Property>
12                  <Property PropertyName="MD_Model.Connections.IsSource">
13                    <Value>True</Value>
14                  </Property>
15                </Properties>
16              </DataItem>
17            </DataItems>
18          </Entity>
19          <Entity Name="Tables" MetadataModelEntityName="MD_Model.Tables">
20            <DataItems>
21              <DataItem Name="Person">
22                <Relationships>
23                  <Relationship RelationshipName="MD_Model.Tables.Connection" RelatedItemName="MD_Instance.Tables.Person" />
24                </Relationships>
25              </DataItem>
26            </DataItems>
27          </Entity>
28        </Entities>
29      </MetadataInstance>
30    </Metadata>
31  </Biml>
```

Figure C-28. *Entity data item properties loaded by MetadataInstanceRetrieveGeneric.biml*

Conclusion

This has been a lengthy and intense chapter on Biml metadata persistence and retrieval. Using metadata for data-related operations saves time and improves quality. Biml itself is metadata-driven. Using Biml metadata is a lot like using "meta-metadata."

In this chapter, you built two schemata for metadata storage: di (for custom metadata storage) and meta (for generic metadata storage). In the custom schema, you built tables to hold metadata entities based on the entity name and properties. The design required you to manage relationships manually, but you could extend the di schema to also manage relationships. In the generic schema, you built tables that represent the Biml metadata instance hierarchy, which allows you to store *any* Biml metadata instance entity.

Our recommendation is to use the generic approach. The generic metadata instance you built in this example is sufficient to store metadata in your example, but it represents a small subset of a design that supports the full Biml metadata instance.

Index

Get the eBook for only $5!

Why limit yourself?

With most of our titles available in both PDF and ePUB format, you can access your content wherever and however you wish—on your PC, phone, tablet, or reader.

Since you've purchased this print book, we are happy to offer you the eBook for just $5.

To learn more, go to http://www.apress.com/companion or contact support@apress.com.

Apress®

Printed in the United States
By Bookmasters